One-stop shopping. That's what makes *The Christian Writer's Manual of Style* so useful. It's what we recommend to students at the Christian Writers Guild (*www.christianwritersguild.com*). Anyone serious about writing needs a copy.

Jerry B. Jenkins, author

During my thirty years in Christian publishing, I've never seen a manual of style so relevant, so accessible, so clear, and so complete. This one stays on my desk.

Gregg Lewis, author

Style is how you do it. Class is where you arrive when you do it right. I've never known a classy writer who was indifferent to style. Robert Hudson is committed to excellence . . . yours! So turn off your word processor. It doesn't matter what you are writing; you'll write it better when you spend some time with Robert Hudson. Strunk & White may be the final authority for style in general, but Robert Hudson is the last, most important word on style for the Christian writer. So give your Christian editor a break. Play by the rules. Write well. Pay attention to style. It's your ticket to class.

Calvin Miller,
Professor of Preaching and Pastoral Studies,
Beeson Divinity School Sanford University,
Birmingham, Alabama

This well-written, comprehensive, and clear guide offers practical wisdom for both new and seasoned writers who want to communicate effectively with today's readers. Robert Hudson and Zondervan have performed an enormous service to the publishing community and to the reading public with this well-organized, easy-to-use version, making this the definitive style manual for religious writers and publishing professionals. I am grateful for this essential addition to my library.

Ann Spangler,
author of *Women of the Bible*

This manual is an invaluable tool—the most significant and thorough go-to guide for Christian writers and editors.

Rick Christian, President,
Alive Communications Literary Agency

With comprehensive and easy-to-find information, *The Christian Writer's Manual of Style* is a must-have resource for all Christian authors.

Brandilyn Collins, author of *Getting into Character:
Seven Secrets a Novelist Can Learn from Actors*

D0289250

A wonderful compendium of information and advice. All religion writers would benefit from keeping this volume close at hand and referring to it often.

Andrew T. Le Peau,
Editorial Director, InterVarsity Press

A practical, helpful resource for beginning and advanced writers and editors and others involved in religious writing and publishing. Walks readers through style-related complexities as well as basic how-tos. Wish I'd had a copy sooner.

Stephen W. Sorenson, author, editor, speaker

Those of us in publishing who have long admired Robert Hudson's qualities as an editor will not be surprised at the dedication to editorial excellence on display in this volume. Kudos to the entire team that contributed to this new edition of a splendid and helpful resource. It will certainly be at the editorial right hand of those of us at Eerdmans.

Jon Pott, Vice President,
Editor-in-Chief,
Wm. B. Eerdmans Publishing Company

I think you could change the title. You could call it *The Only Christian Writer's Reference Book You'll Ever Need*. Putting that incredible amount of detailed information in one place makes the book an invaluable resource for anybody who is writing for the Christian market.

Dick Malone,
Vice President Product Purchasing,
Riverside Distributors

The Christian Writer's Manual of Style is a clear, targeted, and insightful stylebook that answers the rubber-meets-the-road questions unique to Christian writers, editors, and publishers. The A-to-Z format is easy to access and writers and editors will find the breezy tone helpful with even the most challenging editorial decisions.

Carolyn McCready,
Vice President of Editorial,
Harvest House Publishers

The editors at Zondervan have used the previous editions of this manual for our in-house style decisions for nearly three decades—because it meets our needs and answers our questions. Now, this newly updated and expanded edition offers writers and editors everywhere an even more useful and accessible resource and brings Christian writing style fully into the twenty-first century.

Scott Bolinder,
Executive Vice President and Publisher,
Zondervan

THE
Christian
Writer's Manual
OF Style

UPDATED AND EXPANDED EDITION

Robert Hudson

GENERAL EDITOR

GRAND RAPIDS, MICHIGAN 49530 USA

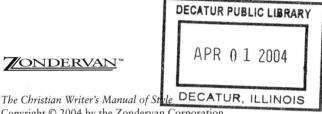

The Christian Writer's Manual of Style
Copyright © 2004 by the Zondervan Corporation

This is a revised, updated, and expanded edition of the book published in 1988 under the title *A Christian Writer's Manual of Style.*

Requests for information should be addressed to:

Zondervan, *Grand Rapids, Michigan 49530*

Library of Congress Cataloging-in-Publication Data

The Christian writer's manual of style / Robert Hudson, general
    editor. —Updated and expanded ed.
        p. cm.
    Includes bibliographical references and index.
    ISBN 0-310-48771-4
    1. Christian literature—Authorship. 2. Authorship—Style manuals. I. Hudson, Bob, 1953-
BR44.C48 2003
808'.027—dc21

                                        2003011917

This book contains advice and information relating to the legal and technical aspects of writing, publishing, and book production. While every effort has been made to achieve a high level of accuracy, this book is not intended to replace legal counsel on issues of copyright, permissions, and fair use. Authors and publishers are encouraged to consult their own attorneys regarding any specific questions and concerns.

The webpage addresses recommended or used as examples throughout this book are offered as a resource to the reader. These websites are not intended in any way to be or imply an endorsement on the part of Zondervan nor this book's compilers, nor do we vouch for their content for the life of this book.

The editors would like to thank the National Association for Visually Handicapped for their kind permission to reproduce their large-print standards and recommendations.

We would also like to thank Abingdon Press for their permission to adapt their list of US Denominations and Associations of Churches from Frank S. Mead, Samuel S. Hill, and Craig D. Atwood's *Handbook of Denominations in the United States* (2001). Copyright © 2003 by Abingdon Press. Used by permission.

All Scripture quotations, unless otherwise indicated, are taken from the *Holy Bible, New International Version®. NIV®.* Copyright © 1973, 1978, 1984 by International Bible Society. Used by permission of Zondervan. All rights reserved.

Interior design by Beth Shagene

Printed in the United States of America

---

04 05 06 07 08 09 10 /❖ DC/ 10 9 8 7 6 5 4 3 2 1

Since misunderstanding even a single word can hinder one's reading, . . . we have carefully annotated the meanings of foreign words; studied the spelling, style, etymology, and syntax of the ancients with untiring care; and taken pains to explain those terms time has obscured—so that the pathway before the reader might be smoothed.

RICHARD DE BURY, *THE PHILOBIBLON*, 1345

Contents

Preface

Why a *Christian* writer's manual of style? Or as humorist Artemus Ward once wryly asked, "Why care for grammar as long as we are good?"

Perhaps G. K. Chesterton provided the best answer. Although referring to spelling, his response is as true of grammar, punctuation, and usage: "If you spell a word wrong, you have some temptation to think it wrong."

Words have special significance in the Judeo-Christian tradition. God spoke his creation into being and wrote his laws on stone. The Bible itself is "the Word," and Christ "the Word Incarnate." Among the earliest printed books in most Western languages was the Bible, and its words have shaped our civilization. Words are full of history and power and spiritual import.

There is, however, a more practical answer to that question as well. Religious writing often requires a different stylistic emphasis and raises many questions not answered in the standard references. The references on which this manual is based are *Merriam-Webster's Collegiate Dictionary, Eleventh Edition* and *The Chicago Manual of Style, Fifteenth Edition.** Updated editions of both those books were published in the summer of 2003, just as *The Christian Writer's Manual of Style* was in its proof stages, which allowed us to incorporate into this manual the many changes in spelling and style outlined in those references. This manual, however, does not pretend to replace those definitive and exhaustive works but merely to supplement them. While compatible with those works, *The Christian Writer's Manual of Style* deviates from some rules spelled out in those works when more clarity and detail are needed, especially in regards to usage and style in religious publications.

Caution is advised, however, in the use of that word *rules*—not because rules of style and usage don't exist (they do) or because they aren't helpful (they are), but because the word implies a certain inviolability. It is all too easy, perhaps especially for religious writers and editors, to equate effective style with a vague sense of moral correctness.

This manual is not a rule book. It can be thought of as a travel guide to a wondrous and often baffling country called Religious Writing and Publishing. Its entries are not that country's legal code but helpful observations about the customs, patois, and etiquette of its inhabitants. Its goal is to equip the user with the linguistic tools to communicate to the greatest number of people most effectively, which, after all, is the goal of writing.

---

* *Note:* In the following pages we often refer to *Merriam-Webster's Collegiate Dictionary* and *The Chicago Manual of Style* by their common abbreviations: *Webster's* and *CMS* respectively.

Authors, editors, and proofreaders are not the final arbiters of style, as much as we might like to think so, nor are the grammarians, professors, linguists, and lexicographers. Rather, the final authority on written English is the reader. Our language, whether we acknowledge it or not, is an elegant anarchy, a sort of democratic gumbo. If any spelling option, punctuation mark, or word choice—even the "correct" ones—causes the average reader to stumble, then it is wrong.

This manual not only offers guidelines for communicating to the average Christian reader but also notes those instances when public taste appears to be split. We outline several alternate systems of style—British, mid-Atlantic, NIV, KJV, academic, popular, and even some advice regarding Jewish, Muslim, and Chinese style—and we also suggest alternatives for specific style points, such as when to capitalize and not capitalize the deity pronoun, options for gender-accurate language, three-dot and three-and-four-dot ellipses, open and close punctuation, and much more.

Our ability to deal with so much complexity seems to have been strained in recent years. The Internet especially has prodded our language in new and often exhilarating directions. While some critics view this new linguistic diversity, along with a perceived erosion of traditional grammatical absolutes, as a reflection of a general moral decline, one need only consider the willow and the oak to decide whether flexibility or rigidity are more able to withstand the storm.

This manual, therefore, does not bemoan diversity, for diversity only enriches the writer. It allows the writer to reach the book's ideal readers— and in greater numbers. Since flexibility is essential for growth, one might almost think of the entries in this book as trellises on which young plants may drape and intertwine. When the trellis is outgrown or broken, it is best thrown into the fire and replaced. This manual will have proved its usefulness when it has to be revised again in five or ten years.

In fact, this manual has thrown out a number of trellises since the last edition, following the recommendations of the most recent edition of *The Chicago Manual of Style*. For instance, we no longer recommend small caps for such abbreviations as *AD, BC, CE, BCE, a.m.*, and *p.m.* Another example is that we now recommend that periods, commas, colons, and semicolons be set in the same font as the larger sentence rather than in the font of the word to which they are attached.

Despite the changing language, one constant remains: *The Christian Writer's Manual of Style* has been compiled with an abiding respect for the literary functions of English, an acknowledgment of the organic nature of the language, and an awareness of the special needs of people who work with words.

Whether we are writers, editors, or proofreaders, our goal is the same— that is, in the charming words of Richard de Bury, "that the pathway before the reader might be smoothed."

ROBERT HUDSON
ADA, MICHIGAN, FEBRUARY 2004

Abbreviations

As a shortened form of a word or phrase, an abbreviation is usually used when the repetition of the full form would be monotonous or distracting, although some words and phrases, such as *Dr.*, *Mr.*, *Mrs.*, and *etc.*, as well as those used by scholars, such as *i.e.* and *e.g.*, are nearly always abbreviated by convention.

When Not to Use Periods. While periods often stand in place of the omitted letters, they are used less often now than in the past. *CMS*'s most recent guidelines are particularly useful: when the abbreviation is made up of all capital letters (*DVD*, *SJ*, *UFO*), no periods should be used. When the abbreviation is made up of some or all lowercase letters (*ibid.*, *Mrs.*, *Rev.*), periods should be used.

Exceptions should be permitted in some instances, such as retaining the periods with personal initials (*C. S. Lewis*, *I. A. Richards*). The periods should be dropped from lowercased acronyms that have passed into common usage as nouns (*jeep*, *laser*), in company names formed from acronyms (*Amoco*, *Texaco*), and in most technical computer and Internet-related abbreviations that use lowercase (*dpi*, *ftp*, *Kbps*, *www*). We recommend dropping the periods in country abbreviations (*UK*, *US*, *USSR*), but retaining the periods is perfectly acceptable as long as consistency is maintained (*U.K.*, *U.S.*, *U.S.S.R.*).

The following list summarizes those instances when periods should not be used and shows some common exceptions as well.

academic degrees: BA, MA, MD, PhD (*Ph.D.* is also acceptable)

acronyms and initialisms: AFL-CIO, AIDS, jeep, NATO, Texaco

agencies and organizations: CRC, GE, IBM, RCC, YMCA

computer- and Internet-related words: CD-ROM, dpi, RAM (see "Abbreviations: Computer- and Internet-Related Terms")

famous people referred to by initials only: GKC (Chesterton), JFK (Kennedy)

French forms of address: Mme, Mlle, though note that M. (*Monsieur*) uses a period

historical eras: AD, BC, BCE, AH, BP

scholarly style for abbreviating books of the Bible (the General Style retains the periods; see "Abbreviations: Bible Books and Related Material")

terms of biblical scholarship: NT, Q

titles of books and periodicals that are commonly abbreviated: *CMS, NYT, OED, TLS*

UK style: UK publishers and editors do not use periods with *Dr, Ltd, Mr, Mrs,* and other abbreviations when the eliminated letters fall in the middle rather than at the end of the word. See "British Style" for more detail.

units of measurement: ft, yd (though note that *in.* usually retains a period to avoid confusion with the preposition)

Acronyms and Initialisms. An acronym is a form of abbreviation in which the first letter or letters of a series of words are combined to create a new word that has the force of a proper name or noun. Acronyms are pronounced as words in themselves, such as *UNICEF* (United Nations International Children's Emergency Fund) and *laser* (light amplification by stimulated emission of radiation).

Initialisms, which are similar to acronyms, are abbreviations pronounced as a series of letters, such as *BBC* (British Broadcasting Company) and *CIA* (Central Intelligence Agency). Most rules of abbreviation apply equally to acronyms and initialisms. (See "Acronyms and Initialisms," however, for more detailed rules on their use.)

Defining Abbreviations in Text. When an abbreviation is likely to be unfamiliar to the reader, the author should define it at the place of its first reference. Since no definitive resource exists to determine what might or might not be familiar to most readers, common sense should guide the writer. When in doubt, spell it out.

George Carey was one of the founders of the BMS, the Baptist Missionary Society. [first usage; thereafter BMS need not be spelled out]

An exception is made when the abbreviation is used in a heading or a title, in which case the abbreviation should be explained at the next occurrence in the text itself.

Personal Initials. Personal names should be abbreviated according to the person's own preference or in the form given in a competent authority such as *Merriam-Webster's Biographical Dictionary* (newly revised in 2003). Among its back matter *Merriam-Webster's Collegiate Dictionary* contains a handy, highly condensed biographical dictionary that can resolve many questions.

Normal word spacing (or a nonbreaking three-to-em or a three-point space) should separate two or more personal initials preceding a second name or surname, though initials should not be allowed to break over line endings, nor should they be allowed to separate from the surname over a line or page. If a person's initials are commonly used as a nickname, they should be set without spaces or periods.

C. S. Lewis, *not* C.S. Lewis
J. R. R. Tolkien, *not* J.R.R. Tolkien
J. K. Rowling
P. J. Zondervan, *or* PJ (nickname)

In many cases well-known people are more popularly identified by the initials of their given names than the names themselves. In casual references, always use the form by which they are most commonly known; for instance, *T. S. Eliot* rather than *Thomas S. Eliot*, or *G. K. Chesterton* rather than *Gilbert Chesterton*.

In a few cases, historical or literary figures have become identified with their initials alone, such as *JFK* (John F. Kennedy) or *GBS* (George Bernard Shaw). In these cases, periods are not used and the letters are not spaced.

Using Rev. Most authorities discourage the use of *Rev.* with a last name alone and recommend that both the word and the abbreviation be used with the article *the*. Various other forms are permissible. (For more details and exceptions, see "*Reverend*.")

the Rev. Billy Graham   Mr. Graham *or just* Graham
the Rev. Mr. Graham   *but not* Rev. Graham

Civil and Military Titles. Spell out a civil or military title in text when used with a surname only. Abbreviate it if the full name is used.

Governor Wallace, *but* Gov. Lew Wallace
General Booth, *but* Gen. William Booth
Lieutenant Colonel McSally, *but* Lt. Col. Martha McSally

Academic Degrees. The abbreviations of academic degrees should be set in capital letters without periods: *BA, MA, MD*, and so on. Even though the general rule states that periods should be used with abbreviations that incorporate lowercase letters, we recommend that such abbreviations as *PhD* and *MDiv* be set without periods. Using periods (*Ph.D.* or *M.Div.*) may be warranted in certain situations as long as consistency is maintained.

For a list of abbreviations of academic degrees, see *CMS*, 15.21. The following list shows only the abbreviations for the most common religious degrees.

ABT   bachelor of arts in theology, or *ABTh*
BCL   bachelor of canon law
BD   bachelor of divinity, or *BDiv*
BHL   bachelor of Hebrew letters
BMin   bachelor of ministry

BRE	bachelor of religious education
BSL	bachelor of sacred literature
BT	bachelor of theology, or *BTh*; *baccalaureus theologiae*
CSB	bachelor of Christian science
CSD	doctor of Christian science
DB	bachelor of divinity; *divinitatis baccalaureus*
DCL	doctor of canon law; *doctor canonicae legis*
DD	doctor of divinity; *divinitatis doctor*
DHL	doctor of Hebrew letters
DMin	doctor of ministry
DRE	doctor of religious education
DST	doctor of sacred theology
DT	doctor of theology, or *DTh*; *doctor theologiae*
JBC	bachelor of canon law
JCD	doctor of canon law; *juris canonici doctor*
MDiv	master of divinity
MMin	master of ministry
MRE	master of religious education
MTS	master of theological studies
STB	bachelor of sacred theology; *sacrae theologiae baccalaureus*
STD	doctor of sacred theology
STM	master of sacred theology
ThD	doctor of theology; *theologiae doctor*
ThM	master of theology

Corporations and Organizations. Like other less familiar abbreviations, the name of a corporation or organization should be given in full on first reference, although the abbreviations *Inc.* and *Ltd.* are usually dropped. Thereafter, the acronym or abbreviated form may be used without further explanation.

Periods are not usually used in the abbreviations of such groups. For example: *GE, IBM,* and *AT&T.* Articles are used before company abbreviations only if they are used when the name is given in full; for example, *the SPCA* (*the Society for the Prevention of Cruelty to Animals*), but *PETA* (*People for the Ethical Treatment of Animals*).

States, Territories, Provinces, and Countries. Whenever possible, the names of US states and territories, Canadian provinces, and countries should be spelled out in text. In lists, footnotes, indexes, bibliographies, or charts, those names are commonly abbreviated with standard abbreviations. Although two-letter postal abbreviations for states and provinces are becoming more common in text (and are slightly preferred by *CMS*), this manual still primarily recommends them for actual mailing addresses. The following list shows state, territory, and province abbreviations in both standard and postal style. Note that some names are traditionally not abbreviated.

State	Standard Abbrev.	Postal Abbrev.	State	Standard Abbrev.	Postal Abbrev.
Alabama	Ala.	AL	Montana	Mont.	MT
Alaska	Alaska	AK	Nebraska	Neb.	NE
Arizona	Ariz.	AZ	Nevada	Nev.	NV
Arkansas	Ark.	AR	New Hampshire	N.H.	NH
California	Calif.	CA	New Jersey	N.J.	NJ
Colorado	Colo.	CO	New Mexico	N.Mex.	NM
Connecticut	Conn.	CT	New York	N.Y.	NY
Delaware	Del.	DE	North Carolina	N.C.	NC
Florida	Fla.	FL	North Dakota	N.Dak.	ND
Georgia	Ga.	GA	Ohio	Ohio	OH
Hawaii	Hawaii	HI	Oklahoma	Okla.	OK
Idaho	Ida.	ID	Oregon	Ore.	OR
Illinois	Ill.	IL	Pennsylvania	Pa. or Penn.	PA
Indiana	Ind.	IN	Rhode Island	R.I.	RI
Iowa	Ia.	IA	South Carolina	S.C.	SC
Kansas	Kans.	KS	South Dakota	S.Dak.	SD
Kentucky	Ky.	KY	Tennessee	Tenn.	TN
Louisiana	La.	LA	Texas	Tex.	TX
Maine	Me.	ME	Utah	Utah	UT
Maryland	Md.	MD	Vermont	Vt.	VT
Massachusetts	Mass.	MA	Virginia	Va.	VA
Michigan	Mich.	MI	Washington	Wash.	WA
Minnesota	Minn.	MN	West Virginia	W.Va.	WV
Mississippi	Miss.	MS	Wisconsin	Wis.	WI
Missouri	Mo.	MO	Wyoming	Wyo.	WY

American Territories	Standard Abbrev.	Postal Abbrev.
American Samoa	American Samoa	AS
Guam	Guam	GU
Puerto Rico	P.R.	PR
Virgin Islands	V.I.	VI

Canadian Province	Standard Abbrev.	Postal Abbrev.	Canadian Province	Standard Abbrev.	Postal Abbrev.
Alberta	Alta.	AB	Nova Scotia	N.S.	NS
British Columbia	B.C.	BC	Nunavut	Nunavut	NU
Manitoba	Man.	MB	Ontario	Ont.	ON
New Brunswick	N.B.	NB	Prince Edward Island	P.E.I.	PE
Newfoundland and Labrador	N.L.	NL	Québec	Qué. or P.Q.	QC
Northwest Territories	N.W.T.	NT	Saskatchewan	Sask.	SK
			Yukon Territory	Y.T.	YT

Although most country names should be spelled out in text, the following common abbreviations are often used. Note that no periods are used nor are letter spaces placed between the letters of these abbreviations.

(the former) Soviet Union—USSR (though *U.S.S.R.* is also acceptable)
United Arab Emirates—UAE (though U.A.E. is also acceptable)
United Kingdom—UK (though *U.K.* is also acceptable)
United States—US (though *U.S.* is also acceptable)

Other Geographical Names. Generally such prefixes to geographical names as *Saint, Mount, Fort, Point, Port, North, South, East,* and *West* are spelled out, not abbreviated. *Saint* may be abbreviated to *St.* according to custom, as in *St. Paul, Minnesota,* or whenever there is a good reason to do so, as long as it is done consistently.

Saint Louis (*or* St. Louis)	Fort Worth	Port Huron
Mount Carmel	Point Barrow	West Memphis

Numbers and Measurements. Generally, units of measurement are not abbreviated in text unless they are used so often as to be unwieldy, and even then they should only be abbreviated when used with a number. Periods should not be used for abbreviations of units of measurement, except for *in.* (*inch*), which retains the period to avoid confusion with the preposition.

In scientific writing, charts and graphs, mathematical texts, and other technical settings, units of measurement should always be abbreviated, though again, only in combination with a number. Also note that the singular and plural forms are the same for any abbreviation of a unit of measurement.

The designer preferred his giant twenty-one-inch monitor. [ordinary text]
but The specifications required precisely 12.5 in. by 16.25 in. [technical]
1 lb [singular]; 20 lb [plural]

Elements of a Book. The elements of a book may be abbreviated in references or bibliographies as follows. Except where noted, plurals of these abbreviations are formed by adding *s*.

appendix(es)	app. (apps.)	note(s)	n. (nn.)
bibliography	bibliog.	number	no.
book	bk.	page(s)	p. (pp.)
chapter	chap.	paragraph	par.
column	col.	part	pt.
figure	fig.	section	sec.
folio(s)	fol. (ff.)	verse(s)	v. (vv.)
introduction	intro.	volume	vol.

Months and Days of the Week. As a general rule, do not abbreviate the names of the months and the days of the week in text. Abbreviate them only in lists, charts, or other graphic settings where space is a concern. In those cases, they are usually abbreviated with periods, as follows: *Sun., Mon., Tues., Wed., Thurs., Fri.,* and *Sat.* The months *May, June,* and *July,* being so short, are not abbreviated even when the context might call for it (as in a graphic or a chart); thus: *Jan., Feb., Mar., Apr., May, June, July, Aug., Sept., Oct., Nov.,* and *Dec.*

Eras. Abbreviations designating historical eras, formerly set in small caps with periods, are now most commonly set in full caps without periods: *AD, BC, BCE, BH.* The small-cap style is still acceptable, however, especially when the designer or editor wishes to convey an atmosphere of high artistic or literary quality to the reader, though, in time, the small-cap style will probably pass from the scene entirely.

Times of Day. Abbreviations designating times of the day, formerly set in small caps, are now most commonly set lowercased with periods: *a.m., p.m.,* though the small-cap style may still be used when a highly artistic or literary feeling needs to be conveyed.

When to Spell Out Abbreviations. Except for initials and other words that are commonly abbreviated in all instances, like *Dr.* or *Mrs.,* spell out an abbreviation if it falls at the beginning of a sentence or is connected to another word with a hyphen:

Dr. Johnson was the toast of London society. [the abbreviation retained]
Old Testament scholars disagree about the meaning of *selah.* [not "OT scholars," even if OT is used elsewhere in the text]
the 3-inch-long tubing, *not* the 3-in.-long tubing

Scholarly Latin Abbreviations. Latin abbreviations used in scholarly writing should be set with periods and in roman, except for *sic*, which is best set in italic to distinguish it from quoted text. When used inside quoted text, *sic* is also usually set in square brackets; hence, [*sic*]. (Note that the brackets are roman while the word *sic* is italic.) The use of scholarly abbreviations is discouraged in books intended for a popular audience, but their use can be of benefit in technical and academic writing. The following list shows the more common abbreviations (and a few words), their Latin form, and their meaning.

Abbreviation	Latin	Meaning
ad loc.	*ad locum*	indicating the place referred to
aet	*aetatis*	aged
ca., or c.	*circa*	approximately, or about
cf.	*confer*	compare with
e.g.	*exempli gratia*	for example
et al.	*et alii (aliae, alia)*	and others
etc.	*et cetera*	and so on
et seq.	*et sequentes*	and the following
fl.	*floruit*	flourished (a person's prime)
ibid.	*ibidem*	in the same source
id.	*idem*	that which was mentioned before, same
i.e.	*id est*	that is
inf.	*infra*	below
loc. cit. (best avoided)	*loco citato*	in the place cited previously
loq.	*loquitur*	he or she speaks
NB, or n.b.	*nota bene*	note well
non seq.	*non sequitur*	does not follow
ob.	*obiit*	died
op.	*opus*	a piece of work
op. cit. (best avoided)	*opere citato*	in the work already mentioned
passim	*passim*	here and there, throughout
q.v.	*quod vide*	referring to the text within a work
sic	*sic*	thus, literally
sup.	*supra*	above
ut sup.	*ut supra*	as above
v.	*vide*	look up, see
v. inf.	*vide infra*	see below
viz	*videlicet*	namely, that is to say
vs., or v.	*versus*	versus

V. *and* Versus. The word *versus* should only be abbreviated as *v.* when it is used in the actual name of a legal case: *Roe v. Wade*. The *v.* is also customarily lowercased in the titles of legal cases. It was once common to set the *v.* in roman while the parties in the legal case were set in italic, but this manual recommends that the entire name of the legal case be set in italic.

With Other Punctuation. When an abbreviation that uses a period falls at the end of a sentence, do not double the period. One period suffices. Otherwise, any punctuation mark can be placed next to any abbreviation.

Abbreviations: Bible Books and Related Material

The names of books of the Bible, the Apocrypha, and pseudobiblical writings are generally spelled out in the text of books written for a popular audience, although they may be abbreviated in parenthetical references, especially when such references are numerous. (Abbreviating parenthetical references is less common in popular books published in the UK than in such books published in the US.) In scholarly books and reference works the names of books of the Bible may be abbreviated in both the text and in parenthetical references as appropriate and at the discretion of the author and editor.

Two Styles. Two styles of abbreviation are offered here: a General, or Popular, Style and a Scholarly Style. In deciding which to use, the author and editor should keep the audience in mind. The General Style is less formal, making it the choice for trade books in which a warmer, less academic atmosphere is desired. Although it is unlikely that a popular book would refer to portions of the pseudepigrapha, the abbreviations for those books are offered here for completeness' sake. The General Style is also useful in academic and reference works that are expected to have a wide appeal among lay readers. Note that some shorter names are not abbreviated at all.

The Scholarly Style, by contrast, is more condensed and technical in appearance, making it especially appropriate for books intended almost exclusively for a scholarly readership. It is sometimes referred to as "Two-Letter Style" even though many contain more than two letters. For most reference works, it is customary to provide a list of the abbreviations used in the book. Such a list is usually not required when the General Style is used.

Another useful system of abbreviating books of the Bible is outlined in *The SBL Handbook of Style: For Ancient Near Eastern, Biblical, and Early Christian Studies*. That system of abbreviation largely resembles the General Style listed below but without periods. That system is highly recommended both for books of a scholarly nature and for books intended for both scholarly and popular audiences.

The titles of the books of the Old and New Testament in the following list are based on the New International Version but may be adapted according to the version used (some alternatives are given below).

Title of Book	General Style	Scholarly Style	Title of Book	General Style	Scholarly Style
Old Testament			Proverbs	Prov.	Pr
Genesis	Gen.	Ge	Ecclesiastes	Eccl.	Ecc
Exodus	Ex.	Ex	or Qoheleth	Qoh.	Qoh
Leviticus	Lev.	Lev	Song of Songs	Song	SS
Numbers	Num.	Nu	or Song of		
Deuteronomy	Deut.	Dt	Solomon	Song	SS
Joshua	Josh.	Jos	or Canticles	Cant.	Cant
Judges	Judg.	Jdg	Isaiah	Isa.	Isa
Ruth	Ruth	Ru	Jeremiah	Jer.	Jer
1 Samuel	1 Sam.	1Sa	Lamentations	Lam.	La
or 1 Kingdoms	1 Kgdms	1Kgdms	Ezekiel	Ezek.	Eze
2 Samuel	2 Sam.	2Sa	Daniel	Dan.	Da
or 2 Kingdoms	2 Kgdms	2Kgdms	Hosea	Hos.	Hos
1 Kings	1 Kings	1Ki	Joel	Joel	Joel
or 3 Kingdoms	3 Kgdms	3Kgdms	Amos	Amos	Am
2 Kings	2 Kings	2Ki	Obadiah	Obad.	Ob
or 4 Kingdoms	4 Kgdms	4Kgdms	Jonah	Jonah	Jnh
1 Chronicles	1 Chron.	1Ch	Micah	Mic.	Mic
2 Chronicles	2 Chron.	2Ch	Nahum	Nah.	Na
Ezra	Ezra	Ezr	Habakkuk	Hab.	Hab
Nehemiah	Neh.	Ne	Zephaniah	Zeph.	Zep
Esther	Est.	Est	Haggai	Hag.	Hag
Job	Job	Job	Zechariah	Zech.	Zec
Psalm(s)	Ps. (Pss.)	Ps(s)	Malachi	Mal.	Mal
New Testament					
Matthew	Matt.	Mt	1 Timothy	1 Tim.	1Ti
Mark	Mark	Mk	2 Timothy	2 Tim.	2Ti
Luke	Luke	Lk	Titus	Titus	Tit
John	John	Jn	Philemon	Philem.	Phm
Acts	Acts	Ac	Hebrews	Heb.	Heb
Romans	Rom.	Ro	James	James	Jas
1 Corinthians	1 Cor.	1Co	1 Peter	1 Peter	1Pe
2 Corinthians	2 Cor.	2Co	2 Peter	2 Peter	2Pe
Galatians	Gal.	Gal	1 John	1 John	1Jn
Ephesians	Eph.	Eph	2 John	2 John	2Jn
Philippians	Phil.	Php	3 John	3 John	3Jn
Colossians	Col.	Col	Jude	Jude	Jude
1 Thessalonians	1 Thess.	1Th	Revelation	Rev.	Rev
2 Thessalonians	2 Thess.	2Th	Apocalypse	Apoc.	Ap.

Title of Book	General Style	Scholarly Style
Apocrypha		
1 Esdras	1 Esd.	1Es
2 Esdras	2 Esd.	2Es
Tobit	Tobit	Tb
Judith	Judith	Jth
The Rest of Esther	Rest of Est.	RE
or Additions to Esther	Add. Est.	AE
The Wisdom of Solomon	Wisd. Sol.	WS
Sirach	Sir.	Sir
or Ecclesiasticus	Ecclus.	Eccus
Baruch	Bar.	Bar
Additions to Daniel	Add. Dan.	AD
The Song of the Three Holy Children	S. of III Ch.	STHC
or Song of the Three Young Men	S. of III YM	STYM
Susanna	Sus.	Sus
Bel and the Dragon	Bel	Bel
Prayer of Manasseh	Pr. Man.	PrM
1 Maccabees	1 Macc.	1Mc
2 Maccabees	2 Macc.	2Mc
3 Maccabees	3 Macc.	3Mc
4 Maccabees	4 Macc.	4Mc
Prayer of Azariah	Pr. Azar.	PrAz
Epistle of Jeremiah	Ep. Jer.	Ep Jer
Psalm 151	Ps. 151	Ps 151
Old Testament Pseudepigrapha		
Assumption of Moses	As. Moses	AM
Syriac Apocalypse of Baruch	2 Bar.	2Ba
Greek Apocalypse of Baruch	3 Bar.	3Ba
Ethiopic Book of Enoch	1 Enoch	1En
Slavonic Book of Enoch	2 Enoch	2En
Hebrew Book of Enoch	3 Enoch	3En
4 Ezra	4 Ezra	4Ezr
Joseph and Asenath	Joseph	JA
Book of Jubilees	Jub.	Jub
Letter of Aristeas	L. Aris.	Aris
Life of Adam and Eve	Adam and Eve	Adam
Lives of the Prophets	Prophets	LP
Martyrdom and Ascension of Isaiah	Mar. and As. Isa.	MA Isa
Odes of Solomon	Odes Sol.	OS
Paralipomena of Jeremiah	Paralip.	PJ
Pirke Aboth	Pirke Aboth	PA
Psalms of Solomon	Pss. Sol.	PS
Sibylline Oracles	Sib. Oracles	Sib

Title of Book	General Style	Scholarly Style
Old Testament Pseudepigrapha cont.		
Story of Ahikar	Ahikar	Ahi
Testament of Abraham	T. Abram.	TAb
Testament of Adam	T. Adam	TAd
Testament of Benjamin	T. Ben.	TBen
Testament of Dan	T. Dan	TDan
Testament of Gad	T. Gad	TGad
Testament of Job	T. Job	TJob
Testament of Joseph	T. Jos.	TJos
Testament of Levi	T. Levi	TLevi
Testament of Naphtali	T. Naph.	TNaph
Testaments of the Twelve Patriarchs	T. Pats.	TPat
Zadokite Fragments	Zad. Frag.	ZF
New Testament Pseudepigrapha		
Acts of Andrew	Acts Andr.	AcA
Acts of Andrew and Matthias	Acts Andr. Mth.	AcAM
Acts of Andrew and Paul	Acts Andr. Paul	AcAP
Acts of Barnabas	Acts Barn.	AcB
Acts of James the Great	Acts Jas.	AcJas
Acts of John	Acts John	AcJn
Acts of John (by Prochorus)	Acts John Pro.	AcJn(P)
Acts of Paul	Acts Paul	AcP
Acts of Peter	Acts Pet.	AcPet
Acts of Peter (Slavonic)	Acts Pet. (Slav.)	AcPet(S)
Acts of Peter and Andrew	Acts Pet. Andr.	AcPetAnd
Acts of Peter and Paul	Acts Pet. Paul	AcPetPaul
Acts of Philip	Acts Phil.	AcPhil
Acts of Philip (Syriac)	Acts Phil. (Syr.)	AcPhil(S)
Acts of Pilate	Acts Pil.	AcPil
Acts of Thaddaeus	Acts Thad.	AcThad
Acts of Thomas	Acts Thom.	AcT
Apocalypse of Dositheus	Apoc. Dosith.	ApD
Apocalypse of Messos	Apoc. Messos	ApM
Apocalypse of Peter	Apoc. Pet.	ApP
Apocalypse of Thomas	Apoc. Thom.	ApT
Apocalypse of the Virgin	Apoc. Vir.	ApV
Apocryphal Epistle of Titus	(Apoc.) Ep. Tit.	ApocTit
Apocryphal Gospel of John	(Apoc.) Gos. John	ApocJn
Apocryphon of John	Ap. John	ApJn
Apostolic Constitutions and Canons	Apos. Con.	AposCon
Apostolic History of Pseudo-Abdias	Ps.-Abd.	PsAbd
Arabic Gospel of the Infancy	(Arab.) Gos. Inf.	ArabInf

Title of Book	General Style	Scholarly Style
Armenian Gospel of the Infancy	(Arm.) Gos. Inf.	ArmInf
Ascents of James	Asc. Jas.	AscJas
Assumption of the Virgin	Assum. Vir.	AsVir
Book Elchasai	Bk. Elch.	BkElch
Book of the Resurrection of Christ by Barnabas the Apostle	Bk. Barn.	ResBarn
Cerinthus	Cerinthus	Cer
3 Corinthians	3 Cor.	3Co
Epistle to the Alexandrians	Ep. Alex.	EpAlex
Epistle to the Apostles	Ep. Apos.	EpApos.
Epistle of Christ and Abgar	Ep. Chr. Abg.	EpChrAbg
Epistle of Christ from Heaven	Ep. Chr. Heav.	EpChrHea
Epistle to the Laodiceans	Ep. Lao.	EpLao
Epistle of Lentulus	Ep. Lent.	EpLent
Epistles of Paul and Seneca	Ep. Paul Sen.	EpPaulSen
Gospel of Barnabas	Gos. Barn.	GosBarn
Gospel of Bartholomew	Gos. Bart.	GosBart
Gospel of Basilides	Gos. Bas.	GosBas
Gospel of the Birth of Mary	Gos. Mary	GosBirMary
Gospel of the Ebionites	Gos. Eb.	GosEb
Gospel of the Egyptians	Gos. Eg.	GosEg
Gospel of Eve	Gos. Eve	GosEve
Gospel of Gamaliel	Gos. Gam.	GosGam
Gospel of the Hebrews	Gos. Heb.	GosHeb
Gospel of Marcion	Gos. Marcion	GosMar
Gospel of Mary	Gos. Mary	GosMary
Gospel of the Naassenes	Gos. Naass.	GosNaass
Gospel of the Nazarenes	Gos. Naz.	GosNaz
Gospel of Nicodemus	Gos. Nic.	GosNic
Gospel of Peter	Gos. Pet.	GosPet
Gospel of Pseudo-Matthew	Gos. Ps.-Mt.	GosPsMt
Gospel of Thomas	Gos. Thom.	GosThom
Gospel and Traditions of Matthias	Gos. Trad. Mth.	GosTradMat
History of Joseph the Carpenter	Hist. Jos. Carp.	HisJos
Hymn of the Dance	Hymn Dance	HmDance
Hymn of the Pearl	Hymn Pearl	HmPearl
Infancy Gospel of Thomas	Inf. Gos. Thom.	InfGosThom
Infancy Gospels	Inf. Gos.	InfGos
Martyrdom of Bartholomew	Mart. Bart.	MartBart
Martyrdom of Matthew	Mart. Mt.	MartMt
Martyrdom of Paul	Mart. Paul	MartPaul
Martyrdom of Peter	Mart. Pet.	MartPet
Martyrdom of Peter and Paul	Mart. Pet. Paul	MartPetPaul

Title of Book	General Style	Scholarly Style
New Testament Pseudepigrapha cont.		
Martyrdom of Philip	Mart. Phil.	MartPhil
Melkon	Melkon	Melk
Memoria of Apostles	Mem. Apos.	MemApos
Preaching of Peter	Pre. Pet.	PrePet
Protoevangelism of James	Prot. Jas.	ProtJas
Pseudo-Clementines	Ps.-Clem.	PsClem
Revelation of Stephen	Rev. Steph.	RevSteph
Secret Gospel of Mark	Sec. Gos. Mk.	SecGosMk
Vision of Paul	Vis. Paul	VisPaul

Abbreviations: Computer- and Internet-Related Terms

With the advent of computerization and the Internet comes a new set of common abbreviations, acronyms, and initialisms, many of which are as appropriate for books and conversation as they are for online communication. Many of these have become part of our daily parlance. The following are some of the more frequently seen and heard. None use periods.

ALGOL	algorithmic language
ASCII	("ASK-ee") American Standard Code for Information Interchange
BASIC	beginners' all-purpose symbolic instruction code
bit	binary digit (sometimes *BIT*)
bps	bits per second
CAD	computer aided design
CAM	computer-aided manufacturing
CC	copies
CD	compact disc
DAT	digital audio tape
DOI	digital object identifier
DOS	disk operating system
dpi	dots per inch
DRAM	dynamic random access memory
DVD	digital versatile disc (or digital video disc)
EDI	electronic data interchange
FORTRAN	formula translator
fps	frames per second
FTP	file transfer protocol
ftp	file transfer protocol (as part of an Internet location)
GB	gigabyte
GHz	gigahertz

GIF	graphic interchange format
GPS	global positioning system
GUI	graphical user interface
HDTV	high-definition television
HTML	hypertext markup language
HTTP	hypertext transfer protocol
Hz	hertz
IP	Internet protocol
IS	information services
ISP	Internet service provider
IT	information technology
K	kilobytes
Kbps	kilobytes per second
KHz	kilohertz
LAN	local-area network
LCD	liquid crystal display
LED	light-emitting diode
MB	megabytes
Mbps	megabytes per second
MIDI	musical instrument digital interface
MIME	multipurpose Internet mail extensions
OCR	optical character recognition
PDF	portable document file
POD	print on demand (a downloaded file printed as a traditional book)
QWERTY	("KWER-tee") standard keyboard layout
RAM	random access memory
ROM	read-only memory
SACD	super audio compact disc (Sony format)
SCSI	("SCUZZ-ee") small computer system interface
SGML	standard generalized markup language
TCP/IP	transmission control protocol/Internet protocol
URL	uniform resource locator
VCD	video compact disc
WWW	World Wide Web
www	World Wide Web (as part of an Internet address)
WYSIWYG	what you see is what you get

Abbreviations: Editorial and Proofreading Terms

Since editors and proofreaders share a common vocabulary, see "Proofreading Abbreviations and Terms" for a list of terms that editors should be familiar with.

Abbreviations: Publishing Terms

Like most industries, publishing has developed its own alphabet soup of abbreviations, acronyms, and initialisms. Terms with asterisks are detailed under their own headings elsewhere in this manual. (See also "Proofreading Abbreviations and Terms.")

ABA	American Booksellers Association
BEA	Book Expo of America (American Booksellers Association annual convention)
B&N	Barnes and Noble
CBA	formerly Christian Booksellers Association, although this organization now goes by the abbreviation only—CBA International; the trade association for Christian retailers and suppliers. Often the abbreviation refers to the annual trade convention sponsored by this organization
CIP	cataloging in publication* (library filing data provided by the Library of Congress)
EAN	European Article Number (book barcode system; now referred to as *International Article Number*)
IAN	International Article Number (book barcode system)
ISBN	International Standard Book Number*
ITPE	International Trade Paper Edition
JIT	Just in Time (an inventory management system; lowercased, refers to the making of more frequent, smaller print runs to minimize inventory)
M&P	marketing and promotion
MS; MSS	manuscript; manuscripts
NYP	not yet published
OP	out of print
OPN	out of print, nonreturnable
OPR	out of print, returnable
OS	out of stock
OSI	out of stock indefinitely
P&L	profit and loss (statement)
POP	point of purchase (counter display)
POS	point of sale (information obtained from retailer's cash register data)
PPB	paper, print, and binding (manufacturing costs)
pre-pub	pre-publication
RBTE	Religious Booksellers Trade Exhibit
sig	signature (bundle of book pages)
SRP	suggested retail price
SSO	sold as set only
subrights	subsidiary rights
S&W	shipping and warehousing
UPC	Universal Product Code (bar code system for all products)

Abbreviations: References and Periodicals

Common References

The abbreviations for some reference books and periodicals have become so common that they could be appropriately used in academic and some nonacademic contexts provided that the full title of the book is given at the point of first usage, in a footnote, or in a list of abbreviations in the front matter of the book. For popular usage all such abbreviations are set in italics, whether they are based on the actual title or the author, editor, or compiler's name. Such books include:

APA	*The Publication Manual of the American Psychological Association*
Bartlett's	*Bartlett's Familiar Quotations,* Justin John and Kaplan Bartlett
Brewer's	*Brewer's Dictionary of Phrase and Fable,* Adrian Room
CMS	*The Chicago Manual of Style, Fifteenth Edition*
Covey	*The Seven Habits of Highly Effective People,* Stephen R. Covey
CPT	*Christian Parenting Today*
CT	*Christianity Today*
CWMS	*The Christian Writer's Manual of Style*
Follett	*Modern American Usage,* Wilson Follett and Erik Wensberg
Fowler's	*Fowler's Modern English Usage,* H. W. Fowler
LMP	*The Literary Market Place*
MLA	*MLA Style Manual and Guide to Scholarly Publishing*
NYT	*The New York Times*
OAD	*The Oxford American Dictionary*
OED	*The Oxford English Dictionary*
PW	*Publishers Weekly*
Roget's	*Roget's Thesaurus* (various editions)
SBL	*The SBL Handbook of Style*
Strunk and White	*The Elements of Style,* E. B. White and William Strunk Jr.
TCW	*Today's Christian Woman*
TLS	*The Times Literary Supplement*
Webster's	*Merriam-Webster's Collegiate Dictionary, Eleventh Edition* (or other versions and editions bearing the name *Webster*)

Theological References and Periodicals

The following list shows the abbreviations for some of the most commonly used reference books, periodicals, and series in the field of biblical and theological studies. These abbreviations are recommended primarily for books of an academic nature. When such abbreviations are used, a key should appear somewhere in the front matter of the book, usually in an introduction or a note to the reader.

Styling. These abbreviations are set without periods. Usually the title of the work is abbreviated, in which case the abbreviation is italicized like any title, but in some cases the name(s) of the author(s), editor(s), or compiler(s) is more commonly abbreviated, in which case the abbreviation is not italicized. The names and abbreviations of series are not italicized. For certain well-known works, an editor's or author's surname stands as a substitute for the actual title. For a more complete list of bibliographic abbreviations, refer to the *Journal of Biblical Literature*'s "Instructions for Contributors" (*www.sbl-site.org/Publications/index.html*).

AB	Anchor Bible
ABD	*Anchor Bible Dictionary*
ANT	Josephus, *Jewish Antiquities*
AUSS	*Andrews University Seminary Studies*
BAR	*Biblical Archaeology Review*
BASOR	*Bulletin of the American Schools of Oriental Research*
BBR	*Bulletin for Biblical Research*
BDAG	W. Bauer, F. Danker, W. Arndt, and F. W. Gingrich, *A Greek English Lexicon of the New Testament and Other Early Christian Literature* (3d ed.)
BDB	F. Brown, S. R. Driver, and C. A. Briggs, *The New Brown-Driver-Briggs-Gesenius Hebrew-English Lexicon*
BDF	F. Blass, A. DeBrunner, and R. Funk, *A Greek Grammar of the New Testament*
Bib	*Biblica*
BJ	Josephus, *Bellum Judaicum* ("The Jewish War")
BSac	*Bibliotecha Sacra*
BTB	*Biblical Theology Bulletin*
CBQ	*Catholic Biblical Quarterly*
ExpTim	*Expository Times*
HTR	*Harvard Theological Review*
ICC	International Critical Commentary (series)
JBL	*Journal of Biblical Literature*
JETS	*Journal of the Evangelical Theological Society*
JSNT	*Journal for the Study of the New Testament*
JSOT	*Journal for the Study of the Old Testament*
JTS	*Journal of Theological Studies*
JW	Josephus, *Jewish War;* same as *BJ*
NAC	New American Commentary
NHC	Nag Hammadi Codices
NICNT	New International Commentary on the New Testament
NICOT	New International Commentary on the Old Testament
NIDNTT	*New International Dictionary of New Testament Theology*
NIDOTTE	*New International Dictionary of Old Testament Theology and Exegesis*

NIVAC	NIV Application Commentary
NTS	*New Testament Studies*
OTL	Old Testament Library
RevExp	*Review and Expositor*
SBLDS	Society of Biblical Literature Dissertation Series
SBLMS	Society of Biblical Literature Monograph Series
TDNT	*Theological Dictionary of the New Testament*
TDOT	*Theological Dictionary of the Old Testament*
TNTC	Tyndale New Testament Commentary
TOTC	Tyndale Old Testament Commentary
TrinJ	*Trinity Journal*
TynBul	*Tyndale Bulletin*
VT	*Vetus Testamentum*
WBC	Word Biblical Commentary
WTJ	*Westminster Theological Journal*

Abbreviations: Religious Organizations and Parachurch Ministries

The following list shows abbreviations for some of the more common religious organizations, past and present, and various parachurch ministries. The abbreviations for denominations are not included here. For those, see "Denominations and Associations of Churches."

AAR	American Academy of Religion (1909)
ABS	American Bible Society (1816)
ACCC	American Council of Christian Churches (1941)
ACE	Academy of Christian Editors
ACE	Alliance of Confessing Evangelicals
ACFP	Association of Christian Fighter Pilots
ACSI	Association of Christian Schools International
AEGM	Anglican Evangelical Group Movement (1906/1923)
AIM	Africa Inland Mission (1895)
APUC	Association for the Promotion of the Unity of Christendom (1857)
ATS	American Tract Society
AWM	Arab World Ministries
BCMS	Bible Churchmen's Missionary Society (1922), now *Crosslinks*
BFBS	British and Foreign Bible Society (1804)
BMS	Baptist Missionary Society (1792)
CA	Church Army (1882)
CARF	Christian Amateur Radio Fellowship
CBA	Catholic Biblical Association
CBA	formerly Christian Booksellers Association, although this organization now goes by the abbreviation only—CBA International; the trade association for Christian retailers and suppliers. Often the abbreviation refers to the convention sponsored by this organization

CBE	Christians for Biblical Equality
CBMW	Council of Biblical Manhood and Womanhood
CBT	Committee on Bible Translation
CCC	Campus Crusade for Christ
CCCS	Colonial and Continental Church Society (1838), later Commonwealth and Continental Church Society
CCCU	Coalition of Christian Colleges and Universities
CCD	Confraternity of Christian Doctrine
CEF	Child Evangelism Fellowship (1937)
CIM	China Inland Mission (1865), now known as *OMF*
CIY	Christ in Youth
CLS	Christian Literature Society
CMDA	Christian Medical and Dental Associations
CMJ	Church's Ministry Among Jewish People (1809)
CMS	Church Missionary Society (1799)
CPAS	Church Pastoral Aid Society (1836)
CSW	Christian Solidarity Worldwide (1979)
CTI	Christianity Today, Inc.
CWM	Council for World Mission (1975), formerly *LMS*
CYO	Catholic Youth Organization
EA	Evangelical Alliance (1846)
ECFA	Evangelical Council of Financial Accountability
ECPA	Evangelical Christian Publishers Association
ECPO	Evangelical Christian Publishers Outreach (a part of *ECPA*)
EEN	Evangelical Environmental Network
EFAC	Evangelical Fellowship in the Anglican Communion (1962)
EFMA	Evangelical Foreign Missions Association
EPA	Evangelical Press Association
ETS	Evangelical Theological Society
FCA	Fellowship of Christian Athletes (1954)
FCM	Fellowship of Christian Magicians
FCS	Family Christian Stores (retailer)
FOCUS	Fellowship of Christians in Universities and Schools (1961)
FOTF	Focus on the Family
GEMS	Girls Everywhere Meeting the Savior (Girls' Club)
HAH	Hearts at Home
IA	International Aid
IBR	Institute for Biblical Research
IBS	International Bible Society
ICCU	Intercollegiate Christian Union (1877; later *IVF*)
ICF	Industrial Christian Fellowship (1918)
ICS	InterContinental Church Society (1823)
IFMA	International Foreign Missions Association

IMC	International Missionary Council (1921)
ITS	Institute of Theological Studies
IVCF; IV	InterVarsity Christian Fellowship (US; 1939)
IVF	InterVarsity Fellowship (Great Britain; 1927), now known as *UCCF*
LMS	London Missionary Society (1795), known since 1975 as *CWM*
LNBA	Layman's National Bible Association
LPEA	Luis Palau Evangelistic Association
MAF	Missionary Aviation Fellowship
MOPS	Mothers of Preschoolers
MTS	Mission to Seafarers (1856)
MU	Mothers' Union (1876)
NAE	National Association of Evangelicals
NBA	National Bible Association (formerly *LNBA*)
NCC	National Council of Churches
NCCJ	National Conference of Christians and Jews
NEC	National Ecumenical Coalition (1976)
NPC	National Prayer Committee
NRB	National Religious Broadcasters
OM	Operation Mobilisation (1962)
OMF	Overseas Missionary Fellowship
PK	PromiseKeepers
RBC	Radio Bible Class Ministries (1938)
RNS	Religion News Service
SA	Salvation Army (1865)
SAMS	South American Missionary Society (1844)
SBL	Society of Biblical Literature
SCLC	Southern Christian Leadership Conference
SCM	Student Christian Movement (1895)
SIM	They now go by acronym only; formerly *Sudan Interior Mission*
SOMA	Sharing of Ministries Abroad (1979)
SPCK	Society for Promoting Christian Knowledge (1698)
SPG	Society for the Propagation of the Gospel (1701), now known as *USPG*
SU	Scripture Union
SVM	Student Volunteer Movement (1888)
TF	TearFund (1968)
TWR	Trans World Radio
UCCF	Universities and Colleges Christian Fellowship
UMCA	Universities Mission to Central Africa (1857)
USPG	United Society for the Propagation of the Gospel
WCA	Willow Creek Association
WCC	World Council of Churches (1948)
WCTU	Women's Christian Temperance Union (1874)

WEC	World Evangelisation Crusade (1913)
WEF	World Evangelical Fellowship
WoF	Women of Faith
YFC	Youth for Christ (1944)
YMCA	Young Men's Christian Association (1844)
YMHA	Young Men's Hebrew Association
YS	Youth Specialties
YWAM	Youth with a Mission International
YWCA	Young Women's Christian Association (1855)
YWHA	Young Women's Hebrew Association

Abbreviations: Religious Terms

Several lists of abbreviations of religious terms can be found elsewhere in this manual.

For	See
Academic degrees, religious	"Abbreviations, *Academic Degrees*"
Apocryphal books of the Bible	"Abbreviations: Bible Books and Related Material"
Bible books	"Abbreviations: Bible Books and Related Material"
Bible in other languages	"Bible Versions and Translations" not in English
Bible versions	"Bible Versions and Translations" in English
Hymn meters	"Hymn Meters"
Ministries	"Abbreviations: Religious Organizations and Parachurch Ministries"
Organizations, religious	"Abbreviations: Religious Organizations and Parachurch Ministries"
Periodicals, religious	"Abbreviations: Reference and Periodicals, *Theological*"
Pseudepigraphal books	"Abbreviations: Books of the Bible and Related Material"
References, theological	"Abbreviations: Reference and Periodicals, *Theological*"

The following abbreviations, which don't fit neatly into any of the categories listed above, are common in both popular and academic books. An asterisk (*) indicates that a more complete discussion of that word can be found under its own entry in the text.

ab.	abbot *or* abbess
ABMC	Ancient Biblical Manuscript Center (Claremont, Calif.)
Abp.	archbishop
AC	Anglican church *or* Anglican calendar
AC	*ante Christum* ("before Christ")
ACN	*ante Christum natum* ("before the birth of Christ")
AD *	*anno Domini* ("the year of [our] Lord"; usually precedes date)
a.d.	*ante diem* ("the day before")
Adm. Rev.	*admodum reverendus* ("very reverend")
Adv.	Advent
AH	*anno Hebraico* ("in the Hebrew year")
AH	*anno Hegirae* ("in the year of the Hegira")
Akkad.	Akkadian
AM	*anno mundi* ("in the year of the world"; precedes date)
AM	*artium magister* ("master of arts")
AMDG	*ad maiorem Dei gloriam* ("to the greater glory of God"), motto of the Jesuits
AME	African Methodist Episcopal
an.	*annus* ("year")
ana., ant.	antiphon
anc.	ancient
Angl.	Anglican
ani.	*anni* ("years")
ap.	apocryphon
ap.	apostle *
Apoc.	Apocalypse
Apocr.	Apocrypha *or* Apocryphal
Ap. Sed.	*Apostolica Sedes* ("Apostolic See")
Aq.	Aquila's Greek translation of OT
Arab.	Arabic
Aram.	Aramaic
ARS	*anno reparatae salutis* ("in the year of our redemption")

AS	*anno salutis* ("in the year of salvation")
Assyr.	Assyrian
AUC	*ab urbe condita* ("after Rome's founding"; precedes date)
B, BB	*Beatus, Beati* (pl.) ("Blessed")
b.	*bar* / *ben* (Aram./Heb. for "son of")
b.	born
BA	Babatha Archive
Bab.	Babylonian
Bapt.	Baptist
BC *	before Christ
BCE	before the Common Era
BCP	Book of Common Prayer
ben.	*benedictio* ("blessing")
benevol.	*benevolentia* ("benevolence")
b.f.	*bona fide* ("in good faith")
bib.	biblical
BK	Bar Kochba
BL	British Library
bl.	blessed
BM	British Museum
bon. mem.	*bonae memoriae* ("of happy memory")
bp.	bishop
Bro.	Brother
BV	*beatitudo vestra* ("your holiness")
BVM	Blessed Virgin Mary (*beata virgo Maria*)
Byz.	Byzantine
C	Cross
Can.	Canaanite
card.	cardinal
CE	Common Era
C. of E.	Church of England (or CE)
CM	common meter—86.86 (hymnody)
CMD	common meter doubled 86.86 86.86 (hymnody)

CME	Christian Methodist Episcopal Church
cod., codd.	codex, codices
comm(s).	commentary (commentaries)
con.	*contra* ("against")
Copt.	Coptic
cr.	*credo* ("creed" in the Breviary)
CRC	Christian Reformed Church
CRL	Canons Regular of the Lateran
CS	Christian Science
D	one of the supposed Deuteronomist sources of Pentateuch
D	*Dominus* ("Lord")
d.	*dies* ("day")
Dec.	deacon
def.	*defunctus* ("deceased")
DG	*Dei gratia* ("by the grace of God")
DN	*Dominus noster* ("our Lord")
DNJC	*Dominus noster Jesus Christus* ("our Lord Jesus Christ")
doct.	doctrine
DOM	*Deo optimo maximo* ("To God the best and greatest")
DP	domestic prelate
DSS	Dead Sea Scrolls
DV	*Deo volente* ("God willing")
E	one of the supposed Elohist sources of Pentateuch
EC	Eastern calendar
eccl.	ecclesiastic *or* ecclesiastical
Egyp.	Egyptian
EO	Eastern Orthodox
ep(p).	epistle(s)
Episc.	Episcopal *or* Episcopalian*
ET	English translation
Eth.	Ethiopic
extrabibl.	extrabiblical

Fr., F.	*frater* ("brother")
frag.	fragment
GARBC	General Association of Regular Baptist Churches
Gk.	Greek
H	Law of Holiness
HB	Hebrew Bible
HC	Holy Communion
Heb.	Hebrew
Hel.	Hellenistic
Hev./Se.	Used for documents earlier attributed to Seiyal
Hex.	Hexateuch
Hitt.	Hittite
IC	Jesus (Greek, based on the first and third letters of his name)
IHS	monogram for Greek name for Jesus
INRI	*Iesus Nazarenus Rex Iudaeorum* ("Jesus of Nazareth, King of the Jews")
J	one of the supposed Yahwist sources of Pentateuch
J"	Jehovah
Jeh.	Jehovah (Yahweh)
Jerus.	Jerusalem
JT	Jerusalem Talmud
Jud.	Judaism
Lat.	Latin
LB	Late Bronze Age
LDS	Latter-Day Saints
lex.	lexicon
LL	Late Latin
LM	long meter—88.88 (hymnody)
LMD	long meter doubled 88.88 88.88 (hymnody)
Luth.	Lutheran
LXX	Septuagint

m., mg.	marginal notes in Scripture version
m(m).	martyr(s)
MB	Middle Bronze Age
MEC	Methodist Episcopal Church
Meth.	Methodist
Mird.	Khirbet Mird
mk.	monk
ML	Medieval Latin
MS, MSS	manuscript, manuscripts
MT	Masoretic Text of OT
Mur.	Murabba'at
ND	*nostra Domina, notre Dame* ("our Lady")
NHC	Nag Hammadi Codex
NS	New Series
NS	*notre Seigneur, nostro Signore* ("our Lord")
NT	New Testament (*Novum Testamentum*)
nup.	nuptials
ob.	*obiit* ("died")
O.Cart.	Order of the Carthusians (*Ordo Cartusiensis*)
OCC	Order of the Carmelites (*Ordo Carmelitarum Calceatorum*)
OCD	Order of the Discalced Carmelites (*Ordo Carmelitarum Discalceatorum*)
O.Cist.	Order of the Cistercians (*Ordo Cisterciensium*)
OFM	Order of the Franciscans, Observant Franciscans (*Ordo Fratrum Minorum*)
OP	Order of Preachers, Dominicans (*Ordo Praedicatorum*)
OS	Old Syriac
OSA	Order of the Augustinians, Eremites (*Ordo Sancti Augustini*)
OSB	Order of St. Benedict, Benedictines (*Ordo Sancti Benedicti*)

OSD	Order of Saint Dominic
OSFC	Order of the Franciscan Capuchins (*Ordinis Sancti Francisci Capuccini*)
OSFS	Oblates of St. Francis de Sales (*Oblati Sancti Francisci Salesii*)
OSM	Order of the Servants of Mary
OT	Old Testament
P	Priestly Narrative, source of Pentateuch
P.	*pater* ("father")
Pal.	Palestine *or* Palestinian
pap.	papyrus
par.	parallel
Patr.	Patriarch
PC	Priestly Code
PCA	Presbyterian Church in America
PCUSA	Presbyterian Church (USA)
Pent.	Pentateuch
Pesh.	Peshitta
PG	preacher general
Phoen.	Phoenician
postbibl.	postbiblical
pr.	priest
pr. bk.	prayer book
Presb.	Presbyterian
Prot.	Protestant
pseudep.	pseudepigrapha *or* pseudepigraphal
Q	Quelle (one of the supposed source of Synoptic Gospels)
Q	Qumran
R	with refrain (hymnody)
r.	rabbi
rab.	rabbinic
RC	Roman calendar
RC	Roman Catholic
RCC	Roman Catholic Church
relig.	religion
Rev.	Reverend *

RIP	*requiescat in pace* ("[may he or she] rest in peace")
Rom.	Roman
Rt. Rev.	Right Reverend
Sab.	*Sabbatum* ("Sabbath," or "Sunday")
Sam.	Samaritan
Script.	Scripture
SCS	*sanctus* ("saint")
SD	*servus Dei* ("servant of God")
s.d.	*sine data* (a book without a date)
SDA	Seventh-day Adventist
Sem.	Semitic
SJ	Society of Jesus, Jesuits (*Societas Jesu*)
SM	*santae memoriae* ("of holy memory")
SM	short meter—66.86 (hymnody)
SM	Society of Mary (*Societas Mariae*)
SMD	short meter doubled 66.86. 66.86 (hymnody)
Sr.	Sister (of a religious order)
SSL	licentiate in sacred Scripture
St.	saint
Sta.	saint (female; Italian)
Ste.	saint (female; French)
STL	licentiate of sacred theology
Sum.	Sumarian

Symm.	Symmachus's Greek translation of OT
Syr.	Syriac
Talm.	Talmud
Tan.	Tanak (Hebrew Scriptures)
Targ.	Targum
Theod.	Theodotion's Greek translation of OT
theol.	theology, theological
TR	Textus Receptus
tr.	translation or translated
UIODG	*ut in omnibus Deus glorificetur* ("that God may be glorified in all things"), motto of the Benedictine order
V	Vatican Library
v(v).	verse(s)
VBS	Vacation Bible School
ven. (or V).	venerable
vers.	vespers
Vulg.	Vulgate (Jerome's Latin Bible)
WWJD	What would Jesus do?
XC (or XCS)	*Christus* (Greek initials for "Christ")
Xmas *	Christmas

Abbreviations of Bible Versions and Translations

See "Bible Versions and Translations."

Accents and Diacritics

As a conglomerate of many languages, English has adopted a number of accents and diacritic marks that are commonly used with certain foreign words. (See also "Foreign Letters and Characters.") Technically, there are only three accent marks: the acute accent, the grave accent, and the circumflex. Apart from the breve and the macron, which are termed *pronunciation marks*, the other marks added to certain letters are true *diacritics*. For most purposes, all are generically referred to as either *accent marks* or *diacritics*. The following is a list of those most commonly used in English:

Mark	Name	Examples and Notes
Accents		
´	acute	canapé, cliché, fiancée, résumé Cézanne, simpático
`	grave	Thomas à Kempis, à la mode, voilà, crèche, Pietà
^	circumflex	château, fête, pâté, Rhône
Pronunciation Marks		
˘	breve	to indicate short vowels
‾	macron	to indicate long vowels
Diacritics		
¸	cedilla	façade, François, Niçoise, français
ˇ	haček	used mostly in Czech; sometimes called an *inverted circumflex*
~	tilde	mañana, señor, señora, São Paulo
¨	umlaut (diaeresis, trema, zweipunct)	Brontë, Köln, naïve [the Scandinavians use a ° symbol instead of an umlaut]

In English-Language Contexts. For foreign words that have become common in English, no simple rules can be given for when to retain an accent, or diacritic, and when to drop it. The language is in flux. It is becoming more common, for example, to see the acute accent and diacritics being dropped from the words *cliché*, *café*, and *naïve*—thus, *cliche*, *cafe*, and *naive*. When a specific word is in question, this manual recommends conforming to the first entry of that word in *Merriam-Webster's Collegiate Dictionary*. If the word is not found there, then retain the accent. In many cases, the accent is best retained to avoid misreading: for instance, *résumé* (or *resumé*) instead of *resume*; *pâté* instead of *pate*.

Accents and diacritics should be retained in foreign place names (such as *São Paulo*, *Göttingen*, and *Córdoba*) and personal names (such as *Salvador Dalí*, *Molière*, and *Karel Čapek*). In many cases, an alternate Anglicized form exists that eliminates the accent or diacritic (such as *Cologne* in place of *Köln*, or *George Mueller* in place of *George Müller*). The editor and author should decide in each case which form would be expected, or more easily understood, by the book's ideal reader. See also "Misspelled Personal Names" for other names of people that have accents and diacritics.

In Hymns, Plays, and Poetry. Occasionally in hymnody, theater scripts, and poetry, a grave accent is used to indicate unexpected syllabification: as in the word *blessèd*. Some actors' editions of early English plays, such as Shakespeare's, use this device (which is not found in the original editions) to alert the actor to the correct pronunciation. Poets too use these accents to indicate the correct number of syllables for proper scansion. Such accents should always be retained in direct quotation, as is the grave accent in this quote:

> For, though I knew His love Who followèd,
> Yet was I sore adread
> Lest, having Him, I must have naught beside.
> Francis Thompson, "Hound of Heaven"

The poet Gerard Manly Hopkins often used the acute accent to indicate a stressed beat within a line of his "sprung rhythm." In this case, the entire syllable or word is stressed, not just the letter over which the accent appears.

> Márgarét, áre you gríeving
> Over Goldengrove unleaving?
> Leáves, líke the things of man, you
> With your fresh thoughts care for, can you?
> "Spring and Fall: To a Young Child"

For Accented Syllables. An acute accent is sometimes used in an explanatory reference or a pronunciation guide to indicate which syllable of a word should be emphasized when spoken. Often the syllables are separated by hyphens or even spelled phonetically as an aid to pronunciation.

> An-ax-á-go-ras
> Cynewulf (kí-nuh-wolf)
> Eurípedes

Acknowledgments

On an *acknowledgments page*, the author credits the people and institutions that helped in conceiving, writing, and producing the book, often including a brief description of their contribution. Some authors opt to incorporate their acknowledgments into the preface rather than providing a separate acknowledgments page; this is especially efficient when very few people are credited.

Placement. The acknowledgments page is customarily placed at the beginning of the book after the foreword or preface (which generally have a looser connection to the book's content) but before an introduction (which has a tighter relation to the book's content).

Although such acknowledgments may be quite important to the author, most readers find them extraneous. For that reason, acknowledgments are more regularly appearing at the end of books, in the same way that a film's credits usually appear at the end of the film. This is especially true when the author or editor senses that the reader may not want to wade through a lot of preliminary matter before tackling the content of the book itself, as in some genre fiction, for example. Setting the acknowledgments at the end of the book is perfectly acceptable when there is good reason to do so. By contrast, some fiction writers prefer to place the acknowledgments at the beginning of the book so that the spell of the narrative won't be broken by encountering extraneous material at the end. The author should communicate his or her preference to the editor.

Type Size. Although acknowledgments pages used to be set in type that is one point smaller than text size, that practice is now much less common, and text-type size is the norm. Still, it can be set smaller when space is a consideration or when there is a reason not to draw too much attention to it, as in fiction.

Tone. In writing an acknowledgments page, the author should be careful to avoid making the reader feel excluded by making too many inside jokes directed at those being acknowledged or by making those acknowledged feel patronized (for example, by overpraising small matters or crediting those whose contributions were marginal). The tone should be both warm and straightforward.

Acronyms and Initialisms

An acronym is an abbreviation that by intention or common usage has come to be pronounced as a word in itself or as a group of letters with the force of a name or noun. Technically, this latter case is termed an *initialism*, but rules governing the use of acronyms and initialisms are identical, so a strict distinction between the two need not be observed for purposes of style. Still, there are some minor differences, which will be specified below.

The names of many companies and organizations are acronyms: among those pronounced as words, for instance, are such organizations as *UNICEF* (United Nations International Children's Emergency Fund), *NOW* (National

Organization for Women), and *NATO* (North Atlantic Treaty Organization). Among those pronounced as groups of letters with the force of a name or noun (initialisms) are such organizations as the *FBI* (the Federal Bureau of Investigation), the *CIA* (the Central Intelligence Agency), and the *NCAA* (the National Collegiate Athletic Association).

Many other kinds of acronyms and initialisms are common, such as those describing diseases—*AIDS* (acquired immune deficiency syndrome) and *SARS* (severe acute respiratory syndrome)—and commercial products—*ATV* (all-terrain vehicle) and *SUV* (sport utility vehicle). Note that the initialism itself is capped even though the fully spelled-out name is not.

Furthermore, the etymologies of many common English words are rooted in acronyms: for instance, *radar* (radio detecting and ranging), *awol* (absent without leave), *laser* (light amplification by stimulated emission of radiation), *jeep* (from GP—general purpose), and *snafu* (situation normal all fouled up). Computer technology has added a large number of new acronyms to the language: for instance, *ROM* (read-only memory), *DAT* (digital audio tape), and *RAM* (random access memory).

Styling. Generally, an acronym that is pronounced as a word and contains four or fewer letters is all-capped, such as *WAC* (Women's Army Corps), *SALT* (Strategic Arms Limitation Treaty), and *SWAT team* (special weapons and tactics).

Organizational acronyms that have five or more letters (and are pronounced as words) are usually cap-lowercased, such as *Nasdaq* (National Association of Securities Dealers Automated Quotations) and *Amoco* (American Oil Company), although there are exceptions, which are established by the organizations themselves, such as *UNICEF*.

Those that have passed into common parlance as nouns are generally all lowercased, regardless of how many letters they contain, such as *sonar* (sound navigation ranging) and *bit* (binary digit). For some reason, some computer-related acronyms continue to be all-capped by convention, such as *RAM* (random access memory) and *DAT* (digital audio tape), perhaps to distinguish them from already existing common nouns (in the case of *RAM*, for instance). See "Abbreviations: Computer- and Internet-Related Terms" for more examples.

Initialisms (abbreviations pronounced as a string of letters) are usually all-capped, regardless of the number of letters they contain: such as, the *SPCA* (the Society for the Prevention of Cruelty to Animals) and the *NAACP* (the National Association for the Advancement of Colored People).

Periods are never used with either acronyms or initialisms.

With an Indefinite Article. When in doubt as to which indefinite article, *a* or *an*, should precede an acronym, choose the one that would ordinarily be used with the acronym as it is actually pronounced: e.g., *an Amoco station*; *a UNICEF worker*; *an ANSI character*.

Introducing. As with other abbreviations, whenever an acronym might be unfamiliar to the reader, it should be defined or spelled out when first used in the text unless it is used in a heading. In that case, the author should explain the acronym at the next opportunity in the running text itself.

> While in graduate school, he was an active member of FOCUS (Fellowship of Christians in Universities and Schools). [first usage]

Note. Lest we think that acronyms are a recent phenomenon, a common acronym familiar to Jewish scholars through the centuries is *Tanak*, which is short for *Torah* (Law), *Nevi'im* (the Prophets), and *Kethuvim* (the Writings), which are the three major sections of the Jewish Bible (the Christian Old Testament).

AD

AD stands for *anno Domini* ("the year of the Lord") and defines the general historical era since the birth of Jesus. It was once considered grammatically improper to use the abbreviation with any but single-year references and to insist that the abbreviation always precede the date. It has now become acceptable, however, to use AD with century designations as well, in which case the abbreviation follows the date.

> AD 90 *but* the first century AD

Formerly *AD* was set in small caps with periods (A.D.) but that form is quickly passing from common use. (See also "BC.")

Ad Card

See "Author Card, or Ad Card."

Addresses

Three ways of showing mailing addresses are in common use, as follows:

Postal Style. The United States Postal Service prefers that addresses on envelopes be rendered in all capital letters with no punctuation. Note also the extra space between the city, state, and zip code.

> LOUISE TAYLOR
> SENIOR EDITOR
> EXTREMELY ROMANTIC BOOKS
> 2200 EAST OF EDEN BLVD SW
> LA JOLLA DUNE CA 12345

List Style. Often one or more addresses are listed in the text of a book or on a website or other electronic medium. For instance, the publisher's address is usually placed on the copyright page (see "Address of Publisher"); sometimes the author wants the reader to write to his or her home or organization; and sometimes a series of addresses are given in a reference or resources section of the book. In these cases, addresses should be set in caps-and-lowercase style with periods.

Louise Taylor
Senior Editor
Extremely Romantic Books
2200 East of Eden Blvd. SW
La Jolla Dune, CA 12345

In Text. When addresses are given in continuous text, as many elements as possible should be spelled out. For instance, spell out such words as Avenue, Drive, Street, and so on, as well as state names. The primary exceptions to this rule are the directional compass points that follow street addresses, such as NW or SE. Also note that commas appear after each element, although no comma should be placed between the state name and zip code.

Such books may be sent to Louise Taylor, Senior Editor, Extremely Romantic Books, 2200 East of Eden Boulevard SW, La Jolla Dune, California 12345.

Style. In general, use numerals for address numbers (*520 Walker Road*). Numeric street names should be spelled out as ordinals for *First* through *Ninth*, though names with higher numbers should use numerals. For example: *Fourth Street*, but *10th Avenue*. The abbreviations *Ave., Blvd.,* and *St.* are used when an address number is used (as in *1 Pennsylvania Ave.*). Otherwise, spell them out when no address number is used (as in *Fifth Avenue* or *Tobacco Road*), and in all cases spell out designations like *Alley, Center, Court, Drive, Highway, Road, Route, Terrace, Way,* etc. (Generally *Road* is preferred to its common abbreviation, *Rd.*, because in Postal Style the abbreviation becomes *RD*, which could be mistaken for *Rural Delivery*.)

Addresses, Spelling Out Numbers In

See "Numbers, Spelling Out Versus Using Numerals, *Street Addresses*."

Address of Publisher

The inclusion of the publisher's mailing address on the copyright page is customary, though not mandatory, among US publishers. If the address does not appear on the copyright page, however, it should appear elsewhere in the book, most commonly on the title page or on a "reader response card" at the end of the book.

The address benefits readers and distributors who may want to contact the publisher with questions, and its presence can result in added income for the publisher since it can lead to book orders from stores or individuals, and since it facilitates contact from people seeking permission to quote material from the book.

Afterword

When used, an *afterword* is the first element of a book's back matter. Usually short, an afterword is written by the author and comments upon either the writing of the book itself or events in the author's life since the writing of the book, or it serves as a sort of extended acknowledgments page. In a sense, it can have some of the same functions as the preface, except that it falls after the body of the book. It can also be termed an *epilogue*, though usually only when it is used to tie up narrative elements in the story itself. (See also "Conclusion" and "Epilogue.")

Agnostic **Versus** *Atheist*

Though often used synonymously, the terms *agnostic* and *atheist* have different shades of meaning. *Agnostic* was coined by nineteenth-century biologist T. H. Huxley, based on the reference to "the unknown god" in Acts 17:23, to indicate a belief that the nature of reality is such that humans cannot definitively determine whether a deity exists. By extension, it has come to mean the general attitude that belief in a creator is irrelevant to living. An *atheist,* by contrast, is more proactive in asserting that a divine being cannot possibly exist.

AH

See "Time and Dates, *AH*"

Alleluia

See "*Hallelujah* Versus *Alleluia.*"

All Rights Reserved Notice

The use of the phrase "all rights reserved" on the copyright page of a book is recommended because it is the accepted formula for protection under the Buenos Aires Convention, recognized by the US and most Latin American countries. Some Latin American countries do not recognize the copyright symbol ©, the word *copyright*, or the abbreviation *copr*. as providing legal copyright protection.

Many publishers place the phrase "all rights reserved" on the same line as their copyright notice. Others place it on a line by itself elsewhere on the copyright page, often accompanying the warning notice. (See "Warning Notice.")

Alms

Although the word *alms* is usually used as a plural, it is also the singular form of the noun as well. Since an article is seldom used with the noun (*The king gave alms to the poor*), the issue of number is seldom a problem. As a subject, however, it can take either a plural or singular verb, as in *The alms were distributed by the steward* (plural); and *The alms given to the monk was one gold coin* (singular). In the latter case, the singular form was preferred because the object of the sentence was also singular and the plural verb would have sounded out of place.

Alphabet: Letters as Words

We forget that the letters of the alphabet are themselves words. We seldom use their actual spellings since the letters alone (often italicized) suffice in nearly all contexts, but when the careful writer needs to distinguish between *tea* and the letter *tee*, for instance, or *are* and the letter *ar*, then this following list might be helpful. Note that the vowels are usually spelled with the letter alone, but if further differentiation is required, the forms in parentheses may be used. See also "Spelling Out Words in Text."

A—a (ay)	H—aitch	O—o (oh)	V—vee
B—bee	I—i (eye)	P—pee	W—double-u
C—cee	J—jay	Q—cue	X—ex
D—dee	K—kay	R—ar	Y—y (why)
E—e (ee)	L—el	S—ess	Z—zee
F—ef	M—em	T—tee	
G—gee	N—en	U—u (you)	

Alphabetization

Styles of Alphabetization. There are two styles of alphabetization: *letter-for-letter* and *word-for-word*. Letter-for-letter style alphabetizes words as though word spaces did not exist, while word-for-word style considers whole words first, stopping at the first word space unless further distinction is needed. Both styles alphabetize as though words with hyphens or apostrophes were set solid, and both alphabetize only those word units that precede any commas. If two words are identical up to the point of the comma, the information after the comma should be used for the basis of arranging the identical words alphabetically. The two styles may be contrasted by examining the following:

Letter-for-letter	Word-for-Word
Old Believers	Old Believers
Oldcastle, Sir John	Old Catholics
Old Catholics	old covenant
old covenant	Old Latin Versions
Oldham, Joseph	Oldcastle, Sir John
Oldham, Martin	Oldham, Joseph
Oldham Library	Oldham, Martin
Old-Home Week	Oldham Library
Old Latin Versions	Old-Home Week
Olds, Benjamin	Olds, Benjamin
Olds, Ditmar	Olds, Ditmar

For most purposes, such as indexes, this manual recommends a letter-for-letter style of alphabetization. Neither style is likely to confuse readers, although letter-for-letter style is slightly more common in popular and trade references, while word-for-word is somewhat more common in academic references.

The Use of Articles and Pronouns in Indexes. In alphabetizing entries and subentries in an index, initial articles (such as *the* and *a*) and initial pronouns (such as *him*, *her*, and *their*) are generally ignored, and the entry is alphabetized according to the key word.

Mac, Mc, *and* St. In both styles of alphabetization, names beginning with the prefixes *Mac* and *Mc* should be alphabetized letter-for-letter. *Mc* should not be listed as though it were spelled *Mac*, as was once commonly done. Likewise, place names that begin with the abbreviation *St.* should be alphabetized letter for letter and not as though they were spelled *Saint.*

A.M. and P.M.

The abbreviations *a.m.* (*ante meridiem*, "before noon") and *p.m.* (*post meridiem*, "after noon") were once commonly set in small caps (A.M. and P.M.) with periods. That style is no longer used as widely as it once was, but it may be retained if applied consistently throughout a publication, especially when an unusually strong artistic or literary mood needs to be conveyed. This manual, however, in accordance with *CMS*, recommends lowercasing those abbreviations, with periods, in most cases.

Noon and Midnight. The question sometimes arises as to whether 12:00 noon, which is sometimes called the *zero point*, is considered a.m. or p.m. The answer is neither. In very technical writing 12:00 noon is marked with an *m.*, which stands for the Latin *meridies*, meaning "noon," or "midpoint." Since few readers are familiar with that abbreviation, however, it should be avoided in ordinary writing. Noon should simply be referred to as *noon*, *twelve o'clock noon*, or *12:00 noon*.

Midnight, however, is considered *12:00 p.m.* or simply *midnight*. Midnight itself is considered the final moment of the day just ending. One second after midnight is the start of the new day.

Amen

This solemnizing Hebrew word, which ordinarily concludes a prayer, means "may it be so" or "so be it." Apart from prayer, it is also used to express strong affirmation. Since it so often stands alone as an interjection— "*Amen!*"—many writers mistakenly capitalize it in all instances. There is no reason to capitalize it, however, when used within a sentence or after a comma in a prayer: *The chorus was followed by a rousing amen*, or . . . *in Jesus' name we pray, amen.*

The word sometimes causes consternation in liturgical settings because it is commonly pronounced two different ways: *ah-men* (short *a*) and *ay-men* (long *a*). Both are correct, although *ah-men* (short *a*) is the more common. That pronunciation is also the one usually used when the word is sung, since diphthongs (two vowel sounds masquerading as one) such as *ay* (a long *a* and long *e* together) are generally avoided in singing whenever there's an alternative.

Curiously, the word is usually accented on the second syllable when spoken but on the first syllable or on both syllables when sung.

Americanizing British Publications

American publishers are increasingly less likely to spend time and money restyling British publications to conform to American English, and vice versa. American and British readers alike are more open to reading books that have not been revised for their own form of English. For details of the many issues involved, see "British Style" and "Mid-Atlantic Style."

There are cases, however, when American publishers feel they have no alternative but to recast British publications for an American readership. The following procedures should help.

Reasons for Americanizing. Perhaps the most common reason to Americanize a book is that the British character of the writing is so extreme that it would simply be incomprehensible to the American target audience. Often the issue is one of reaching younger American readers who might be confused by

British spelling, punctuation, and slang, as was the case, for example, when J. K. Rowling's American publisher edited the Harry Potter books.

There are basically three levels of Americanization.

Level One: Converting Spelling and Punctuation. This level of Americanization simply replaces British typographic and spelling conventions with American ones. This involves converting single quotation marks (*inverted commas*) to American double quotation marks, and the British double quotation marks to the American single. Some British punctuation that rests outside the quotation marks would be moved inside (mostly periods and commas), according to American style. Some British publications use spaced en dashes where US convention uses em dashes, and these would be changed. And finally, but perhaps most importantly, British spellings would be changed to American for all words that are basically the same in both languages: *splendour* would be changed to *splendor*; *theatre* to *theater*; *plough* to *plow*; and so on.

This first level of Americanization is the most superficial, but it has the benefit of causing the least distraction for the American reader while retaining the maximum amount of British character—a factor that would be important in works of fiction, for instance. All other uniquely British words and cultural references are retained.

Level Two: Converting Vocabulary. The second level of Americanization, which would be added to the first, would be the actual conversion of words for common objects that are different in the two styles of English. That is, *lorry* would become *truck* in the American version; *vest* would become *undershirt*; and so on. This can be done to a greater or lesser extent, depending on how much of the British character is intended to remain in the publication. For novels set in England, for instance, it may be important to retain the British flavor of the original. In such cases, the editor would translate only those words that might seriously confuse the American reader. For nonfiction, it might be important to convert weights and measures from metric.

Level Three: Converting Cultural Equivalents. The most thorough level of Americanization, added to the other two levels, would be a complete conversion of all the cultural and topical references. In this level of editing, the editor is, in a sense, disguising the fact that the author is British. This would only be done for books in which the British character is clearly inessential to its appeal, for instance, in some self-help books or technical manuals that for clarity or safety need to be rendered in language as close to that of the target reader's as possible.

The issue here is not so much translating the individual words as it is finding recognizable cultural equivalents. *Prime minister* would become *president*, for example; *Houses of Parliament* would become *Congress*; and *BBC Radio* might be changed to *National Public Radio*.

This level obviously takes more time and work because such cultural equivalents are not always easy to devise. This translating of equivalents must be done with sensitivity and only when the British reference would be too obscure for the majority of American readers, for many British cultural references are equally familiar to Americans: Stonehenge or Shakespeare's birthplace, for instance.

This level of Americanization also runs the risk of making the book dated if the cultural equivalents soon become passé, as would references to television shows, films, or current bestsellers.

Ampersand

An *ampersand* (short for "and per se and" and sometimes called the "tironian sign") is the typographical symbol &. It simply means "and," and in form it is a stylistic rendering of the Latin *et* ("and") developed by medieval calligraphers. Unlike most other letters and symbols, it can take on a wide variety of forms, depending upon the typeface being used.

When to Use It. The symbol is seldom used in text type, although it is still often seen in advertising, on book covers, in display typography, and in headings to charts, lists, and tables where space is limited. If it is used in any of those instances, that use should be spelled out on an editor's style sheet and used consistently throughout the work.

An ampersand may be used, at the discretion of the cover designer, to replace *and* in a book's title as displayed on the cover, even if the *and* is retained elsewhere in the book.

Company Names. The ampersand should be retained in text, however, in the abbreviations of company names, such as *AT&T* and *A&P* (since it would look odd to write *AT and T*), and in the names of those few companies that prefer the ampersand in their official moniker (when such preference is known), such as *Smith & Wesson* and the former *Harper & Row*.

Drop the Serial Comma. Do not use a serial comma before an ampersand, no matter what the context; for instance: *Smith, Gundersen & Klein*, not *Smith, Gundersen, & Klein*.

Anachronism

An *anachronism* is an error of chronology. In writing, it is usually the insertion of an object, concept, or detail from one period of time into another, such as the famous clock that strikes the hour in Shakespeare's *Julius Caesar*. Anachronisms have only been considered contrary to artistic and literary realism since about the eighteenth century, before which it was common to see portraits of the Virgin Mary, for instance, garbed in the clothes of a

Renaissance Dutch lady or a medieval French peasant. The King James Bible translators used anachronisms from time to time, especially when the meanings of the Hebrew and Greek words were fuzzy. For instance, in Genesis 4:21, Jubal is said to be "the father of all such as handle the harp and organ." Most later translations render *organ* as *flute*.

While inadvertent anachronisms can be an embarrassment, most creative writers know that intentional anachronism is but one more tool in the toolkit of communication. They are a common source of humor and satire, as in Mark Twain's *Connecticut Yankee in King Arthur's Court*; they are part of the intrigue of most time-travel novels; and they are implicit in any modern translation of an older work. To give readers a general sense of obsolete concepts and objects, a certain amount of deliberate anachronism is necessary. That is part of the process of finding "dynamic equivalents" in translation, as when the TNIV renders the Bible's "ninth hour" as "three in the afternoon" (Matt. 27:45)—which, when you think about it, is not too far off from Shakespeare's clock in *Julius Caesar*. See also "Archaism."

Anglican Church Versus *Church of England*

Anglican connotes the worldwide body of churches that are either loosely or formally associated with the Church of England, including the Anglican Church of Canada and the Episcopal Church in the US. The usual practice is to use *Anglican Church* for modern references and *Church of England* for historical references or for specifically referring to the church as it exists today in the UK alone. See also "*Episcopal* and *Episcopalian*."

Anglicizing American Publications

The process of restyling American publications for a British audience is similar to restyling British publications for American audiences, only working in the other direction. The principles are the same, and they are outlined in "Americanizing British Publications." See also "British Style" and "Mid-Atlantic Style."

Annotations

See "Notes."

Antichrist

The term *antichrist*, apparently first coined in the epistles of John (1 John 2:18, 22; 4:3; 2 John 7), can mean either "a person who opposes or denies Christ" or "a false Christ." When the term is used to mean the specific individual referred to in the Bible who will be defeated by Christ at the Second

Coming, then the term is capitalized. Otherwise, it is lowercased to mean someone who possesses a general spirit of evil and opposition to Christ. Throughout Christian history, many people, from the Emperor Nero to Mikhail Gorbachev, have been identified as either generic antichrists or the biblical Antichrist himself.

Apostate

The term *apostate* is used to describe a person who once accepted but then rejected the Christian faith altogether. For a fuller discussion see *"Heresy* Versus *Schism."*

Apostles, Twelve

Sunday school students often puzzle over the fact that the twelve apostles (from the Greek *apostolos*, meaning "messenger") actually number fourteen or more. The reason, of course, is that after the death of Judas, a man named Matthias was chosen by lot to replace him, and Paul also applied the term to himself. The New Testament also labels several other people *apostles*: for instance, Barnabas (Acts 14:14), Jesus' brother James (Gal. 1:19), and possibly Andronicus and Junias (Rom. 16:7). Finally, the term *apostle* is popularly used in the pulpit to describe any faithful follower of Jesus.

The meticulous writer, therefore, should only use the phrase *the twelve apostles* when Jesus' original disciples are being referred to: Andrew, Bartholomew, James (son of Alphaeus, also called "James the Less"), James (son of Zebedee, also called "James the Great"), John, Judas Iscariot (replaced by Matthias after the resurrection), Matthew, Philip, Simon (Peter), Simon (the Zealot), Thaddaeus, and Thomas (Didymus). When using the word *apostles* alone, the writer should clarify the intended meaning.

Apostolic Fathers, The

The term *apostolic fathers* (lowercased) is sometimes mistakenly used for Jesus' apostles themselves, but it actually refers to the next generation of Christian writers immediately after the original twelve. They are called the "apostolic" fathers because they most likely knew the apostles personally. They are, notably, Clement of Rome, Hermas, Ignatius, Papias, Polycarp, and the anonymous writers of *2 Clement, Didache, Barnabas,* and *Diognetus.* The writings of these individuals are corporately referred to as the Apostolic Fathers (capitalized, in roman type).

Apostrophe

The *apostrophe* (') is a mark usually used in a word or number to show an intentional omission, possession, or a plural, and its origins date back to Roman and medieval calligraphy.

Contractions. The apostrophe is most commonly used in contractions to indicate the absence of a letter or letters: *shouldn't, ma'am, M'Cheyne.* For more details, see "Contractions."

For Possessives. An apostrophe is used to denote possession (see "Possessives"). An antiquated rule of grammar states that only people, not things, may possess an object and that therefore it is improper to say, "the book's cover." In modern usage this rule may be ignored, and possessives may be used with inanimate objects.

the prophet's writings	the apostles' ministry
the women's advice	George MacDonald's novels

With Plurals of Abbreviations. An *'s* should be used to form the plurals of abbreviations with periods, the plurals of letters in common expressions, and the plurals of letters when it would be confusing if only *s* were added. Note that except when appearing in common expressions, letters used as letters are italicized. In all cases, the *'s* or *s* should be set in roman type.

ThD's
Mind your p's and q's
S's, A's, I's but Ts, Ds, xs, and *ys*

With Gerunds. The possesive *'s* is usually added to any noun that is linked to a gerund, as in *the minister's leaving the church.*

With Numeral Abbreviations. If the numerals in a year reference are abbreviated to two numerals, they should be preceded by an apostrophe, as in *"the blizzard of '78."* No apostrophe, however, should go before the *s* in decade designations in numerals. In most cases the spelled-out form, *eighties, nineties,* etc., is preferred to *80s, 90s,* etc.

They graduated with the class of '02.
It should not have surprised us when the seminarians of the 80s became the ministers of the 90s. [Preferred: "when the seminarians of the eighties became the ministers of the nineties."]

Appendix

An *appendix* is a convenient place to store information that is useful to the reader but intrusive in the main text of a book. An author should avoid, however, the tendency to lump unprocessed and unexplained research or data in an appendix if it has only marginal value to the body of the book. An appendix should contain only information that will be of positive value to the reader.

Design. Since appendixes are meant to be read, they should be set in the same size type as the main text of the book, or possibly one point size smaller. They should be readable and inviting. Also, the titles and headings in an appendix should match those in the main part of the book.

Reference in Text. In the main text of the book, the author should be sure to make a detailed reference to every appendix, including the number and title of the appendix and a brief explanation of why it will be of value to the reader.

Enumerating. Although it was once common to use roman numerals to number appendixes when there are more than one, arabic numerals or capital letters are now predominantly used.

The Plural. The plural form of *appendix* can be either *appendixes* or *appendices,* although this manual recommends *appendixes* as the one appropriate for most books. *Appendices* can appear slightly pretentious in popular writing.

Archaism

If an *anachronism* is a modern word in an old setting (see "Anachronism"), then you might say an *archaism* is an old word in a modern setting. Although for most purposes this manual discourages the use of words marked "archaic" in *Webster's,* archaisms, like anachronisms, are useful tools in the creative writer's hands. They lend authenticity to historical fiction, provide useful etymological illustrations for the nonfiction writer, and create comic effects when necessary.

Among the more interesting archaisms of the Christian faith are such words as *All-welder* ("the Almighty Ruler," that is, God), *holystead* ("holy place"), *housel* ("to receive last rites") and *unhouselled* (not to have received them), *mare* ("demon"; survives in *nightmare*), *rood* ("cross"), *sooth* ("truth"; survives in *soothsayer*), and *wedbreaker* (the Wycliffe Bible's poetic word for "adulterer"). Nearly all of these are Anglo-Saxon words that have been superceded by Latin interlopers.

The anachronistic second person singulars, *thou, thee, thy,* and *thine,* are still commonly used in hymns and elsewhere. (See "*Thou* and *Thee.*")

An entire class of archaisms are remembered only because they survive in popular songs or customs: *ebenezer,* from 1 Sam. 7:12, meaning "monument," survives in Robert Robinson's hymn "Come Thou Fount of Every Blessing"; *langsyne,* "long ago," in Robert Burns's "Auld Langsyne"; *shrove,* "to have confessed," survives in *Shrove Tuesday,* etc.

All modern English words are fossils of the past. An archaism is simply a fossil that has been left undisturbed for many years. When there is a good reason to unearth them, do so. Otherwise, let them lie.

Aureole

The word *aureole* is sometimes mistakenly used as a synonym for *nimbus* or *halo* when speaking of religious art and iconography. *Aureole*, however, is the golden sheen-like background that surrounds the entire body of a figure, as opposed to the *nimbus*, which is the circlet over the head (halo). Both indicate sanctity and holiness.

Author Card, or Ad Card

The *author card*, which is also called the *ad card* or sometimes just the *card*, is a page in a book reserved for listing the author's other published books or major publications (major articles, monographs, or other shorter publications are usually not included). It is most often supplied by the publisher and is intended to promote the author's other books from that publisher, although it may occasionally be to the author's or publisher's advantage to include a more comprehensive list that includes the author's books from other publishers.

Placement and Size. If an author card is used, it is usually placed on page 2 of the book; that is, the verso of the half-title page and facing the title page. It is commonly set in text size or one point smaller.

Style. The list is usually headed by a phrase like "Other books by [name of author]." If the author has coauthored any of the books on the list, the name(s) of the coauthor(s) should be given in parentheses after the title so that it doesn't appear the author is trying to claim sole authorship.

Author Signature

At some time or other, nearly every author has been asked to sign a copy of his or her book for an admiring reader. The signature should be done in black ink and usually takes one of two forms: (1) If the reader is a collector of the author's first editions, it is customary for the author to sign only his or her name on the title page, directly beneath the author's own printed name unless asked to do otherwise. A sole signature with no personalization increases the value of the book if it is ever resold to the collectors' book market. (2) If the author wishes to write a personal message, or if the author is requested to write such a message, it can be done on the title page (if the message is short) or on the half-title page (if the message is longer). Very long messages are best written on the right-hand side of the flyleaf.

Back Matter, Elements of a Book's

The *back matter* of a book is whatever follows the main body of the text. Ideally, all parts of the back matter should begin on recto pages, but they may begin verso if the design or space limitations dictate. The back matter is arranged in the following order, as appropriate:

Afterword or conclusion or epilogue (though in some literary books, a
  conclusion or an epilogue may be the final element of the body matter)
Note from the author
Acknowledgments (if not placed in the front matter)
Appendix(es)
Study questions (if not incorporated into the text)
Notes (if not placed as footnotes or as chapter endnotes)
Glossary
Chronological table(s)
Bibliography, or "For Further Reading"
Index to maps
Proper-name index
Subject index
Scripture index
Author biographical note
Colophon, publisher's note, or reader response page

Banns of Marriage

The term *banns of marriage* is lowercased and nearly always plural in form. *Banns* is sometimes mistakenly thought to mean "bands" or "bonds," however, it means the announcement of an intention to be married and has its origin in the Middle English word for "proclamation." It is plural because of the former English custom of posting in the church an announcement of an impending marriage for three consecutive weeks. It is usually used with the verbs *to post* or *to publish* and passive in construction: "*the banns were posted*," rather than "*they posted the banns*."

Baptismal Name

See "*Christian Name*."

BC

With Year and Century Designations. Since BC is an abbreviation for "before Christ," it logically comes after references to a year or century: *Augustus was born in 63 BC.* Note that the abbreviation *AD* commonly comes before a year designation though after a century designation (see additional details at "*AD*"). The abbreviation *BC* was formerly set in small capitals with periods (B.C.); that form is no longer common but may still be used when a feeling of high literary or artistic quality needs to be conveyed.

Believer

In the US and the UK, the term *believer* has come into vogue in recent decades as a synonym for *Christian.* It is both common and acceptable in Christian writing since, for many writers, it seems an inoffensive way to distinguish practicing Christians from the nominal. Still, in some contexts, it may have acquired a hint of Christian cant.

The term is limited by its generality, however. In a larger context it can refer to a believer in any religion, so caution must be used when targeting a readership made up of Christians and non-Christians or when attempting to distinguish between Christians and the faithful of other religions.

Bible: Online Versions

The Internet is a valuable source for accessing complete Bible texts in various versions and languages. Some of these can be downloaded, while others are read-only. The following list shows only a few of the more common versions from among the scores available online. For online versions of the Vulgate and versions of the Bible in seventeen modern languages, see *bible.gospelcom.net/*.

American Standard Version	*ebible.org/bible/asv/*
	www.christianlibrary.org/bibles/bibles.mv
	bible.gospelcom.net/
Amplified Bible	*bible.gospelcom.net/*
Analytical-Literal Translation	*dtl.org/alt/index.html*
The Bible in Basic English	*bf.org/bfetexts.htm*
The Darby Translation	*bf.org/bfetexts.htm*
	bible.gospelcom.net/
Hebrew Names Version of the World English Bible	*www.ebible.org/bible/hnv/*
International Standard Version	*isv.org/*
Jefferson Bible	*www.angelfire.com/co/JeffersonBible/*
King James Version	*www.ebible.org/bible/kjv/*
	www.christianlibrary.org/bibles/bibles.mv
	www.scriptures.com/
	www.bibles.net/
	bible.gospelcom.net/

King James Version, audio	www.audio-bible.com/Bible/Bible.html
	www.talkingbible.com/
	www.bibles.net/
Modern Literal Version	www.christianlibrary.org/bibles/bibles.mv
New American Standard Bible	www.bibles.net/
	bible.gospelcom.net/
New English Translation	www.netbible.org/
	www.scriptures.com/
New International Version	www.bibles.net/
	bible.gospelcom.net/
New International Version, audio	www.bibles.net/
New King James Version	bible.gospelcom.net/
New Living Translation	bible.gospelcom.net/
Revised Standard Version	www.bibles.net/
	bible.gospelcom.net/
Today's New International Version (NT)	www.zondervanbibles.com/home.asp
Twenty-first Century King James Version of the Holy Bible	bible.gospelcom.net/
Webster's Bible	bf.org/bfetexts.htm
Weymouth's New Testament in Modern Speech	bf.org/bfetexts.htm
World English Bible	www.ebible.org/bible/WEB/
	www.christianlibrary.org/bibles/bibles.mv
	bible.gospelcom.net/
World English Bible, audio	audiotreasure.com/
	www.talkingbible.com/
Young's Literal Translation of the Bible	www.bibles.net/
	bf.org/bfetexts.htm
	bible.gospelcom.net/

Bible Belt

No absolute geographical boundaries can be drawn around the region referred to as the *Bible Belt*, a term that should be capitalized. Suffice it to say that it is broadly synonymous with the American South, extending as far west as Texas and as far north as Kentucky, Virginia, and Maryland, and even portions of the southern Midwest. The term is often used derogatorily to describe conservative fundamentalists and those who hold a largely uncritical view of biblical literalism, regardless of geographic location. Care should be used in using the term since it is generally pejorative.

Bible Permissions, Guidelines for Obtaining

Using Copyrighted Versions. When an author quotes extensively from a copyrighted translation, paraphrase, or other version of the Bible, he or she should write for permission from that version's publisher just as he or she might write for permission to use material from any other book (see "Permissions, Obtaining: Author Guidelines").

Some publishers allow fairly extensive use of their Bibles without requiring the author to obtain written permission or pay fees, but since each publisher has different criteria, the author should be sure to write to the Bible publisher for their guidelines. Any permission notice provided by the Bible publisher should be placed on the copyright page. As a general rule, written permission does *not* need to be obtained when:

1. The use of a Bible version is so minimal as to fall unquestionably under the "fair use" defense category. Only one Bible publisher (*New American Bible*), for instance, requires written permission to quote fewer than 250 verses. Some allow as many as 500, 1,000, or even 2,500 verses to be quoted before written permission is needed or a fee is required.
2. The version or translation is in the public domain (for example, the King James Version). Care should be taken, however, because some public-domain versions have been modernized or altered by their publishers to such an extent that the updated version has been newly copyrighted (for example, the *New King James Version*).

All quotations should be referenced in such a way that it will be clear to the reader which version is being quoted. Usually some form of abbreviation is used with the reference (see "Bible Versions and Translations"). When several quotations are used, a general note can appear on the copyright page, in the acknowledgments, or elsewhere, indicating the version used. Supplying the bibliographic information (publisher, edition, etc.) on the copyright page or elsewhere is also recommended, even for versions for which no written permission is needed.

If more than one version is used, then a statement should be provided to clarify the abbreviations used with the references in the text. For example:

> Scripture verses marked KJV are from the King James Version of the Bible. Those marked NRSV are from the *New Revised Standard Version* [followed by any bibliographic information or permission notice, as appropriate].

Guidelines for Common Copyrighted Versions of the Bible

The following are some of the guidelines for some major versions of the Bible:

The Amplified Bible (AB). Published by Zondervan. The publisher's policy states that up to 500 verses may be quoted without permission as long as the verses quoted "do not amount to a complete book of the Bible, do not comprise 25 percent or more of the total text of the work in which they are quoted, and the verses are not being quoted in a commentary or other Biblical reference work."

The correct credit lines for the Amplified Bible, New and Old Testaments respectively, should read:

> All Scripture quotations, unless otherwise indicated, are taken from *The Amplified Bible*, Old Testament. Copyright © 1965, 1987, by the Zondervan Corporation. Used by permission. All rights reserved.

> All Scripture quotations, unless otherwise indicated, are taken from *The Amplified Bible*, New Testament. Copyright © 1954, 1958, 1987, by The Lockman Foundation. Used by permission.

Requests for permission to quote from the Old Testament should be directed to:

> Zondervan
> Attn: Amplified Bible Permission Director
> 5300 Patterson Ave. SE
> Grand Rapids, MI 49530

Requests for permission to quote from the New Testament should be directed to:

> Director of Rights and Permissions—*Amplified* NT
> The Lockman Foundation
> PO Box 2279
> La Habra, CA 90631

Contemporary English Version (CEV). Published by the American Bible Society. The publisher's policy states:

> The CEV text may be quoted in any form (written, visual, electronic or audio) up to & inclusive of five hundred (500) verses without written permission, providing the verses quoted do not amount to 50% of a complete book of the Bible nor do the verses account for twenty-five percent (25%) or more of the total text of the work in which they are quoted. This permission is contingent upon proper copyright acknowledgment.

The credit lines may read:

> Scripture quotations marked (CEV) are from the *Contemporary English Version* © 1991, 1992, 1995 by American Bible Society. Used by Permission.

Or

> All Scripture quotations in this publication are from the *Contemporary English Version* Copyright © 1991, 1992, 1995 by American Bible Society. Used by Permission.

Permission may be obtained by writing to:

The American Bible Society
1865 Broadway
New York, NY 10023

English Standard Version (ESV). Published by Crossway Books. The publisher's policy states:

> Up to 1,000 verses (inclusive) from assorted books of the English Standard Version (ESV) may be quoted in printed (e.g., book, brochure, magazine, newsletter, lesson outline), visual (e.g., film, video tape), and electronic forms (e.g., computer diskette, CD-ROM, on-line) without written permission, as long as the verses quoted do not amount to 50% of a complete book of the Bible and do not make up 50% or more of the total text of the work in which they are quoted.

> These uses of the ESV must be acknowledged by an appropriate copyright notice.... Permission is contingent upon an appropriate copyright acknowledgment.

Appropriate credit lines read:

> Scripture taken from *The Holy Bible, English Standard Version.* Copyright © 2000; 2001 by Crossway Bibles, a division of Good News Publishers. Used by permission. All rights reserved.

Or

> Scripture quotations marked "ESV" are taken from *The Holy Bible, English Standard Version.* Copyright © 2000; 2001 by Crossway Bibles, a division of Good News Publishers. Used by permission. All rights reserved.

Or

> All Scripture quotations, unless otherwise indicated, are taken from *The Holy Bible, English Standard Version.* Copyright © 2000; 2001 by Crossway Bibles, a division of Good News Publishers. Used by permission. All rights reserved.

Requests for use of the *ESV* in excess of the above guidelines may be addressed to:

Good News Publishers
Attn: Bible Rights
1300 Crescent Street
Wheaton, IL 60187

Good News Translation (GNT; also called *The Good News Bible, Good News for Modern Man,* and *Today's English Version* [TEV]). Published by the American Bible Society, whose policy (updated March 2003) reads:

> The GNT text may be quoted in any form (written, visual, electronic or audio) up to & inclusive of five hundred (500) verses without written permission, providing the verses quoted do not amount to 50% of a complete book of the Bible nor do the verses account for twenty-five percent (25%) or more of the total text of the work in which they are quoted. This permission is contingent upon an appropriate copyright acknowledgment.

The correct credit line should read:

> All Scripture quotations in this publication are from the Good News Translation—Second Edition. Copyright © 1992 by American Bible Society. Used by Permission.

Or

> Scripture quotations marked (GNT) are from the Good News Translation—Second Edition. © 1992 by American Bible Society. Used by Permission.

Within North America, permission requests for commercial use should be sent to:

> Zondervan
> Attn: Good News Translation Permission Director
> 5300 Patterson Avenue SE
> Grand Rapids, MI 49530

Outside North America, permission requests may be addressed to:

> Director of Permissions
> American Bible Society
> 1865 Broadway
> New York, NY 10023

The Message (MSG). The full title of this paraphrastic translation, which is the work of author and scholar Eugene Peterson, is *The Message: The Bible in Contemporary Language.* It is published by NavPress Publishing Group. The publisher's policy states:

> You may quote up to 500 verses without written permission unless the verses quoted amount to:
>
> • A complete book of the Bible.
> • 25% or more of the total text of your project.

You must receive written permission to quote:

- 501 verses or more
- An entire book of the Bible
- Text that accounts for 25% or more of the total project.

You must include copyright information for *The Message* on the title page or copyright page of the project in which verses are quoted.

Appropriate credit lines read:

Scripture quotations from THE MESSAGE. Copyright © by Eugene H. Peterson 1993, 1994, 1995, 1996, 2000, 2001, 2002. Used by permission of NavPress Publishing Group.

Or

All Scripture quotations in this publication are from THE MESSAGE. Copyright © by Eugene H. Peterson 1993, 1994, 1995, 1996, 2000, 2001, 2002. Used by permission of NavPress Publishing Group.

For permission, please write to:

NavPress Publishing Group
Attn: Kristen DiFelice, Rights Assistant
PO Box 35001
Colorado Springs, CO 80935
Kristen.di.felice@navpress.com
Rights@NavPress.com
Fax: (719) 260-7223

The New American Bible (NAB). Published by the Confraternity of Christian Doctrine, whose policy states:

1. Permission must be requested from the Confraternity of Christian Doctrine for each usage regardless of the small amount of text used. A copy of the manuscript should accompany each request. The Scripture selections should be *highlighted*, and reference citations clearly marked.
2. Anyone may use up to 2,500 words of the text in a single non-liturgical publication (including recordings) free of charge. . . .

A credit line should contain the basic information:

Scripture texts used in this work are taken from the *New American Bible* Copyright © 1970 by the Confraternity of Christian Doctrine, Washington, D.C., and are used by permission of copyright owner. All rights reserved.

Or

Scripture texts used in this work are taken from the *New American Bible with Revised New Testament* Copyright © 1986 by the Confraternity of Christian Doctrine, Washington, D.C., and are used by permission of copyright owner. All rights reserved.

Or

Scripture texts used in this work are taken from the *Revised Psalms of the New American Bible* Copyright © 1991 by the Confraternity of Christian Doctrine, Washington, D.C., and are used by permission of copyright owner. All rights reserved.

For permission write:

Publications Development Manager
Office for Publishing and Promotion Services
United States Catholic Conference
3211 Fourth Street NE
Washington, DC 20017–1194

New American Standard Bible (NASB). Published by The Lockman Foundation, whose policy states:

The text of the *New American Standard Bible* ... may be quoted and/or reprinted up to and inclusive of five hundred (500) verses without express written permission of The Lockman Foundation, provided the verses do not amount to a complete book of the Bible nor do the verses quoted account for more than 25% of the total work in which they are quoted.

The standard credit line for the 1977 edition reads as follows:

Scripture taken from the *New American Standard Bible,* © Copyright 1960, 1962, 1963, 1968, 1971, 1972, 1973, 1975, 1977 by The Lockman Foundation. Used by permission.

For the 1995 updated edition, use the above credit line with the addition of "1995" to the end of the series.

Requests for permission to quote from the NASB should be sent to:

The Lockman Foundation
900 S. Euclid Street
La Habra, CA 90631

New Century Version (NCV). Published by Thomas Nelson, Inc. The publisher's policy states:

> Up to 1,000 verses (inclusive) from assorted books of the New Century Version (NCV) may be quoted in printed ... visual ... and electronic forms ... without written permission, as long as the verses quoted do not amount to 50% of a complete book of the Bible and do not make up 50% or more of the total text of the work in which they are quoted.
>
> These uses must be acknowledged by an appropriate copyright notice.... Permission is contingent upon an appropriate copyright acknowledgement.
>
> Use of the NCV text beyond [the above] requires written permission.

Appropriate credit lines read:

> Scripture taken from the New Century Version. Copyright © 1987, 1988, 1991 by Word Publishing, a division of Thomas Nelson, Inc. Used by permission. All rights reserved.

> Or

> Scripture quotations marked "NCV" are taken from the New Century Version. Copyright © 1987, 1988, 1991 by Word Publishing, a division of Thomas Nelson, Inc. Used by permission. All rights reserved.

> Or

> All Scripture quotations, unless otherwise indicated, are taken from the New Century Version. Copyright © 1987, 1988, 1991 by Word Publishing, a division of Thomas Nelson, Inc. Used by permission. All rights reserved.

To request permission, please inquire in writing to:

Thomas Nelson Publishers
Attn: Bible Rights and Permissions
PO Box 141000
Nashville, TN 37214-1000

New International Version (NIV). Published by Zondervan for the International Bible Society. The publisher's policy states:

> The NIV text may be quoted in any form (written, visual, electronic or audio), up to and inclusive of five hundred (500) verses or less without written permission, providing the verses quoted do not amount to a complete book of the Bible, do not comprise 25% or more of the total text of the work in which they are quoted, and the verses are not being quoted in a commentary or other Biblical reference work....

One complete copy of the work using quotations from the New International Version must be sent to Zondervan within 30 days following the publication of the work.

Rights and permission to quote from the NIV text in printed or electronic media intended for commercial use within the US and Canada that exceed the above guidelines must be directed to, and approved in writing by, Zondervan Publishing House.

Rights and permission to quote from the NIV text in printed or electronic media intended for commercial use within the UK, EEC, and EFTA countries that exceed the above guidelines must be directed to, and approved in writing by, Hodder & Stoughton, Ltd., 338 Euston Road, London, NW1 3BH, England.

Rights and permission to quote from the NIV text in media intended for non-commercial use which exceed the above guidelines must be directed to, and approved in writing by, International Bible Society, 1820 Jet Stream Drive, Colorado Springs, CO 80921-3969.

The most current credit line for "fair use" quotations from the NIV is:

> All Scripture quotations, unless otherwise indicated, are taken from the *Holy Bible, New International Version*®. *NIV*®. Copyright © 1973, 1978, 1984 by International Bible Society. Used by permission of Zondervan. All rights reserved.

Note the use of the registered symbol after both the complete and abbreviated titles.

If NIV use falls outside the "fair use" guidelines, requiring a fee and written permission, then a more complete copyright notice is required:

> All Scripture quotations, unless otherwise noted, are taken from the *Holy Bible, New International Version*®. *NIV*®. Copyright © 1973, 1978, 1984 by International Bible Society. Used by permission of Zondervan. All rights reserved.
>
> The "NIV" and "New International Version" trademarks are registered in the United States Patent and Trademark Office by International Bible Society. Use of either trademark requires the permission of International Bible Society.

Letters should be addressed to:

Zondervan
Attn: NIV Permission Director
5300 Patterson Ave. SE
Grand Rapids, MI 49530

In addition, if *NIV* or *New International Version* are to be used in a title or on the cover of a book, special written arrangements must be made with the International Bible Society.

New International Reader's Version (NIrV). Published by Zondervan for the International Bible Society. The publisher's policy states:

> The NIrV text may be quoted in any form (written, visual, electronic or audio), up to and inclusive of five hundred (500) verses or less without written permission, providing the verses quoted do not amount to a complete book of the Bible, do not comprise 25% or more of the total text of the work in which they are quoted, and the verses are not being quoted in a commentary or other Biblical reference work. . . .

> One complete copy of the work using quotations from the New International Reader's Version must be sent to Zondervan within 30 days following the publication of the work.

> Rights and permission to quote from the NIrV text in printed or electronic media intended for commercial use within the US and Canada that exceed the above guidelines must be directed to, and approved in writing by, Zondervan Publishing House.

> Rights and permission to quote from the NIrV text in printed or electronic media intended for commercial use within the UK, EEC, and EFTA countries that exceed the above guidelines must be directed to, and approved in writing by, Hodder & Stoughton, Ltd., 338 Euston Road, London, NW1 3BH, England.

> Rights and permissions to quote from the NIrV text in media intended for non-commercial use which exceed the above guidelines must be directed to, and approved in writing by, International Bible Society, 1820 Jet Stream Drive, Colorado Springs, CO 80921-3969.

The most current credit line for "fair use" quotations from the NIrV reads:

> All Scripture quotations, unless otherwise indicated, are taken from the *Holy Bible, New International Reader's Version®. NIrV®.* Copyright © 1973, 1978, 1984 by International Bible Society. Used by permission of Zondervan. All rights reserved.

Note the use of the registered symbol after both the complete and abbreviated titles.

If NIrV use falls outside the "fair use" guidelines, requiring a fee and written permission, then a more complete copyright notice is required:

> All Scripture quotations, unless otherwise noted, are taken from the *Holy Bible, New International Reader's Version®. NIrV®.* Copyright © 1973, 1978, 1984 by International Bible Society. Used by permission of Zondervan. All rights reserved.

> The "NIrV" and "New International Reader's Version" trademarks are registered in the United States Patent and Trademark Office by International Bible Society. Use of either trademark requires the permission of International Bible Society.

Letters should be addressed to:

Zondervan
Attn: NIrV Permission Director
5300 Patterson Ave. SE
Grand Rapids, MI 49530

The New English Translation (NET). Published online by Biblical Studies Press. The publisher's policy states:

> From our website at www.bible.org, you may download the information and print it for yourself and others as long as you give it away and do not charge for it. In this case *free means free.* It cannot be bundled with anything sold, nor can you charge for shipping, handling, or anything. It is provided for personal study or for use in preparation of sermons, Sunday school classes, or other non-commercial study. . . .
>
> For free distribution of more than 100 copies, you must obtain written permission and comply with reasonable guidelines of content control and include currently valid BSP copyright and organizational acknowledgments.

The publisher's credit line reads:

> Copyright © 1997–2003 Biblical Studies Press. This material is provided for personal use or for use in preparation of sermons, Sunday school classes, or other oral communication. This material may be quoted in written form but give credit where credit is due (author's name and website address: www.bible.org). It may not be reprinted for commercial publication. It may be copied or reprinted for distribution as long as it is given away and no charge is made for copies, shipping or handling.

You may contact Biblical Studies Press for permission for noncommercial use by linking to www.bible.org/email.asp or by calling 1-800-575-2425.

The New Jerusalem Bible (NJB). Published by Darton, Longman & Todd, Ltd. and Doubleday for Random House, Inc. The publisher's policy states:

> We are pleased to grant permission for the inclusion of up to 2,500 words, free of charge (providing such number of words does not constitute more than one-third of your total text), covering rights in the United States and Canada only.

The prescribed credit line reads:

> Excerpt from *The New Jerusalem Bible,* copyright © 1985 by Darton, Longman & Todd, Ltd. and Doubleday, a division of Random House, Inc. Reprinted by Permission.

For permission to use outside the United States and Canada, please write to:

New Jerusalem Bible Permissions
Darton, Longman & Todd, Ltd.
1 Spencer Court
140-142 Wordsworth High Street
London SWL8 4JJ
ENGLAND

New King James Version (NKJV). Published by Thomas Nelson, Inc. The publisher's policy states:

> Up to 1,000 verses (inclusive) from assorted books of the New King James Version (NKJV) may be quoted in printed ... visual ... and electronic forms ... without written permission, as long as the verses quoted do not amount to 50% of a complete book of the Bible and do not make up 50% or more of the total text of the work in which they are quoted.

> These uses of the NKJV must be acknowledged by an appropriate copyright notice. . . . Permission is contingent upon an appropriate copyright acknowledgment.

Appropriate credit lines read:

> Scripture taken from the New King James Version. Copyright © 1982 by Thomas Nelson, Inc. Used by permission. All rights reserved.

Or

> Scripture quotations marked "NKJV" are taken from the New King James Version. Copyright © 1982 by Thomas Nelson, Inc. Used by permission. All rights reserved.

Or

> All Scripture quotations, unless otherwise indicated, are taken from the New King James Version. Copyright © 1982 by Thomas Nelson, Inc. Used by permission. All rights reserved.

For permission requests that exceed the above guidelines, please write to:

Thomas Nelson Publishers
Attn: Bible Rights and Permissions
PO Box 141000
Nashville, TN 37412-1000

New Living Translation (NLT). Published by Tyndale House Publishers, whose policy states:

The text of the *Holy Bible, New Living Translation*, may be quoted in any form (written, visual, electronic, or audio) up to and inclusive of five hundred (500) verses without express written permission of the publisher, provided that the verses quoted do not account for more than 25 percent of the work in which they are quoted, and provided that a complete book of the Bible is not quoted.

When the *Holy Bible, New Living Translation*, is quoted, one of the following credit lines must appear on the copyright page or title page of the work:

> Scripture quotations marked (*NLT*) are taken from the *Holy Bible, New Living Translation*, copyright © 1996. Used by permission of Tyndale House Publishers, Inc., Wheaton, IL 60189 USA. All rights reserved.

Or

> Scripture quotations are taken from the *Holy Bible, New Living Translation*, copyright © 1996. Used by permission of Tyndale House Publishers, Inc., Wheaton, IL 60189 USA. All rights reserved.

Or

> Unless otherwise indicated, all Scripture quotations are taken from the *Holy Bible, New Living Translation*, copyright © 1996. Used by permission of Tyndale House Publishers, Inc., Wheaton, IL 60189 USA. All rights reserved.

For permission to quote in excess of the above guidelines, please write to:

> Tyndale House Publishers, Inc.
> Attn: Bible Permissions
> PO Box 80
> Wheaton, IL 60189

Fax requests are also accepted at (630) 668-8311.

New Revised Standard Version (NRSV). Published by Augsburg Fortress for the National Council of Churches. The NCC's permissions policy states:

> The [New] Revised Standard Version Bible may be quoted and/or reprinted up to and inclusive of five hundred (500) verses without express written permission of the publisher, provided the verses quoted do not amount to a complete book of the Bible or account for fifty percent (50%) of the total work in which they are quoted.

An appropriate credit line reads:

> New Revised Standard Version Bible, copyright 1989, Division of Christian Education of the National Council of the Churches of Christ in the United States of America. Used by permission. All rights reserved.

Permissions inquiries may be addressed to:

Augsburg Fortress
Attn: RSV/NRSV Permissions
Box 1209
Minneapolis, MN 55400-1209
Tel: 1-800-421-0239
Fax: (612) 330-3252

Today's New International Version (TNIV). Published by Zondervan for the International Bible Society. The publisher's policy states:

> The TNIV text may be quoted in any form (written, visual, electronic or audio), up to and inclusive of five hundred (500) verses or less without written permission, providing the verses quoted do not amount to a complete book of the Bible, do not comprise 25% or more of the total text of the work in which they are quoted, and the verses are not being quoted in a commentary or other Biblical reference work....
>
> One complete copy of the work using quotations from the Today's New International Version must be sent to Zondervan within 30 days following the publication of the work.
>
> Rights and permission to quote from the TNIV text in printed or electronic media intended for commercial use within the US and Canada that exceed the above guidelines must be directed to, and approved in writing by, Zondervan Publishing House.
>
> Rights and permission to quote from the TNIV text in printed or electronic media intended for commercial use within the UK, EEC, and EFTA countries that exceed the above guidelines must be directed to, and approved in writing by, Hodder & Stoughton, Ltd., 338 Euston Road, London, NW1 3BH, England.
>
> Rights and permissions to quote from the TNIV text in media intended for non-commercial use which exceed the above guidelines must be directed to, and approved in writing by, International Bible Society, 1820 Jet Stream Drive, Colorado Springs, CO 80921-3969.

The most current credit line for "fair use" quotations from the TNIV reads:

> All Scripture quotations, unless otherwise indicated, are taken from the *Holy Bible, Today's New International Version*®. *TNIV*®. Copyright © 2002, 2004 by International Bible Society. Used by permission of Zondervan. All rights reserved.

Note the use of the registered symbol after both the complete and abbreviated titles.

If TNIV use falls outside the "fair use" guidelines, requiring a fee and written permission, then a more complete copyright notice is required:

> All Scripture quotations, unless otherwise noted, are taken from the *Holy Bible, Today's New International Version*®. *TNIV*®. Copyright © 2002, 2004 by International Bible Society. Used by permission of Zondervan. All rights reserved.
>
> The "TNIV" and "Today's New International Version" trademarks are registered in the United States Patent and Trademark Office by International Bible Society. Use of either trademark requires the permission of International Bible Society.

Letters should be addressed to:

> Zondervan
> Attn: TNIV Permission Director
> 5300 Patterson Ave. SE
> Grand Rapids, MI 49530

The Jerusalem Bible (JB). Published in the US by Bantam Doubleday Dell Publishing Group, Inc. The publisher's policy reads, in part:

> Up to 2,500 words [may be quoted], free of charge (providing such number of words does not constitute more than one-third of the total text), covering rights in the United States and Canada only. For additional territory, please apply to *Jerusalem Bible* Permissions, Darton, Longman & Todd, 89 Lillie Road, London SW6 1UD, England.

The credit line should read:

> Excerpt from *The Jerusalem Bible*, copyright © 1966 by Darton, Longman & Todd, Ltd. and Doubleday, a division of Bantam Doubleday Dell Publishing Group, Inc. Reprinted by permission.

Apply for permission to:

> Director of Rights and Permissions—*Jerusalem Bible*
> Bantam Doubleday Dell
> 666 Fifth Ave.
> New York, NY 10103

The New Jerusalem Bible (NJB). Published in the US by Bantam Doubleday Dell Publishing Group, Inc. The publisher's policy reads, in part:

> Up to 2,500 words [may be quoted], free of charge (providing such number of words does not constitute more than one-third of the total text), covering rights in the United States and Canada only. For additional territory, please apply to *New Jerusalem Bible* Permissions, Darton, Longman & Todd, 89 Lillie Road, London SW6 1UD, England.

The credit line should read:

> Excerpt from *The New Jerusalem Bible*, copyright © 1985 by Darton, Longman & Todd, Ltd. and Doubleday, a division of Bantam Doubleday Dell Publishing Group, Inc. Reprinted by permission.

Requests for permission to quote from the *New Jerusalem Bible* should be sent to:

> Permissions Manager
> Bantam Doubleday Dell
> 666 Fifth Ave.
> New York, NY 10103

New Revised Standard Version (NRSV). Published by the National Council of Churches, whose policy states:

1. As a general rule, if the quotation is less than a full book in length and fewer than 500 verses, permission is granted without application.
2. If a quotation of one portion of the NRSV consists of a full book or more, or if quotations of several excerpts have a combined length of more than 500 verses, or if the quotation is more than 50 percent of the word content of the proposed publication and deemed to be 50 percent or more of the basic message of the proposed publication, it will be necessary for the author or publisher to arrange with the Division for permission.

Credit lines for the various NRSV editions are as follows:

___

New Revised Standard Version Bible:

> The Scripture quotations contained herein are from the *New Revised Standard Version of the Bible*, copyrighted 1989 by the Division of Christian Education of the National Council of Churches of Christ in the United States of America, and are used by permission. All rights reserved.

___

New Revised Standard Version Bible, Catholic Edition:

> The Scripture quotations contained herein are from the *New Revised Standard Version Bible, Catholic Edition*, copyrighted [date to come; not yet in print] by the Division of Christian Education of the National Council of Churches of Christ in the United States of America, and are used by permission. All rights reserved.

___

New Revised Standard Version Apocryphal/Deuterocanonical Books:

> The Scripture quotations contained herein are from the *New Revised Standard Version Apocryphal/Deuterocanonical Books*, copyrighted 1989 by the Division of Christian Education of the National Council of Churches of Christ in the United States of America, and are used by permission. All rights reserved.

New Revised Standard Version Common Bible:

The Scripture quotations contained herein are from the *New Revised Standard Version Common Bible,* copyright [date to come; not yet in print] by the Division of Christian Education of the National Council of Churches of Christ in the United States of America, and are used by permission. All rights reserved.

Permission requests should be addressed to:

The National Council of the Churches of Christ in the USA
Division of Christian Education
Program Ministry on Bible Translation and Utilization
475 Riverside Drive
New York, NY 10115–0050

The Revised Standard Version (RSV). Published by the National Council of Churches, whose policy states:

1. As a general rule, if the quotation is less than a full book in length and fewer than 500 verses, permission is granted without application.
2. If a quotation of one portion of the RSV consists of a full book or more, or if quotations of several excerpts have a combined length of more than 500 verses, or if the quotation is more than 50 percent of the word content of the proposed publication and deemed to be 50 percent or more of the basic message of the proposed publication, it will be necessary for the author or publisher to arrange with the Division for permission.

Credit lines for the various RSV editions are as follows:

Revised Standard Version:

The Scripture quotations contained herein are from the *Revised Standard Version of the Bible,* copyright 1946, 1952, 1971 by the Division of Christian Education of the National Council of Churches of Christ in the USA. Used by permission.

Revised Standard Version Bible, Catholic Edition:

The Scripture quotations contained herein are from the *Revised Standard Version Bible, Catholic Edition,* copyright 1965 and 1966 by the Division of Christian Education of the National Council of Churches of Christ in the USA. Used by permission.

Revised Standard Version Apocrypha:

The Scripture quotations contained herein are from the *Revised Standard Version Apocrypha,* copyright 1957 by the Division of Christian Education of the National Council of Churches of Christ in the USA. Used by permission.

Revised Standard Version Common Bible:

> The Scripture quotations contained herein are from the *Revised Standard Version Common Bible*, copyright 1973 by the Division of Christian Education of the National Council of Churches of Christ in the USA. Used by permission.

Permission requests should be addressed to:

> The National Council of the Churches of Christ in the USA
> Division of Christian Education
> Program Ministry on Bible Translation and Utilization
> 475 Riverside Drive
> New York, NY 10115–0050

Common Public Domain Versions of the Bible

Virtually all English translations of the Bible published in the US before 1923 are in the public domain, although some published in the British Isles before that date may still be protected by copyright in the countries of the British Commonwealth. Naturally, all the classic translations, such as the King James Version, the Tyndale Bible, and the Douay-Reims, can be quoted without restriction.

Many recent editions of the Bible are also public domain. Among the most common are:

> *American Revised Version* (1901)
> *American Standard Version* (1901)
> *Bible in Basic English* (1949; rev. 1962; PD in US but not UK)
> *Hebrew Names Version of the World English Bible* (ongoing; as yet, online only)
> *Modern Literal Version* (recent; in software and online only)
> *Revised Version* (NT 1881, OT 1885, Apoc. 1895)
> *World English Bible* (ongoing; as yet, online only)
> *Young's Literal Translation* (1862)

Bible Style: The New International Version

The translators and editors of the New International Version (NIV) and Today's New International Version (TNIV) of the Bible have established style guidelines that are largely compatible with those outlined in this manual (and by extension *CMS*), but they differ in a few significant ways. These style exceptions are used for both the text of the Bible itself and for all peripheral matter, and they are recommended for books and other publications that are tightly tied to the NIV text or to its supplementary material—so tightly, in fact, that the reader would be confused if these NIV style exceptions were not used. In general, these style rules also apply to the New International Reader's Version (NIrV).

Omit the Serial Comma. The NIV and TNIV texts omit the comma before *and*, *or*, and *nor* in a series unless the comma is required for clarity or to avoid misreading.

Use Three-Dot Ellipses. The NIV and TNIV use only three-dot ellipses unless the fourth dot, which is actually a period preceding the ellipsis, is essential for clarity or to prevent misreading.

Lowercase Prepositions of Three or Fewer Letters in Titles. While *The Christian Writer's Manual of Style*, like *CMS*, now recommends lowercasing all prepositions in titles regardless of length, the NIV style is to lowercase only those of three or fewer letters.

The Deity Pronoun. The NIV and TNIV style differs slightly from *The Christian Writer's Manual of Style* in its recommendation regarding the lowercasing of the deity pronoun. While *CWMS* allows for some exceptions to the universal lowercasing of the deity pronoun, the NIV and TNIV do not. In both the NIV and TNIV texts and in all their supporting material, the lowercase form of the pronoun should be used without exception.

LORD *and* GOD *with Small Caps.* The small-capped forms LORD and GOD, as they appear in the NIV and TNIV, should be retained in all quotations, regardless of context.

Spelling Out Numbers. The NIV and TNIV stylists recommend spelling out numbers through ten in ordinary text. This includes numbers indicating people's ages. Use numerals for all numbers above ten except for large round numbers.

Abbreviations of Chapter(s). The NIV and TNIV abbreviate the words *chapter* and *chapters* as *ch.* and *chs.*, respectively, rather than *chap.* and *chaps.*

Punctuation with Bible References. While both *CWMS* and the NIV/TNIV use an en dash between continuous verse numbers (*Matthew 4:8–10*), the NIV and TNIV use an em dash rather than an en dash between continuous chapter numbers (*Matthew 4—8*) or continuous verses spanning separate chapters (*Matthew 4:8—5:10*). Unlike *CWMS*, the NIV and TNIV do not use a space after a comma in nonconsecutive verse numbers (*Matthew 4:6,8,10*).

Differences of Style between the NIV and the TNIV. Although style continuity was scrupulously maintained between the NIV and TNIV, there are a few differences. The one that received the most attention is the TNIV's use of gender-accurate pronouns when a masculine pronoun is used in the original language to denote both men and women.

Also, to facilitate this, the TNIV accepts third-person plural pronouns in general references when the sense is singular. Although controversial, this usage is largely accepted by grammarians and style experts.

Capitalization. By and large, the NIV and TNIV use the capitalized forms shown in this manual (see "Capitalization: Biblical and Religious Terms"), but there are exceptions.

In general, the NIV and TNIV are less inclined to capitalize occasional epithets for persons of the Trinity, Satan, and some biblical characters, events, and locations. There are exceptions, however, which should be noted below. The NIV and TNIV accept all the capitalized forms shown in the list in "Capitalization: Biblical and Religious Terms," except the following, which are the preferred forms of the editors and translators of the NIV and TNIV:

NIV/TNIV tend to lowercase occasional epithets for persons of the Trinity

advocate	light of the world
bread of life (Bible or Christ)	Lord of hosts
bridegroom	Lord of lords
defender	man of sin
door	man of sorrows
eternal God; Eternal God (used both ways. See Romans 16:26 and Genesis 21:33)	Passover lamb
firstborn	shepherd (though *Shepherd* in Hebrews 13:20 and 1 Peter 5:4)
great high priest	victor
head	vine
high priest (Christ)	water of life
King of glory	way
King of kings	

NIV/TNIV tend to lowercase epithets for Satan

antichrist	enemy
beast	evil one
devil	serpent
dragon	wicked one

NIV/TNIV tend to lowercase some biblical events, people, things, and places

book of life (book of judgment)	patriarch, the (Abraham)
celestial city (abode of the redeemed)	promised land (Canaan or heaven)
Christ-child	sun of righteousness
false prophet (of Revelation)	tower of Babel
high priestly prayer	tree of life (in Garden of Eden and Revelation 22)
Lamb's book of life	word of life
land of promise	word of truth
new Jerusalem (heaven)	

Though some epithets for biblical events, people, things, and places are capitalized

Advent (Christ's first coming)
Battle of Armageddon (final battle)
Children of Israel
Garden of Eden
Garden of Gethsemane
Holy City, holy city (used both ways. See Rev. 21:2, 10 and Rev. 22:19)
Holy Place, holy place (used both ways. See Ez. 45:3 and Ez. 45:4)
Last Judgment, the
Magi
Millennium, the
Nativity, the
Rapture, the
Sheol (italicize when referred to as a Hebrew word)
Tent of Meeting (use lowercase when talking about the construction of the tabernacle but capitalize when the context refers to the finished tabernacle)
Triumphal Entry, the
Virgin Birth, the

NIV/TNIV tend to capitalize descriptive terms for the Bible and portions of the Bible

Apocryphal
Biblical
Book of the Covenant
Book of the Law
Canon, the (Scripture)

Gospel (John's, et al.)
Law of Moses
Mosaic Law
post-Biblical
Scriptural

Miscellaneous

Catholic church (*but* Roman Catholic Church)
Christianize (-ization)
Christology (-ical)
faith-healing
Gentile laws (adj.)
Gnostic (generic)
Good News, the (the gospel)
Judge, judge (used both ways. See James 4:12 and Heb. 12:23)
living word (Bible)

Messiahship
Messianic
Neo-Pentecostalism
Rock, the (Christ); rock, the (used both ways. See Ps. 92:15 and 2 Sam. 22:2)
Satanism
Savior (depends on usage; note on 2 Sam. 22:3: "my refuge and my savior")
twenty-third psalm

Bible Versions and Translations

Kinds of Versions and Translations. Three basic types of Bible translations exist: (1) literal, (2) paraphrastic, and (3) dynamic. These make up, in reality, more of a gradation, or spectrum, than three distinct categories.

1. A *literal* translation attempts to provide an exact linguistic equivalent for each word in the original. While such translations are accurate, they are most useful for academic study. The average reader, however, can find literal translations confusing, and such translations usually require extensive annotations to explain outmoded idioms, vocabulary, and references.

2. At the other extreme is the *paraphrase*, which attempts to render the original in easily understood modern equivalents so that little explanation is required. Its extensive use of contemporary idiom and jargon can result in an extremely readable Bible but one that is also blind to certain shades of meaning and inference in the original. Paraphrases are also more highly susceptible to the paraphraser's own misperceptions and biases.

3. A *dynamic* translation tries to split the difference between the literal and the paraphrase. It attempts to adhere as closely as possible to the original language, but when obscure idioms, vocabulary, and references occur, it attempts to render them in modern "dynamic" equivalents. The challenges of dynamic translation can run in the direction of both the literal translation—that is, obscurity and overexplanation—and the paraphrastic—that is, misleading inaccuracy. Ideally, such problems are minimized, however, and most Bible translations meant for a general readership strive to be dynamic.

Many other adjectives are used to describe many different kinds of Bible translations and versions. The following list will help sort out the most common.

abridgment—a Bible from which certain passages or books have been eliminated to facilitate ease of reading

chronological Bible—a Bible in which the narrative elements are chronologically arranged

condensed Bible—a Bible especially shortened for ease of reading; usually more extensively abridged than an abridgment

inclusive Bible—a Bible in which gender-specific language has been made non-gender-specific, especially in those cases where the gender-specific construction of the original is clearly meant to be generic

interlinear Bible—a Bible in which the translation is given between the lines of the original language lectern Bible—an oversize, often ornamental, Bible designed to be displayed on a lectern or special stand near or on the altar of a church; the type is usually very large so that a standing reader can easily read it

literal translation—a translation that attempts to give literal rather than dynamic equivalents for each word of the original

modernized version—usually refers to an older version of a Bible that has been rendered into more contemporary language

parallel Bible—a Bible in which two or more versions are shown side by side for comparison and study

paraphrase—a modernized version, usually in colloquial language, of an existing translation

paraphrastic translation—a modernized version, usually in contemporary colloquial English, though translated from the original texts

pew Bible—a Bible specially printed and bound to be used by worshipers in a church setting; often the type size is a little larger than normal, and most annotations are eliminated

reading Bible—a Bible printed without verse numbers or intruding annotations; sometimes also called a *reader's Bible*

synchronized Bible—a Bible in which the Gospels or certain OT historical books have been melded into a single continuous narrative; also called a *harmony*

translation—implies that a Bible has been translated freshly from the original languages

updated version—an older version of the Bible that has been revised or altered in some form to keep pace with changing times and tastes; usually more extensive than a *modernized version*, which implies just updating of vocabulary

wide-margin edition—a Bible printed with columns of white space in which the reader may write his or her own notes

What Is the Bible? When you say, "the Bible," most people assume they know what you mean, and yet the book exists in a mindboggling number of versions, paraphrases, and translations in English, to say nothing of the many translations into nearly every language on earth. Beyond that, even its basic canon is a matter of dispute among various traditions. For instance, many people who staunchly defend the King James Version as the authoritative English translation are surprised to find that the Apocrypha was not only included in the original edition of 1611 but was considered canonical at the time. The Apocrypha was also included in the earlier Wycliff and Tyndale translations.

To sort out just what is meant by "the Bible," we offer the following four lists: (1) The Bible Canon According to the Major Religions and Denominations; (2) Bible Translations, Paraphrases, and Significant Editions in English (along with their academic reference abbreviations and as much background information as could be conveniently included); (3) Important Non-English Versions of the Bible; and finally, for fun, (4) Infamous Versions of the Bible (known largely for their errors or eccentricities).

The Bible Canon According to the Major Religions and Denominations

Jewish Bible

Contains 24 books, originally written in Hebrew. It is similar in content to the Christian Old Testament, but the two Samuels are one book, as are the two Kings and the two Chronicles, and the 12 shorter prophetic books are combined into one book called "The Minor Prophets." The Jewish Bible is divided into four large groupings:

The Pentateuch (the Torah): Genesis, Exodus, Leviticus, Numbers, and Deuteronomy

The Former Prophets: Joshua, Judges, Samuel, and Kings

The Latter Prophets (the Former and Latter Prophets together are called the Nevi'im): Isaiah, Jeremiah, Ezekiel, and the Minor Prophets (which incorporates Hosea, Joel, Amos, Obadiah, Jonah, Micah, Nahum, Habakkuk, Zephaniah, Haggai, Zechariah, Malachi)

The Writings (the Kethuvim): Psalms, Proverbs, Job, Song of Songs, Ruth, Lamentations, Ecclesiastes, Esther, Daniel, Ezra, Nehemiah, and Chronicles

The acronym used for the major sections of the Jewish Bible is Tanak (Torah, Nevi'im, Kethuvim).

Greek Old Testament (Septuagint)

Written in Greek, it contains 50 books, including all those of the Jewish Bible, though the minor prophets are separated, and many books are slightly altered in content. Job is shorter in the Greek, for instance; portions of 1 Samuel and Jeremiah are not found in the Greek; and some verses are in a different order in Ezekiel and Jeremiah.

The Septuagint adds the following apocryphal books not found in the Jewish Bible: 1 Esdras, Tobit, Judith, Wisdom of Solomon, Wisdom of the Son of Sirach (Ecclesiasticus), Baruch, Epistle of Jeremiah, Song of the Three Holy Children, Susanna, Bel and the Dragon, 1–4 Maccabees, and Prayer of Manesseh.

The Vulgate

The earliest Latin version of the Bible, based on the work of Jerome and extensively revised and edited throughout the Middle Ages. It contains 73 books, with basically the same order and format as the Catholic Bible (see below), which was based on the Vulgate.

Protestant Bible

Contains 66 books. Translated into many languages.

The 39 books of the Old Testament are traditionally divided as follows:

The Historical Books: Genesis, Exodus, Leviticus, Numbers, Deuteronomy, Joshua, Judges, Ruth, 1 Samuel, 2 Samuel, 1 Kings, 2 Kings, 1 Chronicles, 2 Chronicles, Ezra, Nehemiah, and Esther

The Poetical Books: Job, Psalms, Proverbs, Ecclesiastes, and Song of Songs

Protestant Bible (cont.)

The Prophetic Books: Isaiah, Jeremiah, Lamentations, Ezekiel, Daniel, Hosea, Joel, Amos, Obadiah, Jonah, Micah, Nahum, Habakkuk, Zephaniah, Haggai, Zechariah, and Malachi

The 27 books of the New Testament are divided as follows:

The Gospels: Matthew, Mark, Luke, and John

The Acts of the Apostles

The Epistles, or the Letters: Romans, 1 Corinthians, 2 Corinthians, Galatians, Ephesians, Philippians, Colossians, 1 Thessalonians, 2 Thessalonians, 1 Timothy, 2 Timothy, Titus, Philemon, Hebrews, James, 1 Peter, 2 Peter, 1 John, 2 John, 3 John, and Jude

Revelation

Catholic Bible

Available in many languages and often based on the Vulgate (see above). Contains 73 books (46 OT; 27 NT), which are essentially the same as the Protestant Bible, except with the addition of the writings of the Apocrypha (some of which are separate books and others additions to existing OT books):

The Apocrypha: Tobit, Judith, Additions to the Book of Esther, Wisdom of Solomon, Sirach, Baruch, Additions to the Book of Daniel (Susanna, The Song of the Three Holy Children, and Bel and the Dragon), 1 Maccabees, and 2 Maccabees

Note that in the Catholic Bible and Vulgate, the books of the Apocrypha are interspersed throughout, whereas in some Protestant Bibles, when they are included, they are in a separate section between the OT and NT.

Anglican Bible

The same as the Protestant Bible, except it often includes the apocryphal writings from the Catholic Bible as edifying though not canonical. The books of the Apocrypha usually appear as a separate section between the OT and NT.

Eastern Orthodox Bible

Available in many languages. The same contents as the Catholic Bible, with the addition of two more apocryphal books (1 Esdras and the Prayer of Manasseh) and two OT pseudepigraphal writings (Psalm 151 and 3 Maccabees)

Muslim Bible

Muslims believe that the Jewish Bible and Christian NT are divinely inspired and should be respected. They admire the Torah, the Psalms (called *Zaboor*), and the Gospels (called *Injeel*) in particular but believe both the OT and NT texts are corrupted, with original portions having been lost or tampered with by partisan faiths. They accept specific tenets of the Bible insofar as they are confirmed by the Qur'an, and any tenet contradictory to the Qur'an is rejected as a human corruption.

The Book of Mormon

> The Church of Jesus Christ of the Latter-Day Saints (Mormons) accepts the Protestant Bible as translated by Joseph Smith as authoritative but considers the Book of Mormon, which is called "Another Testament of Jesus Christ," to be equally canonical.

Bible Translations, Paraphrases, and Significant Editions in English

Style. In general, the names for all versions and translations of the Bible are set in roman type—for instance, the King James Bible, the New International Version, the Douay Version—especially when those versions appear in many different editions and formats. When a specific edition of a particular version is referred to, however, it should be italicized as a common book title—*The Good News Bible, The NIV Study Bible, The King James 2000 Bible.*

The abbreviations of Bible translations, paraphrases, and significant editions are usually set in roman type. If the abbreviation is an acronymn incorporating the initial letters of the version, the letters are set in full capitals; for instance, NIV is the correct abbreviation for the New International Version. This is a major change from the former style of setting those abbreviations in small caps. Likewise, if the abbreviation is the last name of the translator or paraphraser, it is set in roman type with an initial capital letter, followed by lowercase letters; for instance, Phillips is the abbreviation for that author's paraphrase, *The New Testament in Modern English.* If the abbreviation is a complete word from the title of a specific edition, then it is set in italics; for instance, *Anchor* is the correct abbreviation for *The Anchor Bible.*

This list presents a standard that can easily accommodate variations in typographic style as needed.

Abbreviation	Title and Information
AB	Amplified Bible; (1958–65, rev. 1987)
ABUV	American Bible Union Version; (1912)
Aitken	Aitken Bible (NT 1777, complete 1782; first English language Bible printed in America; essentially adapted from KJV)
AIV	*An Inclusive Version* (1995; gender-neutral revision of NRSV; Psalms and NT only)
Alford	*New Testament in Basic English* (Alford)
ALT	*Analytic-Literal Translation* (Darkness to Light Ministries; 1999; online literal NT trans.: *dtl.org/alt/index.html*)
Anchor	*The Anchor Bible* (1964)
ARV	*American Revised Version* (1901; US edition of ERV; public domain)
ARV, MG	*American Revised Version*, margin
ASV	*American Standard Version* (1901; US edition of ERV; public domain)
AT	*The Complete Bible: An American Translation* (Goodspeed, Smith, and others; NT 1923; OT 1927; Apoc. 1938)
AV	Authorized Version (1611; same as KJV; used in British references; public domain)

Barclay	*The New Testament* (William Barclay; 1968–69)
Bassendyne	The Bassendyne Bible (first Bible printed in English in Scotland; NT 1576; whole Bible 1579; used the text of the Geneva Bible)
BB	*The Basic Bible* (C. K. Ogden; 1950; uses basic vocabulary of 850 words)
BBE	*The Bible in Basic English* (1949; updated 1962; public domain in US only)
Beck	*New Testament in Language of Today* (Beck; Lutheran; 1963; rev. 1976; reprinted in 1990 as *God's Word to the Nations*)
Bishop	The Bishop's Bible (Archbishop Parker and others; 1568; a revision of the Great Bible; sometimes called "Matthew Parker's Bible"; public domain)
BLE	*Bible in Living English* (1972; used by Jehovah's Witnesses)
BV	*Berkeley Version in Modern English* (NT 1945; OT 1959)
BWE	*Bible in Worldwide English* (Annie Cressman; 1959; also referred to as "Cressman")
Cassirer	*The Cassirer New Testament* (Heinz W. Cassirer; 1989)
CENT	*Common English New Testament* (American Bible Union; 1865; public domain)
CEV	*Contemporary English Version* (American Bible Society; 1995; fifth-grade reading level)
CJB	*Complete Jewish Bible* (1998; David H. Stern, OT)
CLNT	*Concordant Literal New Testament* (1926; A. E. Knoch, NT)
CNT	*The Centenary New Testament* (1924)
Coverdale	Coverdale Bible (Miles Coverdale; 1535; first full English translation to be printed and its 1537 edition was the first full version to be printed in England; incorporates Tyndale's Pentateuch and NT; public domain)
CPV	*The Cotton Patch Version* (1973; loose paraphrase by Clarence Jordan; same as Jordan)
Cranmer	Cranmer's Bible (the 1540 edition of the Great Bible, with prologue by Cranmer)
Cressman	See BWE
CSB	*The Christian Standard Bible* (Southern Baptist Convention; not yet published)
Darby	*The Darby Translation* (1871; Dispensationalist; public domain)
DB	*The Dartmouth Bible* (abridgment of KJV; 1961)
DNT	*Documents of the New Testament* (1934; paraphrase by G. W. Wade)
DV	Douay Version, also called Douay-Rheims Bible (NT 1582; OT 1609–10; based on Vulgate)
Easy	*The Easy to Read Version* (for deaf readers and ESL readers; fourth-grade reading level)
EB	*Emphasized Bible* (Rotherham; NT 1897; OT 1902; public domain)
ERV	English Revised Version (first major revision of KJV; NT 1881; OT 1885; Apoc. 1895; same as RV; public domain)
ERV, MG	English Revised Version, margin
ESV	*The Holy Bible: English Standard Version* (Crossway; 2001)
Geneva	Geneva Bible (first English Bible with verse divisions; trans. by William Whittingham, Anthony Gilby, and Thomas Sampson; 1560; popularly referred to as "The Breeches Bible" for its translation of Gen. 3:7)
GNT	*Good News Translation* (same as TEV; also called *Good News Bible* and *Good News for Modern Man*; NT 1966; OT 1976)
Great	Great Bible (Coverdale's revision of Matthew Bible; 1539; 1539 edition called "Cromwell's Bible" because of his portrait on title page; 1540 edition called "Cranmer's Bible" for his portrait)

GWT	*God's Word Translation* (Luther Bible Society; 1995; update of Beck)
GWTN	*God's Word to the Nations* (1995; same as GWT)
Hammond	*Hammond's Paraphrase* (Henry Hammond; 1653; NT, based on KJV)
HNB	*Holy Name Bible* (1963)
HNV	*Hebrew Names Version of the World English Bible* (rev. of WEB that uses Hebrew names; public domain)
Hooke	*The Bible in Basic English* (Hooke; NT 1940; OT 1949)
ICB	*The International Children's Bible* (1986; same as ICV)
ICV	*The International Children's Version* (original name for NCV; 1986; same as ICB)
ISV	*International Standard Version* (ISV Foundation; NT 1998; OT not yet released)
IV	*Inspired Version* (1867; supposedly "inspired" revision by Joseph Smith, Mormon founder; also called *Joseph Smith Translation*; public domain)
JB	*Jerusalem Bible* (first Catholic Bible translated from original languages rather than from Vulgate; French 1956; English 1966; French version referred to as BJ: *La Bible de Jérusalem*)
Jefferson	Jefferson Bible (Thomas Jefferson's extracted version of KJV NT Gospels; c. 1820; public domain)
JNT	*The Jewish New Testament*
Jordan	*Cotton Patch Version* (Clarence Jordan's dialect paraphrase; 1973; same as CPV)
JPS	*Holy Scriptures: Jewish Publication Society Version of the Old Testament* (1917)
JST	*The Joseph Smith Translation* (Joseph Smith, founder of the Church of the Latter Day Saints; 1867)
KJ2000	*The King James 2000 Bible*
KJ21	*Twenty-first Century King James Version of the Holy Bible* (1994; modernized KJV)
KJII	*King James II Version* (1971)
KJC	*King James, Clarified* (modernized KJV)
KJV	King James Version (same as Authorized Version; 1611; public domain)
Knox	*Holy Bible: A Translation from the Latin Vulgate in the Light of the Hebrew and Greek Original* (Knox; NT 1945; OT 1949)
Lamsa	*Holy Bible from Ancient Eastern Manuscripts* (Lamsa; 1933, 1939, 1940, 1957)
Lattimore	*The Four Gospels and the Revelation* (Lattimore; 1979); *Acts and Letters of the Apostles* (Lattimore; 1982)
LB	*The Living Bible* (Kenneth Taylor; paraphrase; NT 1967; OT 1970; also called *The Book*, and later reprinted as *The Way*)
Leeser	*The Leeser Bible* (a nineteenth century Jewish version by Isaac Leeser; public domain)
LO	*Living Oracles* (Alexander Campbell; 1835; NT; public domain)
Lorimer	*The New Testament in Scots* (Scots dialect NT by William L. Lorimer; 1983)
LTHB	*Literal Translation of the Holy Bible* (Jay P. Green; 1976; only available on software and online)
Matthew	Matthew Bible (Thomas Matthew; 1537; first English Bible printed in England)
MKJV	*Modern King James Version* (J. P. Green; 1999; modernized KJV)
MLB	*Modern Language Bible* (NT 1945; same as NBV; OT 1959)

MLV	*Modern Literal Version* (a software version, updating of the ASV; public domain)
Moffatt	*A New Translation of the Bible* (Moffatt; NT 1913; OT 1924; rev. 1935)
Montgomery	*Centenary Translation of the New Testament in Modern English* (Helen Montgomery and American Baptist Publication Society; 1924)
Moulton	*Modern Reader's Bible* (Moulton; 1907; public domain)
MSG	*The Message: The Bible in Contemporary Language* (paraphrastic translation by Eugene Peterson; NT 1993; whole Bible 2000)
NAB	*New American Bible* (Catholic; NT 1941; OT 1969)
NASB	*New American Standard Bible* (Lockman Foundation; NT 1963; OT 1971; rev. 1995)
NASB95	*New American Standard Bible* (Lockman Foundation; 1995 update of NASB)
NAV	*The New Authorized Version* (1998; updated KJV with Apocrypha; same as TMB)
NBV	*New Berkeley Version in Modern English* (NT 1945; OT 1959; same as MLB)
NCV	*The New Century Version* (third-grade reading level; NT 1978; complete 1986; same as ICB and ICV)
NE	*The New Evangelical New Testament* (1990; NT of GWTN)
NEB	*New English Bible* (NT 1961; OT and Apoc. 1970)
NET	*The New English Translation* (Biblical Studies Foundation; 1997; software and online)
NIrV	*New International Reader's Version* (International Bible Society; 1996; third-grade-reading-level version of NIV; gender-inclusive language of British edition removed in US version. Note the lowercase "r" amid the full capitals)
NIV	*New International Version* (International Bible Society; NT 1973; OT 1978)
NIVSB	*NIV Study Bible* (1985)
NJB	*The New Jerusalem Bible* (update of JB; 1985)
NJPS	*Tanak: The Holy Scriptures: The New Jewish Publication Society Translation According to the Traditional Hebrew Text* (1988; update of JPS)
NJV	*New Jewish Version* (rev. of JPS, 1962–82; Torah rev. 1985)
NKJV	*New King James Version* (loosely based on KJV, though largely new trans.; 1979)
NLT	*New Living Translation* (Tyndale House; 1996; trans. based on LB, but less paraphrastic; sixth-grade reading level)
NLV	*New Life Version* (Gleason H. and Kathryn Ledyard; 1969; third-grade reading level, uses basic vocabulary of 850 words)
NNT	*Noli New Testament* (Albanian Orthodox Church in America; NT; 1961)
Norlie	*New Testament in Modern English* (Norlie; 1951)
Noyes	*The New Testament* (Noyes; 1868; public domain)
NRSV	*The New Revised Standard Version* (National Council of Churches; 1990; rev. of RSV; gender-inclusive)
NSRB	*New Scofield Reference Bible* (KJV; 1967)
NTUV	*New Testament: An Understandable Version* (1998)
NWT	*New World Translation of the Holy Scriptures* (Watchtower Bible and Tract Society [Jehovah's Witnesses]; loosely based on ASV; 1961)
OAB	*Oxford Annotated Bible* (RSV; 1962)
OBP	*Original Bible Project* (literal version was due 2000 online; still in progress)

ORSV	*Oxford Revised Standard Version* (Catholic version of RSV)
Phillips	*New Testament in Modern English* (paraphrase by J. B. Phillips; 1958; later editions less paraphrastic)
PNC	*People's New Covenant* (Christian Scientist; 1925)
RDB	*Reader's Digest Bible* (heavily condensed RSV; 1982)
REB	*Revised English Bible* (the second edition and revision of NEB; 1989)
Rheims	Rheims New Testament (NT of DV; 1582; public domain)
Rieu	*Penguin Bible* (Rieu; 1952)
RSV	*Revised Standard Version* (National Council of Churches; NT 1946; OT 1952; Apoc. 1957; rev. of ASV)
RV	Revised Version (NT 1881; OT 1885; Apoc. 1895; public domain)
RV, MG	Revised Version, margin
SEB	*Simple English Bible* (International Bible Translators, Inc.; NT 1980)
Smith	Joseph Smith Translation (Joseph Smith, Mormon; 1867; public domain; also referred to as the *Inspired Version*, or IV)
SRB	*Scofield Reference Bible* (KJV; 1909)
Taverner	Taverner's Bible (trans. by Richard Taverner; 1537; public domain; revision of Matthew)
TB	*Today's Bible* (retitling of GWTN; 1995)
TCNT	*Twentieth Century New Testament* (based on Weymouth; 1898–1901; public domain)
TEB	*The Everyday Bible* (1986; same as NCV)
TEV	*Today's English Version* (American Bible Society; NT 1966; OT 1976; also called *The Good News Bible* and *Good News for Modern Man*; easy reading level)
TMB	*Third Millennium Bible* (modernized KJV, with some Apocrypha; 1998; same as NAV)
TNIV	*Today's New International Version* (International Bible Society updating of NIV, gender-inclusive; NT 2002; OT 2005)
Tyndale	Tyndale New Testament (1526; based largely on both Erasmus's Greek Testament and Latin version, as well as the Vulgate and Luther's German version; the Pentateuch followed c. 1530; public domain)
WEB	*World English Bible* (based on ASV; currently in progress; public domain)
Webster	Webster's Bible (Noah Webster's rev. of KJV, with updated spelling; 1833; public domain)
Wesley	Wesley New Testament (John Wesley's rev. of KJV; 1790; public domain)
Weymouth	*Weymouth's New Testament in Modern Speech* (Richard Weymouth; 1903; rev. 1924 and 1929)
Williams, C.B.	*New Testament: A Translation in Language of the People* (Charles B. Williams; 1937)
Williams, C.K.	*New Testament in Plain English* (Charles K. Williams; 1963)
Wuest	*Wuest Expanded Translation* (1961)
Wycliffe	Wycliffe Bible (c. 1380; trans. from Vulgate by Nicholas of Hereford and an anonymous translator. Two early versions exist: Bodley [before 1382, catalogued in Bodley Library as MS Bodley 959] and Purvey [c. 1400]. Not actually printed in its complete form until 1810; public domain)
YLT	*Young's Literal Translation of the Bible* (Young; 1862; based on KJV; rev. 1887, 1898, new rev. forthcoming; public domain)

Important Non-English Versions of the Bible

Abbreviation	Title and Information
Aquila	Version of Aquila (c. AD 130; Greek OT)
Bedell	Bedell's Bible (trans. of KJV into Irish)
BHK	*Biblia Hebraica* (Rudolf Kittel; Hebrew OT text; 1925 and others)
BHS	*Biblia Hebraica Stuttgartensia* (Hebrew OT text; 1983 and others)
BJ	*La Bible de Jérusalem* (original French; 1956)
CP	Complutensian Polyglot (first Bible printed in Greek and Hebrew; in six volumes; 1513–17)
Eliot	Algonquin Bible (John Eliot; first Bible printed in America; 1662)
Erasmus	Erasmus New Testament (Latin trans. from Greek of NT by Erasmus; 1516)
Ferrara	Ferrara Bible (first Spanish OT, trans. from Hebrew; 1553)
Gutenberg	Gutenberg Bible (Johannes Gutenberg; first Bible and first book printed on a printing press with movable type; the Latin Vulgate; 1456; sometimes called the Forty-two Line Bible; followed by the Thirty-Six Line Bible, c. 1458–59)
HT	Hebrew Bible (OT; general name for many editions)
Leopolita	Polish trans. of Vulgate by John of Lemberg; 1561
Luther	Luther Bible (Martin Luther trans. into German; 1534)
LXX	Septuagint (3d and 2d centuries BC; Greek version of Hebrew Bible; the four notable editions are the Complutensian, the Aldine, the Grabian, and the Vatican Codex)
Mazarin	A specific copy of the Gutenberg Bible discovered in the Mazarin Library, Paris, in 1760
MT	Masoretic Text (basis for Christian OT; c. 1100)
NA27	*Novum Testamentum Graece*, 27th ed. (Erwin Nestle and Kurt Aland; 1993)
Ostrog	First complete Slavonic Bible, printed in Russia; 1581
Pagninus	First complete Latin translation from original languages by a modern scholar (1528; Santes Pagninus)
Sacy	An early French translation by Louis de Sacy; c. 1670
Sauer	Sauer Bible (German Luther Bible; the first Bible printed in America in a European language; 1743)
Stephanus	Stephanus Greek New Testament (printed in Paris by Robert Stephanus; first NT to have verse numbers; one of the sources for KJV and other translations; 1551)
Symmachus	Version of Symmachus (late 2d. cent.; idiomatic Greek OT)
Theodotion	Version of Theodotion (early 2d cent.; Greek OT; partly a revision of LXX)
UBS4	*The Greek New Testament*, 4th ed. (United Bible Societies; last rev. 2000)
Vulg.	Latin Vulgate (Jerome; 405; also called the Jerome Bible)
WH	*The New Testament in the Original Greek* (B. F. Westcott and F. J. A. Hort; 1881)
Wuyck	Wuyck's Bible (first authorized Polish translation; 1599)
Zurich	The Zurich Bible (1530; incorporates Luther's NT and portions of his OT; predates Luther's complete translation by four years)

Infamous Versions of the Bible

Why include a list of Bibles famous largely for their errors? Admittedly this list is provided largely for whimsical reasons, but they do have a more serious purpose as well. First, they are interesting in themselves. Second, the list will assist the author, editor, and proofreader when a reference is made to one of these Bibles.

Most books don't achieve fame solely for their misprints, but the Bible is an exception because of the aura of sanctity that surrounds it. The only other writings that even distantly compete with the Bible for their number of infamous editions are the works of Shakespeare, which have acquired an aura of sanctity all their own. For instance, in one edition, Hamlet's famous "To be or not to be" was rendered "To be or to be." The edition was dubbed the Optimist's Shakespeare.

Also, there are some fine points to the styling of these titles. For instance, when the misprint itself becomes part of the popular title, it is placed in quotation marks. If it is a generic term describing the mistake, the word is not set in quotes. (In the following notes, the correct word is sometimes provided in brackets.) All of these are set in roman type because they are actually descriptive epithets rather than formal titles.*

Mistake	Description
"Adultery" Bible	A 1631 KJV, printed for Charles I by Robert Barker and Martin Lucas, renders the seventh commandment "Thou shalt commit adultery." Also called the Wicked Bible.
Affinity Bible	A 1923 KJV contains a table of family affinities that includes the line "A man may not marry his grandmother's wife."
"Breeches" Bible	The first Geneva Bible (1560) renders Gen. 3:7 "They sowed figge tree leaves together, and made themselves breeches."
"Bug" Bible	The first Coverdale Bible (1535) translates "terrors" as "bugs" in Ps. 91:5: "Thou shalt not nede to be afrayed for eny bugges by night." In its defense, however, the word *bugges* at that time meant "bogie," or ghosts.
"Camels" Bible	An 1823 KJV translates "camels" for "damsels" in Gen. 24:61: "And Rebekah arose, and her camels."
Denial Bible	A 1792 KJV has Philip denying Christ rather than Peter in Luke 22:34.
"Discharge" Bible	An 1806 KJV reads "discharge" for "charge" in 1 Tim. 5:21: "I discharge thee before God . . ."
"Ears to Ear" Bible	An 1810 KJV renders Matt. 13:43 "Who hath ears to ear, let him hear."
"Fool" Bible	A KJV printed for Charles I renders Ps. 14:1 "A fool hath said in his heart there is a God."

*This list is loosely adapted from both William S. Walsh's *Handy Book of Literary Curiosities* (Philadelphia: Lippincott, 1892) and *Brewer's Dictionary of Phrase and Fable* (New York: Harper & Brothers, n.d.).

"Forgotten Sins" Bible	A 1638 KJV renders Luke 7:47 "Her sins which are many are forgotten [forgiven]."
Harwood's Bible	English minister Edward Harwood (18th century) paraphrased NT in the genteel language of the day. For example, in Rev. 3:15–16, Christ tells the Laodicean church: "Since, therefore, you are now in a state of lukewarmness, a disagreeable medium between the two extremes, I will, in no long time, eject you from my heart with fastidious contempt."
"He" Bible; "She" Bible	The first KJV of 1611 renders Ruth 3:15 "he went into the city," which is, according to the Hebrew, correct. The second printing incorrectly rendered it "she went into the city." Nearly all subsequent English versions reproduced the error until it was corrected in the Revised Version, 1885.
Incunabula Bible	Transposed numbers on the title page of this Elizabethan Bible dated its printing as 1495 rather than 1594.
"Judas" Bible	One printing of the 1611 KJV has Judas rather than Jesus initiating the Last Supper in Matt. 26:26.
Leda Bible	A 1572 Bishop's Bible scandalously borrows decorative woodcuts from an edition of Ovid's *Metamorphoses*, including one of Leda and the swan.
"Lions" Bible	A notoriously error-riddled printing of KJV that, among other errors, renders 1 Kings 8:19 "Thy son . . . shall come forth out of thy lions [loins]."
"More Sea" Bible	A 1641 KJV renders Rev. 21:1 as "there was more sea" rather than "there was no more sea."
"Murderers" Bible	An 1801 KJV renders "murderers" for "murmurers" in Jude 16: "These are murderers, complainers, walking after their own lusts."
"Placemakers" Bible	A 1562 Geneva Bible renders Matt. 5:9 "Blessed are the placemakers [peacemakers]."
"Printers" Bible	A 1702 KJV renders Ps. 119:161 "Printers [princes] have persecuted me without a cause."
"Rosin" Bible	The 1609 Douay Bible translates "balm" as "rosin" in Jer. 8:22: "Is there noe rosin in Galaad?" See also "Treacle" Bible.
"Sin On" Bible	The first English Bible printed in Ireland (1716) renders John 5:14 as "Sin on more" rather than "Sin no more."
"Standing Fishes" Bible	An 1806 KJV renders Ezek. 47:10 "The fishes [fishermen] shall stand upon it."
"To Remain" Bible	In 1805 a proofreader marked on some galleys that a comma was "to remain." His instructions were mistakenly transferred to the text of Gal. 4:29: "Persecuted him that was born after the spirit to remain, even so it is now."
"Treacle" Bible	The first Bishop's Bible (1568) translated "balm" as "treacle" in Jer. 8:22: "Is there no tryacle in Gilead?" See also "Rosin" Bible.
"Unrighteous" Bible	A 1653 KJV leaves out the word "not" in 1 Cor. 6:9: "The unrighteous shall inherit the Kingdom of God."
"Vinegar" Bible	A 1717 KJV titles Luke 20 "The Parable of the Vinegar [Vineyard]."
Wicked Bible	See "Adultery" Bible.
"Wife-hater" Bible	An 1810 KJV renders Luke 14:26 "If any man come to me, and hate not his father and mother . . . yea, and his own wife [life] also . . ."

Bible Versus *Scripture*

See "*Scripture* Versus *Bible.*"

Biblical Time

See "Hours, Biblical" and "*Watches of the Night.*"

Bibliography

See "Sources."

Block Quotations

See "Quotations."

Body Matter, Elements of a Book's

The *body matter* of a book is its essential content, its primary reason for being a book in the first place. The elements of any book's body matter should be arranged in the following order, as appropriate:

Inside half-title page (recto if used, followed by a blank verso)
Prologue
Part title page (on recto page, usually followed by a blank verso)
Part epigraph (if it applies to entire part; on recto, verso, or part-title page)
Chapter title page (on recto page)
Chapter epigraph (if it applies to chapter only; on recto, verso, or chapter-title page)
Chapter number and title (usually on recto page)
Text of chapter (usually starts recto)
Discussion questions (on recto, verso, or last page of chapter)
Chapter endnotes (on recto, verso, or last page of chapter)
Chapter bibliography or "For Further Reading" (on recto, verso, or last page of chapter)
Epilogue or conclusion (on recto page)

Boldface Type

As a rule, authors, designers, and editors should avoid using boldface type in text, although it is commonly used in heads and display type. The kind of emphasis gained from boldface type can usually be achieved with less unevenness of appearance and distraction by using italics.

By contrast, boldface type may be useful and appropriate in reference books, workbooks, and other books in which design aesthetics are of secondary concern and in which extra emphasis is needed.

Boldface type is commonly used in reference materials to indicate cross-references, though, again, italics are often used instead. In place of both boldface and italic, which can equally be confused with emphasis, many academic works use *cf.* (Latin *confer*, to compare), which is an abbreviation commonly used for cross-references. When boldface is used to indicate a cross-reference, that fact should be made clear to the reader in a note at the beginning of the book.

Bookmaking Terminology

Like any trade, the book production industry has developed its own terminology. The list below demystifies some of the more common terms that refer to the physical makeup of the book, as opposed to the typographic or editorial makeup. These should prove helpful to the author when discussing the actual packaging of his or her creation.

absorption—the rate at which ink dries as it is absorbed in paper

accordion fold—paper folded in a zigzag fashion

acetate—transparent plastic laid over artwork on which color separation and other instructions can be written

achromatic colors—black, white, and gray are considered *achromatic colors* for printing purposes

acid-free paper—paper made without acid content (neutral PH); prolongs paper life

advance copies—copies of a book sent to an author or reviewer before publication date

alkaline paper—high quality acid-free paper

antique—a natural or slightly cream-colored paper

antique finish—a slightly rough texture on paper, often used on covers

archival paper—the highest quality acid-free paper, used mostly for documents

back flap—the back (right hand) folded portion of a dust jacket

back lining—a cloth or paper strip glued to the signatures to hold them together

bind—to join pages together with thread, wire, glue, or other adhesives

binding—the gathering and adhering of printed signatures

bleed—when printed material is intended to run off the trimmed edge of a page

blind stamp—embossing a book's cover or dust jacket with a raised image that does not carry ink or metallic leaf; also called *blind embossing*

blowup—to enlarge

broadside—a single sheet, printed flat and either unfolded or folded once

broadside page—a printed page that must be turned on its side to be read

case—the cover of a hardcover book

casebound—a book with a stiff cover; also called *hardcover* or *clothbound*

cast off—to estimate the length of a book before typesetting

chapbook—a single signature book, usually with fewer than 44 pages

clothbound—a book with a hard cover; also called *hardcover* or *casebound*

composition—the setting of the book's type

crash—the piece of cloth sometimes used to reinforce the spine of a book's cover

crop—to trim the edges of a photo or other graphic image

dead copy—once a new set of galleys is run, the previous version is called the *dead copy*; sometimes called *foul proof*

dead matter—the old galleys and papers returned from the printer

die cut—the cutting of holes in paper by using sharp steel rules bent to the appropriate shape

double-page spread—facing pages on which the print or image runs across the gutter

drop shipment—paying to have a shipment sent to another address

dummy—a mockup, or preliminary layout, to give a rough idea of the finished product

dust jacket—the printed and folded paper sheet that wraps around the cover of a hardcover book

embossing—pressing a relief image onto paper, either with or without foil or ink

end paper—also called *end sheet*; the piece of paper glued to the inside of a book's cover to hide the tabs where the case is glued to the signatures. End papers can be printed or colored or left blank.

errata—a loose, printed piece of paper inserted into a book, acknowledging and correcting printer's errors

f & g—short for "folded and gathered"; an unbound copy of a book's signatures

flap—the front or back folded portion of a dust jacket

flap copy—the text printed on a book's dust jacket flaps

flyleaf—the half of the end paper not glued down to the case; it is usually the first and last page in any book

foil—thin metallic material impressed on paper with a stamping die; used on covers

foul proof—see *dead copy*

foxing—brown spotting on old or non-acid-free papers

front flap—the front (left hand) folded portion of a dust jacket

galleys—pages of the book printed out for inspection purposes before the final printing is done

gatefold—a page that folds out; a cover or two facing interior pages that fold out from the book

gutter—the space, or margin, between two columns of text; in most books this falls in the place where the pages are gathered into the spine

halftone—a method of reproducing art of photographs that converts the image into a series of minute, printable dots

hard copy—a paper copy as opposed to a computer or digitized copy

hardcover, or hardbound—a book with a stiff cover; same as *clothbound* or *casebound*

headband—a piece of decorative fabric, formerly sewn, now glued to the top and bottom of a hardcover book, between the case and the gathered pages

hinge—the place where the cover is connected to the spine of the book; also called a *joint*

imposition—arranging the pages so that they will print in the correct order

ink-jet printer—a method of printing by spraying minute dots of ink onto paper

jog—to align paper along the edge

joint—the place where the cover is connected to the spine of the book; also called a *hinge*

keyline—a finished piece of art, showing the final position and color, ready for the printer

laser printer—a method of printing in which a beam of laser light is projected on paper so as to attract ink (called *toner*)

library binding—an especially durable book bound in accordance with standards established by the American Library Association

line art—artwork that contains no gray tones, only black and white; also called *line drawing*

live copy—the most recent and current set of galleys; contrast with *dead copy*

mackle—an intentional double or blurred image on a printed page

markup—marking a paper copy of a book, indicating the elements of a book for the typesetter; in digitized copies of manuscripts, this means the addition of codes to indicate the different elements

newsprint—paper made from raw ground wood

oblong—binding a book along its shorter edge

offprint—a book page or the cover of the book, printed in single sheets for promotional purposes

overrun—copies of a book printed in excess of the planned print run

paperbound—a book with a paper or light cardboard cover; also called *softcover*

perfect binding—a method of binding that uses glue to fasten the pages together after the folds have been trimmed off

prepress—all the steps in production before the actual printing is done

printer-ready copy—a paper or digitized copy of the final book from which the book will be printed ream—500 sheets of paper, regardless of weight or size

recycled paper—previously printed paper than has been pulped, bleached of ink, and made into new sheets of paper

run-around—type that is shaped so as to fit around an image on the page

saddlestitch—a binding method of holding the pages of a single signature together by using a staple, wire, or thread

self-cover—using the same paper for the cover of a book as is used for the text pages

sew-and-glue—holding sewn signatures together with hot adhesive and a glued paper cover

short run—a print run of 100 to 2,000 copies

show through—ink printed on one side of a page but visible from the other; some show through is unavoidable, but the goal of printing is to minimize it

shrink wrap—clear plastic that is heat-shrunk around books to protect them in shipping

signature—large sheets of paper that are printed, folded into booklet-looking bundles, and gathered to make up the book's pages

slip case—a decorated cloth- or paper-covered cardboard box into which a single book or a set of books can be inserted

Smyth sewn—a method of sewing signatures together that allows the book's pages to open flat, with little bend in the gutter

softcover—a book with a paper or light cardboard cover; also called *paperbound*

spine—the part of the book that connects the two covers together and holds in the book's pages

spiral binding—holding pages together by use of a spiral-shaped length of wire

spot varnish—applying a shiny coating to only a specified portion of a book's cover

tapes—strips of paper or cloth added to a book's binding to give it extra strength

tear sheet—a page torn from a book, showing corrections needing to be made

thumb edge—the edge of the book opposite the binding

tip-in—a separate page intended to be glued into a book after printing

trade book—any book intended to be sold to the general public

trim—cutting away the edges of a book or of paper

varnish—a clear protective coating added to paper

vignette—an illustration in which the edges fade

watermark—a faint image impressed on paper by the papermaker to identify the maker; can be seen only when held up to the light

webpress—a printing press that prints on a continuous roll of paper and on both sides of the paper, and cuts and folds sheets into signatures

Born Again

This term, which finds its origin in John 3:3, should be hyphenated as an adjective (*born-again Christian*) but set as two words otherwise (*he was born again*).

While this well-worn term still has credibility among evangelical Christians, it has been somewhat tarnished through overuse. For many people, both inside and outside the church, it has an aura of religious cant. Since the seventies, the popular press has used it sarcastically to describe anyone who has adopted a new creed or enthusiasm with zeal, as in *a born-again fiscal conservative* or *a born-again vegetarian*. For these reasons, the term should be used with care or even avoided if the target readership is wider than the specifically Christian subculture.

Braces

Braces { } are seldom used in ordinary typesetting. Sometimes referred to as *curly brackets*, they are used primarily as a means of grouping a number of items together, such as multiple lines of type. Unlike brackets and parentheses, braces are not necessarily used in pairs, and because of their special function of bracketing many items, they are also extended in length as needed.

Brackets

Types. Four different typographic devices are commonly referred to as *brackets*:

square brackets [ ], usually called simply *brackets*
round brackets ( ), usually called *parentheses*
curly brackets { }, usually called *braces*
angle brackets < >, also called *less than* and *greater than signs*

All of these are used to enclose parenthetical or appended material in various contexts, but since, after parentheses, the square brackets are the most often used in text preparation, the term *brackets*, unmodified, refers to them. (For more detail about round brackets, see "Parentheses.")

Appropriateness. By and large, all brackets, except for parentheses, should be used as seldom as possible since most readers are unfamiliar with their technical functions. Wherever possible, commas or ordinary parentheses should be used for parenthetical elements. In ordinary text curly brackets and angle brackets should never be used. Square brackets, however, are unavoidable in certain situations, such as in quoted material or within parentheses.

Within Quoted Material. Square brackets are most commonly used to contain an editorial comment, substitution, or explanation within quoted material.

The bracketed word may either replace a word in the original or be placed next to a word as an amplification or as a correction to an error.

> "On September 2, 1666, [Richard Baxter] witnessed the Great Fire of London." [Replaces a word in the original.]
>
> "The creed was first proposed by Eusebius [of Caesarea] in AD 325." [Amplifies the meaning of a word.]
>
> "Gutenberg [actually Fust and Shoeffer using Gutenberg's types] completed the Psalter in 1457." [Corrects an error.]

For Parenthetical Thought. Brackets are also commonly used to mark a parenthetical statement made within an already parenthetical context (sometimes called *parentheses within parentheses*).

> Daniel interpreted the mysterious inscription (*"Mene, mene, tekel, parsin"* [Dan. 5:25]) immediately before Belshazzar's death.

When Adjacent to Parentheses. When an open or close square bracket is placed immediately adjacent to an open or close parenthesis, a thin space should be inserted between them.

With Font Changes. All types of brackets should be set in the same font as the surrounding sentence or text, not necessarily in the same font as the material contained within the brackets. For examples, see "Parentheses, *With Font Changes.*")

Brand Names

Often, the distinction between brand names, which are trademarked and therefore capitalized, and their generic equivalents is a useful one. The use of a well-known brand name in writing is generally acceptable as long as the writer has a specific reason for specifying the product by name, though obviously the writer should avoid any negative or defamatory statements about the specific brand. If a product is being singled out for criticism by name, the author or editor should always ask an attorney to review the manuscript before publication. Also, the brand name should never be used in such a way (as in a title or in cover or advertising copy) as to suggest that the brand's maker is endorsing the book or product.

In fiction, brand names are frequently used to give the narrative an air of realism. Again, this is usually acceptable as long as the context is not one that might give offense to the product's manufacturer (such as a character getting sick or dying after using a given product).

Even the above guidelines are no guarantee that an especially aggressive trademark owner won't attempt to sue for perceived damages or to have the publisher cease using the name, but the guidelines offer the best protection for the publisher. Still, litigation, even if unlikely to succeed, can be costly. So caution is recommended.

Trademark Symbol. When a brand name is used in text, the trademark-registration symbol ® does not need to be shown after the brand or trade name. This is distracting to the reader and unnecessary in most contexts. A trademark symbol, ® or ™, should be used, however, whenever a registered trademark name is used on the cover of a book, for instance, or in advertising copy or anywhere else where its use might be taken as an endorsement of the product, and permission for its use must first be obtained in writing from the trademark owner. In most cases, obtaining such permission must be done by contract and an attorney should be consulted.

Word Lists. Two lists follow. The first itemizes some common brand names that are often mistaken for generic terms. The generic name is also given as an alternative. The second list shows brand names that because of their age, common usage, or numerous imitators have passed into general use and are therefore lowercased. The generic terms, as well as the words in the second list, may be used in pejorative or negative contexts if necessary, since no specific manufacturer is implied.

Common Brand Names and Their Generic Equivalents

Alka-Seltzer—effervescent antacid tablets
Anacin—analgesic tablets, aspirin
Autoharp—button-chorded zither
Baggies—plastic bags
Band-Aid—adhesive bandage
Books on Tape—audio book, audio tape
Bufferin—buffered aspirin
Chap Stick—lip balm
Coca-Cola, or Coke—cola, pop, soda, or soft drink
Crock-Pot—slow cooker
Dacron—polyester fiber
Day-Glo paint—fluorescent paint
Dictaphone—dictating machine
Dobro—metal bodied guitar
Dramamine—anti-nauseant
Drano—drain opener
Dumpster—trash bin
Fig Newton—fig cookie
Formica—laminated plastic
Freon—refrigerant
Frigidaire—refrigerator

Frisbee—toy flying disk
Grand Marnier—liqueur
Jacuzzi—whirlpool bath
Jell-O—flavored gelatin dessert
Kitty Litter—cat-box filler
Kleenex—facial tissue or paper tissue
Kodak—film, camera, etc.
Kool-Aid—powdered soft-drink mix
Kotex—sanitary napkin (pl., *Kotex*)
Laundromat—coin-operated laundry
Levi's—denim jeans (note 's)
Librium—tranquilizer
Liquid Paper—correction fluid
Lycra—spandex, a synthetic fiber
Maalox—antacid liquid
Mace—tear gas
Magic Marker—felt-tipped or marking pen
Masonite—hardboard product
Muzak—background music
Naugahyde—vinyl-coated fabric
Novocain—local anesthetic
NutraSweet—aspartame, nutritive sweetener

Olean—olestra, non-fat cooking oil
Pablum—pabulum
Pampers—disposable diapers
Paxil—antidepressant
Pepsi—cola soft drink
Perrier—carbonated mineral water
Ping-Pong—table tennis
Plexiglas—acrylic plastic
Popsicle—frozen dessert bars
Post-It—sticky tags, self-adhesive notes
Prozac—antidepressant
Pyrex—heat-resistant glass
Q-Tip—cotton swab
Rollerblade—in-line skate
Rolodex—desktop address file
Saltines—soda cracker
Samsonite—luggage
Sanka—decaffeinated coffee
Saran Wrap—plastic wrapping film
Scotch tape—adhesive or cellophane tape

Sheetrock—plaster board
Simoniz, Simonize—paste wax
Stetson—cowboy hat
Styrofoam—plastic foam
Sweet'N Low—sugar substitute
Tabasco—pepper sauce
Tampax—tampon
Tang—instant orange drink
Teflon—nonstick surface
Touch-Tone phone—pushbutton phone
Tums—antacid
Tupperware—plastic storage container
U-Haul—rented moving truck or trailer
Valium—tranquilizer
Vaseline—petroleum jelly
Velcro—fabric fastener
Wite-Out—correction fluid
X-Acto—modeler's knife, layout knife
Xerox—copier, duplicating machine, photo
copier

Former Brand Names Now Considered Generic

aspirin	kerosene	mason jar	shredded wheat
cellophane	lanolin	milk of magnesia	thermos
celluloid	linoleum	mimeograph	trampoline
escalator	linotype	nylon	yo-yo
hula hoop	mah-jongg	raisin bran	zipper

"Britishizing" American Publications

See both "Americanizing British Publications" and "British Style."

British Style

Oscar Wilde once wrote that the British have "everything in common with America . . . except, of course, language." Until a few years ago, British and American publishing seemed mutually exclusive. It was thought that a British book had to be Americanized to succeed in the US, and American books Anglicized in the UK. This is still true to a degree, as evidenced by the differences between the British and American editions of J. K. Rowling's Harry Potter books.

But increasingly, boundaries are falling. Publishers are not nearly as concerned as they once were about styling books to conform to a particular brand of English and are increasingly exporting them without "translation."

Many Americans expect British authors to *read* like British authors, "odd" words and all, and vice versa. Even Harry Potter was not Americanized nearly as much as he would have been ten years earlier. The contrasts between the two styles are relatively straightforward, and readers, whether British or American, find they adapt quickly to the other's style. (See also "Mid-Atlantic Style.")

Only marginally more difficult is the challenge of vocabulary, especially the slang and regional dialects of each language. Kipling's dialect stories are as baffling to Americans as Joel Chandler Harris's are to the British.

While it is a mistake to overemphasize these differences, a few guidelines, given below, will help editors and proofreaders navigate the contrasts between American English and British English (a term disliked by many in England, by the way, who prefer the term *standard English*). At the end is a short vocabulary list that will offer a few common words in both styles.

British Spelling. The differences in spellings between common British and American words can be loosely categorized as follows:

Type	British	American
ae and *oe*	anaemia, anaesthetic, oedema	anemia, anesthetic, edema
-augh and *ough*	draught, plough	draft, plow
-ce / *-se* endings	defence, offence	defense, offense
double l / *single l*	counsellor, jeweller, travelling	counselor, jeweler, traveling
-ize / *-ise* endings	analyse, criticise, paralyse (though *-ize* endings are gaining ground in the UK)	analyze, criticize, paralyze
-our / *-or* endings	colour, honour, labour, savour	color, honor, labor, savor
-re / *-er* endings	centre, spectre, theatre	center, specter, theater
-t / *-ed* for some verbs	burnt, dreamt, learnt	burned, dreamed, learned
-xion / *-tion*	connexion, inflexion	connection, inflection

There are many exceptions to the patterns shown above, however. The word *glamour* is *not* spelled *glamor* in the United States, for example, and American orthography has retained such British *-re* words as *acre*, *euchre*, *lucre*, and *mediocre*. Also note that the British are increasingly using *-ize* endings for such words as *organize* and *agonize*, and the Americans have never discarded the British *-ise* ending in such shared words as *advertise*, *chastise*, *compromise*, *enterprise*, *exercise*, and *supervise*. The British have also largely shifted toward the American *inflection*, *connection*, etc.

American Episcopalians spell the word for morning prayer *matins*, while the Church of England spells it *mattins*. For religious publishers, probably the most noticeable spelling difference is the word *Saviour*, which is usually spelled *Savior* in the United States, although many writers, basing their preference on the King James Bible, use *Saviour* when referring to Christ (but revert to *savior* for all other uses). Also note the difference between *baptise* (UK) and *baptize* (US).

Many other spelling differences exist, but they follow no clear pattern. In general these don't pose a cross-cultural problem because most American readers have little trouble adapting to such alternate spellings as *catalogue*, *cheque*, *enquire*, *fulfil*, *gaol* (for "jail"), *kerb* (for "curb"), *mum* (for "mom"), *programme*, *skilful*, *storey*, *tyre*, *waggon*, and many others.

The words *towards* and *afterwards* tend to be the forms preferred in the UK, whereas both those forms and *toward* and *afterward* are used interchangeably in the US. In either case, maintain consistency.

Collective Nouns Are Often Plural in Number. Although the usage is not entirely consistent in the UK, the British tend to view organizations and other collective nouns for groups of people as plural, whereas Americans usually view them as singular.

> The corporation are braced for a takeover. [British, though sometimes *is*]
> The government have issued checks. [British, though sometimes *has*]
> The couple are travelling to Scotland after the wedding.

Do Not Use the Serial Comma. Most often, the British do not use the serial comma in lists with *and* or *or*.

Use a Spaced En Dash in Place of an Em Dash. It is common in British typography to use an en dash, with spaces on either side, where American typography uses the em dash.

Three-Dot Ellipsis. Use only three-dot ellipses, never in combination with a period, and always with a word space (or 3-to-em space) on either side. This contrasts with the American style, which sometimes uses a period with the ellipsis (called the *three-and-four-dot ellipsis* style). (See also "Ellipses.")

Use Hyphens for Prefixes. In those cases when a prefix begins with the same letter as the word it precedes, the British insert a clarifying hyphen: *co-ordinate*, *re-evaluate*, *pre-eminent*, *no-one*. This was frequently done in the US until the mid-twentieth century, at which time such words began to be run together (as in the case of *coordinate*) or separated (as in the case of *no one*).

Use Single Quotation Marks for Quotes. The British sometimes use single quotation marks (which they refer to as *inverted commas*) wherever Americans would use double quotation marks, most commonly in direct quotations, dialogue, some titles, and so on, although many British publishers also use double quotation marks as a matter of house style. The British use single quotation marks for primary quotations and double quotation marks for "quotes within quotes."

Punctuation with Quotation Marks. In British style as in American, if a complete sentence is set in quotation marks, the periods (called *full stops*) and commas are placed inside the quotation marks. Likewise, in dialogue, the punctuation goes with the spoken words in quotes.

When a fragmentary quotation or a single quoted word, however, is run into a larger context, the punctuation is set outside the quotation marks:

> The publisher said that 'Adrian is our bestselling author.' [full quote]
> The publisher said, 'Adrian is our bestselling author.' [dialogue]
> The publisher said that Adrian is 'our bestselling author'. [fragmentary quote]
> The publisher referred to it as a 'bestseller'. [single word]

In both British and American style, exclamation points (called *exclamation marks* in England) and question marks are only set inside the quotation marks if they are part of the original quotation itself. In both systems, most double punctuation marks (colons and semicolons) are set outside.

In other words, the general rule is this: Only those punctuation marks found with the original source quotation should go inside the quotation marks; all others go outside.

Fewer Periods in Abbreviations. The British rule is to not use a period in abbreviations when internal letters are eliminated (like *Ltd, Mr, Mrs, Revd*). Like the Americans, however, the British retain the periods when the ending of the word has been cut off (such as *Corp., Gen., Inc., Prof., Rev.*) and for personal initials (such as *C. S. Lewis* and *J. R. R. Tolkien*). UK stylists, like those in the US, avoid periods in abbreviations of organizations, famous people referred to by initial, terms of scholarship, units of measurement, acronyms, and computer-related terms; but in addition, the British also tend to eliminate the periods in:

> time designations: AM, PM [often small-capped in the UK]
> scholarly abbreviations: eg, ie, cf

Books of the Bible. The names of books of the Bible are nearly always spelled out in British publications rather than abbreviated.

Use Periods in Expressions of Time. The British use a period (*full stop*) rather than a colon in expressions of time: *3.30 AM*, for instance. Also, they tend to drop the zero (*nought* or *cipher*) before a single-digit designation for minutes: *7.5 PM* rather than the American *7:05 PM*. Also note that the British use the twenty-four-hour clock more frequently than Americans: *15.00* rather than *3:00 PM*.

Dates. The British use the European style of referring to specific dates by giving the day of the month first, followed by the month and the year with no internal commas: *12 February 1953.*

Footnotes. The British system of academic footnoting uses superior numbers, with no periods, for both the callout and the bottom-of-page reference. The style of both the Oxford and Cambridge Universities' presses is to begin the numbering of footnotes with *1* on every new page, unlike the US system that begins the numbering with *1* with every new chapter, or, more rarely, sometimes numbering consecutively throughout the book. Alternatively, if footnotes are relatively few, the asterisk-and-dagger system may also be used as in American publishing.

British Numbering. British and American terms for numbers are identical through the millions, but thereafter they differ significantly, as follows:

British	American
one milliard, or one thousand million	one billion
one billion	one trillion
one thousand billion	one quadrillion
one trillion	one quintillion
one thousand trillion	one sextillion
one quadrillion	one septillion
one thousand quadrillion	one octillion
one quintillion	one nonillion
one thousand quintillion	one decillion

Also note that when these numbers are set in numerals, the American *zero* (0) is referred to as a *cipher* or *nought* in England. Cross-cultural discussions of high finance need to be carefully enumerated to verify accuracy. Several famous law cases are on the books because the differences in number style were not accounted for.

Authorized Version. The Bible issued by King James's printers in 1611 is called the Authorized Version in the British Isles and the King James Version in the United States. A strict adherence to these uses is not essential since readers in each country are likely to be familiar with the other's terminology, but the difference is usually observed whenever possible.

British Vocabulary. Many common objects have different names in England and the United States. While many Americans know that the British *lift* is the American *elevator*, fewer realize that the British *vest* is not part of a three-piece suit, but an undershirt. If a British play is a *bomb*, it is a success, while an American theatrical *bomb* is a failure. Entire dictionaries have been compiled to list the differences between the two vocabularies (the best of which is *British English A to Zed* by Norman W. Schur), and their entries run into the thousands. The following list contains only a few familiar differences by way of example.

British	American	British	American
aerodrome	airfield	lift	elevator
berk	jerk	loo	toilet
biro	ball-point pen	lorry	truck
biscuit	cracker or cookie	mince	ground meat
bonnet	hood (car)	motorway	highway
boot	trunk (car)	nappy	diaper
brackets	parentheses	overdraft	bank loan
candy floss	cotton candy	petrol	gasoline
caravan	trailer	plaster	Band-aid
car-boot sale	trunk sale	post	mail (verb)
carriage	railroad car	pram	baby carriage
charity	junk shop	queue	line (of people)
chemist	druggist	return	round trip
chips	french fries	roadway	pavement
clothes-peg	clothespin	spanner	wrench
cookery book	cookbook	tarmac	asphalt
crisps	chips	tea towel	dish towel
drawing pin, push-pin	thumbtack	tinned	canned
dustbin	garbage can	torch	flashlight
engage	hire	tram	streetcar
first floor	second floor	trolley	shopping cart
flyover	overpass	tube	subway
football	soccer	turn-ups	cuffs
Girl Guide	Girl Scout	underground	subway
headlamp	headlight	vacuum flask	thermos bottle
interval	intermission	vest	undershirt
inverted commas	quotation marks	Wellingtons	rubber boots
jumble sale	rummage sale	windscreen	windshield
knock-on effect	side effect	winge	whine, or cry
larder	pantry	zed	the letter *z*
lead, or flex	electric cord		

Bullets

Bullets are dot-like typographic devices used to call attention to items in a list. They should be modest in appearance, neither too bold nor too light, and they are usually separated from their accompanying text with a word space. Ideally, they should be set so as to center on the height of the letter that immediately follows them; that is, higher for a capital, lower for a lowercase letter.

Bullets are usually not used for lists of items that contain only single words or for short lines that do not carry over to a second line. A single row of dots running down the left-hand side of text is unsightly.

Usually, bullets are set to the left of the listed items, and the runover lines are set flush with the first word. This too can be unpleasant to the eye, so some designers recommend that the bullet be indented but not allowed to hang at the left.

If the list has only two or three items in it, indent the bullet from the left margin. If it has more, allow the bullet to set flush with the left margin.

C

Call Versus Calling

The words *call* and *calling* have a special meaning in Christian usage, and while they are similar, some distinctions should be observed. *Call* is the more specific and temporal of the two, often being synonymous with one's specific job. A seminarian, for instance, *receives a call* to become a pastor of a church. This term is often rendered as a passive verb: The seminarian *was called* to be the church's pastor.

A *calling*, by contrast, has larger implications and is most often synonymous with one's life path or core identity. This is the sense of the word as used by Paul when he advises the Ephesians to "live a life worthy of the calling you have received" (4:1). That same seminarian, for instance, may have realized early in life that it was *his calling* to someday serve as a pastor, but at that point he had not yet *received a call*.

Canticles

In some older references, the Song of Songs is referred to as *Canticles* or *the Book of Canticles* or *the Canticle of Canticles*, the latter used in English as early as the Wycliffe Bible of the fourteenth century. Though that usage is now largely outdated, it is still often found in literary contexts or when the plainer *Song of Songs* doesn't seem to convey the exotic tone of the text itself. *Canticles* retains the Middle Eastern flavor of the original. Like *Psalms*, *Canticles* as a title has the form of a plural but takes a singular verb, since it refers to a single book: *Canticles is part of the Old Testament canon.*

One argument for avoiding the term altogether is that other portions of the Bible are also commonly referred to as *canticles* (lowercased), notably those poetic portions that have been transformed into common liturgical songs, such as the Psalms and the Magnificat (Luke 1:46–55).

Capitalization

No surer sign of insanity exists than an attempt to formulate inviolable rules of capitalization. The following rules attempt to bring some order to this topic. As in every other area of life, general consistency as well as flexibility are often the best one can hope for.

Reasons for Capitalizing. Aside from reasons of typographic convention, the purpose of capitalization is to show that a given word has a specialized or specific meaning rather than a general one. This would include such words as place names or proper names, the titles of books or works of art, specialized vocabulary, and so on.

Capitalization was not developed as a way of conferring status or respect. We capitalize *Baker*, for instance, to signify the name of the carpenter who lives down the street so that we may distinguish him from the baker next door, whose name happens to be *Carpenter*. The recent tendency in editing practice has been to avoid capitalization whenever it is not needed for such purposes of specification, and many words formerly capitalized are now commonly lowercased without any loss of clarity.

As a purely typographic convention, capitalization is used to distinguish the beginning of sentences, some quoted material, special emphasis, and other uses.

Specialized Vocabulary. Authors occasionally capitalize terms as part of a special vocabulary. Authors should inform the editor of these special uses and should in all cases establish a consistent pattern of capitalization throughout the work.

Titles. Capitalize the first and last words of titles of books, software, or other major publications or works of art. Also capitalize the first word following a colon or a dash in a title.

All other words in titles should be capitalized, except for articles (*a, an,* and *the*); prepositions of any length; and coordinating conjunctions (*and, but, or, for,* and *nor*), all of which should be lowercased. An exception should be made in the case of any preposition that is used adverbially or emphasized. For example: *Miss Julia Takes Over* and *One Flew Over the Cuckoo's Nest.*

The ordinary rules of capitalization in a title should be ignored, however, when an existing work has been purposely titled to go against common style (for example, E. E. Cummings's books *EIMI* and *is 5* or the ezine *WorkingPOET*). Caution should be exercised in the case of some books, though, because for design reasons titles are often rendered differently on the cover. Generally, if the title is listed on the copyright page, accompanying the copyright notice, then that should be considered the correct version to be used in all references to that book. Do not use the version in the Library of Congress Cataloging in Publication Data, however, since that uses a different capitalization style altogether. If no title is shown accompanying the copyright notice, then consider the title as given on the title page to be definitive (though a colon should be inserted when a subtitle is used, since such colons are commonly dropped on title pages).

Titles with Compound Words. The first word of a hyphenated compound in a title or heading is always capitalized. The subsequent words in the compound are capitalized unless they are articles, prepositions, or coordinating conjunctions. Also, when a hyphenated number is used in a title, the second element is lowercased.

Orange-Red Leaves
"Ninety-five Theses"
King-Sized Mistakes

Old-Fashioned Gospel Hymns
Two-for-One Sale

Adverbs in Titles. An adverb in a title should always be capitalized, even though the same word might not be capped when used as a preposition.

Looking Up to Jesus
Coming In Out of the Rain

Steady As She Goes
A Walk in the Rain

Titles with Words Beginning with A-. There is sometimes a question as to how to capitalize titles with the prefix *a-*, a sort of old-fashioned way of expressing that the action of the verb to which it is attached is ongoing, as in *a-hunting* or *a-sailing*. Such formulations are common in folk songs. There are three ways of rendering such words when they appear in titles. Penguin Press, in its seminal *Penguin Book of English Folk Songs*, opts to lowercase the *a* and cap the letter following it: "Ships Are a-Sailing." Other presses cap the *a* and lowercase the following letter: "Ships Are A-sailing." Oxford University Press in its extensive publishing on music and folklore has elected to cap both elements: "Ships Are A-Sailing." While there is no strong argument for any one method, as long as consistency is maintained throughout a publication, we recommend the Oxford system.

"A-Hunting We Will Go"
"Here We Come A-Wassailing"
"The Times They Are A-Changing"

After a Colon. Capitalize the first word after a colon only if that colon introduces two or more sentences in close sequence, announces a definition, presents a proverb or quotation, or introduces a question or formal statement. Otherwise, the first word should be lowercased after a colon.

Here are the directions: Turn right at the first stoplight. Drive three miles and make a left.

William Carey will be remembered for this phrase: Expect great things from God; attempt great things for God.

Merton's conflict was this: he didn't know whether the Trappists would even accept him or whether the army would draft him first.

Racial Designations. As racial designations, the terms *black* and *white* are low-ercased both as adjectives and nouns unless they form part of a phrase that would require capitalization. Some contexts may require capitalization for consistency, for instance, when those terms are included in a list of other racial designations that are commonly capitalized. Also capitalize when the racial designation is included in a general area of academic study or a social movement.

> Many blacks and whites marched together in the sixties.
> The group included Blacks, Whites, Native Americans, and Hispanics.
> a black gospel choir
> the Black Studies program
> the Black Muslims

Particles with Proper Names. Consult a dictionary or a biographical reference book if in doubt about foreign names that use particles (connecting words, such as *von*, *de*, etc.). The following guidelines, though somewhat confusing, should help in some cases: (1) Particles in well-known English and North American names adapted from other cultures are usually capped (*Mark Van Doren, Bernard De Voto*) unless the individual prefers a lowercase form (*Walter de la Mare, Aubrey de Vere*). (2) French, Italian, Portuguese, Spanish, Dutch, and German particles are usually lowercased if a name or title precedes them (*Baron Manfred von Richtofen*). (3) In French names *Le, L', La,* and *Les* are usually capped (*La Bruyère*), but *de* and *d'* are not capitalized (*Honoré de Balzac, Charles d'Orléans*). (4) For some names, the particle is commonly dropped when the last name is used alone (*Vondel*, rather than *van den Vondel*). When a particle is not preceded by a first name or a title (except for French names using *de* or *d'*), capitalize it (*Le Corbusier*). A particle is always capitalized at the beginning of a sentence (*De la Mare was born in Charlton, Kent, in 1873*) or when used as an author name at the beginning of a bibliography.

Here are some further examples:

Charles de Gaulle	Ludwig van Beethoven, *but* Beethoven
Catherine de Médici	Corrie ten Boom, *but* the Ten Boom family
Werner von Braun	Leonardo da Vinci, *but* Da Vinci
Thomas De Quincey	Henry Van Dyke

Personal Titles. When a title directly precedes a person's name, it is capitalized. When it follows or when it is used in place of the person's name, it is lowercased.

President George W. Bush; George W. Bush, president of the United States; the president of the United States; the president

Gen. H. Norman Schwarzkopf; General Schwarzkopf; the general

Elizabeth II, queen of England; Queen Elizabeth; the queen

Traditional titles of the nobility, however, are often capitalized even when they follow the person's name or when the personal name is not given at all. When the full title is given, it may be capitalized according to custom: for instance, *the Duchess of York's latest children's book* or *an exhibition of paintings by the Prince of Wales.*

Organizations. Like personal names, the names of businesses, educational institutions, and other organizations are capitalized and otherwise styled according to the individual organization's preferences, even if those stylings go against common sense or usage.

This is sometimes tricky since the advent of the Internet because major online businesses often style their names differently in their logos than in their running text. When in doubt, style the name according to that company's usage in text rather than in their logo (for example, *eBay* rather than *ebay*; *Amazon.com* rather than *amazon.com*). To further complicate this situation, the names of some Internet companies incorporate the .com while others do not (*Ask Jeeves*, but *Go.com*). If absolute accuracy is needed, query the online company.

While authors should always adhere to the organization's own styling of its name, there is one exception: the article *the* should not be capitalized even if that organization insists that it should be. Such "in-house" styles should be reserved for official publications emanating from those organizations alone. Some organizations, such as the University of Michigan, insist that the article be capitalized when referring to the entire statewide network of universities under its umbrella (*The University of Michigan*) and lowercased when referring to a particular campus (*the University of Michigan at Ann Arbor*). The problem is that this distinction will simply be lost on the majority of readers, rendering adherence to the rule meaningless. The reader should not have to depend on a typographical device to make such distinctions clear. Lowercase the article in all cases and qualify if further distinction is needed.

Compass Arts

eBay [company prefers closed spelling with interior capital]

HarperCollins [company prefers closed spelling with interior capital]

the Favorite Poem Project [even though the organizers capitalize *the*]

Governmental Bodies. Generally, the formal names of governmental organizations and bodies are capitalized; however, as adjectives they are lowercased. Generic terms and informal terms for governmental bodies are lowercased.

United States Congress; Congress; congressional
House of Representatives; the House; the lower house of Congress
Committee on Foreign Affairs; Foreign Affairs Committee; the committee
Parliament; parliamentary; early parliament; Houses of Parliament
General Assembly of Illinois; Illinois legislature; assembly

administration	government
cabinet	ministry
the crown	office
district	precinct
electoral college	state
federal government	state's attorney

Political Organizations. Names of official political organizations are capitalized. The word *party*, however, is only capped when it is part of the official name.

Common Market	Grand Old Party (GOP)
Communist Party	Holy Alliance
Communists	Republican convention
Democratic platforms	Republican National Committee
Fascist party	Republican Party
Fascist	

Eras. Most period designations are lowercased (except for those derived from proper nouns and a few that have come to be capitalized by tradition).

Age of Reason	first century
age of steam	information age
ancient Greece	Middle Ages
Christian Era	Paleolithic times
colonial period	space age
Eighteenth Dynasty	Stone Age
Era of Good Feeling	the twenties *but* the Roaring Twenties
fin de siècle	Victorian era

Historical Events and Epithets. Most names for specific historical events, as opposed to broad historical eras, are capitalized. Popular epithets and nicknames for most cultural or historical moments or events are capitalized.

Bamboo Curtain	Iron Curtain
California Gold Rush	Kentucky Derby
Cold War	Pickett's Charge
Fall of Rome	Prohibition
Great Depression; the Depression	Reconstruction
but a depression; a recession	Vatican Council
Holocaust	World War I
Industrial Revolution	

Systems of Thought. To indicate broad systems of economic, philosophic, or political thought, the noun or adjective should be lowercased. If the word is derived from a proper name, however, it should be capitalized.

Likewise, most nouns and adjectives referring to general artistic, academic, religious, or philosophic schools of thought are lowercased. When they are derived from proper nouns, however, they are capitalized. Discretion is required, and in any given work a particular term must be treated consistently.

Aristotelian	Malthusianism
baroque	Marxist-Leninism
bolshevism	modernism
Cartesian	Nazism
classical	neoclassicism
communism	neoconservatism
conservatism	neo-Nazi
cubism	Neoplatonism
democracy	Platonism
environmentalism	postmodernism
expressionism	religious right
Gregorian chant	romanticism
impressionism	socialism
liberalism	transcendentalism
Machiavellian	

Personification. When abstract concepts are personified or made into allegorical characters, they should be capitalized as though they were proper names.

Then a thousand men thronged together, crying aloft to Christ and his Virgin Mother, that Grace might go with them in their search for Truth. (William Langland, *Piers the Plowman*)

Place Names. The rules for the capitalization of geographical nouns and adjectives are many and varied. Most specific questions can be answered by referring to a reference work such as *Merriam-Webster's Collegiate Dictionary.* The following brief summary and the list that follows it should help with most standard names.

Capitalize *Western, Eastern,* etc. when they are part of a formal place name or are used in the sense of political division. *Continent* and *Continental* are capitalized to designate Europe. Such terms as *mountain* and *lake* are capitalized when they are part of a formal place name.

the Arctic Circle *but* the equator
the Continent (Europe) *but* the Australian continent
the East; Far East(ern); the Near East
the East Coast or the West Coast
Lake Michigan; Lakes Huron and Michigan
the Midwest
the North
the North Atlantic *but* northern Atlantic
the Northwest
Ohio River; the Ohio and Wabash Rivers *but* the river Nile
the South, the Old South, the Deep South
Southerner (Civil War) *but* southerner (common usage)
the Tropics *but* the tropic of Cancer
the Western world *but* the western plains
a westerner (from either the Western Hemisphere or the western United States)

When the article *the* is a traditional part of a place name, it should be lowercased. The one exception to this rule is *The Hague,* the capital of the Netherlands, from the Dutch *Den Haag.*

the Hebrides
the Lesser Antilles
the Netherlands, *but* The Hague
the People's Republic of China

Family Relationship. A term indicating a family relationship is lowercased when used generically or when preceded by a modifier. It should be capitalized when used as a family member's common appellation, that is, when used as if it were a proper name.

"Will Cousin Ed lead the singing, Dad?" his son asked hopefully.
"No, Son, but Mother's brothers and her sister Carol will sing solos."

Terms of Affection. Common terms of affection, such as *honey, dear, sweetheart,* and so on, are lowercased unless they are used so often as to have the force of a nickname.

Brand Names. The distinction between brand names, which are trademarked and therefore capitalized, and their generic equivalents, which are lowercased, should be observed. For an outline of the rules for using trademarked names in writing and a list of examples, see "Brand Names."

Adjectives Derived from Proper Names. No rule satisfactorily resolves all doubt about when to capitalize adjectives derived from proper names and nouns. Usually, adjectives of direct biographical and geographical reference (*Socratic, Hawaiian*) are capitalized, although there are some common exceptions; for instance, *platonic* and *romanesque*, which are lowercased probably because they have come to have primary meanings far removed from the proper names from which they were derived.

When an adjective's connotation is no longer immediate, a decision must be made. It is usually a question of evocation. On one hand, the quintessentially American term *french fries* does not evoke France, so the adjective is lowercased. On the other hand, *French cuisine* does evoke French food, so it is capped. By the same token, *brussels sprouts* does not evoke Brussels any more than *lima beans* evokes Lima, Peru, the city for which they were named. Such lowercasing is more common with geographical adjectives, though it occasionally happens with biographical adjectives as well; for example, most style manuals lowercase *cesarean section*, which was named for Julius Caesar. When in doubt, check the dictionary.

> Byzantine (referring to Constantinople) *but* byzantine (meaning devious or labyrinthine)
> cesarean section—*but note*: C-section
> Ferris wheel
> Molotov cocktail
> moroccan leather
> russian dressing

Parts of a Book. Only capitalize the parts of a book when that part appears in a title, heading, or caption. Otherwise, lowercase parts of a book in text.

> "Appendix A [title]"
> "Refer to chapter 3 for more information."
> "See figure 12"
> "Turn to page 48"

Capitalization: Biblical and Religious Terms

Few matters of style have caused as much consternation to writers and editors of religious books as the capitalization of biblical and religious terms. Since Victorian times, religious books have tended to overcapitalize, a style that looks religiose and antiquated to most readers in the twenty-first century. The recent trend has been to undercapitalize. In an effort to bring some consistency to capitalization and to offer a rationale for adhering to a contemporary style, the following guidelines are offered.

The Persons of the Trinity and Deities of Other Religions. Capitalize all commonly accepted names for the persons of the Trinity. Also capitalize names of deities from other faiths and from mythology. Lowercase, however, the pronouns referring to persons of the Trinity (and deities of other religions). For a focused discussion of this issue, see "Deity Pronoun: Capitalization."

Adonai	Holy Spirit	Messiah
Allah	Isis	Paraclete
Christ	Jehovah	Ra
El	Jesus	Shiva
God	Jupiter	Yahweh

Epithets. Common epithets for persons of the Trinity, biblical characters, or figures in church history should be capitalized.

Judgment must be exercised in determining which words and phrases are epithets that have the force of a proper name and are therefore capitalized, and which are merely descriptive and are lowercased. When in doubt, the lowercase form is usually preferred, and in all cases, when a style is decided upon, consistency throughout the manuscript should be the rule.

Alpha and Omega	Man of Sorrows
Ancient of Days	Saint John the Divine
Comforter	Son of Man
Divine Doctor	Venerable Bede
King of Kings	Virgin Mary

the Twelve *but* the twelve disciples
the Evangelists *but* the four evangelists
the Almighty *but* almighty God
the Good Shepherd *but* the second person of the Trinity

Apostle *and* Prophet. The words *apostle* and *prophet* are lowercased unless used as part of a common epithet that has come to have the force of a proper name.

> the apostle John *but* the Beloved Apostle
> Paul the apostle *but* the Apostle to the Gentiles
> the prophet Jeremiah *but* the Weeping Prophet

Pharaoh *as a word*. The word *pharaoh* should be capitalized only when it is used as a proper name, which is, in most cases, when it is used without an article. When an article precedes it, it is lowercased as a common noun.

> Moses was raised in Pharaoh's household.
> At first he was afraid to address the pharaoh.

Religious Titles. Official religious titles of modern or historical personages are capitalized according to the same rules as secular titles. When an official title precedes a person's name, it is capitalized. When it follows or when it is used in place of a person's name, it is lowercased. General names for religious offices are lowercased, as are purely descriptive titles.

> Archbishop Rowan Williams *but* the archbishop of Canterbury; the archbishop
> Father Patrick O'Neil *but* the father
> Bishop John Shelby Spong *but* John Shelby Spong, bishop of Newark
> Pope John Paul II *but* the pope
> the ministry, the papacy, the bishopric, the pastorate
> evangelist Billy Graham

Names for Satan. Names and common epithets for Satan are capitalized.

Beast	Dragon	Evil One
Beelzebub	the Enemy (Satan, *but,*	Father of Lies
the Devil *but* a devil	the enemy, meaning	
	the forces of evil at large)	

Adjectives Derived from Proper Names. Many, but not all, adjectives derived from proper names are capitalized. Adjectives and adverbs derived from the words *God* and *Satan*, however, are usually lowercased, though for a fuller discussion, see "*God* Compounds." Also see, "Personal Names, Adjectives Derived from."

Aaronic priesthood	Isaian passages
Augustinian arguments	Matthean version
Christlike	miltonic verse [*but* Petrarchan sonnet]
godlike power	Pauline writings
godly woman	satanic rites

Epithets for the Bible. All names and common epithets for the Bible and for the sacred writings of other traditions are capitalized and set in roman type. Note, however, that the word *bible* is lowercased when used in a figurative sense: *The* OED *is the bible of English-language studies.*

Good Book	Scripture	Vedas
Qur'an	Talmud	the Word

For more details, see "Titles of Common Texts of the World's Religions."

Adjectives Indicating the Bible. Adjectives and adverbs derived from names for the Bible or other sacred writings are usually lowercased, although the terms *Qur'anic (Koranic)*, *Mishnaic*, *Pentateuchal*, and *Vedic* are commonly capitalized since they have not come to have a general meaning beyond the works to which they refer.

apocryphal	scriptural
biblically	talmudic

Names for Versions of the Bible. Names and nicknames of well-known or important versions and editions of the Bible, especially when they exist in a multiplicity of editions and formats, are capitalized and set in roman type. When a specific edition of a particular version is referred to, however, it should be set in italics like any other ordinary book title. See "Bible Versions and Translations."

The King James Version	The Vinegar Bible	The New International Version
The Syriac Version	The Vulgate	The New King James Version

but: *The King James 2000 Bible*
The NIV Study Bible

Books of the Bible. Names for all books of the Bible, the Apocrypha, and pseudobiblical writings are capitalized. The words *book, gospel, letter, psalm,* and *epistle* are generic terms that specify different forms of written documents. They are lowercased unless they form part of the actual title of a book as given in the specific translation of the Bible being used. (For a full discussion of the capitalization of the word *gospel,* see "*Gospel: Capitalization.*")

Job, the book of Job [NIV], *but* the Book of Job [MLB]
John, John's gospel, the gospel of John [NIV], *but* the Gospel According to John [KJV], the Gospel of John [Phillips]
Corinthians 1, First Corinthians, Paul's first epistle to the Corinthians, the first book of Corinthians, *but* the First Letter of Paul to the Corinthians [RSV]
the Gospel of Thomas [actual title]

the Protevangelion
Psalm 139
the Twenty-third Psalm *but* a psalm of David

Parts of the Bible. Names for specific parts, groupings, or passages of the Bible are capitalized when those names have come to be used commonly as the equivalents of titles in theological and devotional writing. (Note that in this instance *The Christian Writer's Manual of Style* departs from *CMS*, which lowercases most parts, groupings, and passages of the Bible. The *CMS* alternative is recommended, however, for books intended for a broad or secular readership. The capitalized system is best used when a solely Christian audience is intended.) Judgment must be exercised in determining whether a name is generic or used as the equivalent of a title. For instance: *David's psalms*, but *the Davidic Psalms.* When in doubt, lowercase.

Accession Psalms	New Testament
General Epistles	Olivet Discourse
Gospels	Pentateuch
Historical Books	Poetical Books
Lord's Prayer	Synoptic Gospels
Love Chapter	Upper Room Discourse
Minor Prophets	Wisdom Literature

the Ten Commandments *but* the first commandment
the Gospel According to Matthew [RSV] *but* Matthew's gospel
the Gospels *but* the four gospels
the Epistle of Paul to the Romans [MLB] *but* Paul's Roman epistle
the Book of Jeremiah [RSV] *but* Jeremiah's book of prophecies

Law as a Word. The word *law* is capitalized only to clarify that it refers to the Pentateuch as a whole or to the Ten Commandments.

the Law [Pentateuch] *but* the law [as opposed to grace]
Mosaic law
law of Moses
Davidic law

Parable as a Word. Unless used in an actual title, the word *parable*, like the words *book*, *gospel*, *letter*, *psalm*, and *epistle*, is lowercased as a descriptive term, as are any descriptive words that accompany it. Words describing specific parables should only be capitalized when they are proper nouns.

the parable of the prodigal son
the parable of the wicked serving men
the parable of the good Samaritan

Biblical Events. Accepted names for major biblical events, such as events in the life of Christ, are set in lowercase.

> the advent of Christ [*but* Advent, meaning the season]
> the captivity
> the captivity of the Jews
> the creation [both the act and the things created]
>> How long were the six days of creation?
>> God looked over all his creation and said, "Very good!"
> the creation of the universe
> the crucifixion
> the crucifixion of Jesus
> the nativity
> the nativity of Christ

Biblical and Sacred Objects. Names for important biblical objects are generally lowercased. Many specific names of sacred concepts and objects of veneration, especially those associated with the persons of the Trinity, were once capitalized. The modern practice is to lowercase them. Care must be taken to distinguish between those words that are common nouns and therefore lowercased, and those that form parts of epithets for people, which should be capitalized. Note that the names for a very few legendary sacred objects have become so common in imaginative literature that they are traditionally capitalized and should continue to be so: *the True Cross, the Holy Grail.*

> the blood of Christ
> the brazen altar
> the cross [both the wooden object and the event]
> the golden calf
> the holy name of Jesus
> the light of Christ in the world, *but* the Light of the World
> Noah's ark
> the seven seals
> the star of Bethlehem
> the tent

Biblical Eras. Names for biblical eras are lowercased.

> the age of the prophets
> the exile
> the exilic period
> the last day
> the last days
> the millennial kingdom
> the millennium

Historic Documents. The titles of creeds, confessions, and other important documents of church history are capitalized and set in roman type.

Apostles' Creed	Thirty-nine Articles
Heidelberg Catechism	Westminster Confession

Religious Observances. Common names for religious seasons, holy days, feast days, saints' days, and religious festivals and observances are capitalized.

Advent	Epiphany	Michaelmas
Ash Wednesday	Holy Communion	National Day of Prayer
Christian Unity Week	Holy Week	Passover
Conversion of Saint Paul	Lent	Saint Valentine's Day

Sacraments and Rites. Names of specific sacraments and rites are commonly lowercased, except those indicating Communion, or the Eucharist, which are traditionally capitalized. The seven sacraments recognized by the Roman Catholic Church are baptism, confirmation, the Eucharist, penance, anointing of the sick (which is the term preferred to *extreme unction*), holy orders, and matrimony. Names for general systems of religious rites (such as Latin Rite, Roman Rite, Eastern Rites, and Western Rites) are capitalized. For more details, see "*Sacraments.*"

Holy Eucharist	Lord's Table	Sacred Host
last rites	Masonic Rites	sacred rites

Names of Denominations. Names of official denominations and the common adjectives derived from them are capitalized according to denominational usage. The article *the* should not be capitalized, even if that is the group's preference. See also "Denominations and Associations of Churches."

Baptist	Church of God	Roman Catholic
Brethren	Episcopal	Seventh-day Adventism
Christian Reformed	Methodism	

Church *as a Word.* The word *church* is lowercased unless it is part of the formal or official name of a specific denomination. For instance, since there is no official denomination called "the Reformed church," *church* is lowercased. In "the Christian Reformed Church," however, it is capped as part of the official name of the denomination. *Church* is also lowercased when used in a general sense or to refer to the universal church of all believers.

Baptist church	church and state
Christ's church	Episcopal Church
the church	invisible church

Methodist church	Reformed Church in America
Protestant church	Roman Catholic Church
Reformed church	United Methodist Church

Names for Places of Worship. Words such as church, chapel, temple, meeting, synagogue, tabernacle, mission, ministry, hall, fellowship, cathedral, congregation, and assembly are capitalized when they form part of the official name of a local religious meeting place. Otherwise, as common nouns they are lowercased. The article *the* should never be capitalized in front of a church or denomination's name, even if that church or denomination insists that the article be capitalized. Like names for other organizations, it would be too unwieldy to keep a definitive list of which churches and denominations prefer the capitalized article. Such "in-house" styles should be reserved for official publications emanating from those churches and denominations.

> Church of the Servant, *but* the church
> Brick Bible Chapel, *but* the chapel
> Temple Emmanuel, *but* the temple
> St. Paul's Cathedral, *but* the cathedral
> Westminster Presbyterian Church, *but* the local Presbyterian church
> Holy Spirit Catholic Church, *but* a Catholic church
> the Brooklyn Tabernacle (even though the church prefers The Brooklyn Tabernacle, with the article capped)

Religious Groups and Movements. The names for major historical religious groups and movements, and the adjectives derived from them, are generally capitalized. This includes the historical heresies and schisms. (See also "*Heresy* Versus *Schism*.")

Adoptionism	Pentecostal(ism)
Antinomianism	Pharisees
Donatism	Protestant(ism)
the Great Schism	Puritan(ism)

The names of broad modern religious movements that are not official denominations, the names of general religious philosophies, and the adjectives derived from all such words should be lowercased. By the same principle, the terms *liberal* and *conservative* usually have a generic or relative use and should be lowercased.

agnostic(ism)	evangelical(ism)
charismatic renewal	secular humanism
charismatics	theistic
conservative church	theologians
ecumenical, ecumenism	

Movement *as a Word.* The word *movement* is capitalized only if the adjective that precedes it is capitalized. Tradition may be a factor in whether to capitalize; recognized historical movements are more likely to be capitalized, while contemporary movements are less likely to be.

> the Holiness Movement *but* the ecumenical movement
> the Pentecostal Movement *but* the charismatic movement
> the Temperance Movement

Religious Historical Eras. Common names for major periods and events in church history are generally capitalized unless they are purely descriptive.

> Great Awakening *but* the age of revivalism
> Middle Ages *but* the medieval era
> Reformation

Heaven, Hell, *Etc.* Although place names in the Bible are ordinarily capitalized, terms like *heaven, hell, gehenna, sheol, tartarus,* and *hades* are lowercased as common nouns. This is done to accord with the style used by most of the popular versions of the Bible. The seven heavens of Islamic tradition are also lowercased: *the first heaven, the second heaven,* and so on. The word *paradise* is capitalized only when it refers specifically to the garden of Eden. The word *kingdom* is usually lowercased.

> Abyss *but* hades, sheol
> garden of Eden
> kingdom of God, Christ's kingdom
> New Jerusalem *but* heaven, paradise, the abode of the saints
> seventh heaven

In classical and Western literary tradition, however, names for heaven and hell are often capped, as in the Greek mythological *Hades*; Dante's *Inferno, Purgatorio,* and *Paradiso*; and Milton's terms *Heaven, Hell,* and *Paradise* (as used in *Paradise Lost*). Other literary place names and geographical locations within heaven, hell, and the other various abodes of the dead are capitalized as though they were ordinary geographical references.

Acheron	Olympus
Cocytus	Pandemonium
Elysium	Phlegethon
First Circle of Hell	Styx
Lethe	

Epithets for Place Names. Common epithets for geographical places are capitalized. Care must be exercised to distinguish between those words and phrases that are epithets and are therefore capitalized, and those that are merely descriptive and are lowercased.

> the City of David *but* the city where David reigned
> the Eternal City
> the Holy Land *but* the land of Jesus
> the Land of Promise *but* the land of Canaan

Capitalization of Common Religious Terms

Aaronic priesthood
Aaronide (geneology of Aaron)
Abba
abomination of desolation
Abrahamic covenant
Abraham's bosom
Abraham's side
Abyss, the
Achaemenid
Adonai
advent, the
Advent season
Advocate, the
Agabah
agape
age of grace
age to come, the
agnosticism
Ahiram Inscription
Almighty, the
almighty God
Alpha and Omega (Christ)
amillenarian
amillennial(-ism)(-ist)
ancient Near East(ern)
Ancient of Days, the (God)
angel (cap if theophany)
angel Gabriel, the
angel of the Lord (cap if
    theophany)
annunciation, the (the event)
Annunciation, the (the holiday)
Anointed, the (Christ)

Anointed One, the (Christ)
anointed Savior
anointing of the sick
ante-Christian
antediluvian
ante-Nicene fathers
anti-Catholic
antichrist (the general spirit)
Antichrist (the person)
anti-Christian
antichurch
anti-God
antilegomena
anti-Semitism
anti-Trinitarian
Apocalypse, the (Revelation of
    John)
apocalyptic
Apocrypha, the
apocryphal
apostle Paul, Peter, et al.
apostles, the
Apostles' Creed, the
Apostle to the Gentiles (Paul)
apostolic
apostolic age
apostolic benediction (2 Cor. 13)
apostolic council (Acts 15)
apostolic faith
apostolic fathers (the men)
Apostolic Fathers, the (the group
    of writings)
Arabah

Aramaean
archangel
archbishop of Canterbury (*but* Archbishop Smith)
ark, the (Noah's)
ark of the covenant
ark of the testimony
Arminian(-ism)
ascension, the
Ascension Day
Athanasian Creed
atheism, -ist
atonement, the
Atonement, the Day of (Yom Kippur)
Augsburg Confession

Baal
baalism
babe in the manger, the
baby Jesus, the
Babylonian captivity (Jews)
Babylonian Empire
baptism
baptism, the (of Christ)
Baptist, the (John the Baptist)
battle of Armageddon (final battle)
Beast, the (Antichrist)
beatification
beatific vision (theology)
beatitude, a
Beatitudes, the
bedouin (sing. and pl.)
Beelzebub
Beelzebul
Begaa
Being (God)
Beloved Apostle, the
betrayal, the
Bible, the
Bible Belt, the
Bible school
biblical
bidding prayer
bishop of Rome (*but* Bishop Jones)

blessed name (Christ)
Blessed Virgin
blood of Christ
body, the (of Christ)
body of Christ (the church)
Book, the (Bible)
book of Genesis, et al.
Book of Life (book of judgment)
book of the covenant
book of the law
Book of the Twelve, the
Book of Truth
boy Jesus, the
brazen altar
Bread of Life (Bible or Christ)
Bridegroom, the (Christ)
bride of Christ (the church)
brotherhood of man
bulla (pl. *bullae*)
burning bush, the (Ex. 3)
burnt offering

Calvary
Calvinist(ic), -ism
Canon, the (Scripture)
canonical
Canonical Epistles, the (James, et al.)
canonical hours
canonization
canon law
canon of Scripture, the
captivity, the (of the Jews)
catechumen
catholic (universal)
Catholic church, a (the building)
Catholic Church, the (the Roman Catholic Church)
Catholic Epistles (James, et al.)
Catholicism
Celestial City (abode of the redeemed)
cereal offering
charismatic
charismatic church

charismatic movement
cherub(im)
chief priest
Chief Shepherd (Christ)
child Jesus
children of Israel
chosen people (Jews)
Christ
Christ child
christen(ing)
Christian (n. and adj.)
Christian Era
christianize, -ization
Christianlike
Christian socialism
Christlike
Christlikeness
Christmas Day
Christmas Eve
Christmastide
christocentrism
christological
Christology
christophany
Chronicler, the
church, the (body of Christ)
church (building)
church (service)
church age
church and state
church father(s)
church in America
church invisible
church militant
Church of England
Church of Rome
church triumphant
church universal
church visible
City of David (Jerusalem, Bethlehem)
Code of Hammurabi
College of Cardinals
Comforter, the (Holy Spirit)
commandment (first, et al.)

Commandments, the Ten
Communion (sacrament)
compline
confirmation
co-regency
Council of Trent
Counselor, the (Holy Spirit)
Counter-Reformation
covenant, the (old, new)
covenant of grace
covenant of the Lord, the
covenant of works
creation, the (both the act and the result)
Creator, the
creator God, the
creed, the (Apostles' Creed)
cross, the (both the wooden object and the event)
crown
Crucified One, the (as name; lc as descriptor)
crucifixion, the
crucifixion of Christ, the
Crusades, the
cupbearer
curse, the

Daniel's Seventieth Week
Davidic covenant
Davidic law
day hours (first seven canonical hours)
Day of Atonement (Yom Kippur)
day of grace
day of judgment
day of Pentecost
day of the Lord
Dead Sea Scrolls
Decalogue (Ten Commandments)
Defender (God)
deism, -ist
Deity, the
deity of Christ
deluge, the (the flood)

demiurge
demon(ic)
deuterocanonical
Deuteronomic
devil, a
Devil, the (Satan)
Diaspora (the event and the
  people)
diglot
disciples
dispensation(alism)(alist)
dispensation of the Law
dispersion, the
divided kingdom (period of
  history)
divine
Divine Doctor (Christ)
Divine Father (God)
divine guidance
Divine King
Divine Liturgy (Eucharist, Eastern
  Orthodox)
divine office (canonical hours)
Divine Providence (God)
divine providence (God's
  providence)
Divinity, the (God)
divinity of Christ, the
doctor(s) of the church
Door, the (Christ)
doxology
Dragon, the (Satan)

early church
early church fathers
Early Church Fathers (title of work)
Eastern church
Eastern Orthodox church, an (a
  building)
Eastern Orthodox Church, the
Eastern religions
Eastern Rites
Easter Sunday
ecumenism, -ical
Eden

El
elect, the; God's elect
Eleven, the
Elohim
Elohist source
El Shaddai
Emmaus road
emperor, but Emperor Nero
empire, the (Babylonian)
end-time (adj.)
end time(s), the
Enemy, the (Satan)
enemy, the (satanic forces)
Epiphany
epistle (John's epistle, et al.)
epistle to the Romans
Epistles, the (NT apostolic letters)
eschatology, -ical
Eternal, the (God)
Eternal City, the (Rome)
eternal God, the
eternal life
eternity
Eucharist
eucharistic
Evangel (any of the four gospels)
evangelical (adj.)
evangelicals, -ism
evangelist (someone who
  evangelizes or a gospel writer)
Evangelists, the (the Gospels)
evensong
Evil One, the (Satan)
exile, the
exodus, the (from Egypt)
extrabiblical
extreme unction (prefer anointing
  of the sick)

faith, the (Christianity)
faith healing
fall, the
fall of humanity
fall of Jerusalem
false christs

False Prophet (of Revelation)
false prophet(s)
Farewell Discourses (John)
Father (God)
fatherhood of God
Father of Lies (Satan)
Fathers, the (fathers of the church)
fathers of the church, the
Feast (meaning Passover)
Feast of Booths (Sukkoth)
Feast of Esther (Purim)
Feast of Firstfruits
Feast of Tabernacles
Feast of the Dedication
    (Hanukkah)
Feast of the Lights (Hanukkah)
Feast of the Passover (Pesach)
Feast of Unleavened Bread
Fertile Crescent
fertility god(dess)
first Adam, the
first advent
Firstborn, the (Christ)
firstborn Son of God
First Cause, the
First Estate (Second Estate, etc.)
firstfruits
first person of the Trinity
First Vatican Council (1869–70)
flood, the
footwashing
four evangelists, the
four gospels, the
fourth gospel, the
free will
Friend (Quaker)
fundamentalist(s), -ism
fundamentals of the faith

Galilean, the (Christ)
garden, the (Eden or Gethsemane)
garden of Eden
garden of Gethsemane
gehenna
Gemara

General Epistles
General Letters
Gentile, a (distinguished from Jew)
Gentile laws
Gloria Patri
gnostic (generic)
Gnostic(ism) (specific sect)
god (pagan)
God (Yahweh)
God Almighty
God-given
Godhead (essential being of God)
godhead (godhood or godship)
God is spirit
godless
godlike
godliness
godly
God-man
God Most High
godsend
God's house
Godspeed
God's Son
God's Spirit
God's word (his statement or
    promise)
God's Word (the Bible)
godward
golden calf, the
golden candlesticks, the
Golden Rule, the
Good Book, the
Good Friday
good news, the
Good Samaritan, the (but the
    parable of the good Samaritan)
Good Shepherd (Jesus)
good shepherd, the parable of the
gospel (see *"Gospel"*)
gospel (John's gospel, et al.)
gospel of Matthew
Gospels, the
gospel truth
grain offering

Great Awakening, the
Great Commandment, the
Great Commission, the
Great High Priest, the
great judgment, the
Great Physician, the
Great Schism (of 1054)
Great Shepherd, the
great tribulation, the
great white throne, the
Ground of Being
Guide, the (Holy Spirit)
guilt offering

Hades (Greek mythology)
hades (hell)
Haggadah
hagiographa
hagiographer
hagiographic
Hail Mary
halakah
Hallel
hallelujah
Hanukkah (Feast of the Dedication)
Hasidic
Hasidim
Head, the (Christ, head of the church)
heaven (abode of the redeemed)
heavenly Father
Hebraism
Heidelberg Catechism
Heilsgeschichte
hell
Hellenism (-istic)
hellenize
Heptateuch
Herodian
Herod's temple
Hexapla
high church
high priest, a
High Priest, the (Christ)
High Priestly Prayer, the

Historical Books, the (of Bible)
Hittite Law Code
holiness
Holiness Movement, the
Holy Bible
Holy Book (Bible)
Holy City (present or New Jerusalem)
Holy Communion
holy day of obligation (Roman Catholic)
Holy Eucharist
holy family
Holy Father (pope)
Holy Ghost (*prefer* Holy Spirit)
Holy God (*but* a holy God)
Holy Grail
Holy Island (Lindisfarne)
Holy Joe (slang for parson)
Holy Land (Palestine)
Holy League (1510–11)
Holy of Holies
holy oil
Holy One, the (God, Christ)
holy order(s)
Holy Place
Holy Roller
Holy Roman Empire
Holy Saturday
Holy Scriptures
Holy See
Holy Spirit
Holy Thursday
Holy Trinity
holy war
holy water
Holy Week (before Easter)
Holy Writ (Bible)
Holy Year (Roman Catholic)
homologoumena
house of David
house of the Lord

imago Dei
immaculate conception, the

Immanuel
incarnation, the
incarnation of Christ
Indo-Eurpoean
infancy gospels, the
infant Jesus, the
Inklings, the (Lewis, Tolkien, et al.)
inner veil
Intercessor, the (Christ)
intertestamental
Isaian or Isaianic

Jacob's trouble
Jehovah
Jehovah's Witness
jeremiad
Jeremian or Jeremianic
Jesus Prayer, the
Jewish Feast (Passover)
Jewish New Year (Rosh Hashanah)
Johannine
John the Baptist
John the Beloved
John the Evangelist
Jordan River (*but* the river Jordan)
Jubilee (year of emancipation)
Judaic
Judaica
Judaism, -ist, -istic
Judaize, Judaizer
Judean
Judeo-Christian
judges, the
judgment day
judgment seat of Christ

Kaddish
kerygma
King (God or Jesus)
King David (etc.)
kingdom, the
kingdom age
kingdom of God
kingdom of heaven
kingdom of Israel

kingdom of Satan
King James Version
King of Glory (Christ)
King of Kings (Christ)
kingship of Christ
kinsman-redeemer
koinonia
Koran, Koranic (*prefer* Qur'an)

Lady, our
lake of fire
Lamb, the (Christ)
Lamb of God
Lamb's Book of Life
land of Canaan
Land of Promise
last day(s), the
last judgment, the
last rites
Last Supper, the
last times, the
Latin Rite
Latter Prophets, the
lauds
laver
law (as opposed to grace)
Law, the (Pentateuch)
Lawgiver (God)
law of Moses
Lent(en)
Levite
Levitical
Levitical decrees
liberal(ism)
Light (Truth or Christ)
Light of the World (Christ)
Litany, the (Anglican)
living God
living Word, the (Bible)
loanword
Logos, the
Lord, the
Lord Almighty, the
Lord of Hosts
Lord of Lords

Lord's Anointed, the (Christ)
Lord's anointed Savior, the (Christ)
Lord's Day, the
lordship of Christ
Lord's Prayer, the
Lord's Supper, the
Lord's Table, the
Lost Tribes
lost tribes of Israel
Love Chapter, the
low church
Lucifer (Satan)
Lukan

Maccabean
Maccabees
magi
Magnificat, the ("Song of Mary")
Majority Text
Major Prophets, the (div. of OT)
major prophets (people)
mammon (cap for the god)
Man, the (Jesus)
Man of Sin (Satan)
Man of Sorrows
Markan or Marcan
Masorete
Masoretic text
Mass, the (liturgy of the Eucharist)
Master, the (God)
matins
matrimony (sacrament)
Matthean
Mediator, the (Christ)
medieval
menorah
mercy seat
Messiah, the (Christ)
messiahship
messianic
Middle Ages
midtribulation(al)
millenarian(ism)(ist)
millennial kingdom
millennium, the

minor prophets (people)
Minor Prophets, the (div. of OT)
Miserere, the
Mishnah, Mishnaic
modernist(s), -ism
moon-god
Mosaic
Mosaic law (Pentateuch or Ten
    Commandments)
Most High, the
Mount of Olives
Mount of Transfiguration
Mount Olivet
Mount Olivet Discourse
Mount Sinai
Muhammad (preferred)
Muslim (preferred)

Nag Hammadi codices
name of Christ, the
name of God, the
nativity, the
nativity of Christ, the
Near East
Neo-Babylonian Empire
neoorthodox(y)
neo-Pentecostalism
neoplatonic
new birth
New City (part of modern
    Jerusalem)
new covenant (NT)
new heaven and new earth
New Jerusalem (heaven)
New Testament church
Nicene Creed
Nicene fathers
night office (canonical hour)
Ninety-five Theses
noncanonical
non-Christian (n. and adj.; but
    unchristian)
Nonconformism, -ist
none (canonical hour)
non-Pauline

northern kingdom
Nunc Dimittis

Old City (part of modern
   Jerusalem)
old covenant (OT)
Olivet Discourse
Omega, the
omnipotence of God
Omnipotent, the
One, the (*but* the one true God
   and God is the one who . . .)
Only Begotten, the
only begotten of the Father
only begotten Son of God
orders (sacrament)
Original Sin
orthodox(y)
outer court (of the temple)

Palestinian covenant
Palm Sunday
papacy
parable of the prodigal son, etc.
Paraclete, the
Paradise (garden of Eden)
paradise (heaven)
parousia
partial rapture
Paschal Lamb (Jesus)
passion
Passion Sunday (fifth Sunday in
   Lent)
Passion Week
Passover
Passover Feast
Passover Lamb (Jesus)
Pastoral Epistles
Pastoral Letters
patriarch, a
Patriarch, the (Abraham)
patriarchs, the (church fathers)
Pauline Epistles
Paul's epistles
Paul's letters

Paul the apostle
peace offering
penance
Pentateuch
Pentateuchal
Pentecost
Pentecostal(ism)
person of Christ
persons of the Trinity (the three)
Pesach (Passover)
Petrine
Pharaoh (when used as name
   without article)
pharaoh, the (general)
pharisaic (attitude)
Pharisaic (in reference to Pharisees)
Pharisee
Pilgrim Fathers
Pilgrims, the
pillar of cloud
pillar of fire
Poetical Books, the
pope, the
Pope John Paul II
postbiblical
post-Christian
postexilic
postmillennial(ism)(ist)
postmodern
post–Nicene fathers
pre-Christian
predestination
premillenarian
premillennial(ism)(ist)
pretribulation(al)
priesthood of believers
priesthood of Christ
prime (canonical hour)
Prime Mover
Prince of Darkness
Prince of Peace (Christ)
Prison Epistles
Prison Letters
Prodigal Son, the (*but* the parable
   of the prodigal son)

Promised Land (Canaan or
    heaven)
Promised One, the (Christ)
Prophetic Books, the
prophet Isaiah, et al., the
Prophets, the (books of OT)
prophets, the (people)
Protestant(ism)
Providence (God)
providence of God
providential
psalm, a
Psalm 119 (etc.)
psalmic
psalmist, the
Psalms, the (OT book)
Psalter, the (the Psalms)
pseudepigrapha(l)
purgatory
Purim (Feast of Esther)

Qumran
Qur'an, Qur'anic (*preferred*)

rabbi
rabbinic(al)
rapture, the
real presence
Received Text, the
Redeemer, the
Reformation
Reformed church
Reformed theology
Reformers
Renaissance
resurrection, the
resurrection of Christ
rite(s)
River of Life, the (Christ)
Rock, the (Christ)
Roman Catholic Church
Roman Rite
Rosh Hashanah (Jewish New Year)
Sabbath (day)
sabbath rest (for the land)

Sabbath rest (for the people
    of God)
sabbatical (n. and adj.)
sacrament(s)
sacramentalism, -ist
Sacramentarian(ism)
sacrament of baptism,
    confirmation, etc.
Sacred Host
sacred rite(s)
Sadducee
Sanhedrin
Satan
satanic
satanism
Savior
scribe
scriptural
Scripture(s) (Bible; n. and adj.)
scripture(s) (other religions)
Sea of Galilee
second Adam, the (Christ)
second advent, the
second coming, the
second coming of Christ
second person of the Trinity
Second Vatican Council (1962–65)
seder
Semite, -ic, -ism
Septuagesima
Septuagint
seraph(im)
Sermon on the Mount
Serpent, the (Satan)
seven deadly sins, the
seven sacraments, the
Seventh-day Adventist
seventh heaven
Seventieth Week
sext (canonical hour)
Shabuoth (Pentecost)
shalom
shalom aleichem
shekinah

sheol (italicized only when referred
   to as a Hebrew word)
Shepherd Psalm, the
shofar
Shulammite
Sinai Desert
Sinai peninsula
Sin-Bearer, the
sin offering
Solomon's temple
son of David
Son of God
Son of Man
sonship of Christ
southern kingdom
Sovereign Lord
Spirit, the (Holy Spirit)
star of Bethlehem
stations of the cross
Sukkoth (Feast of Booths)
Sunday school
Sunday school teacher
sun-god
Sun of Righteousness
Supreme Being, the
Sustainer (God)
synagogue
Synoptic Gospels
Synoptics, the
synoptic writers, the

tabernacle, the (OT building)
table of shewbread
Talmud, talmudic
Tanak
Targum, targumic
Te Deum
temple, the (at Jerusalem)
temptation, the
temptation in the desert, the
temptation of Christ, the
Ten Commandments (*but* the
   second commandment, etc.)
tent
Tent of Meeting

Tent of the Testimony
Ten Tribes, the
ten tribes of Israel, the
terce (canonical hour)
Testaments, the
tetragrammaton
Textus Receptus
third person of the Trinity
Thirty-nine Articles (Anglican)
throne of grace
Thummim
time of Jacob's trouble
time of the Gentiles, the
time of the judges, the
tomb, the
Torah
Tower of Babel
transfiguration, the
Transjordan
Tree of Knowledge of Good and Evil
Tree of Life
tribe of Judah
tribulation, the (historical event)
Trinitarian
Trinity, the
triumphal entry
triune God
True Cross, the
Twelve, the
twelve apostles, the
twelve disciples, the
Twenty-third Psalm

unchristian
ungodly
Unitarian
united kingdom (of Israel)
universal church
universalism, -ist
unscriptural
Upanishads
upper room, the
Upper Room Discourse
Urim

vacation Bible school
Vedas, Vedic
vespers
viaticum
Victor, the (Christ)
Vine, the (Christ)
Virgin, the
Virgin and child
virgin birth, the
Virgin Mary, the
visible church
voice of God
Vulgate

Wandering Jew, the (legend)
Water of Life (Christ)
Way, the (Christ)
way, the truth, and the life
Weeping Prophet, the (Jeremiah)

Western church
Western Rites
Westminster Catechism
Wicked One, the (Satan)
Wisdom Literature, the
wise men
Word, the (Bible or Christ)
Word made flesh (Christ)
word of God (his statement or promise)
Word of God (the Bible)
Word of Life
Word of Truth, the
Writings, the

Yahweh (italicized only when referred to as Hebrew word)
Year of Jubilee
Yom Kippur (Day of Atonement)
Yuletide

Caption

Captions are brief descriptions that appear with illustrations or other graphic matter. The author should be careful to make them as brief as possible.

Type Size. They are usually set two point sizes smaller than the size of the text type when the illustrations are set in the text, although they should be the same size and face when set outside the text, on their own pages. Still, if a caption runs more than two lines, it should be reduced in size to save space.

With Periods. Periods should be used only when the caption forms a complete sentence.

When the Illustration Is Turned on Its Side. If the graphic material needs to be placed on its side to fit within the format of the book, then the caption should run along the right-hand side of the page, that is, from the bottom of the page to the top.

From Left *and* From Right. When identifying people in a photograph, say *from left* or *from right* rather than *left to right* or *right to left.*

Carol

In popular usage, especially in the US, the term *carol* has become synonymous with Christmas song; however, it is correctly applied to a song for any seasonal celebration. Only about half of the nearly two hundred songs in *The Oxford Book of Carols* (1965 edition) relate to Christmas. Also, a carol is most precisely defined as a song, usually with traditional words or lyrics, that is used ceremonially or as part of a traditional seasonal celebration. While the songs "White Christmas" and "Frosty the Snowman" are commonly regarded as Christmas carols in the US, for instance, they are more accurately called *Christmas songs*. In its earliest meaning, *carol* described a specific poetic form, consisting of four lines, rhymed AAAB, and often the last line was either short or one of two repeating refrain lines.

Cataloging in Publication Data (CIP)

Cataloging in publication (CIP) data is the accurate cataloging information for a book as it will appear in the card catalog of the Library of Congress. Providing this information on the copyright page of the book helps libraries catalog and access the book easily—in both their card and electronic files. Although placing CIP information in a book is not legally mandated, its use is strongly urged. Many libraries will not buy a book unless this information appears on the copyright page.

Note that the Library of Congress uses the unhyphenated form, *Cataloging in Publication Data*, whereas many publishers use the hyphenated compound-adjective form, *Cataloging-in-Publication Data*. There seems to be no reason for preferring one form over the other.

Placement. Ordinarily, the CIP data appears on the copyright page of a book. If a book's copyright page is already too crowded or if there are other reasons for displacing the CIP data, it may appear elsewhere in the book (on another page in the front or in the back), although a note stating where to find the CIP data should appear on the copyright page as a courtesy to the librarian.

Accuracy. CIP data should be printed line-for-line and space-for-space as it appears on the official paper or electronic form received from the Library of Congress. The typeface, however, should conform to that of the rest of the copyright page. The Library of Congress makes no other specifications than legibility.

Occasionally mistakes creep into the CIP data due to errors on the publisher's originally submitted form, an error at the Library of Congress itself, or an error in keying the data. Mistakes in birth date or in the spelling of an author's name, for instance, are not uncommon, and all CIP data should be proofread carefully at every proof stage. The publisher may correct any such error as long as the Library of Congress is informed of the change.

Changes. Other changes in the CIP data may be made by the publisher. For instance, if the author prefers not to reveal his or her birth date, the publisher may substitute the word *date* for the birth year (although the actual birth year should be provided on the application form for CIP). Also, if a pseudonymous author prefers that no one know his or her actual name, then a long dash may be substituted for the author's real name on the CIP data. Again, all such changes should be reported to the CIP Division of the Library of Congress. In this last case, CIP should probably be registered in the author's pseudonym to begin with.

For Multi-authored Books. For multi-authored books, only the first author is listed as the main catalog reference (that is, on the first line of the CIP data itself). That is not a mistake, as many coauthors think. Coauthors are listed as secondary catalog references.

For Reprints. In a reprint edition of a book, if no bibliographic information (title, author, publisher, ISBN, page count, format, etc.) other than the year of publication has changed, then a new CIP need not be applied for. This means, for instance, that a reprint that has received a new cover does not need a new CIP. If the book has gone from hardcover to paper, however, then a new CIP should be applied for because a new ISBN also has to be obtained. If a publisher is reprinting another publisher's book, then a new CIP is needed even if there are no other changes in the content of the book.

Publications That Do Not Need CIP. Printed matter of an ephemeral nature (tracts, pamphlets, catalogs, etc.) and books that are not likely to be purchased by libraries (such as workbooks, some Bible studies, cartoon books, comic books, and some series books) do not need CIP data. In some of these cases, the Library of Congress will refuse to provide data for such books.

Contact. Questions concerning any aspect of CIP data will be answered by the Copyright Office:

Copyright Office
Library of Congress
Washington, DC 20559
Telephone: (202) 287-8700

Catholic

Many a Protestant eyebrow has arched over the line "I believe in the holy, catholic, and apostolic church" from the Apostles' Creed. The word *catholic,* when lowercased, means "universal, or general." Hence, the New Testament epistles of James, 1 and 2 Peter, 1 John, and Jude are known as the *Catholic Epistles*, because they are not addressed to any individual or church. Otherwise, *Catholic*, when capitalized, refers exclusively to the Roman Catholic Church.

CE and BCE

The scholarly abbreviations *CE* ("common era") and *BCE* ("before the common era") are synonymous with *AD* (*anno Domini*, "year of our Lord") and *BC* ("before Christ") respectively and are used primarily when a writer feels the reader might be offended by the christocentric forms, as in writing for Jewish, Islamic, or secular readers. Most Western scholars still prefer AD and BC as the most commonly understood by the greatest number of readers in English, though CE and BCE are rapidly gaining ground.

To CE and BCE, Muslim scholars also add the abbreviation *AH* (*anno Hegirae*, "in the year of the Hegira"), which relates to the year AD 622 when Muhammad fled Mecca for Medina, a key turning point in the history of Islam. (See "Islamic Religious Terminology.")

Celebrant

In general usage, the term *celebrant* is used to mean anyone who celebrates. In Protestant contexts it can loosely refer to any worshiper at a religious service. Care should be taken, however, when using the word in the context of the Roman Catholic Mass, in which *celebrant* refers specifically to the person who officiates at the celebration of the Eucharist. In that case, the word does not refer to those in the congregation.

Change of Title

See "Title Changes."

Chapter Endnotes

See "Notes."

Chapter Opening Pages

The first page of a chapter, called the *chapter opening page* or *chapter opener*, should be designed with more flair than the standard text page; it should feel to the reader like an invitation to the chapter's content. As such, it is an exception to the general rule that text typography should be invisible. (See "Typography, The Elements of Basic Book.")

Ideally, and where space allows, opening pages should be set recto with the chapter number, chapter title, and text starting lower on the page than a normal text page. Oftentimes in mass-market-size books, the chapter will need to begin flush to the top of the text area.

Chapter *as a Word*. As in the table of contents, the word *chapter* is often omitted on a chapter opening page since a numeral alone usually suffices. The exception is for those cases when the word is actually designed in such a way as to be a part of the page's artistic composition.

Chapter Number. Arabic numerals are standard for chapter numbers, but roman numerals are sometimes used when there are very few chapters (no more than about ten). Chapter numbers may be spelled out for design reasons, but in books with many chapters, the higher numbers are cumbersome. Use arabic numerals unless there is a good design reason not to do so.

The title, if the chapter has one, should be the dominant element in the design, not the chapter number. If the number is spelled out, it should be set in a contrasting type or located well apart from the title so that it won't appear that the number is actually the first word of the chapter title.

Also keep in mind that if the word *chapter* is used and is set in all caps, Roman numerals should certainly not be used, since the numbers cannot be distinguished from the all-cap lettering.

Chapter Titles. If the chapter titles in a book tend to be long, the designer should set them in caps-and-lowercase rather than all caps. Also, a period should never follow a chapter title.

Initial Capitals. The first letter of the first word of a chapter is commonly given a special treatment. An enlarged cap sitting on the baseline of the first line is called a *standing cap*. If it is cut into the text so that it stands on the baseline of the second, third, or other succeeding line, it is called a *drop cap*. These may be indented for design reasons, but they can be set flush left or even hung out in the left margin. The entire first word can also be given this sort of display treatment at the discretion of the designer. If the chapter actually begins with a quotation mark, the mark is dropped if any kind of enlarged initial cap is used.

First Line of Text. When no oversized initial cap is used, and occasionally when it is used, the first line of text may be given a special treatment. The first word, phrase, or line may be set in small caps, italics, or a special font. Alternatively, the first word, phrase, or line can be set cap-lowercase like the rest of the text.

Running Heads and Folios. Running heads should not appear on a chapter opening page. If the design calls for the folio to appear in the running head, then an alternate location for the folio needs to be found, customarily centered below the text in the lower margin (called a drop folio), although that can be altered to suit the needs of a particular design.

Charismatic

In the broadest sense the word *charismatic* means "personally attractive and compelling." In the stricter and more religious sense, it has come to mean "characterized by an emphasis on the gifts of the Holy Spirit." The careful writer should make clear which meaning is intended. For both uses, it should be lowercased. The reason that *charismatic* is lowercased while *Pentecostal* is capitalized is that *Pentecostal* is actually used in the official names of a denomination and association of churches, whereas *charismatic* is not.

Children's Books: Style and Format

Christianity has a special relationship with children's books, for most scholars credit European Christian educators with having developed the idea of a separate literature for children to provide both entertainment and moral education. The *Orbis Senualum Pictus* (1658) by Jan Amos Comenius, a bishop in the Moravian Church, is generally credited as being the first children's picture book.

Although children's books in our own time vary widely in length, format, age of readership, and content, a few general guidelines are offered below.

Type Size. Even though children can read small type more readily than adults (type as small as 8 point), larger types (12 point and above) are usually used for children through the age of ten. For the very youngest readers, about ages five through seven, type as large as 18 point is not inappropriate. At a fifth-grade level or higher, children are fully capable of reading faces in adult type sizes: 9 point through 12 point. By and large, the younger the audience, the larger the type, even if a publisher expects the parent to read the book to the child.

Type Face. Generally, familiar medium- to heavy-weight typefaces are preferred by children themselves, especially in easy readers and some picture books that young children are expected to read by themselves. Serif faces are the most often used: Times New Roman, Bookman Antique, Century Schoolbook, and similar typefaces that are also common in adult books.

Picture books for preschool-age children are sometimes set in attractive sans-serif fonts such as Arial, Eras, Lucida Sans, and others on the theory that "block" letters are easier for children to identify and closer to a child's own block letters. Books that are especially design intensive often sport handwritten text, elaborate fonts, or exotic calligraphy to achieve special effects. Typographic design of children's books is an opportunity for the author, editor, and designer to work together.

Word Breaks and Justification. Generally, words should not be hyphenated or broken over lines in books for younger readers. Hyphens tend to confuse early readers. This also suggests that ragged-right setting is the most reader friendly. In some cases—as in picture books, for instance—lines can even be set so that each line ends with a complete phrase or sentence.

Word and Letter Spacing. Occasionally, for books intended for beginning readers, a larger than normal word spacing can be used—up to a full em. The compositor should also be sure that no kerning is used, since letters that are artificially squeezed together can cause problems for young readers. By the same token, no extra letter space should be added. The type should be allowed to letter-space itself as it was designed to do.

Paragraphing. In picture books and simple chapter books for beginning readers, it is common to avoid using paragraph indents, since it is felt that they confuse young readers unnecessarily. This adds a special burden on the writer, who has to be careful that the speakers in dialogue are kept distinct and that "said references" are placed early in dialogue rather than later. Appellations, if placed in the middle of a character's speech, should not come at a full stop. They should come midsentence so that it will be clear to the child or adult that the character is continuing to speak and that the sentence that follows is not a new character speaking. If dialogue issues are too complicated or cause confusion in an unparagraphed setting, then traditional paragraph indents should be used.

Margins. The margins in books for young readers should be wider than normal. Research has shown that narrow margins can actually lead the child's eyes off the page.

Lengths. The length of a children's book should be age-appropriate. Although firm rules cannot be established (who would have thought eight-year-olds would be reading a 700-page *Harry Potter* novel?), the publishing industry has developed some standards for length and age. Keep in mind that, especially for picture books and easy readers, part of the page count is taken up with title pages, copyright information, dedications, and sometimes author and artist information. So in the following chart, subtract four to six pages from the total to estimate the number of pages available for the actual text.

Type of Book	Age	Approximate Number of Pages	Approximate Number of Words
Board books	0–3	8, 12, 16	0–20 per two-page spread
Picture books (to be read to children)	3–8	24–32	0–1,000 (with 0–40 per two-page spread); 100–500 average for youngest readers (with 4–20 per two-page spread)
Easy [early] readers			
level 1 (can read and write with help)	4–5	32	300–500
level 2 (can almost read and write)	5–8	32, 48	500–1,000
level 3 (can read and write alone)	7–8	48, 56, 64	1,000–1,500
Chapter books	8–12	80, 96, 112, 128	18,000–25,000 total, unless there is a lot of design or art
Young adult books (teenage readers; teens who read at their level should be able to read adult books by age 16 or 17)	13+	varies, usually 144+	30,000–40,000

Other kinds of children's books have parameters that are not as easily quantifiable. For example, "hi-lo readers" are for children of various ages whose interest in reading is exceptionally high although their skills are below average for their age level. There are also "family readers," which are picture books with higher-than-average word or page counts that are meant to be read to children in several sittings. "Novelty," or "special format" books for children can take whatever shape the imaginations of the author and designer can conceive, and they follow no set pattern. In this last group are foldout books, pop-up books, scratch-and-sniff books, and books enhanced with computer chips to play music or make sounds.

Copyright Page. Because of the design-intensive nature of picture books and some other kinds of children's books, the copyright page is often shifted to the end of the book. There is no legal requirement for the location of the copyright page, so this practice is acceptable and common. Publishers often put only the bare minimum of information required on the copyright pages of their children's books—the copyright notice, the country of printing notice, and the all rights reserved notice.

Dedication Page. Again, because space is limited in books for young children, the dedication is commonly incorporated on either the copyright or title pages.

Chinese Transliteration

Two major systems of rendering Chinese words into English are now in common use: the older *Wade-Giles* and the more recent *pinyin*. This manual recommends pinyin for most purposes. Not only is it preferred by the greater number of Chinese-English speakers and readers, but it is also easier in many ways. It is the system endorsed by the People's Republic of China, although the government in Taiwan continues to use the Wade-Giles system. In addition, British and American libraries are slowly converting to pinyin so that, eventually, most book, subject, and author references will be catalogued according to that system.

For the time being, however, an exception should be made when a highly familiar Chinese word or name already has a long-established romanized form, such as, for instance, the names of classic literary works and certain historical personages. Few English readers recognize the pinyin *Kong Fuzi*, but most readers will immediately know who Confucius is. Still, because of the library cataloguing conversion, even that may eventually change. (See also "Titles of Common Texts of the World's Religions.") It is not always easy to judge which forms are "long-established" and which aren't. When in doubt, use the pinyin. Also, render the names of even well-known modern Chinese personages in pinyin: *Mao Zedong* rather than *Mao Tse-tung*.

Here is a short sampling of some of the differences between pinyin and Wade-Giles. An asterisk follows the preferred forms.

Pinyin	Wade-Giles	Pinyin	Wade-Giles
Beijing*	Peking	qi*	ch'i
Chan	Zen*	Qin dynasty*	Chin dynasty
Dao, Daosim	Tao, Taoism*	Quanyin*	Kuan Yin
Daodejing	Tao Te Ching*	Sichuan Province*	Szechwan Province
do fu	tofu*	Taichiquan	T'ai Chi Ch'uan*
Du Fu	Tu Fu*	Tang dynasty*	T'ang dynasty
Gongfu	Kung Fu*	Yangzi River*	Yang-tse River
Laozi	Lao Tzu*	Yi Ching	I Ching*
Li Bai	Li Po*	Zhou dynasty*	Chou dynasty
Mao Zedong*	Mao Tse-tung	Zhou Enlai*	Chou En-Lai
Nanjing*	Nanking		

The primary disadvantage of pinyin comes when it is pronounced, but if a few rules are observed, those problems are easily resolved.

pinyin character	pronounced
c	*ts* (as in *its*)
q	*ch* (as in *chin* but a little softer)
u	(similar to the French *u* or the German *ü* when it follows *j*, *q*, *x*, or *y*)
x	*sh* (as in *she* but a little softer)
z	*dz* (as in *adz*)

For a very helpful chart of Wade-Giles and pinyin conversions, see Table 10.2 in *CMS*.

Christendom versus *Christianity*

Writers commonly use *Christendom* and *Christianity* synonymously to mean the Christian faith as a whole. In precise usage, *Christianity* is applied to the Christian faith as practiced around the world, but *Christendom* is more limited to those parts of the world where Christianity has been a dominant historical and cultural force. Christianity, for instance, is widely practiced in Asia and Africa, but those continents are not usually considered part of Christendom, although that is rapidly changing as the demographic weight of the Christian faith shifts toward Asia and Africa.

Still, the term *Christendom* has geopolitical overtones, and some writers, including Malcolm Muggeridge, use it to mean nominally Christian Western culture in contrast to genuine Christian faith worldwide. In using this term, which can have such different meanings, a writer should clarify his or her definition.

Christian Holidays, Feasts, and the Liturgical Year

Movable and Immovable Feasts. There are eight primary *movable feasts* in the historical Christian tradition, all of which are determined in relation to the date of Easter: they are Sexagesima Sunday (sixty days before Easter), Palm Sunday, Ash Wednesday, Good Friday, Easter, Ascension Day (or Holy Thursday; forty days after Easter), Pentecost, and Trinity Sunday.

All the other feast days and holidays are considered *fixed*, or *immovable feasts*, though the four primary ones are the Annunciation (March 25), the Nativity of John the Baptist (June 24), Michaelmas (September 29), and Christmas (December 25). These are also called the *quarter days*, because they roughly correspond to the changing of each season.

The following list shows those holidays, and the preferred calendar placement, spelling, and styling of those holidays, that have had historical importance to the worldwide church.

Advent. Advent spans the period between Advent Sunday and Christmas. Advent (from Latin *adventus*, meaning "coming") is the season of remembering Christ's nativity and, by extension, his return to earth.

1. *Advent Sunday.* In Western churches, Advent begins on the fourth Sunday before Christmas (which is also the Sunday closest to November 30). That Sunday is generally considered the beginning of the church year, or calendar.

2. *Christmas (December 25).* Christmas (short for *Christ Mass*) is the day on which the birth of Jesus is traditionally commemorated. It is referred to as the *Feast of the Nativity of Jesus Christ* in some traditions, and although it actually ranks after Easter, Pentecost, and Epiphany in liturgical importance, it is the most popular of the holidays of the church year.

3. *Boxing Day (December 26 or 27).* Though not part of the church's celebration of Advent, *Boxing Day* is observed in the UK and much of its Commonwealth on the day after Christmas unless Christmas falls on a Saturday, in which case Boxing Day is observed on the following Monday. It was formerly the day on which families distributed boxes of gifts to the household servants. Today the tradition survives by remembering those who perform other public services, such as the mail carrier and trash collector.

Epiphany (January 6). Epiphany (from Greek *epiphainein*, "to manifest") is the celebration of Christ's manifestation to the Magi and to the Gentile world in general. This is a particularly important holiday in the Eastern church, where it is the commemoration of Christ's baptism. In England, the evening before Epiphany is referred to as *Twelfth Night.* Since in the church calendar, the new day actually begins at sunset, Twelfth Night was considered the beginning of Epiphany itself, the twelfth day after Christmas. The span of days from December 26 to January 6, inclusive, are the traditional *twelve days of Christmas.* On the old style Julian calendar, Epiphany was, in fact, Christmas day, and it is still a day of gift giving among some Christians.

Lent. The primary church season, Lent (from Anglo-Saxon *lencten*, meaning "spring" or "March") is traditionally a period of penitence and fasting commemorated between Ash Wednesday and Easter in preparation for Easter. The modern dating of Ash Wednesday and Easter were determined at the time of the Gregorian calendar reforms in 1582. The following are the major dates of the Lenten season.

1. *Shrove Tuesday.* The day before Ash Wednesday; generally a time of preparation for Lent. Outside the church, the day is better known as *Mardi Gras*, the traditional day of feasting before the Lenten fast.

2. *Ash Wednesday.* A day of penance and the official beginning of Lent, Ash Wednesday falls forty-six days before Easter. Commonly, Ash Wednesday is considered to be forty days before Easter, but that traditional way of determining the date of Ash Wednesday does not count the Sundays on the calendar.

3. *Laetare Sunday,* also called *Mothering Sunday* and sometimes *Refreshment Sunday.* This is the fourth Sunday of Lent, on which some small breaks in the Lenten penances were allowed.

4. *Passion Sunday.* The fifth Sunday of the Lenten season. In some traditions, the last two weeks of the Lenten season, from Passion Sunday to Holy Saturday, are referred to as *Passiontide.*

5. *Palm Sunday.* The sixth Sunday of the Lenten Season, that is, the Sunday before Easter, on which Christ's triumphant entry into Jerusalem is remembered. The seven-day period beginning on Palm Sunday is called *Holy Week.*

6. *Maundy Thursday.* The Thursday before Easter, traditionally the day on which Christ's institution of the sacrament of Communion, or the Eucharist, is commemorated. This day is sometimes referred to as *Holy Thursday,* although in some traditions the term *Holy Thursday* refers to Ascension Day (forty days after Easter). The word *maundy* is taken from the Bible verse read for that day: *"Mandatum novum do vobis"* ("A new command I give you"—John 13:34).

7. *Good Friday.* The Friday before Easter. On this day Christ's crucifixion and death are remembered.

8. *Holy Saturday.* This day commemorates the resting of Christ's body in the tomb and is honored in some churches with a Paschal Vigil Service, which begins late on this day and ends in the early hours of Easter Sunday morning.

Easter, Easter Sunday. Sometimes called the *Feast of the Resurrection of Christ,* Easter is the celebration of Christ's resurrection. Technically not part of Lent, which ends at midnight on Holy Saturday, Easter Sunday is meant to be a day of joy and celebration.

All dates preceding Easter in the Lenten season are established in relation to Easter Sunday. Several factors determine the date of Easter from year to year. Easter is always on a Sunday, and that Sunday is the first to fall after the fourteenth day of the "paschal moon" (which is a new moon). The paschal moon is determined by considering which spring new moon will have a full moon (fourteen days after the new moon) that either falls on or closest after the vernal equinox (always March 21 for this calculation). These somewhat confusing conditions being met, Easter can never occur before March 22 or later than April 25.

The following chart shows the dates for Ash Wednesday and Easter.

Year	Ash Wednesday	Easter
2004	February 25	April 11
2005	February 9	March 27
2006	March 1	April 16
2007	February 21	April 8
2008	February 6	March 23
2009	February 25	April 12
2010	February 17	April 4
2011	March 9	April 24
2012	February 22	April 8
2013	February 13	March 31
2014	March 5	April 20
2015	February 18	April 5
2016	February 10	March 27
2017	March 1	April 16
2018	February 14	April 1
2019	March 6	April 21
2020	February 26	April 12
2021	February 17	April 4
2022	March 2	April 17
2023	February 22	April 9
2024	February 14	March 31
2025	March 5	April 20
2026	February 18	April 5
2027	February 10	March 28
2028	March 1	April 16
2029	February 15	April 1
2030	March 6	April 21
2031	February 26	April 13
2032	February 11	March 28
2033	March 2	April 17
2034	February 22	April 9
2035	February 7	March 25

Pentecost. Celebrated on the seventh Sunday after Easter, this holy day commemorates the descent of the Holy Spirit on the apostles at Pentecost (Acts 2). Pentecost Sunday is also called *Whitsun*, or *Whitsunday*, in England. In the Roman Catholic Church, *Paschaltide* is the period between Easter Sunday and Pentecost.

Trinity Sunday. This day is set aside to honor the Trinity and is celebrated the Sunday after Pentecost Sunday. In the Church of England, *Paschaltide* is the period between Easter Sunday and the Saturday before Trinity Sunday.

Other Religious Holidays and Feast Days.

Week of Prayer for Christian Unity (January 18 to 25)
Conversion of Saint Paul (January 25)
Presentation of Christ, or Candlemas (February 2)
Annunciation, or Lady Day (March 25)
National Day of Prayer (first Thursday of May; interfaith observance in US; mandated by act of Congress)
Ascension Day (the fifth Thursday after Easter)
Nativity of John the Baptist (June 24)
Feast of Saint Peter and Saint Paul (June 29)
Visitation (July 2)
Transfiguration of Our Lord (August 6)
Assumption of the Blessed Virgin Mary (August 15)
Michaelmas (September 29)
Worldwide Communion Sunday (first Sunday in October)
Reformation Sunday (Sunday nearest October 31)
Reformation Day (October 31)
All Saints' Day (November 1)
All Souls' Day (November 2)
Feast of the Immaculate Conception (December 8)
Feast of the Conception of St. Anne (December 9)
Saint Lucy's Day, or Santa Lucia (December 13)
Saint Stephen's Day (December 26)
Holy Innocents' Day (December 28)

Christian Name

Although the term *Christian name*, which simply means *first name*, has been common in English since the sixteenth century, most stylists disapprove of its use in most contexts. Like the synonymous *baptismal name*, it presumes that a person is Christian or has been baptized. Use the terms *first name* or *given name* instead, unless specifically referring to a ceremony of baptism at which a child receives a name.

Church

The word *church* should only be capitalized when used in the actual name of a denomination or a specific congregation's meeting place: as in *the Church of England* or *Saddleback Church*. When used to mean believers as a whole, the historical church, or organized religion in general, the term should be lowercased: as in *the church in the Middle Ages* or *the worldwide church*.

Church Fathers

See "*Fathers of the Church* or *Church Fathers*."

Citations

See "Sources."

Citing Electronic Sources (CD-ROMs, etc.)

See "Sources."

Citing Webpages

See "Sources."

Clerical Titles and Positions

Clerical titles are formal titles given to religious officials of various kinds; they differ from *clerical positions*, which are common words used to describe religious officials but usually do not have the status of a formal title. Confusion occurs because many clerical titles shared by different denominations have slightly different meanings; therefore, the same word can be a title to some believers and a position to others. The two lists below attempt to sort out some of the confusion.

Clerical Titles

archbishop—*Eastern Orthodox* and *Roman Catholic*: leads an archdiocese or ecclesiastical province. Also a title of honor in the Roman Catholic Church for the head of an important ecclesiastical see.

archdeacon—*Roman Catholic* and *Anglican*: the assistant to a diocesan bishop.

auxiliary bishop—*Roman Catholic*: assists an archbishop or bishop.

bishop—*Eastern Orthodox* and *Roman Catholic*: heads a diocese. *Anglican*: heads a diocese or sometimes other posts. *General Protestant*: one who supervises other clergy in a specific region. *Mormon*: heads a ward.

canon—*Anglican*: connected with a chapter, a cathedral, a collegiate church, or sometimes assisting a bishop.

cardinal—*Roman Catholic*: a high-ranking bishop appointed by and ranking just below the pope. (The term is no longer placed between a given name and a surname in official titles.)

deacon—*Anglican* and *Roman Catholic*: a stage on the way to becoming a priest. Some deacons do not advance farther and instead serve in the church in unpaid positions. Addressed as "Rev." in Anglican Church. *Mormon*: the lowest grade of the Aaronic priesthood.

dean—*Anglican*: heads a cathedral or a seminary.

father—*Eastern Orthodox* and *Roman Catholic*: the title given to most priests. *Anglican*: a title preferred by some Anglican priests.

general secretary—*World Council of Churches*: oversees the general assembly.

metropolitan—*Eastern Orthodox*: a bishop who ranks just below patriarch and oversees an ecclesiastical province.

pastor—*General Protestant*: leads a congregation or local church. *Roman Catholic*: heads a parish.

patriarch—*Eastern Orthodox*: title given to a high-ranking bishop who oversees other bishops. *Mormon*: clergy of the Melchizedek priesthood able to perform certain prescribed duties. *Roman Catholic*: next in rank to the pope, a titular head of a given region.

presiding bishop—*Episcopal*: heads the Episcopal Church.

rabbi—*Jewish*: the leader of a congregation. Also, a teacher qualified to expound and interpret the Law.

suffragan bishop—*Anglican*: assists a bishop.

Clerical Positions

canoness—*Roman Catholic*: a woman living in a religious community but not under binding vows.

deacon—*General Protestant*: a lay officer, sometimes elected, who performs pastoral care or administrative duties or oversees ministries or maintenance duties in a church.

elder—*General Protestant*: A lay church officer, based on the principles set forth in 1 Timothy 5:17. There are two kinds: a *ruling elder* assists a pastor in administrative functions, while a *teaching elder* has pastoral and educational duties as well.

minister—*General Protestant*: describes most Protestant clergy.

pastor—*General Protestant*: a general term describing the person with the primary authority over a local church, congregation, or parish.

priest—*Roman Catholic, Eastern Orthodox*, and *Anglican*: the person authorized to perform religious rites and ceremonies, usually as an intermediary between God and the congregants. In rank, a priest is between a bishop and a deacon.

primate—*Roman Catholic* and *Anglican*: a bishop who has special authority over other bishops or whose ecclesiastical area has primary importance.

rector—*Anglican*: heads a parish.

Cliché, Religious

See "Jargon, Religious."

Colon

As a Pointer. A colon acts as a pointer to something that follows a particular word, phrase, or sentence. It can introduce a question, quotation, example, or amplification. In the case of a salutation to a letter, it can point to the entire text of the letter itself. It may act as a substitute for such expressions as *that is, namely, for instance*, and *for example*. Today a semicolon is used more often than a colon between two closely related sentences.

That is what faith is: God perceived intuitively by the heart, not by reason.
—Pascal

Remember the words of Augustine: "Hasten more slowly."

Many Christian writers have been instrumental in shaping the genre of prison literature: Paul, Boethius, and Bunyan.

It was the golden age of revivalism: Moody, Torrey, and Sunday were the familiar names of the time.

It was the golden age of revivalism; Moody, Torrey, and Sunday were the familiar names of the time. [with semicolon]

With Direct Quotations. A colon may introduce a direct quotation when no verb-of-saying is used.

Luther's answer was unapologetic: "Here I stand; I cannot do otherwise."

Capitalization. Capitalize the first word after a colon only if that colon introduces two or more sentences in close sequence, announces a definition, presents a proverb or quotation, or introduces a question or formal statement. Otherwise, the first word should be lowercased after a colon.

To Introduce a Quotation or a List. Use a colon when quoted material or a list is placed in a separate paragraph after an introductory statement. An introductory statement should not be followed by a colon if the series completes the sentence.

> Consider this passage from Arthur Dent's *Plain Man's Pathway to Heaven*: [. . .]
> The three areas of Tolkien studies are
> 1. The works of fantasy
> 2. The literary criticism
> 3. The personal writings

Between Titles and Subtitles. In bibliographies and other references, a colon is used between a title and subtitle—even when no punctuation appears on the original title page, since publishers commonly drop the colons before subtitles on such pages. But when a dash is used in the title instead of a colon, the dash should be retained in any reference to that work.

Between Volume and Page Numbers. In bibliographies and notes, a colon is used to separate a volume number (and an issue number, if present) from a page number. If no volume or issue numbers are given, a comma precedes the page number.

> Karen Burton Mains, "Healing the Wounds of Long Ago," *Christian Herald* 110, no. 11 (December 1987): 22.
> Tom Carson, "Baring the Celtic Soul of U2," *Los Angeles Times Book Review* (March 27, 1988), 15.

In Scripture References and Times. Place an unspaced colon between chapter and verse designations in Scripture references and between hours and minutes in time references.

> John 3:16   7:21 a.m.

Colophon

A colophon is a short printed notice, usually at or near the end of a book, on which the publisher or, formerly, the printer gives details of the book's production, such as its typeface or the type of paper used. The colophon has a long history in publishing, appearing at the advent of movable type, when it was first used in the Mainz Psalter of 1457. Though not as common now as it once was, a colophon is appropriate for any book of which the publisher is particularly proud or whose production values are unusually high.

Customarily, a colophon appears as a single page at the back of a book, though for space reasons it may appear on the copyright page. It can be as short or as long as can conveniently fit onto one page, though shorter is usually better. Colophons are usually set in type one or two point sizes smaller than the text type. A colophon can contain any or all of the following information:

> Notes on the typeface(s) used in the book, including:
>   style, size, and leading
>   reasons why that typeface was used
>   the provenance of the face (designer, year, first use, etc.)
>   system on which it was set
> Credit lines for the compositor and/or the designer
> Notes on the paper used (weight and maker)
> Credit line for the printer (including location)
> Credit lines for the graphic artists or illustrators who contributed to the book
> A general note on the series or imprint of which the book is a part

Comma

A comma serves several functions in writing. It can introduce a direct quotation, separate clauses of a sentence, indicate parenthetical statements, separate items in a list, and perform other uses. The word *comma* comes from Latin and Greek roots, meaning "a piece cut off," which indicates, metaphorically, the sort of uses to which the comma is put.

With Coordinating Conjunctions. A comma is placed before a coordinating conjunction (such as *and, but, or, nor, for*) in a compound sentence. No comma is needed when both clauses of the compound sentence are fairly short. When one or both of the clauses are long or contain internal punctuation, a semicolon should be used before the conjunction in place of the comma. Bear in mind, however, that a compound sentence differs from a sentence with a compound predicate (that is, two or more verbs with the same subject), in which case a comma should not be used.

> True Christian love can sometimes get angry, but it is also constantly wary of anger's pitfalls. [compound sentence]
> We seek a human Christ but we also seek a transcendent Christ. [short compound sentence; no comma needed]
> The pagan philosophers gave many admirable precepts, both for resigning blessings and sustaining misfortunes; but lacking the motives and sanctions of Christianity, however, they produce little practical effect.—Hannah More [complex compound sentence with other internal punctuation; substitutes semicolon for the comma]
> God teaches us patience and produces in us whatever other virtues we may exhibit. [compound predicate]

With Restrictive Clauses. Commas should not be used to set off adjectival clauses or phrases that restrict the meaning of the noun they modify. Commas should be used, though, when the phrase or clause does not strictly identify (restrict) the noun. The most helpful guiding principle is this: when the modifying phrase could be eliminated without essentially changing the reader's basic understanding of the sentence, commas should be used.

> The translation proposed to King James I in 1604 became known as the Authorized Version. [The phrase "proposed to King James I in 1604" restricts the noun.]
> This version, translated from the original languages, was not printed until 1611. [The phrase "translated from the original languages" does not restrict the noun.]

With Appositives. When a word or phrase is placed in apposition to a noun, it is set off by commas. If the word or phrase is restrictive, however, no commas should be used. Again, when the word or phrase can be eliminated without changing the basic meaning of the sentence, commas should be used.

> John Wycliffe, the great fourteenth-century Bible translator, has been called "the Morning Star of the Reformation."
> her husband, Robert Pearsall Smith
> his brother, Charles [indicates that Charles is the only brother]
> his brother Charles [indicates that there is more than one brother]
> the poet Milton
> the short story "Revelation" by Flannery O'Connor

With a Series of Elements. A comma is placed before *and*, *or*, and *nor* connecting the last two elements in a series of three or more. This is known as the *serial comma*.

> Though John is known for his sermons and Charles for his hymns, both Wesleys were prolific writers of letters, journals, sermons, and hymns.

Many manuals, especially those intended for periodical writing and those for writers in the UK, recommend dropping all serial commas. If done consistently, they can usually be dropped without noticeable effect, though this manual recommends retaining it for several reasons. First, it is still the most common style in American book publishing and, therefore, apt to be the one most familiar to the largest number of readers. Second, experience has shown that misreading can occur more often without the serial comma than with it. Since it is a long-established book custom in the US, keep it until the major style manuals recommend otherwise. (See "Ampersand, *Drop the Serial Comma.*")

With Namely, That Is, *Etc.* A comma should follow such expressions as *namely*, *that is*, and *for example* (including the abbreviations *i.e.* and *e.g.*, although these abbreviations are discouraged in nonacademic books). These expressions should be preceded with a comma, a semicolon, or an em dash, depending on how great the break in thought is.

> She wrote her thesis on the major English mystics, namely, Richard Rolle, Walter Hilton, and Julian of Norwich.

With Dependent Clauses. A comma usually follows a dependent clause (either restrictive or nonrestrictive) when that clause comes before the main clause of the sentence. A comma is also used before nonrestrictive dependent clauses that follow the main clause. A comma should not be used, however, when a restrictive dependent clause follows the main clause.

> Although Merton entered the monastery in 1941, he continued to write poetry throughout his life. [dependent clause preceding main clause]
> Galileo finally agreed to recant, although he was later rumored to have recanted his recantation. [dependent clause following the main clause]
> Dorothy Sayers was not allowed to graduate after earning her "first" at Oxford. [restrictive, dependent clause that follows the main clause]

With Adverbial Phrases. When an adverbial phrase comes before the main clause of the sentence, the phrase is usually followed by a comma, although it may be omitted when the phrase is short and when the omission will not result in confusion. The comma should also be omitted when the introductory adverbial phrase is immediately followed by the verb it modifies.

> Not many years after surviving a storm at sea, John Newton committed his life to Christ.
> After the decree Latimer was free to preach anywhere in England. [short adverbial phrase]
> Two years before, his ministry had ended. [were the comma omitted, misreading would result.]
> On the altar stood the completed carving of the nativity. [adverbial phrase followed by the verb]

With Multiple Adjectives. Two or more adjectives in sequence should be separated by a comma (or commas) when each, by itself, modifies the noun— that is, if the word *and* could be inserted between them without changing the basic meaning of the phrase. If an adjective modifies both a subsequent adjective (or adjectives) and the noun, however, a comma should not be used.

> Margaret Fell proved to be a faithful, sincere friend.
> Caedmon was the first great devotional poet to write in English. [no comma needed]

With Numerals and Names. A comma should be placed between unrelated numerals, although rewriting is often the best way to deal with such situations. A comma should also be used when confusion would result from the juxtaposition of two unrelated proper names or when a word is juxtaposed to itself.

> In August 1670, 450 people heard William Penn preach in front of his padlocked church. [original]
> In August 1670, William Penn preached to 450 people in front of his padlocked church. [rewritten]
> For Walton, Donne was the premier poet of his day.
> His theology seemed to echo Pope's opinion that whatever is, is right.

To Show Ellipsis. In some cases a comma may indicate that a word or phrase has been dropped. If the meaning is clear without it, the comma is not necessary.

> Newman contributed twenty-four tracts to the series; Keble, nine; and Pusey, four.
> We know that the Corinthians received at least two letters from Paul, and the Ephesians one.

With Quotations and Sayings. Commas may be used to set off quotations or sayings, whether or not quotation marks are used. If the quotation is long or formal, a colon should be used instead of a comma. When the entire quotation is used as though it were a noun (for instance, as a subject of a sentence or as a predicate nominative), it should not be set off by commas.

> Meister Eckhart said, "The eye with which I see God is the very same eye with which God sees me."
> The minister was fond of the old saw, Too heavenly minded to be any earthly good.
> "I forgive you" is a primary assertion of the Christian life.

With Oh. Use a comma after *oh* when other words follow it, but not after the vocative *O*, which is usually only used in direct address. Phrases such as *oh yes* and *oh no* are so common, particularly in dialogue, that the comma is not used after *oh* in these combinations.

> Oh, Jerusalem!
> O mighty king!
> Gary Davis sang, "Oh yes! I belong to the band! Hallelu!"

With Too. Use commas with *too* only when the word is used in an odd or unexpected place in a sentence, often for rhetorical effect. Otherwise, do not use commas around *too* in the middle of a sentence or before it at the end of a sentence.

> Saint Colm too was noted for his love of animals.
> Saint Colm was noted for his love of animals too.
> Saint Colm was, too, noted for his love of animals. [rhetorical effect]

To Show Disruption in the Flow of Thought. Adverbs, interjections, and other similar words should be set off by commas when they interrupt the flow of thought. Commas are not necessary, however, when these words do not disrupt the continuity.

> Margery Kempe, not surprisingly, was too impulsive to attract disciples.
> The sincerity of Constantine's faith, alas, has often been questioned.
> Eventually Cowper contributed to the *Olney Collection*.
> "Sinners in the Hands of an Angry God" was indeed Jonathan Edwards' most famous sermon.

With Jr., Sr., *Etc.* Do not use a comma to separate *Jr., Sr., I, II, III,* and so on from a proper name. This constitutes a major shift from the previous style.

> Martin Luther King Jr.
> Pope John Paul II

After the Last Element in a Series. It is not necessary to use a comma after the last element of a series with no conjunction. Likewise, a comma is not needed after expressions such as *etc., and so on,* or *and so forth* if they are the last element of a series.

> Pretentiousness, boasting, arrogance are all symptoms of pride.
> Pretentiousness, boasting, arrogance, etc. are all symptoms of pride.

With Two or More Verbs. Two verbs with the same object should not be separated by commas. A series of verbs with the same object, however, should be separated by commas, as would a series of nouns. In a sense, this is the rule of the "serial comma" applied to verbs.

> Jesus touched and healed the man with leprosy.
> Jesus comforted, healed, and taught many people.

Computer- and Internet-Related Words

Computers and the Internet have added words to the language so quickly that no dictionary or style manual can hope to keep pace. Although online style need not dictate print style, it has certainly had a great influence on it and that influence will only increase. One of the primary difficulties has been agreeing on a consistent style. In most cases, efficiency and brevity—that is, the fewest number of keystrokes—are the goals of most online communication. For instance, *email* rather than *e-mail* and *website* rather than *Web site*.

E- Combinations. The *e* prefix poses special problems. This manual recommends dropping the hyphen in the most common words (*email*, *ebook*, *ezine*). Since new *e-words* are being invented almost daily (*e-trading*, *e-community*), however, we recommend hyphenating all combinations that are clearly temporary (*e-thinking*, *e-storage*) and all instances in which the lack of a hyphen might cause misreading (as in *e-edition*, *e-empire*, or *e-editing*). Still, since the use of the *e* prefix has reached the level of cliché, this manual recommends that writers avoid such neologisms whenever possible. *E-combinations* will most likely vanish in the future as books and ebooks increasingly overlap and as commerce and e-commerce become synonymous.

Capitalization. Only time will tell whether some Internet-related words now commonly capitalized will eventually be lowercased. There are, for instance, some technical differences between *Internet* and *internet*, and *Web site* and *website*, differences that are, for the most part, not clearly understood by the majority of people who access websites on the Internet. This manual recommends lowercasing *website* and most other *web-* combinations, on the general principal of minimizing keystrokes. *Internet* should be capped. To add to the confusion, *World Wide Web* should be capitalized, even though its abbreviation is always lowercased as *www* in webpage address. Also capitalize *the Web* and *the Net*.

List of Words. Here are a few computer- and Internet-related terms in their most common style:

A drive (B drive, etc.)

backup (noun and adj.)
back up (verb)
bandwidth
barcode

cell phone (cellular telephone)
cyberspace

desktop
dialup (adj.)

dial up (verb)
disc (for CDs, CD-ROMs, laserdiscs, DVDs, SACDs, etc.)
disk (for hard drives and floppy disks)
dotcom
download

ebook (preferred; but *e-book* is also common; avoid *e:book*)
e-church

e-commerce
email (preferred; but *e-mail* is
    also common)
e-money
emoticon
Ethernet (capped)
e-trading
ezine

floppy disk

gridline

handheld
homepage
hyperlink
hypertext

icon
information highway (lc)
internet, the (any large network
    made up of smaller ones)
Internet, the (the worldwide
    research network)

laptop
logon, logoff (noun and adj.)
log on, log off (verb)

mailbomb
menubar
morph
motherboard
mouse (singular)
mouses, or mouse devices
    (plural)
multimedia

Net, the (synonymous with the
    Internet)
netiquette

offline
offscreen
online
onscreen

palmtop
plaintext
pop-up
printout (noun)
print out (verb)
pulldown

real-time (adj.)
real time (noun)
richtext

screensaver
search engine
shareware
spam (lc)
spellcheck, spellchecker
spelling checker
stand-alone
startup
supercomputer

telecommute
telnet
toolbar
touchpad
touchscreen
trackball

upload

V-chip
videogame
voicemail

Web, the
webcam
webcast
webmail
webmaster
webpage
website (though *Web site* is
    common)
webzine
word processor
workstation
World Wide Web, the

Conclusion

A *conclusion* falls at the end of the book and is a place for the author to summarize the main themes, fill in additional details, and tie up loose ends of the story or discussion. It is usually longer than an afterword and more integral to the reader's understanding of the body matter. (See also "Afterword" and "Epilogue.")

Concordance

A *concordance* is a reference book that alphabetically lists the words used in a given book, along with their references and often a short quotation to show how that word is used in context. The term is most commonly applied to Bible concordances, the most famous of which was *Cruden's Concordance* of 1737, though there are many scholarly concordances of literary works and sacred writings of other traditions.

Several types of Bible concordances exist:

analytical concordance—analyzes according to Greek and Hebrew words

compact concordance—abridged, in a pocket-size binding

complete concordance—contains many words, but not such common words as articles, prepositions, etc.

concise concordance—abridged for ease of use

condensed concordance—abridged, synonym for *concise concordance*

critical concordance—synonym for *analytical concordance*

exhaustive concordance—unabridged, contains every occurrence of every word and analyzes according to Greek and Hebrew words

handy concordance—abridged, synonym for *compact concordance*

keyword concordance—abridged, using only words of special significance

red-letter concordance—the words spoken by Jesus are printed in red

thematic concordance—organizes entries by theme

topical concordance—organizes entries by chief topics, generally synonymous with *thematic concordance*

unabridged concordance—a complete concordance, contains all words but does not analyze according to Greek and Hebrew words

An entry in a Bible concordance is typically formatted as follows (although punctuation is not retained exactly as in the original quotation):

Book

Ecc   12:12 Of making many *b* there is no end,

Da   7:10 and the *b* were opened.

Jn   21:25 for the *b* that would be written.

Rev   20:12 the throne, and *b* were opened.
        20:12 they had done as recorded in the *b*.

Confession

Largely because of Augustine of Hippo's famous and personally revelatory autobiography called *The Confessions* (c. 400), the term *confession*, as a literary genre, has come to suggest a personal narrative in which the author admits to misdeeds and indiscretions. We commonly forget, however, that Augustine used the word to mean "praises" and "thanksgivings," a series of declarations of his faith in God. This sense of the word is still with us when we say that someone is a "confessing Christian" or "confesses faith in Christ."

Eventually the word was applied to the admission of sin as part of the Catholic penitential process, and as a modern literary genre it came to imply an author's (somewhat self-justifying) moral self-assessment, as in Jean-Jacques Rousseau's seminal *Confessions*.

Contents Page

See "Table of Contents."

Contractions

Contractions (*can't, don't, won't, it's,* and so on) are customarily reserved for dialogue and informal writing in which it is important to preserve a speaker's or author's colloquial tone. Although the rule of avoiding contractions in fine writing is becoming much less common than it once was, contractions should be used sparingly in formal and academic writing.

The tone, style, and genre of the book will usually dictate the extent to which contractions should be used. Memoirs, for instance, in which an author's spoken cadences and voice are particularly colorful may require the use of contractions. Academic books usually avoid contractions in an effort to elevate the tone and authority of the author's voice.

Contractions, of course, are always preserved in direct quotation.

> I'm not tempted by despair; where there's life, there's hope. [informal, colloquial]
>
> I am reminded of Sir Thomas More's idea that there is no sorrow on earth that heaven cannot heal. [formal; *"I am"* and *"there is"* are not contracted]
>
> "Here's to us all—God bless us every one," said Tiny Tim. [direct quotation]

Copyright Holder and Copyright Owner

Usually, the *copyright holder* is the author or creator of the book or software. Such a person (or persons) is sometimes called the *owner of copyright*. Under current laws, that person owns the copyright from the instant the work is written or created. This person may then transfer some or all of those rights (to a publisher, for instance, to print and distribute). The person or organization to whom the author or creator has given legal responsibility to reproduce the book and usually to sell other rights (film rights, serial and subsidiary rights, etc.) is called the *copyright owner*.

Copyright Notice

A copyright notice is the publisher's and author's legal declaration that they alone have the right to reproduce and sell the book or other printed material in which that notice is given.

The Essentials. A legal copyright notice for books consists of three essential elements:

1. The copyright symbol (©) (and/or the word *copyright* or the abbreviation *copr.*)
2. The year of publication
3. The name of the owner of copyright

For works published after March 1, 1989, a notice of copyright is not required in order to protect the copyright of the book, but most sources recommend its use nonetheless—to make the legal status of the copyright unambiguous. Use of the correct copyright notice will generally defeat the defense of "innocent infringement," should anyone infringe on the copyright; and without the notice, the publisher may not be able to collect damages from an infringer.

The order of the three elements is not prescribed, though they should be juxtaposed in some fashion. The most common order is *copyright / year / by copyright owner*:

Copyright © 2003 by Joni Eareckson Tada
[for the book *The God I Love: A Memoir*]

Although it is not necessary to use both the word *Copyright* and the © symbol together, it is often done as a convention.

Name of Copyright Holder. In the copyright notice, the first and last name of the copyright holder, usually the author, should be used. Commonly used middle initials or middle names are acceptable. Abbreviations of names (*Wm.* for William, for example) are acceptable as long as it is still obvious to whom the name refers. In one case, an author named Frederick abbreviated his name as Fr. in order to mislead people into thinking he was a Catholic monk. Such a practice, of course, should be avoided.

Commonly used pen names are acceptable. If the owner of the copyright is commonly known by a pseudonym, single name, or single initial, then that is acceptable as well. When in doubt, the original contract should be consulted to find the most accurate form of name of the copyright holder.

Incorrect Copyright Notice. If one of the three essential elements is entirely missing from the copyright notice, the notice could be considered legally invalid, and a company lawyer should be contacted. Under the current copyright laws, this does not usually mean that copyright is forfeited, but it can result in some limitations to certain privileges or protections.

If a single element is merely inaccurate, then the copyright is still valid, and most privileges and protections are not affected. A copyright attorney should be consulted nonetheless, and the correction made in subsequent editions.

If the name of the copyright holder is misspelled or wrongly given, then it should be corrected in the next printing. This is not usually a serious problem, although again, an attorney should be consulted.

If the wrong year of publication is given, it is usually not a serious problem if the date is off by only one year before or after the actual date of publication. The publisher should be sure, however, to correct the error when applying for copyright registration after publication.

If the date in the notice is two or more years before or after the actual publication date, however, then the law treats the entire notice as omitted, and the publisher's lawyers should be contacted.

Placement. While the Copyright Act of 1976 does not insist that the copyright notice be placed on the copyright page, most publishers still do it since it is the most convenient and obvious place to do it. The law states that the copyright notice should be placed in such a way so as to be "perceived visually" on all copies of the work reproduced. This may seem obvious, but it is stated in order to cover certain ambiguities, such as unreadable material on video, DVD, or other electronic media. A mechanical aid to visual perception may be assumed, such as a projector or video player. In the case of video tape, DVD, and CD-ROM, the copyright notice must be printed on the cassette or disc itself or on its accompanying cassette case as long as the case is not meant to be thrown away. A performance copyright should be obtained for any sound recordings also contained.

Copyright Dates for New Editions. Whenever a new edition of a book contains material that might not be covered under the previous edition's copyright, the entire copyright should be renewed and a new date provided in the copyright line. In that case, both the original copyright date and the new one should appear in the copyright notice. Technically, the first date need not be shown, but for a number of reasons it is advisable to provide it. When more than one year is given in the copyright notice, the lowest number is given first.

If the owner of the copyright has changed, then both the old and new dates—along with the name of the old and new owners—should be shown. This is needful especially when an author dies and the copyright is transferred to a surviving spouse, family member, or estate.

Compilations. Copyright experts recommend that in those cases in which contributors to a compilation or an anthology retain the copyrights to their own works, the safest procedure is for each individual copyright holder to be listed in addition to the compiler's collective copyright for the whole work. This can be done on the copyright page although it may mean providing additional pages at the front or back of the book to list all the copyrights for the individual pieces. In this sense, they are treated the same as any permissions notice would be treated.

Copyright Page

The copyright page is prepared by the publisher. It contains the legal copyright notice for the book in which it is contained. The essential content of this copyright notice consists of the copyright symbol, the year, and the name of the copyright holder. (See "Copyright Notice.") An "all rights reserved" notice and a declaration of the country in which the book was printed should also appear. (See "All Rights Reserved Notice.")

At the publisher's discretion, the copyright page may also include the Library of Congress Cataloging in Publication Data, which is used for library classification; the International Standard Book Number (ISBN), which references a coding system used worldwide; any credits and permissions; disclaimers and other brief notes from the editor or author; a brief printing and publishing history of the volume; edition and printing reference numbers; and any other information deemed necessary.

Placement. The customary location of the copyright page is on the verso of the title page. Occasionally, especially in some art books, gift books, children's picture books, or other books in which graphic elements are dominant, the copyright page may be placed at the back of the book. The functional purpose, however, is that the copyright page should be easy for the reader to find. The law states that it must provide the reader with "reasonable notice" of copyright.

A unique problem is posed by page-a-day calendars. In this case, it is recommended that the copyright page be placed at the very end of the calendar, so that it won't be thrown away at the beginning of the year. This provides the reader with "reasonable notice" of the copyright and ensures that the copyright notice may be "visually perceived" for the maximum amount of time.

Country of Printing Notice

For all books printed in the United States, the copyright page should carry the notice: "Printed in the United States of America." Any time the actual book is printed in a foreign country (whether by a foreign printer or by a foreign division of a US printer), the name of that country should be specified on the copyright page. Even if only the dust jacket of a domestically printed book were to be printed in a foreign country, a notice of the country of printing should appear on the dust jacket.

This notice is provided on printed material for customs reasons, and failure to do so could cause the shipment of books or other material to be impounded by the US Customs Service.

Cover Copy

The cover of a book is basically a billboard. It is an advertisement for the book's contents and is designed to get attention. The interior of the book, by contrast, is usually more subtle. Too much distraction inside will diminish the reader's appreciation for the contents. The interior design of a book, as designer Beatrice Ward used to say, should be a crystal goblet through which the color of the wine can be seen without distortion. (See "Typography, The Elements of Basic Book.")

The same is true for the words themselves, those that appear outside and inside the book. The cover copy is basically a sales pitch for the book, and the writer of such copy should be granted a great deal of freedom in the way that pitch is expressed. The writer should be free to break rules of grammar and punctuation when there is a good reason to do so. In fact, a good copywriter should be breaking the rules.

It is common for editors, authors, and proofreaders to complain that cover copywriters and designers have made mistakes, and they are right in doing so when clear error is involved. But in many cases, the copywriter has broken a rule for good reason, and his colleagues should be sensitive to that. Ideally, the book's cover copy should largely echo the style used in the text of the book itself, but when there's a reason not to, so be it. Call it "copywriter's license." For example, serial commas may be dropped in display copy to save space, numerals may be used when necessary to facilitate rapid communication, and fragmentary sentences are common in cover copy.

Titling. Book designers should have the freedom to "fiddle" with the style of a book's title as it will appear on the cover of the book. A subtitle usually does not need to be preceded by a colon on the cover even though it appears with the colon on the copyright page. The title may be set in all caps or all lowercase letters. Some words may be emphasized in unusual ways. Punctuation can be tampered with; for instance, a serial comma can be dropped from a list in the title if there is a design reason to do so.

Crucifixion, the, and Resurrection, the

Unlike *CMS* and some other manuals of style, *The Christian Writer's Manual of Style* does not urge writers and editors to capitalize such terms as *the crucifixion* and *the resurrection* in most writing for the general reader. Such capitalization is a holdover from a time when devotional books commonly capitalized many religious objects, ideas, and events that are no longer capitalized. While capitalization is legitimately used to distinguish specific objects from generic ones, we feel the article *the* does enough to distinguish which crucifixion and which resurrection are being referred to. When writing of *the crucifixion*, there is little doubt as to whose crucifixion is meant.

There is the added disadvantage that the capitalized terms may appear to hold special meanings for the author not clearly understood by readers, especially those who may not be Christians. For instance, in a popular book that attempts to argue for the historicity of the crucifixion of Jesus or an apologetic that tries to make an objective case for the resurrection, capitalizing those terms may make the reader feel that the writer has a preconceived bias toward one point of view and cannot, therefore, be objective. Typographic style should not suggest partisanship in a book purporting to be objective.

Like most of the rules in this manual, however, this one may be broken when appropriate. The terms may be capitalized when the author and editor agree that they should be, for instance, in scholarly works in which the crucifixion and the resurrection are discussed as largely theological concepts, or, like the deity pronoun, in devotional works intended to have a somewhat antiquated feel.

Crusade and Crusades

The terms *crusade* and *crusades* are legitimate words in most contexts, although they should be avoided when used figuratively for Christian evangelism, modern military campaigns, or any effort to promote beliefs or values cross-culturally. There are two reasons for this. First, the terms have acquired negative overtones in the popular press, suggesting extremism or zealotry, as in *the parents' crusade to ban* Huckleberry Finn *from the school library*. Second, and perhaps more importantly, the terms are an affront to Muslims worldwide.

The terms still strongly evoke the Crusades of the eleventh, twelfth, and thirteenth centuries because they were specifically coined to describe those wars (from the French *croisade* and Spanish *cruzada*, meaning "blessed by, or marked with, a cross"). If evidence were needed to prove that the use of those terms is now considered culturally insensitive, one need only remember the criticism President George W. Bush received in late 2001 when he characterized the war against terrorism as "a crusade." Even before then, the Billy Graham Association had distanced itself from the term *crusade*.

When in doubt, find another word. Such words as outreach, campaign, event, and appeal can usually be substituted, as in: *a city-wide evangelism outreach* or *a spiritual campaign to bring nonbelievers into the church*.

Dash

Five Kinds of Dashes. Five kinds of dashes, varying in length and function, are commonly used. If a word processor does not allow for these distinctions, they may be indicated on the printout as follows:

Kind of dash	Typed	Typeset
hyphen	-	-
en dash	–	–
one-em dash	--	—
two-em dash	---	——
three-em dash	----	———

After the hyphen (see "Hyphenation"), the em dash (—) is the most frequently used dash in ordinary writing. When used alone, the word *dash* usually refers to an em dash.

Em Dash

Em Dash for Sources. An em dash can be used to indicate the source or credit line of a quote when that quote is set off from the text, as in an epigraph or block quotation. Note that in these cases the period should be used in conjunction with the em dash in order to avoid misreading.

> Alms are but the vehicles of prayer.—John Dryden
> A man without religion is like a beast without a bridle.—Latin proverb

Em Dash for Break in Continuity. An em dash can indicate an abrupt shift in the continuity of a sentence or a thought or a strongly rhetorical turn of phrase.

> Nothing in this world is to be taken seriously—nothing except the salvation of a soul.—Bishop Fulton Sheen
> Feel for others—in your pocket.—C. H. Spurgeon

Em Dash for Parenthetical Thought. A dash may be used to insert parenthetical matter that carries special emphasis or importance to the main thrust of the sentence. Commas usually set off parenthetical matter that has a close affinity to the rest of the sentence but does not carry any special emphasis.

Parentheses should be used for extraneous matter that is not essential to the argument of the sentence.

> We must become so pure in heart—and it needs much practice—that we shall see God.—Henry Drummond
>
> Mistress Anne Bradstreet—a woman and a Puritan no less—may be regarded as the first major American poet.
>
> Helen Waddell, who also wrote *Beasts and Saints* and the novel *Peter Abelard,* is probably best remembered for her translation of *The Desert Fathers.*
>
> Erasmus Darwin (grandfather of Charles) and Lamarck postulated the inheritance of acquired characteristics.

Em Dash for Summary of List. When several items are listed and then summarized as a group by a single word in a concluding sentence or clause, a dash should separate the list from the concluding sentence or clause.

> Wycliffe, Tyndale, Coverdale—all had a dream of seeing the Bible generally available in English. [*All* is the summarizing word in this case.]

Em Dash as a Pointer. Occasionally the dash may be used, like a colon, as a kind of pointer to direct the reader to something that follows an introductory phrase. It should be reserved, however, for those instances when a special emphasis is being placed on the words that follow the dash. In most cases a colon will suffice.

> That is what we are here for—to do God's will.—Henry Drummond

Em Dash with Other Punctuation. In some circumstances the dash may be used in combination with other punctuation. When a dash immediately concludes a quotation and is immediately followed by the speaker reference, a comma should follow the dash. Often dashes are used in place of commas to introduce a parenthetical idea into a sentence; in these cases a question mark or exclamation point can be used in combination with the dash when appropriate.

> "Mine is comic art—," Flannery O'Connor quipped.
>
> Southwell knew the dangers—who more than he?—of returning to England.

Em Dash in Dialogue. In dialogue, broken, hesitating, or interrupted speech is indicated by an em dash. An en dash is used to indicate stuttering.

> "I can't—don't even ask—swear such an oath!" [Em dash]
>
> "What was—" A peal of thunder interrupted him. [Em dash]
>
> "I s–see. B–but why?" asked Brother Juniper. [En dash]

Avoid Overusing the Em Dash. Writers of advertising copy often lean heavily on em dashes to give a sense of immediacy and excitement to their copy. Like exclamation points and italics, the em dash is emphatic, but if any of those devices is used too often, they can prove counterproductive by numbing the reader's attention.

Even when not overused, em dashes have a tendency to cause the reader to pause a fraction of a second while reading. Too many of them can lead to what one editor refers to as "stop-and-start" reading, something that every author should be careful to avoid.

Authors and editors should be wary of overusing em dashes. Commas can be substituted for the em dash when a mildly parenthetical thought is intended, or parentheses can be used when the parenthetical thought is more tangential. When used as a pointer, the em dash can usually be replaced with a colon without any loss of sense.

Em Dashes at the Ends of Lines. When an em dash falls at the end of a line of type, it should be set on the right-hand margin rather than allowed to begin the next line (at the left margin). An em dash, which is often very thin, set on the left-hand margin can be mistaken for an indent.

En Dash

The British Dash. In the very same places where American editors would place an unspaced em dash in running text, British editors often use an en dash with a word space on either side – as in this famous prayer by Dag Hammarskjöld:

> Night is drawing nigh – For all that has been – Thanks!
> For all that shall be – Yes!

The advantage of this style is that the dashes appear less emphatic and blend more smoothly with the type. Because in some fonts the em dash is actually lighter in weight than the en, many typographers complain that the em dash, if used too frequently, can make a page of type look like Swiss cheese – full of holes! Also, in some fonts, unless the em dash is hair spaced, it can appear to touch the letters on either side of it.

Even in American publishing, the British en dash style can be used effectively – and without apology or hesitation – in books that require an especially refined appearance, are of a high literary quality, or contain an inordinate number of dashes.

En Dash with Numbers and Dates. In American publishing, the en dash is primarily used to indicate successive, inclusive, or continuing numbers, as in dates, page numbers, or Scripture references. See "Numbers, Inclusive (Elision)" for special rules governing elision of numbers.

    1852–53   May–June 1967   pp. 29–41   John 4:3–6:2

En Dash in Compound Adjectives. An en dash should replace a hyphen in a compound adjective if one of the adjectives is already hyphenated or is made up of two words.

    the Norman–Anglo-Saxon church
    pre–Civil War
    an Old Testament–New Testament contrast

Two-Em Dash

A two-em dash indicates that an entire word or name has been omitted from a sentence.

    A certain pastor in the village of —— was known to have cooperated with the Nazis.

A two-em dash can also indicate that a series of letters has been omitted from within a word.

    A dilapidated sign caused the confusion; it read, "Bay View Church; R——ent [Repent] Now!"
    The book was signed C. W——s [Williams?].

Three-Em Dash

A three-em dash indicates a name that is repeated in a bibliography.

    Jansson, Tove. *Comet in Moominland.* London: Ernest Benn, 1951.
    ———. *The Exploits of Moominpappa.* London: Ernest Benn, 1952.
    ———. *Finn Family Moomintrool.* London: Ernest Benn, 1950.

Dates

See "Time and Dates."

Dedication

Authors often dedicate their work to a specific person or persons and sometimes include a short sentiment by way of appreciation. This is the *dedication*. It has its roots in those times when authors actually had to find patrons to finance the publication of their work.

The dedication usually appears on a page by itself just after the copyright page but before the epigraph, contents page, and any other introductory material. It is customarily centered line-for-line on the page, and a little above the center of the page, unless the designer has decided to alter its setting. The words *dedication* or *dedicated to* should not be used in the dedication itself, nor is it necessary to use the heading *Dedication*. A dedication page should not bear a folio number or running head, nor should it be listed in the table of contents. Customarily, no period is used at the end of a dedication.

In some cases, where space is of special concern, a dedication may be placed at the top of the copyright page and can even be set a point size or two larger than the type on that page as long as there is sufficient visual space between the two blocks of copy.

Deity Pronoun: Capitalization

The capitalization of pronouns referring to persons of the Trinity has been a matter of debate for many decades. Should *He* be capitalized when referring to God or not? Impassioned arguments have been offered up on both sides of the question. The following paragraphs outline Zondervan's policy and the reasoning behind it.

In Most Cases, Lowercase the Deity Pronoun. Although both the lowercase and capped styles have long and deeply rooted pedigrees in English literature, this manual advocates the use of lowercase pronouns in nearly all situations.

Reasons for Lowercasing. Many religious publishers and most general publishers have adopted the lowercase style, in large part to conform to the styles of the most commonly used versions of the Bible (the King James Version, the New International Version, and the Revised Standard Version). It is the style recognized as contemporary by the greatest number of readers and writers both inside and outside the church.

Because capitalizing the deity pronoun, as well as a vast number of other religious terms, was the predominant style in late nineteenth- and early twentieth-century publishing, it gives a book, at best, a dated, Victorian feel, and at worst, an aura of complete irrelevance to modern readers.

Contrary to popular opinion, capitalization is not used in English as a way to confer respect (we capitalize both God and Satan, Churchill and Hitler). As pointed out elsewhere (see "Capitalization: Biblical and Religious Terms"), capitalization is largely used in English to distinguish specific things from general. Jesus is no more specific, in that sense, than Peter, and both should therefore be referred to as *he*.

Some writers argue that the capitalized style should be used to avoid confusion of antecedents in closely written text (for instance, whether Jesus or one of the disciples is being referred to as *he* in a given passage). Even in this last case, a careful writer should be able to make the meaning clear without capitalization. After all, the writer should be able to distinguish between the twelve disciples without resorting to typographic tricks.

Many readers, especially the younger ones, do not recognize the reasons for such typographic conventions, and the capitalized pronoun may actually cause confusion or be read as emphasis when none is implied.

Finally, an insistence on the capped style can introduce unintended religiopolitical overtones into a publication. When *He* is capped for God or Jesus, it can appear to younger readers especially, as though the author is purposely emphasizing the maleness of the deity, in direct response to feminist theologians who argue for the inclusiveness of God. Apart from the merits of either side of that debate, the capitalized deity pronoun introduces a polemical overtone that may wholly detract from the topic at hand.

Is Capitalization Ever Justified? There are some situations in which the capitalization of deity pronouns is preferred, for instance, in books that have a deliberately old-fashioned tone or when the author quotes extensively from a Bible version that uses the capitalized style (such as the New King James Bible or the New American Standard Bible). When deity pronouns are capitalized, though, the words *who*, *whom*, and *whose* should not be.

If a publication falls under one of those categories, the author should discuss his or her preference with the editor ahead of time, and the preferred style should be specified on a style sheet so that the other editors and proofreaders involved in the project will be informed.

In Quotations. Even when lowercasing the deity pronouns in a given publication, the capitals should be retained in any quotations from other books that use the capped style. Likewise, if the deity pronoun is capped in a publication, the lowercase should be retained in all quotes where it is found in the original source. Quotations should always retain the style of the original as a matter of accuracy (or unless otherwise noted in a footnote or on the copyright page). See "Quotations."

Denominations and Associations of Churches*

Because of the array of religions and religious denomintations in the US, confusion often exists about correct names and spellings of certain denominations. The following list is adapted from *The Handbook of Denominations in the United States* and should provide a good basis for accuracy and consistency. Also, following some of the major denominations are the abbreviations by which they are known.

Adventist Churches
    Advent Christian Church
    Branch Davidians
    Church of God General Conference
    Church of God (Seventh Day)
    Seventh-day Adventist (SDA)
Bahá'i
Baptist Churches
    Alliance of Baptist Churches
    American Baptist Association
    American Baptist Churches in the USA
    Baptist General Conference
    Cooperative Baptist Fellowship
    General Association of General Baptist Churches
    General Association of Regular Baptist Churches (GARBC)
    National Association of Free Will Baptists
    National Baptist Convention of America, Inc.
    National Baptist Convention, USA, Inc.
    National Missionary Baptist Convention of America
    National Primitive Baptist Convention, USA
    North American Baptist Conference
    Primitive Baptist
    Progressive National Baptist Convention, Inc.
    Reformed or Sovereign Grace Baptists
    Separate Baptists in Christ (General Association)
    Seventh Day Baptist General Conference
    Southern Baptist Convention (SBC)
Brethren and Pietist Churches
    Brethren Church (Ashland)
    Brethren in Christ Church
    Church of God (Anderson, Indiana)
    Church of the Brethren
    Church of the United Brethren in Christ
    Evangelical Covenant Church
    Evangelical Free Church of America
    Fellowship of Grace Brethren Churches
    Moravian Church (*Unitas Fratrum*)
    Old German Baptist Brethren (Old Order Dunkers)
    Unity of the Brethren

* Frank S. Mead, Samuel S. Hill, and Craig D. Atwood, *The Handbook of Denominations in the United States*, Eleventh Edition (Nashville: Abingdon, 2001), 7–14. Used by permission.

Catholic Churches
   American Catholic Church
   Eastern Rite Catholic/Uniate Churches
   Liberal Catholic Church
   Mariavite Old Catholic Church, Province of North America
   Old Catholic Churches
   Polish National Catholic Church of America
   Roman Catholic Church (RC)
Christian Churches (The Stone-Campbell Movement)
Christadelphians
Christian Church (Disciples of Christ)
Christian Churches and Churches of Christ
Christian Congregation, Inc.
Churches of Christ
Church of Christ, Scientist (Christian Science) (CS)
Church of God and Saints of Christ
Community Churches, International Council of
Community of God and Saints of Christ
Congregational Churches
   Congregational Christian Churches (National Association)
   Conservative Congregational Christian Conference
   United Church of Christ (UCC)
Divine Science
Episcopal/Anglican Churches
   Anglican Catholic Church
   Episcopal Church
   Episcopal Orthodox Christian Archdiocese of America
   International Communion of the Charismatic Episcopal Church
   National Organization of the New Apostolic Church of North America
   Reformed Episcopal Church
   Southern Episcopal Church
Friends (Quaker)
   Evangelical Friends International
   Friends General Conference
   Friends United Meeting
   Religious Society of Friends (Conservative)
Fundamentalist/Bible Churches
   American Evangelical Christian Churches
   Baptist Bible Fellowship International
   Baptist Missionary Association of America
   Berean Fundamental Church
   Bible Fellowship Church
   Bible Presbyterian Church
   Christian and Missionary Alliance
   Christian Brethren (Plymouth Brethren)
   Conservative Baptist Association of America (CB America)
   Grace Gospel Fellowship
   Independent Fundamentalist Churches of America (IFCA International Inc.)

Holiness Churches
  Apostolic Christian Church of America
  Apostolic Faith Church
  Apostolic Overcoming Holy Church of God
  Churches of Christ in Christian Union
  Church of Christ (Holiness) USA
  Church of God (Holiness)
  Church of the Nazarene
  Wesleyan Church
Hutterian Brethren
Islam
  Nation of Islam
  Shi'ism
  Sufism
  Sunnism
Jehovah's Witness (JW)
Judaism
  Conservative Judaism (United Synagogue of Conservative Judaism)
  Hasidic Judaism
  Orthodox Judaism (Orthodox Union)
  Reconstructionist Judaism (Jewish Reconstructionist Federation)
  Reform Judaism (Union of American Hebrew Congregations)
Latter-day Saints (Mormons)
  Church of Christ (Temple Lot)
  Church of Jesus Christ (Bickertonites)
  Church of Jesus Christ of Latter-day Saints (LDS)
  Reorganized Church of Jesus Christ of Latter-Day Saints
Lutheran Churches
  Apostolic Lutheran Church of America
  Association of Free Lutheran Congregations
  Church of the Lutheran Brethren of America
  Church of the Lutheran Confession
  Evangelical Lutheran Church in America (ELCA)
  Evangelical Lutheran Synod
  Lutheran Church—Missouri Synod
  Wisconsin Evangelical Lutheran Synod
Mennonite Churches
  Beachy Amish Mennonite Churches
  Bruderhof Communities
  Church of God in Christ, Mennonite
  Conservative Mennonite Conference
  Evangelical Mennonite Church
  Fellowship of Evangelical Bible Churches
  Mennonite Church Canada
  Mennonite Church US
  Missionary Church
  Old Order Amish Churches
  Old Order (Wisler) Mennonite Church

Methodist Churches
  African Methodist Episcopal Church (AME)
  African Methodist Episcopal Zion Church
  Christian Methodist Episcopal Church (MEC)
  Congregational Methodist Church
  Evangelical Church of North America
  Evangelical Congregational Church
  Evangelical Methodist Church
  Free Methodist Church
  Free Methodist Church of North America
  Pillar of Fire
  Primitive Methodist Church, USA
  Southern Methodist Church
  United Methodist Church (UM)

Native American Religion

Orthodox and Oriental Orthodox Churches
  African Orthodox Church
  Albanian Orthodox Archdiocese in America
  American Carpatho-Russian Orthodox Greek Catholic Church
  Antiochian Orthodox Christian Archdiocese of North America
  Armenian Church
  Bulgarian Eastern Orthodox Church
  Greek Orthodox Archdiocese of North America
  Holy Eastern Orthodox and Apostolic Church in North America, Inc. (EO)
  Malankara Orthodox Syrian Church and Mar Thoma Orthodox Church in
    America (Indian Orthodox)
  Orthodox Church in America (Russian Orthodox)
  Romanian Orthodox Episcopate of America
  Serbian Eastern Orthodox Church
  Syrian Orthodox Church of Antioch (Archdiocese of the USA and Canada)
  Ukrainian Orthodox Church of the USA

Pentecostal Churches
  Assemblies of God, General Council of
  Assemblies of the Lord Jesus Christ
  Bible Way Church of Our Lord Jesus Christ, World Wide, Inc.
  Christian Catholic Church
  Christian Church of North America, General Council
  Church of God (Cleveland, Tennessee)
  Church of God in Christ
  Church of God of Prophecy
  Church of Our Lord Jesus Christ of the Apostolic Faith, Inc.
  Church of the Living God, Christian Workers for Fellowship
  Church of the Living God, The Pillar and Ground of the Truth, Inc.
  Congregational Holiness Church
  Elim Fellowship
  Full Gospel Fellowship of Churches and Ministers, International
  Independent Assemblies of God, International
  International Church of the Foursquare Gospel

International Pentecostal Church of Christ
International Pentecostal Holiness Church
Open Bible Standard Churches, Inc.
Pentecostal Assemblies of the World, Inc.
Pentecostal Church of God
Pentecostal Free Will Baptist Church, Inc.
United Holy Church of America, Inc.
United Pentecostal Church International
Vineyard Churches International

Presbyterian Churches
Associate Reformed Presbyterian Church
Cumberland Presbyterian Church
Cumberland Presbyterian Church in America
Evangelical Presbyterian Church
Korean-American Presbyterian Church
Orthodox Presbyterian Church
Presbyterian Church (USA) (PCUSA)
Presbyterian Church in America (PCA)
Reformed Presbyterian Church of North America

Reformed Churches
Christian Reformed Church in North America (CRC)
Hungarian Reformed Church in America
Netherlands Reformed Congregations in North America
Protestant Reformed Churches in America
Reformed Church in America (RCA)
Reformed Church in the United States

Salvation Army (and related organizations)
American Rescue Workers
Salvation Army (SA)
Volunteers of America, Inc.

Schwenkfelder Church

Spiritualist and Theosophical Bodies
National Spiritual Alliance of the USA
National Spiritualist Association of Churches

Swedenborgian Church (The General Convention of the New Jerusalem
in the USA)

Triumph the Church and Kingdom of God in Christ, International

Unification Church

Unitarian Universalist Association

Unity School of Christianity and Association of Unity Churches

Universal Fellowship of Metropolitan Community Churches

Worldwide Church of God

Devotional Books

At one time, most books of nontechnical religious reflection were termed *devotional reading*, since they were meant to be read in conjunction with a believer's "devotions," or times of prayer and meditation. But since the Victorian era, the term *devotional book*, or just *devotional*, has come to mean a specific genre of religious literature. Growing out of the medieval books of hours, which gathered together prayers to be recited at specific hours of the day (see "Hours, Canonical"), the *devotional book* now most commonly refers to a book of short daily readings. The earliest known daily devotional reader is probably the *Feliré*, written in Gaelic verse in the early ninth century by an Irish monk known as St. Oengus the Culdee.

The conventional, though by no means mandatory, elements for a daily devotional reading are (1) a Bible verse; (2) a meditation, which may or may not relate to the Bible verse; and (3) a closing prayer, which incorporates some theme of the verse or meditation. Other elements can include (1) an epigraph or quote from another author; (2) an assigned reading, in which the reader is directed to read a portion from some other book or from the Bible; (3) a directed activity, in which the author suggests to the reader an activity that would put the message into practice; and (4) a blank or rule-lined workbook section, in which the reader is encouraged to write his or her responses and reflections in the book itself.

Forms. The following are the most common forms of devotionals, although they may be creatively adapted into any number of forms:

Type of devotional	Description
daily devotional	This term most often refers to a complete year's worth of daily readings—usually 366, accounting for leap years (February 29). This is the most common and successful type of devotional book.
classics devotional	A book of daily readings from classic Christian authors
devotional journal	A devotional in which rule lines are provided for readers to write out their own responses
three-month devotional	Usually rounded off to 90 daily readings
two-month devotional	Usually rounded off to 60 daily readings
one-month devotional	Usually rounded off to 30 daily readings
devotional Bible	The text of the Bible divided into daily readings or expanded with daily reflections on the Bible text; most often 366 readings

Format and Design. By and large, devotional books are trimmed smaller than the average book in order to convey a feeling of intimacy and worshipfulness. They should be hand sized. The challenge is that daily devotionals usually contain 366 readings, which can result in books that are extremely thick. Smaller, more condensed type fonts and thinner papers like those used for Bibles are sometimes used, and the margins around the text area are often reduced.

Since devotional books are to be sipped rather than drunk in long draughts, their page design allows for considerable graphic flourish—which would prove too distracting in books like novels that are meant to be read in long stretches. Such flourishes can include decorative borders, dingbats, florets, and even illustrations.

Indexes. Many devotional books include a Scripture index, an author index (in a compilation), a topical index, or a subject index, depending on the uses to which the reader might put the book.

Diacritics

See "Accents and Diacritics" and "Foreign Letters and Characters."

Dialogue, Paragraphing

See "Paragraphing Dialogue."

Dictionaries

This manual recommends the use of *Webster's Third New International Dictionary* (often referred to as *Webster's Unabridged*) and *Merriam-Webster's Collegiate Dictionary, Eleventh Edition* (2003) as helpful standard references. They are descriptive rather than prescriptive dictionaries; that is, they list words in common use without making strict judgments as to which are acceptable.

The editors of these dictionaries have listed the definition of each word according to historical sequence, so that the first definition is usually the oldest, though not necessarily the most common.

For writers and editors to agree on matters of consistent spelling, meaning, and capitalization, this manual recommends a few rules in the use of these dictionaries (rules that are applicable to most standard dictionaries):

Use First Alternative. When alternate spellings are given, use the first. In some cases, the editors of the dictionary list the preferred alternative first; in other cases, all the alternatives are so common that they are simply listed alphabetically. In either case, the principal of the "first alternative" should resolve most inconsistencies.

Use Main Entries Only. Use spellings given in main entries only. Do not use spellings from alternative entries that are followed by such phrases as *var of* (variant of).

Use Standard English. In most cases, do not use words whose definitions or spellings are qualified by such terms as *archaic*, *nonstand* (nonstandard), *obs* (obsolete), *slang*, or *substand* (substandard) unless those words are specifically intended, as in a quotation from an older source. Such other-than-standard words, however, can be effectively used in humor, historical fiction, dialect, and other kinds of writing that require special vocabulary.

Capitalization. Unless otherwise specified by the publisher's manual of style, capitalize all words marked *cap* (capitalize) or *usu cap* (usually capitalized), but lowercase all words marked *sometimes cap* (sometimes capitalized). Words marked *often cap* (often capitalized) may be capitalized or lowercased according to preference, context, and common sense.

Disability Designations

For most uses, the term *disability* is preferred to the term *handicap*. *Disability* refers to an individual's particular condition while *handicap* refers to the person's specific limitation in a particular instance. A disability is not necessarily a handicap. For instance, a person's blindness is a disability, but it is only a handicap in those instances when vision is required (in reading street signs, for example). That person would not be considered handicapped when reading Braille or doing any other activity that can be done without sight. A person in a wheelchair is not handicapped if his or her workplace is wheelchair accessible. All of us are handicapped when our environment imposes limitations on our abilities.

Focus on People. When writing about people with disabilities, the best policy is this: Define them as people first. It is demeaning to use the disability as the primary descriptor for the person. For instance:

Use	Not
people with disabilities	the disabled
a child with epilepsy	an epileptic child
people with visual impairment	the blind
a woman with quadriplegia	a quadriplegic
adults with mental retardation	the retarded
a man with schizophrenia	a schizophrenic

At times the writer needs to use a brief descriptor to define a group in terms of their specific disability, as in a medical or sociological study. If using terms that focus on the people first, like the ones in the preceding list, is simply too cumbersome in context, then terms *challenged* and *impaired*, combined with the disability, may be used: as in *the mentally challenged* or *the hearing impaired*. Whenever possible, however, the "people first" rule should be used.

Avoid Emotionally Charged Terms. In writing about people with disabilities, avoid the tendency, common to those who do not share the disability, to assume the person is necessarily suffering because of it. Unless referring to a particular instance of struggle or hardship, avoid falling into locutions such as: *a victim of epilepsy*, *suffering from hearing impairment*, *the burden of deafness*, or *afflicted with mental retardation*.

Avoid Antiquated and Insensitive Terms. Do not use epithets that express insensitivity to people with disabilities, such as crazy, crippled, deaf mute, deformed, hare-lip, lame, lunatic, mongoloid, paranoid, retarded, and so on.

The Use of the Word Normal. The writer should also avoid using the term *normal* to describe those who do not have a given disability. That term assumes that the disabled person is somehow abnormal. Use such terms as *those without this disability* or *a non-disabled person* instead.

Disclaimer

A disclaimer is the publisher or author's written declaration, usually placed on a book's copyright page, that while every effort has been made to make the content of the book accurate and safe, the publisher and author cannot be personally liable for unintentional errors that may result. It can also be used to assert that the publisher does not endorse products, companies, or websites that may have been referenced by the author. Though a disclaimer is not usually legally protective, it puts the reader on notice that he or she is expected to take responsibility for the way the content of the book is understood and applied.

Unlike most of the information on the copyright page, which only needs to achieve a basic level of legibility, a disclaimer should be prominently placed so as to be clearly noticeable to the average reader. They are often positioned either at the very top or immediately after the copyright notice.

In general, any book that an editor feels might require a disclaimer should be carefully reviewed by an attorney. While many publishers do not use disclaimers, most experts recommend that publishers err on the side of over- rather than underuse of disclaimers.

Some types of books that might benefit from disclaimers are shown in the following list, although these are only examples, not an exhaustive list:

Cookbooks, where ingredients might be easily confused or create hazards

Health and fitness books, in which certain exercises, diets, or medications might cause injury

How-to books, in which some procedures might lead to injury

Books of advice, in which a reader's financial status, reputation, or health could be affected

Novels, in which a person might feel he or she is being personally libeled in the guise of a fictional character

A standard disclaimer for a book of health advice, for instance, might read as follows:

This book contains advice and information relating to health and medicine. It is not intended to replace medical advice and should be used to supplement rather than replace regular care by your physician. Readers are encouraged to consult their physicians with specific questions and concerns.

A disclaimer of nonendorsement for a product, company, or website mentioned in the text might read something like the following:

The [products, companies] recommended in this book are offered as a resource to the reader. They are not intended in any way to be or imply an endorsement on the part of the publisher.

Often, disclaimers must be individually shaped for each instance, and it is best to have an attorney review the phrasing and content. This manual of style carries disclaimers on its copyright page.

Websites. In this age of the Internet, publishers are increasingly adding disclaimers to their copyright pages, stating that the Web addresses cited in the book are for information purposes only and not necessarily accurate or endorsed by either the author or publisher. This is done because popular domain names, if allowed to lapse, have been taken over by pornography or gambling enterprises in an attempt to lure unsuspecting Web surfers. Thus, the following disclaimer might be appropriate in some books:

> The Web addresses (URLs) recommended throughout this book are solely offered as a resource to the reader. The citation of these websites does not in any way imply an endorsement on the part of the author(s) or the publisher, nor do the author(s) or publisher vouch for their content for the life of this book.

Ditto

Ditto marks indicate the repetition of a printed element from one line to the next. In form they differ from quotation marks by being straight instead of curled. On those rare occasions when ditto marks are needed, a double prime mark (″) is used in typeset copy whenever possible. In typewritten copy, ordinary quotation marks are used.

Divine Office

See "Hours, Canonical."

Doctor of the Church

While the term *doctor of the church* is loosely used to mean any of the early theologians of the Christian faith, originally only four were so called in the Western tradition (St. Jerome, St. Ambrose of Milan, St. Augustine of Hippo, and St. Gregory the Great) and four in the Eastern tradition (St. Athanasius of Alexandria, St. Basil the Great of Caesarea, St. Gregory of Nazianzus, and St. John Chrysostom). The writings of these individuals proved especially important in the forging of Christian doctrine as it has been handed down to us today. Now, more than thirty individuals are considered to be doctors of the church. When using the term, it is best to define whether the narrow or general sense is being referred to. See also *"Fathers of the Church or Church Fathers."*

Dot

A *dot* is simply a period that is used in a webpage address. Technically, it is not a punctuation mark but a character that separates elements in a URL.

Confusion with Periods. Some editors are concerned that when a webpage address appears at the end of a sentence in text, the final period might be mistaken as a final dot in the address. Though a few readers may make that mistake, most will understand the period in its correct context. Also, most search engines know to ignore periods mistakenly typed at the end of a URL. See "Webpage Addresses (URLs)."

Spelling Out. Spell out *dot* in the term *dot-com* (an online company).

Doxology

Lowercased, the term *doxology* (from the Greek *doxa* for "glory") refers to any general expression of praise and glory to God, most often in a liturgical setting and usually short. Capitalized, it becomes the title of any specific such expression. Most doxologies are addressed to God, as contrasted with blessings and benedictions, which are largely addressed to worshipers.

People often refer to "The Doxology" as though there were only one, when in fact many are commonly used. Among Protestants, "The Doxology" usually refers to what is formally known as the *Lesser Doxology* or, in Roman Catholic tradition, the *Gloria Patri*. There is also the *Greater Doxology*, known to Roman Catholics as the *Gloria in Excelsis*.

Here are a few of the most well-known doxologies:

The Greater Doxology ("Gloria in Excelsis"; based on Luke 2:14)
Glory to God in the highest and on earth peace, good will to men.

The Lesser Doxology ("Gloria Patri")
Glory be to the Father, and to the Son, and to the Holy Spirit. As it was in the beginning, is now, and ever shall be, world without end. Amen.

The Trinitarian Doxology
Through him, with him, in him, in the unity of the Holy Spirit, all glory and honor is yours, almighty Father, for ever and ever.

Thomas Ken's Doxology ("The Benediction"; based on Psalm 103)
Praise God, from whom all blessings flow;
Praise Him, all creatures here below;
Praise Him, above ye heavenly host;
Praise Father, Son, and Holy Ghost.

The Doxology of the Lord's Prayer (Matthew 6:13)
For thine is the kingdom and the power and the glory forever. Amen. (KJV)

Paul's Doxology (Ephesians 3:20–21)
Now to him who is able to do immeasurably more than all we ask or imagine, according to his power that is at work within us, to him be glory in the church and in Christ Jesus throughout all generations, for ever and ever! Amen.

Other Biblical Doxologies
Romans 16:27, Jude 25

E

Eastern Orthodox Versus *Orthodox*

When capitalized, the term *Orthodox* refers to those Christian denominations listed under *Orthodox and Oriental Orthodox Churches* in the *Handbook of Denominations in the United States* (see "Denominations and Associations of Churches" for complete reference). But since some readers may miss the capital letter and assume the term simply means "conforming to established religious teaching," a careful writer should use the term *Eastern Orthodox* in a first reference. Otherwise, the terms *Eastern Orthodox* and *Orthodox* are used interchangeably.

The terms cover the eleven national churches and four patriarchs of those churches, which came into being after the Great Schism of 1054. Some writers mistakenly refer to just one of the national churches, usually Greek Orthodox or Russian Orthodox, to mean Eastern Orthodoxy as a whole. This is an error. It is also a mistake to refer to Orthodox denominations as Protestant. Orthodoxy predates Protestantism by several centuries. (See "*Catholic*" and "*Protestant.*")

Ebook, Elements of the

Ebooks and other texts designed to be viewed on handheld readers, computer screens, or other display devices pose interesting problems for the designer, editor, and, in some cases, the author. Unlike print books that display two pages (called a spread), most reading devices for ebooks can legibly display only a single page at a time. This means that chapter openers cannot start on right-hand pages, for instance, nor can the folios or running heads alternate position right-to-left as in the traditional book. Blank pages that often appear on the back of such pages as the dedication and the half-title page are superfluous in the ebook and should be eliminated since there is no reason to make a reader turn a blank page in an ebook. Traditional page numbering becomes irrelevant insofar as any ebook element can begin on either an odd- or even-numbered page, whereas in print books, most elements begin on odd-numbered rectos. Because of the greater flexibility in text sequencing, page numbers may be less important than the reader's own electronic "bookmarks." Ebooks can use color more liberally than print books, simply because no actual printing ink is involved.

Not the least of the differences between the ebook and the traditional book can be found on the opening page. The ebook's front cover is its first page, usually obviating the need for a traditional half-title page and sometimes even a title page. Cross-references, footnotes, endnotes, and indexes may work quite differently in the ebook, for they may be electronically linked to other portions of the book or embedded in the text itself.

The future of ebooks is a matter of debate. They could well become more like Internet webpages and less like the traditional book. In fact, with continuing advances in wireless communications, it is possible that the line between ebooks and websites could become quite thin indeed. On the other hand, due to a lack of both a standard reader and a universal format, at present the promise of ebooks seems to be foundering. For the foreseeable future, readers may prefer that their books, even their ebooks, look as much like the traditional book as possible. For sustained reading many readers prefer paper to handheld devices, and research is already underway to make magnetized paper that can carry downloadable text so that the electronic books of the future may, in fact, look like the paper books of the present, except that the text can be continually changed.

With the form and future of ebooks so much in flux, here are at least some general design suggestions, which can be contrasted with the standards listed in the entry titled "Typography, The Elements of Basic Book." In many cases, a designer may wish to modify a print design when transforming a print book into an ebook. On the other hand, those electronic texts that are destined to be printed out as *print-on-demand* (POD) books should probably continue to be formatted like the traditional print book.

Keep in mind that the following lists of elements of the ebook are merely extrapolations of traditional print-book typography. These are offered as default elements, in a sense, and may be liberally modified as appropriate.

Ebook Front Matter. The following are the elements of the front matter of an ebook, as appropriate.

Cover (the book's cover is the ideal first page)

Title page (a half title page can also be used, but it is usually preferable to allow the full title page to be the first text page in an ebook after the cover; if the title page is simply a reiteration of the cover, however, the title page can be dropped altogether)

Ad card (list of author's other books) or Frontispiece

Copyright page (in some cases, publishers move the ebook's copyright page to the end of the book so as not to distract the reader)

Dedication

Epigraph (if it applies to the entire book)

Contents (entries may be linked to the beginnings of the parts, chapters, or other elements themselves)

List(s) of maps, illustrations, or charts (may be linked to their locations in the text)
List of abbreviations
Foreword (usually by someone other than the author)
Preface (usually by the author)
Acknowledgments
Introduction (usually by the author)
Inside half title (optional, though it serves as a good marker that the actual text is about to begin)

Ebook Body Matter. The following list shows the elements of an ebook's body matter, as appropriate.

Part title page
Part epigraph (if it applies to the entire part)
Chapter title page
Chapter epigraph (if it applies to the chapter only)
Chapter number and title
Text of chapter
Discussion questions
Chapter endnotes (may be linked to a separate endnote file)
Chapter bibliography or "For Further Reading"

Ebook Back Matter. The following is a list of elements of the back matter of an ebook, as appropriate.

Appendix(es)
Study questions (if not incorporated into the text)
Notes (may be linked to their locations in the text)
Glossary (may be linked to words used in the text)
Chronological table(s)
Bibliography, or "For Further Reading"
Index to maps (may be linked)
Proper-name index (may be linked)
Subject index (may be linked)
Scripture index (may be linked)
Author biographical note
Colophon or publisher's note

The Author and the Ebook. Already the writing of an ebook is demanding that authors rethink the traditional writing process, especially if the ebook is to take advantage of its unique strengths and be more than just a print book squeezed into an electronic format. Since ebooks allow for different elements and possibilities, the author who knows ahead of time that his or her manuscript will be published as an ebook may want to keep the following things in mind even before the writing of the book begins.

Ebooks allow for almost instantaneous linking of different portions of the text. This can be as simple as shifting between a chapter title on the contents page and the beginning of that chapter itself; or it may be as complex as providing glosses, cross-references, or secondary references for information given in the text. In the writing of a book, the author should be aware of what portions of the text might be conveniently linked to each other for the benefit of the reader. Also, explanatory notes, definitions of terms, and other information can be embedded in the text or as drop-down boxes to aid readers when needed.

Footnotes, for example, instead of appearing at the bottom of the page, might become a small window that opens when the highlighted callout symbol is clicked. Instead of traditional cross-referencing, the reader might be given the option of actually moving to the part of the text referred to in the cross-reference. Words can be defined, biographic and bibliographic information can be provided, and multimedia files can be opened with a click of the mouse.

Since the seventies, an entire generation of experimental novelists has explored the possibilities of "hypertext" fiction, which depends far less on linear structure than the traditional novel. Authors may eventually learn to take advantage of the nonlinear possibilities of the ebook, allowing the reader to jump around in the text, creating a unique experience with each reading.

E-church

The word *e-church*, like so many other *e* combinations, should probably continue to be hyphenated for the time being. Odds are the *e-* prefix will become closed over time if it doesn't disappear entirely before then.

Ecumenical

The word *ecumenical* is commonly used to mean one of three distinct things. First, it has been used by the Roman Catholic Church to mean "all the inhabited world" or "worldwide" Catholicism (from the Latin *oecuminicus*). A convocation of Catholic bishops from around the world is considered an *ecumenical convocation*. This use of the term became particularly popular during the Second Vatican Council, 1962–65.

The term has also come to mean "worldwide" in the sense of "interdenominational," or representing all the different Christian faiths. There is a worldwide *ecumenical movement* that seeks to promote dialogue and unity among different Christian denominations.

Finally, the word has also come to imply "inter-faith," or representing the various major religions of the world. Often an *ecumenical conference* might be attended by Christians, Muslims, Jews, Buddhists, and Hindus alike.

The careful writer should make sure that the written context clarifies which of these meanings is intended.

Editing

Other than the author, no one should be more familiar with a book than its editor. Editing is the process by which a book's content is shaped into its finished, most reader-friendly form. It involves a comprehensive overview and analysis of a book's content, structure, style, elements, and design. Editors are responsible for combining all aspects of the book, interior and exterior, into a cohesive whole that expresses the author's ideas most clearly, is consistent with the publisher's standards and mission statement, and fulfills the book's implied promise of excellence to the most important person of all, the reader.

Although H. G. Wells once said, "There is no greater joy than to correct another's copy," editing is far more than correcting. It can be compared to conducting an orchestra. The conductor does not necessarily know how to play every instrument in the orchestra, but he or she knows enough about each to be able to bring them together into a harmonious whole. Similarly, an editor need not be an author, printer, designer, salesperson, marketer, and copywriter, but he or she should be familiar enough with those functions to create the best book possible. Books are verbal and visual symphonies.

Just as music is a link between the composer and the listener, books connect the author with the reader. As the middle person in that process, the editor becomes an advocate for both. Any editorial task that does not facilitate that connection is not worth doing. In the face of a publisher's financial interests in the book, the editor is often the person most devoted to ensuring that neither the author nor the reader's interests are lost. A strong editorial voice in behalf of the author is, in many cases, a crucial reason that some writers remain at a publishing house. It keeps them coming back and bringing new readers with them. And ultimately, if the authors and readers are happy, the publisher's accountants will be as well.

Levels of Editing

Good editing requires that editors visualize at the outset what the finished product will look like and seek to capture that image in word, format, style, illustration, and symbol. At least three functions are commonly referred to as *editing*, though quite different in intent and responsibility. They are sometimes called "the levels of editing."

1. *Macro editing.* This is the broadest level of editing. The editor reads the manuscript, usually the writer's preliminary draft or in some cases a partial manuscript or proposal, and responds with no more than a few pages of critique.

On this level, the editor shares her or his most basic responses to the author's work: first impressions, needs for major cuts or additions or restructuring, and suggestions for revision. This is perhaps the most creative level of editing because the editor can sometimes assist the author in shaping the book itself.

2. *Substantive, or content, editing.* A substantive, or content editor is usually responding to an author's first complete draft of the book. The editor focuses on the structure of the author's ideas and their arrangement into words. Good content editing requires changes to, and queries concerning, specific words, phrases, sentences, or even long passages to make a book accurate, complete, clear, and precise. Content editors seek to eliminate discrepancies, buttress viewpoints, clarify the obscure, provide missing information, and reorganize material as needed. They work directly with the author by suggesting revisions. The editor is responsible to suggest ways of enhancing the aesthetic qualities of the author's language. Good literary style is inevitably intertwined with content because the subject matter and author's purposes affect tone, reading level, and degree of formality.

Content editing is dynamic and interactive. It usually takes place on a copy of the complete manuscript itself, whether hard copy or electronic. Since each book requires individual treatment, many editors provide authors with a printout or a marked-up copy of the edited manuscript.

3. *Copy editing.* The copy editor is responsible for the details of "house style," or "press style," which deal with such mechanical aspects of language as capitalization, spelling, grammar, use of numbers, outline style, punctuation, and so on. This manual attempts to establish a standard of style for religious publishing.

When possible, a copy editor checks the accuracy of dates, quotations, references, and factual information, although the accuracy of such information is ultimately the author's responsibility. A copy editor's opportunities for making changes in an author's manuscript are restricted to obvious errors, inaccuracies, ambiguities, and inelegancies; and the copy editor's interaction with the author is often limited to occasional queries. In recent years, however, as content editors find themselves more rushed, copy editors often become an author's primary contact person, especially in matters of manuscript preparation. Unless authorized to do so, the copy editor should not presume to make the kinds of dynamic revisions or suggestions that are properly the domain of the author, the macro editor, and the content editor. You might say that the copy editor's job is to "micro edit."

Editing and Correcting on Computer

In spite of what computerization has long promised, the "paperless book" remains a largely unattainable ideal. While theoretically it is possible to write, edit, proofread, and even publish books without using a single sheet of paper, it is seldom practical or even possible. For instance, many publishers require their authors to provide a paper copy of the manuscript for reference purposes; proofreaders still prefer to read paper copies, and tests seem to show that proofreading on paper is more accurate; and salespeople and marketers are more likely to ask for a paper copy when they wish to familiarize themselves with the manuscript. The one process that seems to have made the transition to computerization most smoothly is editing itself, though some challenges still remain.

Every editor should be familiar with the following computerized tools:

Revision Tracking. Editing and word-processing software systems allow the editor to switch a revision-tracking function on and off. When turned on, the tracking function records every editing change made to the manuscript, changes that can be viewed in a printout and in the data itself. Many authors prefer to see every change made and to respond to each one individually, although authors can also become unnecessarily alarmed if they feel attacked for every minor change that is made. (For instance, simply adding the serial comma throughout a manuscript can make the manuscript look very heavily edited.) In a sense, revision tracking enshrines the negative by making the positive very difficult to see.

As a result, many authors are happy for their editors to turn off the tracking software so that both of them can focus on a clean, edited copy. The burden, however, remains with the editor to outline the general changes made in the manuscript (style matters, types of corrections made, and so on). A style sheet of corrections can be provided to an author to clarify some of these issues. The use or non-use of editorial revision tracking is a matter that should be left either to company policy or to an individual agreement between the author and editor.

Annotations and Queries. One of the most useful tools on the editor's computer desktop is the author-query function. This allows the editor to insert numbered callouts into the manuscript, to which embedded queries are attached. Those queries can then be printed on a separate sheet of paper or sent digitally to the author. Internal queries (intended only for others within the publishing house to see) can also be incorporated into the data. These tools are highly recommended.

Spelling and Grammar Checkers. Spelling and grammar checkers are only as smart as the people using them. In spite of the manufacturer's claims, they are never as good as human spelling and grammar checkers. Of the two, editors often use spell-checking programs to catch missed typos. They are helpful, for instance, in catching proper names that may have been misspelled or spelled two different ways in the course of a manuscript. Still, their value is limited, since they are unable to distinguish between homonyms (*two, too, to,* for instance) and are impotent in the face of correctly spelled words in the wrong place (as in *more gist for the mill*).

In the opinion of most professionals, most grammar-checking programs are only a hair better than none at all. They are primarily designed for business-writing purposes, and most editors do not use them because they are not only time-consuming but they subtly train the editor to "edit for the checker" rather than for the reader. Most grammar software programs don't like long sentences, passive constructions, split infinitives, and complex and unconventional syntax, not taking into account that there are often excellent stylistic reasons to allow these. Grammar checkers, if taken too seriously, lead to writing as colorless as a box of crayons with only shades of white to choose from.

Editing and Correcting on Paper

Although most manuscripts are now prepared and edited electronically, some editing, proofreading, and correction checking are still done on paper printouts. The following guidelines offer suggestions for hand-rendering corrections.

Clarity. Since either the author or a keyboard operator will have to enter the editor's paper-copy changes into the electronic data, the editor should make sure that all notations and queries are as clear and as clean as possible.

Colored Pens or Pencils. The content editor, the copy editor, and the proofreader, if they are all working on the same set of galleys, should use pens or pencils of different colors so that their corrections can be distinguished. Pencil allows for erasure and is therefore preferred by many editors, but pencil also smudges more easily than pen. Pen, on the other hand, is often cleaner but does not allow for erasure. It's a toss-up, though this manual recommends pen as long as the editor thinks through the change thoroughly before committing it to paper.

Handwritten Corrections. For corrections and annotations made to a paper copy of a manuscript, block printing is preferred to handwriting because it is more legible. Authors, editors, and proofreaders should print. This also aids in keeping changes, queries, and annotations concise.

Insertions. Lengthy insertions in a paper manuscript, whether by the editor or author, should be typed on a full-size page and inserted after the page on which the insertion is to be made. Again, the placement of all insertions should be clearly marked. Inserted pages should be given the same number as the page they follow but with the addition of a lowercase *a, b, c,* and so on. The data generated by those insertions should be saved to a disk so that they can be easily added to the authoritative data copy.

Queries on a Paper Manuscript. Editorial queries and notes are most conveniently listed on a separate sheet of paper with page and line references. Queries and notes in the margins of the manuscript can easily confuse the keyboard operator, causing the queries to be inserted into the text. If an occasional short query or note is inserted in margins of the text, the editor should remember the proofreader's rule that anything not meant to be typeset should be circled.

Editorial Markup. On paper, editorial notation uses symbols and markings similar to standard proofreading symbols but with one difference: editorial work is done in the text itself, while proofreading corrections are indicated in the text with a symbol and in the margin with an annotation.

Editing Terminology

See "Proofreading Abbreviations and Terms."

Electronic Manuscripts

See "Manuscript Preparation: Author Guidelines."

Elision of Numbers

See "Numbers, Inclusive (Elision)."

Ellipsis

An ellipsis (...) is a typographic device that indicates when words are missing from a direct quotation. Ellipses are also frequently used to show a trailing off or an indecisiveness in thought or speech.

Two styles are common in writing and editing: (1) the three-dot style and (2) the three-and-four-dot style. For fiction books in which quotations from other sources are rare, this manual recommends the simpler three-dot style (though it formerly recommended the three-and-four-dot style). For all other books, especially those containing quotations from other sources and for most academic books, this manual recommends the three-and-four-dot style. Both styles are described in detail here. The basic difference between the two is how they handle periods.

The Three-Dot Style. A three-dot ellipsis can indicate (1) that words within a sentence have been omitted; (2) that words at the beginning or end of a sentence have been omitted, whether or not it leaves the sentence grammatically complete; or (3) that the end of a sentence has been left unfinished to indicate a trailing off of thought or speech. In the three-dot style, in other words, the ellipsis replaces any period that may have been present in the original context. When the ellipsis follows a complete sentence or thought, no period should appear before the ellipsis, though the first letter of the word following the ellipsis should always be capitalized to show the beginning of a new sentence or thought. Generally, no other punctuation is used with three-dot ellipses in this style, except for question marks and exclamation points. Normal word spaces should be placed on both sides of the three-dot ellipsis in all cases.

> "The more often he feels without acting . . . the less he will be able to feel," wrote Screwtape to Wormwood. [Words within the quotation are omitted.]
> Job focuses on God, not on God's questions. He shows this by beginning his answer by saying, "I know that you . . ." (Job 42:2). [shows omission in incomplete sentence]
> "I am cold and weary, ink is bad . . . The day is dark." [omission between complete sentences]
> "My only friend is God; I have no drinking cup or goblet other than my shoe! . . ." [exclamation point used with three-dot ellipsis after complete sentence]

The Three-and-Four-Dot Style. In this style, a three-dot ellipsis is used to indicate (1) that words within a quoted sentence have been omitted or (2) that words at the beginning or end of a sentence have been omitted, but only when it leaves the sentence grammatically incomplete. Otherwise, a four-dot ellipsis (which is simply a period followed by a three-dot ellipsis) indicates an omission that does not render the sentence grammatically incomplete. In other words, use a four-dot ellipsis when the context would ordinarily call for a period (that is, after a grammatically complete sentence). While the "fourth dot" (the period) should be spaced evenly with the other three dots, it should be set without space next to the word it follows.

> "Mother Teresa . . . is one such woman. . . . Malcolm Muggeridge has given her . . . the most beautiful tribute."—Kari Torjesen Malcolm
> "In 1007 the great gospel of Colmcille was stolen from the sacristy of the church of Cenannus. . . ."

Split Over Line. It is acceptable for an ellipsis to fall either at the end or the beginning of a typeset line, as long as it does not stand on a line by itself (as at the end of a paragraph). Most typographers, however, prefer that the ellipsis fall at the end of a line if there is an option. If the four-dot ellipsis is used, it may split over the line break, with the first dot (the period) remaining on the end of the first line and the three subsequent dots carrying over to the next line, again, as long as the three-dot ellipsis never stands on a line by itself. The dots in a three-dot ellipsis may never be split.

> Sheldon's preface began, *"In His Steps* was written in 1896.
> . . . The book has been translated into twenty-one languages."

With Other Punctuation. When a question mark or exclamation point precedes the omitted portion of the quotation, that punctuation mark is retained and followed by a three-dot ellipsis. Other punctuation, such as a comma, may be retained before or after the three-dot ellipsis if it helps clarify the meaning of the sentence or better shows what has been omitted.

> "But now, Lord, what do I look for? . . . Do not make me the scorn of fools"
> (Ps. 39:7–8).
> "For he spoke, . . . he commanded, and it stood firm" (Ps. 33:9).

For Trailing Off of Thought. An ellipsis is used to indicate a trailing off of thought, daydreaming, or hesitation, although frequent use of ellipses for this purpose is discouraged. Also, do not use an ellipsis to indicate a sudden interpolation or an external interruption of thought or speech; in those cases, use an em dash instead.

> *If only the people would read the Bible . . . if only . . .* , thought Frelinghuysen, *then God would bring about revival.*
> Niebuhr—Reinhold, that is, not Richard—was a pastor in Detroit in the twenties.

Before or after Bible Quotations. Unless the context demands it (usually with a sentence fragment), do not place ellipsis points before or after a verse or a portion of a Bible verse. An introductory word such as *and, for, but, verily,* or *therefore* may be omitted from the beginning of a Bible verse without inserting ellipsis points.

> "God so loved the world that he gave his one and only Son" (John 3:16). [The word *For* has been omitted.]

Rigorous Style. CMS adds a third style, the *rigorous style*, which is used only when extreme precision is needed when quoting from other sources, that is, in academic and scholarly books that require letter-for-letter accuracy in quotations or when manuscripts are reproduced or quoted that contain lacunae. The rigorous style is basically the three-and-four-dot style, though in addition, brackets are placed around any initial letters that, for the sake of the context, have changed case (caps to lowercase and vice versa) and an ellipsis surrounded by brackets indicates words missing from an original manuscript source (lacunae). (See *CMS* 11.62–11.65 for more details.)

> "[R]emember my commands; . . . [D]o what is pleasing in his sight"—Tobit 4:19, 21. [brackets used to indicate change of case]
>
> "They could not enter its gates, nor could they [. . .] could not overrun its walls [. . .] nor [. . .] would they see her treasure ruined. . . ."—Levi's "Teaching in Praise of Wisdom" from the Dead Sea Scrolls. [brackets used with ellipses to indicate lacunae]

Em Dash

See "Dash."

Emmanuel Versus *Immanuel*

See "*Immanuel* Versus *Emmanuel*."

En Dash

See "Dash."

Endnotes

See "Notes."

Epigraph

An *epigraph* is a short line or small block of type, most often a quotation from another author, which is set by itself on a page, usually at the beginning of the book (this is called the *book epigraph* and is usually placed before the table of contents) or somewhere at or near the beginning of each chapter (called a *chapter epigraph*). It is usually set in the same type size as the text or one size smaller. In most instances, quotation marks should not be placed at the beginning and end of an epigraph, though internal quotation marks should be retained as in the original.

Book Epigraph. A book epigraph can have several functions: to make a wry comment on a book's content; to summarize a book's thesis; to identify a recognized authority; to whet the reader's appetite; and, at times, to acknowledge the quote from which the title of the book itself is taken. When used at the beginning of a book, an *epigraph page* should not contain a running head or a folio number. The epigraph should stand alone. Only as a last resort, when space is very limited, should it be relegated to the copyright page.

Chapter Epigraph. A chapter epigraph is more limited in function, usually simply glossing the content of the chapter in some way. By the time the reader has finished the chapter, there should be no doubt as to the appropriateness of the chapter epigraph. A good epigraph can attract or even mystify the reader, but it should never confuse.

Gathering Epigraphs. Some disciplined writers who read widely keep "commonplace books" or journals of their favorite quotations for use in their own writing and as epigraphs. Workingman's philosopher Eric Hoffer once said that he kept a notebook with him at all times, just to write down favorite quotes as he read. He assumed, he said, that he would otherwise remember nothing.

The Pitfalls. While the judicious use of epigraphs can enhance a book, some authors use them as a means of appearing more erudite than they are. A serious reader can usually distinguish between the writer who has actually *read* Pliny the Younger, for instance, and the one who has simply lifted an appropriate quotation from some reference like *Bartlett's Familiar Quotations*.

Credit Line. For most epigraphs only the author's name needs to be given as the source. It is usually not necessary to list the title of the author's work as well. The title should be given, however, if it helps the reader understand the context of the quotation more fully or is, for some other reason, essential to the quotation. Also, if the author's name is not known or when quoting the Bible, then the title or chapter-and-verse reference alone should be used as the source.

Citing Sources. It is not necessary for the author to cite the precise source of an epigraph in a footnote or endnote. This may seem overly pedantic to many readers. An epigraph should serve as something of a flourish to a piece of writing and need not be cited, unless the author has a special reason for doing so (for instance, if the quotation is copyrighted and the original publisher has required that a source and credit line be given).

Epilogue

An *epilogue* is generally synonymous with the terms *afterword* and *conclusion*, though it has a somewhat more literary tone. In some literary works, such as fiction, drama, biography, history, and other narrative nonfiction, an epilogue summarizes the events that take place after the main action of the story, just as a prologue fills in the narrative background before the story begins, and is therefore distinct from both the afterword and the conclusion. Despite its name, a literary epilogue is not part of a book's back matter but is the final element of the body matter.

Such a literary epilogue is often, though not always, written in the same voice as the main part of the book, that is, in the narrator's or character's voice rather than the author's, when those voices are distinct. If written in the author's voice while the rest of the book has a different narrative voice, it should be called an *afterword* or, if more lengthy, a *conclusion*. (See also "Afterword" and "Conclusion." Contrast with "Prologue.")

Episcopal and *Episcopalian*

Episcopal is the adjective, *Episcopalian* the noun; as in: *The Episcopalian spoke with the Episcopal minister.* When capitalized, both terms refer to the Protestant Episcopal Church, which is the name given in the US to the Anglican Church. When lowercased, the terms refer to bishops or the governing authority of bishops, which is usually called the *episcopacy*.

Errata

Although less frequently used now than formerly, an *errata* slip or page is provided when the publisher feels that certain mistakes in a book's print run are important enough to warrant bringing the reader's attention to them even before those mistakes can be corrected in the next printing. This is accomplished by inserting a small, loose slip of paper, bookmark-like, into the front matter of the book, usually immediately following the contents page. In especially large print runs or for especially important books, the slip, or even a full-size errata page, is "tipped in" (glued in) to the book perpendicular to the book's spine.

The word *errata*, by the way, even though it is the Latin plural of the word *erratum* (mistake) is considered a singular noun in publishing convention: *An errata is called for.*

Customarily, the notice is kept as simple as possible, with the errors given first, followed by the corrections. The italicized words *for* and *read*, along with the page number, are used to indicate the incorrect and corrected versions respectively.

Page 55, *for* Chuck Berry *read* Wendell Berry

Note that no punctuation should be used unless the punctuation is actually part of the corrected copy.

In his book *Language on a Leash*, editor and writer Bruce O. Boston defined errata as "flecks of spinach on the flashing editorial smile" (114).

Ethnic and Racial Designations

Terms used to describe ethnic and racial groups should be chosen with care and should only be used when those designations are essential to the context. They should also be limited to only those terms used by the groups to describe themselves or terms used as legal designations by the government. Generally, hyphenate them as adjectives but set them as two words when used as nouns.

> an African American, *but* African-American children
> Alaska Native
> Arab American
> Asian American
> Caucasian
> Lebanese American, Scandinavian American, and so on
> Puerto Rican
> Part-Hawaiian (US Government legal status)
> > *but otherwise*: part-Japanese, part-Chinese, and so on

Specificity. Whenever possible, be specific. Even generic terms can have negative connotations in the wrong contexts. As appropriate, use *Lakota*, for instance, rather than *Native American* or *American Indian*; *Mexican* rather than *Hispanic*; *Saudi* rather than *Arab*.

Self-determination. Allowing ethnic groups, racial groups, and other social communities to define their own terms of reference has become a common and accepted practice. While this is sometimes difficult to determine when some subgroups within the larger group disagree with the designation, nevertheless, to honor people is to honor their preferred forms of self-reference, whenever that can be determined. For example:

Use	Rather than
African American	colored person, Negro
Asian	Oriental
Caucasian	white
Native American	Indian

Black *and* White. The term *black* is less often used for people of African descent in the United States than it once was, having given way to *African American* as the preferred form. Still, *black* is common in sociological discussions when contrasted with *white* as a racial designation. The term *black* is lowercased unless it is used in phrases like *Black English*, *Black Power Movement of the sixties*, and *Black Studies*.

To describe Caucasians, *white* is acceptable but seems to be waning in use, though still common in sociological contexts. Like *black*, it is lowercased. The term *white* is appropriate when it is used as a specific term of contrast and comparison to *black*, as in discussions of culture or social issues.

Avoid Derogatory Terms and Stereotypes. Needless to say, derogatory terms for ethnic and racial groups should be scrupulously avoided except, possibly, in fiction when such terms might be used in dialogue as a way of characterizing the speaker (as bigoted or racist, for instance). Even then care must be taken so that the reader understands the views are those of the fictional character, not the author.

Evangelical

The term *evangelical* is lowercased in all its forms (*evangelicalism*, *evangelicals*, and so on), though it should be capped when referring to a specific name of a church or denomination or, in the case of the *Evangelical Church in Germany*, to specify the Lutheran Protestants as opposed to the Calvinists.

Even though those who describe themselves as *evangelicals* do not always agree on its definition, it can generally be used to mean those Protestants since the Reformation, and especially since the time of John Wesley, who stress the importance of (1) the four gospels, (2) the inerrancy of the Bible, (3) personal conversion, and (4) salvation by faith in the atoning death of Christ. Their worship tends to focus on preaching rather than ritual, and they emphasize each believer's responsibility in evangelization.

The term *evangelical* often needs to be used with caution when writing for a mixed audience of believers and nonbelievers. People outside the Protestant church often see *evangelical* as a synonym for *fundamentalist* or *the religious right*, largely with political overtones; whereas people inside the church accept the term more as a description of a personal theological viewpoint.

Exclamation Point

The form of the exclamation point, or exclamation mark, is said to have been developed by early printers as a sort of graphic abbreviation of the Latin word *io*, meaning joy. The character was originally rendered "$\frac{!}{o}$" and was later simplified to the mark as we know it today.

An exclamation point is used after a sentence or a word to express surprise, enthusiasm, astonishment, or special emphasis. Along with the period and the question mark, it is considered an "end stop" (a mark that ends a sentence). The use of exclamation points is traditionally minimized in formal writing, since overuse tends to limit the effectiveness of the device. Using too many exclamation points is the typographic equivalent of crying wolf. Still, they are especially useful in fictional dialogue and in colloquial and informal writing.

With the Question Mark. Oftentimes an exclamation point is needed in the same place in the sentence that a question mark is needed. Since the general rule states that the stronger of two punctuation marks is retained when two might seem to be appropriate, the exclamation mark is usually retained.

> Was it Quasimodo who shouted, "Sanctuary!" [Question mark not placed at end of sentence]

Spanish Exclamation Points. In Spanish-language writing and publishing, an inverted exclamation point (¡) precedes an emphatic statement while a regular exclamation point (!) follows it. This device should not be reproduced when translating Spanish quotations into English, although it may be retained at the author's and editor's discretion when reproducing the quotation in Spanish.

Explicit

Sometimes, at the very end of a book, an author will provide his or her name and the date of the completion to give the work a formal sense of closure. Sometimes the location of the book's completion is also provided. This is called an *explicit*. In former times, an explicit would also provide the name of the scribe who copied the book, although that function has been largely replaced by the modern colophon. (See "Colophon.") An explicit is still occasionally used with works to which the author wishes to lend an air of special gravity or significance.

F

Fathers of the Church or Church Fathers

The terms *fathers of the church* or *church fathers* are often loosely used to mean those theologians who forged the early doctrines of the Christian faith, especially in the first twelve centuries after Christ. In stricter usage, however, the fathers of the church were not only those who forged the doctrines but those, especially of the first six centuries, whose lives were of exceptional holiness and orthodoxy. The primary early and later fathers of the church are:

Early Fathers

first century: Clement of Rome
second century: Cyril of Jerusalem, Ignatius of Antioch, Justin Irenaeus, Polycarp
third century: Cyprian, Dionysius
fourth century: Hilary, Ephraem the Syrian, Optatus, Epiphanius
fifth century: Peter Chrysologus, Pope Leo the Great, Cyril of Alexandria, Vincent of Lerins
sixth century: Caesarius of Arles

Later Fathers

seventh century: Isidore
eighth century: John the Damascene, the Venerable Bede
eleventh century: Peter Damian
twelfth century: Anselm, Bernard

Fathers is not capitalized unless it is used alone to stand for *church fathers*.

First Estate

The church used to be referred to as the *First Estate* (capitalized). In England it was commonly said that three "estates" ruled the lives of the people: the First Estate was the "Lords Spiritual" (the church); the Second Estate was the "Lords Temporal" (the king and nobility); and the Third Estate was the "Commons" (the people). An added Fourth Estate, according to a famous quip by Edmund Burke, was said to be the most powerful of all—the press. In modern usage, only the Fourth Estate is referred to, and any attempt to refer to the church as the First Estate will only be met with confusion.

Folio

Folios Versus Page Numbers. The *folio* is the number actually printed on the page. This differs from a *page number* in that while all pages follow each other in a numerical order, not all those numbers are actually printed on the page. For instance, page numbers are usually not printed on nontext pages, such as title pages, copyright pages, epigraphs, dedications, and part-title pages. An example would be a book's half-title page, which is always page 1, but since no number is actually printed on that page, it cannot be said to have a folio. A folio will ordinarily appear on any page that also has a running head, except for chapter openers, which usually have a folio but no running head.

In general practice, the distinction between folios and page numbers is not an important one. But it becomes problematic in some academic and reference books in which the folio of the front matter are given in roman numerals and in which the actual body text begins with arabic numeral 1. In that case, the first page of body text might actually be the eleventh page in the book (*page number 11*), but it bears the *folio 1*. If an introductory text page preceded it, that introductory page would be referred to as *page 10*, or *folio X* (*roman numeral 10*).

Blind Folio. When a folio is customarily not printed on a page, such as the part title, copyright, or contents pages, it is said to be a *blind folio.*

Drop Folio. When a folio is printed at the bottom of a page or as part of a running footer, it is called a *drop folio* or *foot folio.*

Footnotes

See "Notes."

Foreign Letters and Characters

Many foreign languages that use the Latin alphabet use unusual characters, most of which can be accommodated in type with the use of diacritical marks. (See "Accents and Diacritics.") But there are a few special letters and punctuation marks that are used, though infrequently, in English typesetting. It is useful to know what to call them and how they look. The following is a list of these:

Character	Name	Example or Explanation
Å, å	Danish *a*	Danish and Norwegian, as in *Ångström*; the Scandinavian form of the umlaut; replace with *aa* if the character *å* is not available

Character	Name	Example or Explanation
Æ, æ Œ, œ	ash (ligature)	Old English; as in *Ælfric*; formerly used in Latin words, such as *Cæsar*; also used in Danish and Norwegian; the Œ, œ form is still common in French
Ø, ø	Danish o	Danish and Norwegian; as in *Søren Kierkegaard*
ß	double s, s-set	German for the sound *ss*; replace with *ss* if the character ß is not available
ſ	the long s	not an *f* but an *s*, formerly used in English; usually lacks all or part of the crossbar (ſ)
þ, Þ	thorn	Icelandic and Old and Middle English for the *th* sound as in *three*
ð, Ð	eth, or edh	Old and Middle English for the *th* sound, as in *them*
ȝ, ȝ	yogh	Middle English for the *y* sound in *year* or the *gh* sound in *right*
ω or ƿ	wynn	Old English; for the sound *w*

Foreign Phrases Common to Christian Life and Worship

The pervasive influence of Christianity can be seen in the number of foreign phrases relating to Christian life and worship that have become common in English. The plethora of Latin phrases in the following list is due to the many centuries when Latin was the official language of the church.

Adeste Fideles—(Latin) "O Come, All Ye Faithful." A popular Christmas hymn.

ad majorem Dei gloriam—(Latin) "To the greater glory of God." Motto of the Jesuits. Often abbreviated, *AMDG*.

agape—(Greek) "Love." Used to imply a nonsensual kind of love; charity.

Agnus Dei—(Latin) Short for *Agnus Dei, qui tolles peccata mundi* ("Lamb of God, who takes away the sins of the world.") Also, the portion of the Catholic Mass or Episcopal Communion when these words are spoken or sung.

agrapha—(Greek) "Unwritten sayings." This usually refers to statements of Jesus that are not found in the four gospels.

Anima Christi—(Latin) "Soul of Christ." A well-known Eucharistic prayer: "Soul of Christ, sanctify me."

Anno Domini—(Latin) "In the year of our Lord." (AD) Used for year designations after the time of Christ.

apologia pro vita sua—(Latin) "apology for one's life." A confession, or self-justification. Capped, the title of Cardinal Newman's spiritual autobiography.

Ars Moriendi—(Latin) "The art of death." The shortened title of a fifteenth century religious text, which eventually grew into an entire genre of books of meditations about death. Lowercased, the term refers to the general spiritual practice of meditating upon one's own death.

auto-da-fé—(Spanish) "Act of faith." The formulaic religious rites of the Spanish Inquisition, which preceded the judgment portion of a heresy trial. Has come to be synonymous with the burning at the stake of a person accused of heresy.

Ave, Maria—(Latin) "Hail, Mary." Traditionally, the first words of the angel's greeting to Mary at the annunciation (Luke 1:28). Also, the small beads of the Roman Catholic rosary. (The large beads are the *Paternosters*.)

benedicamus Domino—"Let us bless the Lord." Used in some Roman Catholic offices. The response is *Deo Gratias* ("Thanks be to God").

benedicite—(Latin) "Bless [the Lord]." A common blessing or grace. Also, capitalized, a song of praise based on Daniel 3:28–29.

Benedictus—(Latin) "Blessed." The first word of Zechariah's song of thanksgiving in Luke 1:68–79.

Benedictus qui venit—(Latin) The first words of *Benedictus qui venit in nomine Domini* ("Blessed is he who comes in the name of the Lord," Matt. 21:9). Capitalized, a portion of the Sanctus of the Roman Catholic Mass.

biblia pauperum—(Latin) "Bible of the poor," referring to medieval picture books illustrating Bible stories for the illiterate.

Capitalavium—(Latin) "Washing of the head." An early medieval name for Palm Sunday.

confessio fidei—(Latin) "Confession of faith."

confiteor—(Latin) "I confess." The opening words of the Roman Catholic confession.

contemptus mundi—(Latin) "Contempt for the world."

credo—(Latin) "I believe." A creed. Sometimes refers specifically to Augustine's paradox: "I believe because it is impossible."

Dei gratias—(Latin) "By the grace of God." Abbreviated DG.

Dei judicium—(Latin) "The judgment of God."

Deo favente—(Latin) "With God's favor."

Deo gratia—(Latin) "Thanks to God."

Deo optimo maximo—(Latin) "To God the best and greatest." Its abbreviation, *DOM*, is inscribed on bottles of wine made by the Benedictines.

Deo volente—(Latin) "God willing." Sometimes abbreviated *DV.*

de profundis—(Latin) "Out of the depths." The first words of Psalm 130. The phrase is used to express general spiritual despair, and the psalm is sometimes used at burial services.

Deus absconditus—(Latin) "Hidden God." The idea that it is not possible to grasp God with human understanding.

Deus vult—(Latin) "God wills it." The (misguided) motto of the First Crusade.

Dies Irae—(Latin) "Day of Wrath." The name of a medieval hymn about the Last Judgment, based on Joel 2:31.

Dieu avec nous—(French) "God with us."

Dieu et mon droit—(French) "God and my right." Motto of the British monarchy.

Dieu vous garde—(French) "May God protect you."

dixit Dominus—(Latin) The first words of *Dixit Dominus Domino meo* ("The Lord says to my Lord," Ps. 110:1, or Ps. 109:1 in Vulgate). Capitalized, the first of five psalms sung on certain feast days in Roman Catholic vespers.

Dominus vobiscum—(Latin) "The Lord be with you."

dona nobis pacem—(Latin) "[Lord,] grant us peace." Used liturgically as a prayer response and, when capped, as the title of numerous musical compositions.

Ein Feste Burg Ist Unser Gott—(German) "A Mighty Fortress Is Our God." A hymn of Martin Luther's.

ex cathedra—(Latin) "From the throne." Often applied to any pronouncement of great authority; originally refers to papal announcements.

felix culpa—(Latin) "Happy fault." The idea that Original Sin was providential in that it provided a means for Christ's coming into the world.

fiat lux—(Latin) "Let there be light" (Gen. 1:3).

Formgeschichte—(German) "Form criticism." The study of determining the date and origins of Bible passages by their structure and form.

Fratres Minores—(Latin) "Little [or Inferior] Brothers." A term of intentional self-abasement with which Franciscan monks describe themselves.

gloria in excelsis—(Latin) "Glory to God in the Highest." Sung by the angels announcing Christ's birth (Luke 2:14); the basis for the "Doxology." The *Gloria* is a portion of the Ordinary of the Roman Catholic Mass.

Gott ist über all—(German) "God is over all."

Gott mit uns—(German) "God with us."

hic jacet—(Latin) "Here lies . . ." Used before a name on a tombstone inscription.

imago Dei—(Latin) "The image of God."

in hoc signo vinces—(Latin) "In this sign you will conquer." The words of Constantine the Great, referring to the cross on his military banners.

jubilate Deo—(Latin) "Shout for joy to the Lord." Capitalized, it is used as the title for any number of liturgical songs based on Psalm 100.

jus divinum—(Latin) "Holy law."

kirk—(Scottish) "Church."

kyrie eleison (Greek) "Lord have mercy." A prayer used in Western and Eastern churches as a response during Mass. Also, capitalized, the title of any musical setting of this prayer.

laborare est orare—(Latin) "To work is to pray."

Lasciate ogni speranza, voi ch'entrate—(Italian) "Abandon all hope, you who enter." The words over the entrance to hell in Dante's *Inferno*.

laus Deo—(Latin) "Praise God."

Legenda Aurea—(Latin) "The Golden Legend." A thirteenth-century collection of Bible stories and saints' tales, categorized by feast days and compiled by Jacopo da Voragine.

magnificat—(Latin) First word of "My soul glorifies the Lord," the words of Mary to Elizabeth (Luke 1:46–55). Capitalized, a reading or song long used in church services.

mea culpa—(Latin) "Through my own fault." Used to acknowledge one's own guilt for sin, often accompanied by the gesture of striking one's fist to one's chest.

memento mori—(Latin) "Remember that you will die." Used as a noun, it refers to any object, such as a skull, that aids in the contemplation of mortality.

miserere—(Latin) The first word of Psalm 51, "Have mercy on me, O God." Capitalized, the name for a service during Lent when these words are sung. Also, a place in the church choir for kneeling.

Missa solemnis—(Latin) "High Mass" in the Roman Catholic Church.

nunc dimittis—(Latin) The beginning of *"Nunc dimittis servum tuum, Domine"* ("Sovereign Lord, . . . you now dismiss your servant in peace"), the words of Simeon at the presentation of Jesus in the Temple (Luke 2:29–32). Capitalized, it has become a common canticle sung at the concluding of services in both the Anglican and Roman Catholic Churches. Also, a general term for dismissal.

obiit—(Latin) "He [or she] died."

ora pro nobis—(Latin) "Pray for us."

oremus—(Latin) "Let us pray."

Pater noster—(Latin) First words of the Lord's Prayer, "Our Father" (Matt. 6:9–13). Also, closed up, the large beads of the Roman Catholic rosary.

pax vobiscum—(Latin) "Peace be with you."

pietà—(Italian) "Pity." An artistic representation of Mary holding Jesus' dead body across her lap.

prie-dieu—(French) "pray God." A small prayer desk with a sloping top and a kneeling board. Pl.: *prie-dieux*.

quo vadis?—(Latin) "Where are you going?" From the pseudepigraphal Acts of Peter, in which Peter, while fleeing Rome, encounters Christ. Peter asks, "Where are you going?" Christ answers, "To be crucified again." Peter is convicted and returns to face his own martyrdom. Capitalized, the title of a popular novel by Henry K. Sienkiewicz.

requiem—(Latin) First word of the prayer *Requiem aeternam dona eis, Domine* ("Give the eternal rest, O Lord"). Sung at the beginning of the Roman Catholic Mass for the Dead.

requiescat in pace—(Latin) "Rest in peace" (RIP). Used on gravestone inscriptions.

salve, Regina—(Latin) First words of "Hail, holy Queen, mother of mercy," a hymn sung in the Roman Catholic Church from Trinity Sunday to Advent.

Sanctum Sanctorum—(Latin) "The Holy of Holies" in the Jewish temple, into which only the high priest can enter. By extension—the presence of God.

sanctus—(Latin) "Holy." The first word of *Sanctus, sanctus, sanctus, Dominus Deus Sabaoth* ("Holy, holy, holy, Lord, God of Sabaoth"). Capitalized, a portion of the Ordinary of the Roman Catholic Mass.

similitudo Dei—(Latin) "The likeness of God."

sola scriptura—(Latin) "Scripture only." The Bible as sole authority in matters of faith.

stabat Mater—(Latin) The opening words of a Latin hymn in the Roman Catholic Church recounting the seven sorrows of Mary at the cross ("The Mother was standing"). Capitalized, the title of the hymn sung the week before Easter.

Te Deum—(Latin) Opening words of a Latin hymn: *Te Deum laudamus* ("You, Father, we praise).

ut in omnibus Deus glorificetur—(Latin) "that God may be glorified in all things." The motto of the Benedictine order.

Via Dolorosa—(Latin) "Way of Sorrow." Name of the path through the streets of Jerusalem taken by Christ on the way to the cross.

via negativa—(Latin) "Way of denial." Refers to an approach to the Christian faith that denies worldly pleasures as distractions from God.

via positiva—(Latin) "Way of affirmation." Refers to an approach to the Christian faith that affirms the physical world as a gift from God to be enjoyed.

vita nuova—(Italian) "New life."

vox populi vox Dei—(Latin) "The voice of the people is the voice of God."

Foreword and Preface

A *foreword* and a *preface* are two types of introductory material placed at the beginning of a book, usually relating to the main text of the book but not necessarily essential to its understanding. The main difference between the two types is authorship. Generally, a *foreword* is written by someone other than the author. The name of the person who wrote it should appear either after the title, especially if that person is well known, or at the end of the foreword itself.

A *preface*, by contrast, is usually written by the author. It is not necessary to place the author's name either before or after the preface if its authorship is clear; that is, when the front matter contains no material by anyone other than the book's author. If two or more prefaces are reprinted from various editions of the book, the preface for the most recent edition usually appears first, followed by the next most recent, and so on. Unless there is a compelling reason for presenting the prefaces in some other order, the original preface should appear closest to the text itself. The same rule applies to forewords and introductions. (See also "Introduction.")

Formatting Electronic Manuscripts

See "Manuscript Preparation: Author Guidelines, *Formatting Conventions.*"

Forms of Address, Religious

The following list shows the common titles of religious occupations and the forms of address used for such people in various circumstances. Last names or place names are used in the blanks unless otherwise specified.

Abbot
    written: "The Right Reverend [first and last name], Abbot of ——"
    salutation: "Right Reverend" or "Dear Father Abbot" or "Dear Father"
    spoken: "Father"
    introduction: "The Right Reverend [first and last name], Abbot of ——"

Archbishop
    written: "The Most Reverend [first and last name], Archbishop of ——"
    salutation: "Your Excellency" or "Dear Archbishop ——"
    spoken: "Your Excellency" or "Archbishop ——"
    introduction: "His Excellency" or "Archbishop ——"

Bishop, Episcopal
    written: "The Right Reverend [first and last name], Bishop of ——"
    salutation: "Right Reverend Sir" or "Dear Bishop ——"
    spoken: "Bishop ——"
    introduction: "The Right Reverend [first and last name], Bishop of ——"

Bishop, Roman Catholic
written: "The Most Reverend [first and last name], Bishop of ——"
salutation: "Your Excellency" or "Dear Bishop ——"
spoken: "Your Excellency" or "Bishop ——"
introduction: "His Excellency" or "Most Reverend Sir" or "Bishop ——"

Brother
written: "Brother [first name]" or "Brother [first and last name]"
salutation: "Dear Brother" or "Dear Brother [first name]"
spoken: "Brother [first name]" or "Brother"
introduction: "Brother [first name]"

Cardinal
written: "His Eminence, [first name] Cardinal ——, Archbishop of ——"
salutation: "Your Eminence" or "Dear Cardinal ——"
spoken: "Your Eminence" or "Cardinal ——"
introduction: "His Eminence, Cardinal ——"
Note: The Roman Catholic Church no longer sanctions placing the title *Cardinal* between a given name and a surname.

Clergy, Protestant (Minister)
written: "The Reverend [first and last name]" or "The Reverend [last name]"*
salutation: "Dear Dr. [or Mr. or Ms.] ——"
spoken: "Dr. [or Mr. or Ms.] ——"
introduction: "Dr. [or Mr. or Ms.] ——"
*"DD" is customarily added to the written form of address if the person holds a doctorate of divinity

Monk
written: "Brother [first name], OSF [or other order initials]"
salutation: "Dear Brother [first name]" or "Dear Brother"
spoken: "Brother [first name]" or "Brother"
introduction: "Brother [first name]" or "Brother [first and last name]"

Monsignor
written: "The Right Reverend Monsignor ——"
salutation: "Right Reverend Monsignor" or "Dear Monsignor ——"
spoken: "Monsignor" or "Monsignor ——"
introduction: "Monsignor ——"

Nun
written: "Sister [first name], SC [or other order initials]"
salutation: "Dear Sister [first name]" or "Dear Sister"
spoken: "Sister [first name]" or "Sister"
introduction: "Sister [first name]" or "Sister [first and last name]"

Pope
>written: "His Holiness, the Pope" or "His Holiness, Pope —— "
>salutation: "Your Holiness" or "Most Reverend Father"
>spoken: "Your Holiness" or "Most Holy Father"
>introduction: "His Holiness" or "The Holy Father" or "The Pope" or "The Pontiff"

Priest
>written: "The Reverend [first and last name]"
>salutation: "Reverend Father" or "Dear Father —— "
>spoken: "Father" or "Father —— "
>introduction: "Father —— "

Rabbi
>written: "Rabbi [first and last name]"
>salutation: "Dear Rabbi [or Dr.] [first and last name]"
>spoken: "Rabbi" or "Rabbi [or Dr.] —— "
>introduction: "Rabbi [or Dr.] [first and last name]"

Sister
>written: "Sister [first name]" or "Sister [first and last name]"
>salutation: "Sister [first name]" or "Dear Sister"
>spoken: "Sister [first name]" or "Sister"
>introduction: "Sister [first name]"

Superior, Father
>written: "The Very Reverend [first and last name], CP [or other order initials], Superior of —— "
>salutation: "Reverend Father" or "Father Superior"
>spoken: "Father [first name]" or "Father"
>introduction: "The Very Reverend [first and last name], Superior of —— "

Superior, Mother
>written: "The Reverend Mother Superior, Convent of —— " or "Reverend Mother [first and last name], SM [or other order initials], Convent of —— "
>salutation: "Reverend Mother" or "Dear Reverend Mother"
>spoken: "Mother [first name]" or "Mother"
>introduction: "Reverend Mother [first and last name], Convent of —— "

Forms of Christian Books

While Christians have written novels, memoirs, poetry, and so on, they have also invented genres and forms of books that are unique to the faith or at least primarily associated with it. In the list below, those marked with asterisks are discussed in more detail under their own entries elsewhere in this manual.

apocalyptic fiction—subgenre of science fiction and fantasy genre dealing with the end of the world, the tribulation, and the imminent return of Christ. Inspired by Revelation, Daniel, and the apocryphal writings that discuss apocalyptic events. (Example: C. S. Lewis's *That Hideous Strength*)

Bible study—a book that interprets the meaning of Bible passages verse by verse, most often in an attempt to apply that meaning to day-to-day living. Bible studies often include a basic interpretive essay for each passage, study and discussion questions, and blanks or rule lines for readers to record their thoughts.

book of hours—books, often elaborately decorated, that contain prayers for each of the divine offices, short meditations, records of saints' days and holy days along with short lives of the saints, selected Bible passages, and liturgical readings. These were especially popular in the Middle Ages and the Renaissance. (Example: *Les Très Riches Heures de Duc de Berry*, early fifteenth century)

clerical novel—a novel describing the daily life of a priest or minister, often, but not necessarily, in rural settings. (Examples: Georges Bernanos's *Diary of a Country Priest* and Jan Karon's Mitford Series)

commentary—like the Bible study, the commentary seeks to interpret Bible passages verse by verse, but its focus is not so much on application as it is on the precise meanings of words, phrases, and sections.

* concordance—an alphabetical listing of words used in the Bible, along with their specific verse reference and a short quote to show how the word is used in context. Concordances are helpful in tracking down references or doing word or thematic studies in the Bible. (Example: *Cruden's Concordance*, 1737)

* devotional—a daily devotional contains a short reading or meditation for each day, to be used as part of the reader's devotional exercises. Each reading commonly includes a Bible verse, a meditation, and a prayer. (Example: Mrs. Charles E. Cowman's *Streams in the Desert*, 1926)

illuminated manuscript—refers to the form rather than the book's content; often a unique copy of a Bible or a book of hours that has been rendered in calligraphy with marginal drawings and elaborate initial letters. They are considered works of art in themselves. (Example: *The Book of Kells*, ninth century)

martyrology—collections of stories of noted martyrs. (Example: *Acts and Monuments*, familiarly known as *Foxe's Book of Martyrs*, 1563)

prayer book—a collection of prayers and rites either for private devotions or public liturgy. (Example: *The Book of Common Prayer*, 1549)

* red-letter Bible—an edition of the Bible in which the words of Jesus are printed in red. The majority of modern Bibles use this device.

saint's life—also called a *hagiography*, the saint's life is an inspirational biography of noted saints. Most common in the Roman Catholic Church. (Example: Butler's *Lives of the Saints*, 1756–59)

spiritual thriller—a subgenre of fiction that describes supernatural forces being unloosed in everyday life, it usually follows the ways in which believers and nonbelievers react to the situation. The Christian counterpart to the *supernatural thriller*. (Example: Charles Williams's *War in Heaven* and Bill Myers's *Blood of Heaven*)

Four Cardinal Virtues, The

The phrase *the four cardinal virtues* is lowercased in most contexts. The virtues are, in order, (1) prudence, (2) justice, (3) temperance, and (4) fortitude. (See also "*Seven Deadly Sins, The.*")

Frontispiece

The *frontispiece* is a graphic element, sometimes a photo of the author or biographical subject of the book, that is placed across from the book's title page. Traditionally, it is printed on high quality photographic paper and glued ("tipped") in, in which case it is not considered part of the book's pagination. Most commonly and more economically, it is set as a halftone or piece of line art on the verso of the half-title page, where the author ad card usually appears. In those cases, the frontispiece is included in the book's pagination and may be included in the table of contents. If there is a list of illustrations, it should be listed first.

Front Matter, Elements of a Book's

A book's front matter is made up of all the pages preceding the textual content of the book itself. These preliminary elements are traditionally arranged in the order shown in the following list, where appropriate, and usually only deviate from this order when there is a compelling reason for doing so, such as a limitation of space or idiosyncratic design. For more information, see the entries for each different kind of front matter.

Half title (on recto page)
Author card (sometimes called *ad card*; lists the author's other books) or
    frontispiece (on verso page) or series title page
Title page (on recto page)
Copyright page (on verso page; can be moved to the end of the book if space
    or design warrant it)
Dedication (usually on recto page)
Epigraph (if it applies to the entire book; usually on recto page)
Contents page, or Table of Contents (usually begins on recto page)
Errata (if any, slipped in or set on verso of contents page)
List(s) of maps, illustrations, or charts (usually on recto page)
List of abbreviations (usually on recto page)
Foreword (by someone other than the author; usually begins on recto page)
Preface (by the author; usually begins on recto page)
Acknowledgments (usually begins on recto page)
Introduction (usually by the author; usually begins on recto page)
Inside half title (on recto page)
Prologue (comes immediately before chapter 1 and is properly considered the
    first element of the body matter)

Fundamentalist

It is curious that the term *fundamentalist* has come to describe radical theological conservatives of nearly any faith, including Islam and Hinduism—curious because the term originally described a very specific movement within Christianity. Early in the twentieth century, a group of Christians formulated what they believed to be the five nonnegotiable "fundamentals" of the Christian faith: (1) the inerrancy of the Bible, (2) the divinity of Christ, (3) the virgin birth, (4) the atonement, and (5) the physical resurrection and imminent return of Christ.

As with so much Christian terminology, *fundamentalist* and *fundamentalism* should be used carefully and with an awareness of how a particular group of readers views those terms. Beyond the confines of Christian readership, and often even within that readership, the terms imply religious zealotry, even extremism, of all stripes and is usually considered pejorative.

Gender-Accurate Language

Since the 1970s, an awareness of subtle sexist messages in the English language has demanded that writers and editors develop a new sensitivity to the implications of common words. So attuned have most writers become that they largely take the following rules for granted.

Writers should strive for accurate, unbiased communication and avoid debasing terms, stereotypes, and language that expresses an inherent superiority of one sex over the other. Not only are the words themselves important but so is the overall tone of a written passage. The following guidelines can help writers and editors be more sensitive to sexist language so they might affirm through words and attitudes the worth of all people.

Simple Accuracy. For the sake of accuracy, words and phrases should be gender neutral when the sex of persons is unknown, immaterial, or consisting of both male and female. Good substitutes may be difficult to devise but seldom impossible. Gender-accurate language should improve communication and not result in awkwardness, inexactness, or obscurity.

chairperson (for a man or woman when the gender is immaterial to the context or unknown)

chairpersons (referring to a group of mixed gender or possibly mixed gender)

chairman (when it is important to the context to specify that the chairperson is a male)

chairwoman (when it is important to the context to specify that the chairperson is a female)

Man *as a Generic Term.* The use of *man* as a generic term for both men and women is best avoided whenever possible. Although this preference originally began in the 1970s as a consciousness-raising rule among some in the women's movement, it has passed into general usage and is no longer just a matter of "political correctness." While most older readers are not confused by the generic *man*, after thirty years of writers' generally avoiding its use, younger readers now often take the gender specification quite literally. When a text reads, "Blessed is the man who does not walk in the counsel of the wicked" (Ps. 1:1), many take it to refer exclusively to a male. Here are some generally outmoded terms and some alternatives:

	use:
man, mankind	humanity, people, human beings, humankind
common man	the average person, the ordinary citizen
manhood	maturity, adulthood
manpower	work force
spokesman	spokesperson, representative
forefathers	forerunners, forebears, ancestors

Vocational Terms. Many vocational terms unnecessarily focus on gender and should be avoided.

	use:
fireman	firefighter
foreman	supervisor
housewife	homemaker, consumer
insurance man	insurance agent
pressman	press operator
steward, stewardess	flight attendant
waiter, waitress	server, serving person
watchman	guard

In the case of the word *firefighter*, representatives for the firefighters themselves prefer the gender neutral term as the most accurate reflection of what both men and women in that profession do. They fight fires. Beyond that, the sex of the firefighter is immaterial in most cases. When gender specificity is absolutely essential to a written passage, the terms *male firefighter* and *female firefighter* should suffice.

Double Standards. Avoid double-standard semantics, such as describing a behavior as acceptable for one sex but not for the other. Connotations as well as denotations must be carefully considered. For example, don't use the word *domineering* to describe a wife if a husband displaying similar behavior would be described as *authoritative*.

assertive businessman, pushy businesswoman
thrifty woman, miserly man
cautious woman, spineless man
spirited little boy, unruly little girl

Negative Overtones. Select words carefully to indicate gender. Many widely used terms have negative overtones and should not be used in fine writing.

	use:
ladies, gals, girls (for adults)	women
old maid, spinster	single woman
the little woman, my better half	wife, spouse
women's libber	feminist
my old man	my husband, spouse
little old lady	elderly woman
dirty old man, little old man	elderly man
man and wife	man and woman, or husband and wife

When Gender Is Significant. Do not hide gender if it is significant for the reader.

Grammar. Do not violate essential rules of grammar simply to avoid a gender-specific word or phrase.

Disclaimers. In certain works that do not allow for reediting, such as reprints of classics or other previously published works or quotations from such works, it may be advisable to place a disclaimer somewhere in the front matter, perhaps on the copyright page, although this is probably only necessary when the quoted author's opinions are of such an inflammatory nature as to be offensive to a large number of readers.

Deliberate Sexism. It should be noted that "sexist" language can be appropriate to evocative communication in certain circumstances, such as when used to add color to a fiction writer's palette. Such language can be especially effective in dialogue to characterize the speaker's assumptions and background. This manual is far from saying that such language is forbidden, merely that it should be used consciously and for a desired end. Still, since each publisher has its own policy regarding sexist speech, a writer should check with the editor first.

Neutral Pronouns. Use neutral pronouns instead of the generic *he* whenever possible. Changing a phrase or recasting an entire sentence usually yields an acceptable alternative. Many people ask why we should avoid male generic pronouns. One answer is that an entire generation has now been raised with little awareness of that linguistic custom in English. Some common, acceptable solutions are offered here:

1. *Alternate "he" and "she."* One solution is to alternate gender-specific pronouns (*he* and *she*) as they are needed in different contexts throughout a work.
2. *Use the Third-Person Plural Pronouns.* Sometimes changing the pronouns from the singular to the plural remedies the problem: *He asked any student who knew the answer to raise their hand.* (Although that usage is still frowned upon by some experts, the majority of style manuals now list it as acceptable.)

3. *Change Entire Reference to Third-Person Plural.* By changing the neutral "he" to "they," the male-only reference can become inclusive without changing the meaning: *He asked students who knew the answer to raise their hands.*

4. *Change to First-Person Plural.* Often, shifting a "he" to a "we" is a helpful solution.

5. *Use "he or she" and "him or her."* Although these wordy constructions grow tiresome after only a few uses in close proximity, they can be used in place of a generic *he* to express that the discussion concerns both males and females. The problem with this solution is that it can quickly look stiff, formulaic, and distracting if used too often.

6. *Use Passive Voice.* Occasionally a sentence may be restructured into passive voice to avoid the male-only generic pronoun. Since this is perhaps the least satisfactory of the solutions, use it only as a last resort.

7. *Use "one."* Curiously, English has a longstanding generic pronoun, *one,* although it is seldom used now because it sounds a bit stuffy. In the right context, however, it can be effectively used but should not be repeated too often.

Here are some examples of these solutions:

[Original sentence] A Christian needs to be concerned about his witness before the watching world. [*Problem:* the neutral subject *Christian* is followed by the male pronoun *his,* presuming that Christians are invariably male.]

[Solution 1: alternate *his* and *her*] A Christian needs to be concerned about her witness before the watching world. [*She* is used. In the next instance, *he* would be used.]

[Solution 2: *their* with singular reference] Each Christian needs to be concerned about their witness before the watching world. [Acceptable, though some reject this solution.]

[Solution 3: third-person plural] Christians need to be concerned about their witness before the watching world. [Preferred to solution 2, whenever possible.]

[Solution 4: first-person plural] As Christians we need to be concerned about our witness before the watching world.

[Solution 5: *his* or *her*] A Christian needs to be concerned about his or her witness before the watching world. [Acceptable, although *his or her* can become awkward if used frequently.]

[Solution 6: passive voice] A Christian's witness before the watching world should be a matter of concern. [Acceptable, although the passive construction can sound convoluted and artificial if not handled well.]

[Solution 7: Use *one*] As a Christian, one needs to be concerned about one's witness before the watching world. [Acceptable, although *one* can sound stiff in many contexts.]

Do not use the forms *s/he, he/she, him/her,* or other such combinations when a neutral pronoun is needed. These forms only distract the reader.

God Compounds

When compound words are formed with the word *god*, they are usually set solid (without a hyphen) and lowercased: such as *godchild, goddaughter, goddess, godfather, godhood, godless, godlike, godling, godly, godmother, godparent, godsend,* and *godson.*

When God as deity is specifically being referred to, then the compounds are usually hyphenated and the word *God* is capitalized: *God-fearing, God-forsaken, God-inspired,* and *God-given.*

A few conventional compounds do not fit this general rule, however: *god-awful* (colloquial), *godforsaken* (colloquial), *Godspeed* (customarily capped).

Gospel

The word *gospel* (from the Old English *godspel,* meaning "good tale" or "good news") has come to have several common meanings: (1) the general message of Christ's kingdom; (2) one of the first four books of the New Testament canon; (3) any of the several apocryphal books about the life or sayings of Jesus; (4) a liturgical reading from one of the first four books of the New Testament; (5) any statement that is said to be infallible, as in *the gospel truth* or *If he said it, it's gospel*; (6) a specific style of religious music. As a result, the word is subject to imprecision and misreading. A careful writer should make his or her meaning clear whenever the term is used.

Capitalization. Many different rules have been suggested for the capitalization of the word *gospel,* most of which are confusing and contradictory. This manual, therefore, advises that the word *gospel* be lowercased in all contexts and for all uses except when contained in an actual title ("The Gospel According to Saint Matthew" [KJV]), when used as a collective title for the four canonical gospels as a whole ("the Gospels"), or, obviously, in headings and titles. This style is consistent with the King James Version, the New International Version, and Today's New International Version, and it will also keep authors, editors, and readers from having to split hairs over the different shades of meaning the word can have in particular contexts.

gospel music	the gospel of Christ
gospel revival	the true gospel
gospel tent	the gospel of salvation
the gospel writer	to preach the gospel

but the Gospel of Thomas (if that is the title in the Bible version used; otherwise, *John's gospel* or *the gospel of John*)

The Gospel According to Peanuts

the Gospels, *but* the four gospels

the Synoptic Gospels

The Term Gospel Side. The term *gospel side* of a church or cathedral formerly meant the left side of the altar as one faces the front. This was the side of the chancel from which the gospel was traditionally read. The term is now archaic and is best avoided unless defined for the reader.

The Term Gospeler. The term *gospeler* once referred to anyone who read from Scripture in a liturgical setting, a meaning that is now archaic. While the term is now rare, it is still occasionally used pejoratively to refer to an overly zealous evangelist.

Graphics

Position. In both the electronic and paper copies of a manuscript, the author should clearly indicate the placement of photos, diagrams, tables, and other graphic material. In printed materials, the editor and compositor should strive to place full-page graphics and illustrations on the right-hand page whenever possible; this gives them more presence and emphasis than a left-hand placement allows.

Originals. Valuable original photographs, artwork, or other documents should not be submitted with the manuscript. Photocopies will suffice until such time as the publisher needs to reproduce the originals, usually at first proofs. When submitting valuable original documents for reproduction, the author should always compile a thorough checklist, one copy accompanying the documents themselves and another copy remaining with the author.

Sideways Placement. If a graphic needs to be turned sideways to fit within the book's format, the bottom of the graphic should run along the right-hand side of the upright page.

Reductions. Authors often worry that graphics will not look as good when reduced to the size of the book page, but there is what has been called "the graphic artist's secret": most line art and photographs actually look better when reduced.

Folios. Folios, or page numbers, do not need to be placed on pages with full-page graphics, especially if the number will look lost or out of place. On the other hand, page numbers should be retained if there is a list of illustrations in the front matter. If page numbers are not used, the list-of-illustrations page can use "facing page numbers"; for instance, *Illustration 1, facing page 10.*

Greek and Hebrew Transliterations

Various systems are used for transliterating Hebrew and Greek. The following chart should be helpful in most cases.

Greek

Letters

α	*a*	ζ	*z*	λ	*l*	π	*p*	φ	*ph*
β	*b*	η	*ē*	μ	*m*	ρ	*r*	χ	*ch*
γ	*g*	θ	*th*	ν	*n*	σ, ς	*s*	ψ	*ps*
δ	*d*	ι	*i*	ξ	*x*	τ	*t*	ω	*ō*
ε	*e*	κ	*k*	ο	*o*	υ	*u, y*		

Special Characters

γγ	*ng*	γξ	*nx*	ῥ	*rh*
γκ	*nk*	γχ	*nch*	ʽ	*h*

Hebrew

Letters

א	ʾ	ו	*w*	כ	*k*	ע	ʿ	שׂ	*ś*
ב	*b*	ז	*z*	ל	*l*	פ	*p*	שׁ	*š*
ג	*g*	ח	*ḥ*	מ	*m*	צ	*ṣ*	ת	*t*
ד	*d*	ט	*ṭ*	ן נ	*n*	ק	*q*		
ה	*h*	י	*y*	ס	*s*	ר	*r*		

Vowels

◌ֲ	*a*	◌ֵ	*ē*	◌ֹ	*ō*	◌ְ	*e*
◌ָ	*ā*	◌ֵי	*ê*	וֹ	*ô*	◌ֲ	*a*
הָ	*â*	◌ִ	*i*	◌ֻ	*u, ū*	◌ֱ	*e*
◌ַ	*e*	◌ִי	*î*	וּ	*û*	◌ֳ	*o*

Hagiography Versus *Hagiographa*

These two technical terms for different kinds of religious literature are sometimes confused. *Hagiography*, which is set in lowercase roman, is the study and compiling of what is commonly called "lives of the saints." As a group, that literary genre is called *hagiology*. In ironic usage, *hagiography* has also come to mean any biography that is effusive or tends to gloss over the subject's weaknesses and foibles.

Hagiographa, which is always capitalized as a formal title and set in roman type, is sometimes referred to simply as the Writings, or Kethuvim. It is one of the three major divisions of the Old Testament, the portion that is neither the Law (Pentateuch, or Torah) nor the Prophets (or Nevi'im). The Hagiographa includes Psalms, Proverbs, Job, Ruth, Lamentations, Song of Songs, Ecclesiastes, Esther, Daniel, 1 and 2 Chronicles, Ezra, and Nehemiah. Some scholars in some traditions also include Tobit and other similar apocryphal books.

Half-Title Page

The half-title page is actually an interesting holdover from an earlier era of printing history when books were sold without covers. (The poor could read the book as a paperback, the wealthy could have the book bound in leather.) The half-title page identified the book in lieu of any other outside covering. It also served to protect the interior pages from dirt and wear.

If present, the half-title page is usually page 1 of any book. Only the title of the book, without the subtitle, appears there. In some books, the half-title page may be replaced by endorsements, quotations from reviews of earlier editions of the book, descriptive copy, or the author's biography. If space is a consideration, the half-title page may be dropped altogether. See also "Second Half-Title Page."

Hallelujah Versus *Alleluia*

Ambiguity exists concerning the correct spelling of the Hebrew liturgical interjection *halelu-Jah*, "praise the Lord (Jehovah)," which occurs primarily in Psalms and once in Revelation. Is it *hallelujah* or *alleluia*?

Most authorities consider *alleluia* to be the most accurate rendering of the term, relating most closely to the Greek (Septuagint) and Latin (Vulgate).

But that does not take into consideration the longstanding traditional use of *hallelujah* in English, which dates back to the early sixteenth century.

Generally, though not exclusively, *hallelujah* is used in most Protestant churches, while the Latin *alleluia* is preferred by the Roman Catholic, Anglican, and Eastern Orthodox churches.

Within the context of a particular book, when in doubt, go with the spelling of the predominant Bible version being used. In the absence of that, use *hallelujah* as a spoken interjection (*"I may be a sinner but, hallelujah, I'm saved"*) and for general conversation and low-church settings. Use *alleluia* in formalized liturgical settings (*"The congregation responded with rousing alleluias"*), since that is the form most often used in worship and liturgical song. One exception to this last rule, however, is found in Handel's famous oratorio, *The Messiah*, in which the word is spelled *hallelujah* in the well-known chorus of that name.

Here is the breakdown of which spelling is used by the major Bible versions:

Hallelujah—AB, LB, MLB/NBV, NASB, NCV, NET, NIrV, NIV, NLT, NRSV, RSV, TNIV
Alleluia—JB, KJV, NAB, NEB, NJB, NKJV
Neither—TEV ("praise God")

Headings and Subheadings

Chapters of nonfiction books are often divided into sections, each with its own *heading*, the theory being that the occasional breaks will give the reader a breather that will encourage further reading. Often, those sections are broken down into subsections, each of which bears its own *subheading*.

Levels. The various levels of headings are referred to by letters: *A-heads*, *B-heads*, *C-heads*, and so on. Since readers do not often recognize the various levels of subheads within a chapter, however, authors and editors are encouraged to minimize the number of levels. At its worst, a book with too many subheads reads like it is merely an annotated outline.

Style. Cap-lowercase setting is usually preferred for headings and subheadings, since that style is more readable and less obtrusive than all-caps.

Spacing. More white space should be placed over the heading than under it. It should always visually appear to be part of the text for which it serves as the heading. If the paragraph immediately preceding the heading ends with very few words, the line spacing can be reduced somewhat to keep the spacing from looking too large.

Breaking Over Lines. When a heading or subheading is long enough to break over a line, it should be broken by sense, that is, at the end of a phrase.

Hebrew Transliterations

See "Greek and Hebrew Transliterations."

Helpmeet **and** *Helpmate*

Although accepted in most dictionaries, the now-archaic words *helpmeet* and *helpmate* are best reserved for informal, colloquial, or humorous contexts, based as they are on a misreading of Genesis 2:18 (KJV): "I will make him an help meet for him." *Meet*, in the Jacobean English of the King James Version, means "suitable," not "mate."

Heresy **Versus** *Schism*

Though the line between *heresy* and *schism* often seems blurred in early church history, there is a distinction. The basis for a heretic's break with the church is usually doctrinal, whereas that for a schismatic's is not. Heretics have unorthodox beliefs but can, and often do, perceive themselves as remaining within the main body of the church. Schismatics can be entirely orthodox in their beliefs while willfully separating themselves from the church as a sort of alternative to the faith, usually for reasons other than doctrine. The line does become blurred, of course, when a schism has its roots in a heresy.

The term *apostate*, which is different in meaning from both *heretic* and *schismatic*, applies solely to a person who has willfully rejected the Christian faith. Heretics and schismatics usually perceive of themselves as followers of Christ, while an apostate does not.

Although all of these terms were liberally applied as late as the Reformation and Counter-Reformation, they are generally considered too harsh and strong to apply to major historic branches of the Christian faith today. By and large, it is best to leave them to the historians. When applied to specific groups in our time, the word *cult* has come to have some of the same weight as *heretical sect*.

As a matter of consistent style, the names of important heretical movements and schisms in the early church are always capitalized, whether or not they find their etymology in a person's name. Here is a brief list of a few of the major heresies and schisms of the first millennium of the Christian faith:

Heresies of the Early Church

Adoptionism—(eighth century) the doctrine that Jesus was not God's true son but adopted as an inspired human

Apollinarianism—(fourth century) the doctrine that Christ possessed a divine Logos rather than a human mind

Arianism—(fourth century) the belief that Christ was a superior but wholly created human being and therefore not divine

Heresies of the Early Church cont.

Cainites—(second century) a sect that rejected the NT in favor of the Gospel of Judas, believed the earth to be the creation of an evil force, and identified with Cain of the OT

Docetism—(first century) a Gnostic doctrine rejecting the OT; it taught that Christ's sufferings were apparent, not real

Ebionitism—(first century) a doctrine that denied the divinity of Christ and the virgin birth

Gnosticism—(late second century) emphasized an esoteric revealed knowledge as the way to salvation; maintained that the material world was evil and, therefore, Christ's human and divine natures were separate

Macedonianism—(fourth century) the doctrine that denied the Holy Spirit as a fully divine part of the Trinity

Manicheanism—(second century) followers of Mani; actually a distinct religion, but its strong influence on Christianity was considered heretical. Their doctrine was dualistic, giving nearly equal weight to good and evil.

Marcionism—(second century) a Gnostic offshoot that maintained that the OT God was different than the NT God and that Christ was not born of a woman

Millenarianism—(second century) also called the *Chiliasts,* for whom an essential doctrine was a belief in Christ's earthly one-thousand-year reign over the faithful after his return. This belief was revived in many forms throughout the nineteenth century.

Monarchianism—(second century) emphasized the unity of God at the expense of the Trinity

Monophysitism—(fourth century) the doctrine that Christ's incarnate nature was purely divine

Montanism—(late second century) the apocalyptic personality cult of its leader, Montanus

Nazarenes—(second century) a sect for whom it was essential to assert that Christ, while divine, conformed to all the Mosaic rites and customs

Nestorianism—(fifth century) the doctrine that Christ's human and divine natures were separate, not unified

Pelagianism—(fourth century) the theological system asserting that the human will seeks salvation apart from divine grace

Sabellianism—(early third century) the doctrine that Christ was identical in nature to God the Father, a later form of Monarchianism

Schisms of the Church

Donatist Schism—(fourth century) followers of Donatus, who believed their sect to be the true, uncorrupted church, and that only those achieving exceptional holiness could belong

Great Schism of 1054—the historical point at which Eastern Orthodoxy and Roman Catholicism officially split though the origins of their differences considerably predate that era

Novatianist Schism—(third century) followers of a Roman presbyter Novatian, who was orthodox in doctrine but felt he could not accept the cultural and political compromises of the church at large

Holidays, Christian

See "Christian Holidays, Feasts, and the Liturgical Year."

Holidays, Jewish

See "Jewish Holidays and Feasts."

Holy Bible

We forget that the full name of the Bible in many English versions is *The Holy Bible* (in Latin, *Biblia Sacra*, the formal title of the Vulgate). In writing, the full title is perfectly acceptable, although if overused, it can sound falsely pious. Use *the Bible* in most ordinary writing unless one occasionally needs the ring of extra authority implied by the full term.

The term is usually set in roman type—the Bible—unless a specific edition is referred to, such as *The NIV Study Bible*.

See also "*Scripture* Versus *Bible*."

Holy City

In Christian and Jewish contexts, the *Holy City* (capped) is nearly always Jerusalem. That term, however, is applied not only to the earthly Jerusalem but also to the New Jerusalem, that is, heaven. To some readers, the term can alternatively suggest Rome, the seat of the papacy. The written context should make the meaning clear.

Also keep in mind that many other religious faiths have their own holy cities.

Faith	Sacred City
Christian, Protestant	Jerusalem or New Jerusalem
Christian, Roman Catholic	Jerusalem, New Jerusalem, or Rome
Hindu	Banaras
Incan	Cuzco
Jewish	Jerusalem
Muslim, Indian	Allahabad
Muslim, worldwide	Mecca

Holy Grail

The term *Holy Grail* is used to describe a legendary bowl, or in some versions a wide-brimmed cup, which the apocryphal Gospel of Nicodemus identifies as both the wine bowl of the Last Supper and the receptacle in which Joseph of Arimathea is said to have caught the blood of Jesus as he hung on the cross. As such, it achieved great mythical significance, possessed of life-giving qualities. Even the remote possibility of such a relic existing fired the imaginations of numerous medieval writers, and stories of knights going on quests to recover it soon became symbols of the soul's quest for union with God. It plays an important part in many of the Arthurian tales.

The term, which can be referred to, interchangeably, as *the Holy Grail* or *the Grail*, is always capitalized, even when used metaphorically: *The Gutenberg Bible is the Holy Grail of book collectors.*

Holy Land

The term *Holy Land* is capitalized as an epithet for the geographic region of roughly 14,000 square miles, bound on the south by the Sinai Desert, on the east by Syria and Jordan, on the north by Lebanon, and on the west by the Mediterranean Sea.

In using the term, it is important to remember that the land is "holy" to each of the three great monotheistic religions: Judaism, Christianity, and Islam. For Jews it is the land of Israel, as promised to them by God in the book of Exodus; for Christians, it is the place of Jesus' life and ministry; and for Muslims, it is the place from where Muhammed is said to have ascended to heaven. The term is always capped in all such references. When referring jocularly to other locations, the term is lowercased: *He had finally arrived at that holy land for gamblers—Las Vegas.*

Holy Writ

The term *Holy Writ*, referring to the Bible, has a long history in English, dating back to before the twelfth century, though it now has a sort of anti-quarian mustiness to it and is seldom used.

It is also used, semi-jocularly, to refer to any writing that has undeniable authority; and when used in that sense, it is usually lowercased: *Though the First Folio contains numerous errors, it is still regarded as holy writ by Shakespeare scholars.*

Hosanna Versus Hosannah

Hosanna and *hosannah* are variant spellings of a liturgical and biblical interjection that is used as an expression of adoration and praise. The word is found in Matthew 21:9 and elsewhere. It is lowercased unless it stands alone or begins a sentence. The form without the final *h* is the first option given by *Webster's* and is also the form used in the NIV, but either spelling is acceptable as long as it is used consistently and conforms to the major Bible version used.

Hours, Biblical

Anyone who has read the Bible knows that the NT writers had a different way of telling time. Many readers have puzzled over exactly what times *the ninth* or *eleventh hour* are. One of the advantages of Today's New International Version, following its stated goal of dynamic equivalence, is that it translates the biblical hours of the day into modern "clock time," following this scheme:

Biblical Time	Modern "Clock Time"
first hour	7:00 a.m.
second hour	8:00 a.m.
third hour	9:00 a.m.
fourth hour	10:00 a.m.
fifth hour	11:00 a.m.
sixth hour	12:00 noon
seventh hour	1:00 p.m.
eighth hour	2:00 p.m.
ninth hour	3:00 p.m.
tenth hour	4:00 p.m.
eleventh hour	5:00 p.m.
twelfth hour	6:00 p.m.

This scheme is only roughly equivalent, however, because it falsely suggests that biblical time was as rigidly measured as is modern time. The NT writers divided the daylight portion of the day into twelve hours, but as the days grew shorter or longer with the seasons, the hours themselves changed length. Thus, the *third*, *sixth*, and *ninth hours* (the three used most often in the Bible) are more generally equivalent to midmorning, midday, and midafternoon respectively. No clocks struck the hour in Bible times, and to say "the ninth hour" meant an approximate time, give or take about half an hour either way. Also, *the first hour* usually implies sunrise, which in the earth's temperate zones is closer to 6:00 a.m. in the summer than to 7:00 a.m.

The term *the eleventh hour* had the same metaphorical implications for the Bible writers as it does for us today—that is, a final, critical moment of decision—but for different reasons. In our time, *the eleventh hour* suggests the hour before midnight, a crucial time when Cinderella must return home before midnight, for instance, or when Dr. Faustus, in Christopher Marlowe's play of the same name, delivers his famous "Eleventh Hour Soliloquy" one hour before midnight, at which time the demons are scheduled to carry him off to hell. In Bible times, by contrast, *the eleventh hour* was late afternoon, an hour before sunset, when a field worker's usable daylight hours were soon to expire. The day's business had to be concluded, and the traveler needed to find shelter. Similar symbolism; different time of the day.

Hours, Canonical

Confusion exists regarding the names and times of the canonical hours of the divine office, that is, the assigned daily prayers that priests and laity of some denominations (Roman Catholic, Anglican, and Eastern Orthodox) are encouraged to pray throughout the day. This confusion arose because the hours of the Roman Catholic Church have changed over time, because the number of hours differs from denomination to denomination, and because the *matins* is the last prayer of the day in Roman Catholic tradition, while it is the first prayer of the day in the Anglican tradition.

From about the fifth century until the Reformation, there were eight traditional hours of the Roman Catholic Church. The first seven were considered the day hours; the last one, *matins*, the night hour.

Hour	Description
lauds	prayer upon rising
prime	the first hour, or 6:00 a.m.
terce	the third hour, or 9:00 a.m.
sext	the sixth hour, or 12:00 noon
none	the ninth hour, or 3:00 p.m.
vespers	late afternoon or early evening
compline	late evening
matins	late night

This system was later simplified, and the modern Roman Catholic hours specified in the official Breviary of 1971 are *lauds, a midday prayer* (either *terce, sext,* or *none*), *vespers,* and *compline.*

The Church of England simplifies this even further, including only a morning prayer (called *matins,* spelled *mattins* in England) and an evening prayer (*evensong*).

A question also arises concerning the capitalization of these terms. Although this manual recommends lowercasing the names of the hours in general usage, they are sometimes capped in the traditions to which they are associated. If readership is confined to a specific tradition, follow the capitalization of that tradition.

Hymn Meters

Authors often quote hymn lyrics and other old or traditional songs from musical tablature, but it is often hard to determine where the lines should be broken. Even in those hymnals that capitalize the first letter of each line— and they are becoming fewer—indentation patterns can still be difficult to interpret. The list below shows the most common stanza forms, with line breaks and indentation patterns indicated.

Meter Abbreviations. In parentheses after each term, the common hymnbook abbreviation is given for that stanza form as well as the number of syllables in each line. The periods between the numbers indicate the most common caesuras, that is, the strong breaks in the lines so that the singers can catch their breath. A solidus (slash) is sometimes used between the verse and chorus (as in *8888/88*).

Interchangeability. The lyrics to any song can be sung to the tunes of any other song in that same form—a favorite trick of church music directors. For instance, the words of "Amazing Grace" (in Common Meter) can be sung to the tune of "All Hail the Power of Jesus' Name" (whose tune, "Coronation," is also in Common Meter). Also note that traditional Christian hymnody is almost exclusively iambic.

Indentations. In hymns with lines of varying lengths and whose lines vary by two or more syllables (as in *86.86* or *66.86*), the shorter lines are indented. Differences of one syllable between varying lines (as in *87.87*) do not usually result in any indentation.

Rhyme scheme can also be a factor in determining indentation. While hymns with series of repeating couplets (*aabb*), as in Long Meter, are usually aligned left, many Long Meter songs with alternating rhymes (*abab*) or alternating unrhymed and rhymed lines (*abcb*), indent the even numbered lines (as in the Long Meter Double Meter example below).

The following are examples of the most common metrical forms of hymnody, all of which are taken from the great American shape-note hymnal, *The Sacred Harp* (1860).

Common Meter (CM—86.86)

Amazing grace! (how sweet the sound)
    That saved a wretch like me!
I once was lost, but now am found,
    Was blind, but now I see.
    ("Amazing Grace")

Common Meter Double (CMD—86.86.86.86)

> As on the cross the Savior hung,
>> And bled and wept and died;
> He poured salvation on a wretch
>> That languished at his side.
> His crimes, with inward grief and shame,
>> The penitent confessed;
> Then turned his dying eyes to Christ,
>> And thus his prayer addressed.
>> ("Converted Thief")

Long Meter (LM—88.88)

> Lift up your hearts, Immanuel's friends,
> And taste the pleasure Jesus sends;
> Let nothing cause you to delay,
> But hasten on the good old way.
>> ("The Good Old Way")

Long Meter Double (LMD—88.88.88.88)

> The busy scene of life is closed,
>> And active usefulness is o'er;
> The body's laid in calm repose,
>> And sin shall ne'er distress it more.
> The happy soul is gone to rest,
>> Where cares no more shall spoil its peace:
> Reclining on its Savior's breast,
>> It shall enjoy eternal bliss.
>> ("Paradise Plains")

Short Meter (SM—66.86, rhymes *abcb*)

>> He wept that we might weep,
>> Each sin demands a tear;
> In heav'n alone no sin is found
>> And there's no weeping there.
>> ("Jesus Wept")

Other Forms

Determining the line breaks and indent patterns for the following meters is a matter of common sense and applying the principles set forth in the meters listed above.

Common Proper Meter (CPM—886.886)

Short Hymnal Meter (SHM—66.86; same as Short Meter but rhymes ABAB)

Hallelujah Meter (HM—66.66.88)

Long Proper Meter (LPM—88.88.88)

Proper Meter (PM—no general pattern. *The Geneva Psalter* had a different meter for nearly every psalm; thus, each had its own "proper" meter.)

Miscellaneous. All other stanza forms are indicated by syllable counts alone: for instance, 664.6664 ("My Country 'Tis of Thee"), 77.78 ("Just a Closer Walk with Thee), and 87.87 ("In the Cross of Christ I Glory").

Hyphen

See "Hyphenation," "Dash," and "Spelling Out Words in Text."

Hyphenation

Standard Reference. To resolve problems of word division, the hyphenation of compound words, and other uses of the hyphen, this manual recommends *Merriam-Webster's Collegiate Dictionary* as an authoritative and accessible standard. Because of frequent revision, college editions of dictionaries, like *Webster's*, tend to include newer words and a more current hyphenation style than unabridged editions. Other dictionaries are as comprehensive, but once an editorial standard has been chosen, it is important for a publisher's editors and proofreaders to use it consistently.

In many instances an author must use personal discretion in hyphenating, and editors must constantly adopt additional words as they gain currency. Only the most basic rules of hyphenation are given here. More detailed information can be found in sections 7.33–7.45 in *The Chicago Manual of Style, Fifteenth Edition.*

Compound Adjectives. When two or more words form an adjectival unit (compound adjective) precede a noun, hyphens are placed between the words. Compounds that are so familiar as to preclude the possibility of misreading need not be set with hyphens (such as *high school prom, Sunday school class, Old Testament translation*). When the compound adjective is used as a predicate, it is set with no hyphens. Since some familiar compound adjectives are always hyphenated, it is best to check the dictionary. A hyphen is not used when an adverb ending in *-ly* is combined with an adjective.

R. A. Torrey's well-timed anecdote was effective.
R. A. Torrey's effective anecdote was well timed. [predicate; no hyphen]
The nineteenth-century liturgy sounded strange to our ears; it seemed so old-fashioned. [*old-fashioned* is always hyphenated]
a badly needed reform
a highly effective testimony

Syntactical Use. Hyphenation frequently depends on the syntactical use of a phrase or expression.

Is he born again? [predicate adjective]
Is he a born-again Christian? [adjective]
Soul winning is not a negotiable duty of the Christian life. [noun]
Graham's inspired soul-winning sermons reached many. [adjective]

Prefixes and Suffixes. Many common prefixes and suffixes are set without hyphens, although *Webster's* should always be consulted for exceptions. Among the prefixes and suffixes that do not commonly use hyphens are *anti-*, *co-*, *non-*, *out-*, *over-*, *post-*, *pre-*, *pseudo-*, *re-*, *semi-*, *super-*, *-fold*, and *-like*. Keep in mind, though, that if confusion or misreading will result, or if a prefix is added to a proper name, proper adjective or noun, or numeral, then a hyphen should be used. Also use a hyphen if the added prefix or suffix results in a double vowel (unless the word already appears in *Webster's* without the hyphen).

anti-intellectual	postwar
antimonarchic	preestablished [*Webster's*]
childlike	preexist [*Webster's*]
coauthor	pre-1939
coworker	pre-Reformation
non-Christian	prewar
nonviolent	reelect [*Webster's*]
out-Herod Herod	re-enumerate [double vowel]
outperform	threefold

Exceptions to the Prefix and Suffix Rule. The main exceptions to the previous rule are the prefixes *all-*, *ex-* (meaning former), *half-*, and *self-*, which generally use hyphens unless the word is listed otherwise in *Webster's.*

all-faiths meeting	half-pint
all-weather arena	half-smile
ex-missionary	halfway [*Webster's*]
ex-pastor	self-sacrifice

Changes in Meaning. Keep in mind that the meanings of some words will change depending on the insertion or deletion of a hyphen.

> They worked to recover the ministry's losses.
> They worked to re-cover the pews.
> God, in essence, brings about a re-creation of his church.
> We need recreation to refresh ourselves.

Noun Pairs. When two nouns of equal importance are temporarily yoked, they should be hyphenated. It should be emphasized that the use of a solidus (slash) is incorrect insofar as it can create ambiguity. (For instance, although the solidus used to stand for *or*, many readers are unaware of that fact and read it to mean *and*.)

poet-priest	pastor-father	parent-guardian

Word Division. Hyphens are used to indicate a word that has been broken for copy-fitting purposes over two lines of type. For a full discussion of when and how this is done, see "Word Division."

Spelling Out Words. A hyphen is used to spell out words in text or dialogue.

> "I can't remember; is Niebuhr spelled N-I-E or N-E-I?"

Immanuel Versus *Emmanuel*

Though the names for Christ *Immanuel* and *Emmanuel* are generally interchangeable, being different romanized versions of the Hebrew word found in Isaiah 7:14, *Immanuel* is preferred since it is the form common to the most widely used versions of the Bible (KJV, RSV, NIV, and others). *Emmanuel* (from the Septuagint's *Emmanouel*) is acceptable, however, in the many Christmas stories and carols (for instance, "O Come, O Come, Emmanuel") that use that form. When in doubt, use *Immanuel*.

Imprimatur

Roman Catholic Imprimatur. An *imprimatur*, which is the Latin word for "let it be printed," is used in Roman Catholic publishing. It is the official notice placed on a blank front-matter page (usually facing the title page, in place of the author ad card) or on the copyright page that declares that a bishop and his representatives have reviewed the book and found nothing in it contrary to Catholic doctrine or general morals.

In its most common form, the entire phrase *Nihil obstat quominus imprimatur* ("Nothing stands in the way of allowing this to be printed") is given, along with the date and the bishop's name and full title, all usually rendered in Latin.

Other Imprimaturs. The word *imprimatur* can also refer to an official license granted to a publisher in those countries in which government review and approval are required whenever a book is published. The word is also used metaphorically to mean "an official stamp of approval."

Inclusive Language

See "Gender-Accurate Language."

Indexes

Although many kinds of indexes exist, all serve the same function: to make portions of text more accessible to the reader. Not all books need an index. Fiction, devotional, gift, and general inspirational books, for example, usually do not contain the kind of information that would necessitate an index, though even among those genres there are exceptions. But any work containing facts that the reader might need to locate quickly, such as works of reference or scholarly research, can benefit from a good index.

Who Prepares an Index? The author is the ideal indexer, since no one else has so clear and comprehensive an understanding of the book's contents. In many cases, the author is contractually responsible for preparing the index, in which case, the author may opt to hire a professional or have the publisher hire a professional to compile the index, the expense in either case being borne by the author. When the publisher hires the indexer, the fee can usually be deducted from the author's royalties. In either case, the index is prepared from a clean set of final galleys provided by the publisher. (For a thorough review of techniques for compiling indexes, authors should be sure to read Chapter 18 of *The Chicago Manual of Style, Fifteenth Edition.*)

Types of Indexes. There are two principal types of indexes common to religious publishing: the subject–proper-name index and the Scripture index.

Subject–Proper-Name Index. This kind of index lists references and page numbers to all major subjects and proper names discussed in the text of the book itself. In some cases, there may be an advantage to splitting the index into separate indexes: a subject index and a proper-name index.

Typographic Considerations. Indexes are most commonly set in double columns to conserve space, but specific designs may differ. An even white column of space (from 1 to 1-1/2 picas) rather than a rule line should be used to separate the columns.

There are two typographical styles: the paragraph style and the column style. Paragraph style is convenient when space is a consideration; column style, however, tends to make each entry slightly easier to read. In both styles, commas are used before page numbers. In the paragraph style, a colon separates the main heading from the subentries, while in column style, no additional punctuation is generally used. The following examples illustrate the two styles:

Paragraph Style	Column Style
Heaven: NT conceptions of, 28–32; OT conceptions of, 32–33; pagan views of, 20–25; theological implications of, 33	Heaven 　NT conceptions of, 28–32 　OT conceptions of, 32–33 　pagan views of, 20–25 　theological implications of, 33
Helen, St. (mother of Constantine): abandonment of, 133; advocacy of Christianity, 160, 167, 180–84; birth of Constantine, 126; her marriage, 120; her restoration under Constantine, 150–52, 160	Helen, St. (mother of Constantine) 　abandonment of, 133 　advocacy of Christianity, 160, 167, 　　180–84 　birth of Constantine, 126 　marriage, 120 　restoration under Constantine, 150–52, 　　160

For issues relating to alphabetization in indexes, see "Alphabetization."

Subentries in Indexes. Subentries under each index heading may be listed in three ways: (1) alphabetically, which, as the most common and most versatile, is the preferred method for most indexes; (2) chronologically, used mainly for indexes of predominantly biographical information; and (3) numerically by page number, which should be reserved for simple indexes that do not contain a large number of subentries. Only one style should be used throughout an index. If the index is set in paragraph style, a colon separates the entry heading from the subentries, and semicolons separate subentries from each other.

Cross-references. Cross-references are an important element of any thorough index. They indicate where alternate entries or additional information might be found under other headings. In a paragraph-style index, a cross-reference that includes the whole entry is placed at the end of the entry; in column style, such an inclusive reference is placed after the main-entry heading. In both styles, when only a subentry is being cross-referenced, the cross-reference appears immediately after the subentry. The word *see* indicates that an entirely different heading should be referred to, and the words *see also* indicate that additional information may be found under another entry. The word *see*, whether alone or in the phrase *see also*, is usually capped, set in italics, and preceded by a period. In paragraph style, however, the cross-reference is placed in parentheses and the word *see* is lowercased when only the subentry is being cross-referenced.

Paragraph Style	**Column Style**
Bird, William. *See* Byrd, William	Bird, William. *See* Byrd, William
Bishop's Bible, the, 182, 188. *See also* Bibles: before 1611	Bishop's Bible, the, 182, 188. *See also* Bibles: before 1611
Blake, William: paintings of, 228–30; poetry of, 233–39 (*see also* Religious Poetry); his visions, 211. *See also* Artists; Painters	Blake, William. *See also* Artists; Painters paintings of, 228–30. poetry of, 233–39. *See also* Religious Poetry, his visions, 211

Scripture Indexes. Scripture indexes inform the reader of all the Bible quotations used in a book. Most often they only contain references to those verses that are actually quoted, although for some scholarly works the index may also include those Bible verses that are referred to but not quoted. The Scripture index is usually set in double columns and is arranged in the same order as the books of the Bible itself. Within each book of the Bible, entries are listed numerically by chapter and verse numbers; a chapter-only reference precedes any chapter-and-verse references for that same chapter. When continuous references begin with the same verse number, the one with the lower ending number precedes one with a higher ending number. Although leader dots are no longer used for tables of contents and subject–proper-name indexes, they are still common in Scripture indexes. The most common form is as follows:

Genesis		Exodus	
1	113–14	6	27
1–3	71	6:14–25	28
1:1	7, 12, 117	15:21	33
1:1–19	7, 18	20:1–17	98, 100–101
1:1–13	189		
2:4–7	60–61		

Other Kinds of Indexes. Other kinds of indexes are the title-and-first-line index (for books of hymns and poetry), the concordance (common to Bibles), the index of place names (common to atlases), and the author or contributor index (for compilations, reference works, and anthologies). An index can be tailored, in fact, for almost any kind of book in which information needs to be organized for accessibility.

Initialisms

See "Acronyms and Initialisms."

Initials, with Periods

See "Period, *With Initials and Abbreviations*."

Inklings

The group of writers who clustered around C. S. Lewis and J. R. R. Tolkien from the mid-1930s to the late 1940s used the term *Inklings* to describe themselves. Among the other members were Owen Barfield, J. A. W. Bennett, Lord David Cecil, Nevill Coghill, Jim Dundas-Grant, Hugo Dyson, Adam Fox, Colin Hardie, R. E. Havard, Warren H. Lewis, Gervase Mathew, R. B. McCallum, C. E. Stevens, John Wain, Charles Williams, and Charles Wrenn.

The term *Inklings* is capitalized when referring to the group and is always used in the plural, as in *He was one of the Inklings*, rather than *He was an Inkling*.

Because some Christian bookstores occasionally include George MacDonald and G. K. Chesterton in their Inklings section, it is sometimes assumed they were themselves part of that group. They lived before the Inklings' time, however, and were simply influences. Dorothy Sayers and Joy Davidman are also sometimes listed, but as women, they were never, in fact, invited to join the men.

Another common mistake is to refer to the Inklings as a group of "Christian writers." Not all of the Inklings would have described themselves as such. Barfield, for instance, was a philosophical anthroposophist who long debated matters of faith with Lewis.

Inside Half-Title Page

See "Second Half-Title Page."

Interjections

An interjection is a specialized part of speech, usually independent of any grammatical construction, that is used as an exclamation or a sudden expression of emotion. The Bible and the church use many special interjections that are termed *liturgical interjections*, such as *amen, alleluia,* and *hosanna.*

Uses. Interjections are particularly useful for fictional dialogue, where they lend immediacy and realism. While a nonfiction writer can spice up his or her exposition with an occasional authorial interjection, the use of interjections should be limited since they call too much attention to themselves and can make the writing seem self-conscious.

Repetition of Letters. Some writers tend to repeat letters ("Ahhhhh," "h'mmmm," or "ho-hoooo"), which is acceptable if a comic effect is intended. By and large, however, such extended words not only draw too much attention to themselves but also do not communicate well to readers, who can even perceive such spellings as errors. Most stylists advise that the letters not be extended beyond three repetitions ("Ahhh," "h'mmm," or "ho-hooo"). In fact, using only two usually suffices.

Spelling. Since the spelling of interjections can vary from author to author and from dictionary to dictionary, the following list offers a standard styling for some of the most common conversational interjections in English.

ah	expression of satisfaction, delight, content; can have negative connotation of regret or longing
aha	exclamation of discovery, contempt, triumph, irony, etc.
ahem	clearing the throat; drawing attention to oneself; interrupting
ahoy	greeting, hailing someone, often thought of as a sailor's term
ai, aie, aiee	expression of grief, despair, pain
alas	expression of grief or woe; now considered comically melodramatic and antiquated
argh, aargh	an expression of despair, often mock or exaggerated frustration (one of Charlie Brown's favorites)
aw	expressing sympathy, either feigned or sincere; incredulity, disgust, or disappointment
ay, ay me	expression of regret or sorrow. Not *aye*, which is an affirmative vote (as in *aye* and *nay*)
bah	expression of disdain or contempt (as in Scrooge's "bah humbug")
brr	a whirring sound with the lips; the state of being cold
duh	expression of dim-wittedness; currently used by teenagers as a mocking accusation of stupidity
eek	a shriek or scream of fright, usually comic (*Eek! A mouse!*)
eh	used as a question, "Is that right?" or to beg the listener's agreement; often used as Canadian locution
er	expressing a pause, searching for words, inarticulateness. Be careful not to double the *r*, since it will be misread as the verb *to err* (to commit an error)
glub	sound of drowning or of water in a drain; sometimes repeated, usually comic in effect
gulp	the act of swallowing, usually expressing anxiety or fear
ha, hah	expression of contempt, surprise, triumph, joy, or discovery
ha-ha	laughter, derision, or amusement
harrumph	communicates indignation, a dissatisfied turning away, a certain self-righteousness, a blustering clearing of the throat
hee, hee-hee	laughter or giggling
h'm, hum	thoughtful pondering, musing
ho	surprise, calling attention to something (as in *land ho*)
ho-ho	expression of discovery or laughter (used by Santa Claus)
huh	usually followed by a question mark; expression of surprise, doubt, disbelief, confusion; also an expression of wondering
humph	expression of disdain or disgust, doubt or uncertainty
hup	shout of a marching cadence
hurrah, hurray	cheer; expression of joy, excitement, etc.; also *huzzah*, which has an antiquated feel
hut	a marching cadence or a football quarterback's directive
ick	expression of disgust
mm	expression of content with taste of food or drink; also can be thoughtfulness, similar to h'm

oh	expression of surprise, pain, abashment, or understanding; used often in direct address
oho	taunting, discovery, contempt
oops	dismay or surprise, usually involving a mistake or accident
ouch	usually followed by exclamation point; expression of sudden pain
ow	intense pain
oy, oy vey	Yiddish expression of a sigh
pew	expression of disgust, as with a bad odor
phew	expression of relief, fatigue; sometimes an expression of sensing an unpleasant smell
phooey	expression of disappointment, indignation, or dismissal
rah, rah-rah	a cheer, a shout of encouragement
sh, shh	request for someone to be quiet
sheesh	euphemistic expression of surprise or exasperation
tee-hee	laughter or giggling
tsk-tsk, tsk	expression of scolding; "For shame!"
ugh	expression of disgust, aversion, or fright
uh	expression of pause, filling time, searching for words
uh-huh	positive; saying yes; also mock agreement
uh-oh	same force as "Oh, no!"; favorite expression of toddlers when something falls
uh-uh	negative; saying no
um	hesitation, doubt, searching for words
whew	expression of relief after a close scrape
whoa	"stop" or "slow down"; usually said to horses
wow	expression of being impressed; powerful emotion, either good or bad
yech, yecch	an expression of disgust
yo	getting someone's attention
yow	expression of pain or dismay
yuck, yuk	expression of disgust, distaste
yum, yummy	expression of content with taste of food or drink
zz	suggesting sleep or snoring; is considered comic no matter how many times the letter is repeated

International Standard Book Number (ISBN)

An International Standard Book Number (ISBN), which is a standard part of the CIP data, should be obtained for every publication. (See "Cataloging in Publication Data [CIP].") If no CIP is used in a particular book or if the CIP is located elsewhere in the book, then the ISBN should still be shown somewhere on the copyright page. The ISBN should also always appear somewhere on the cover or flap of the book (it is customarily included in the EAN, or barcode).

Cloth and Paper Editions. If a book is to be published in both cloth and paper editions, then each edition should have its own ISBN.

Series. Each book in a series should have its own ISBN. If a multivolume set of books is to be sold only (and invariably) as a unit, then a single ISBN can be assigned to the set, though this is fairly rare. An example of this would be when volume one contains a text and volume two contains the annotations to that text, or when two or more closely related books are available only as a boxed set.

Reprints and Revisions. If a book will be reprinted with a new format or binding style or is being heavily revised (as opposed to only simple corrections being made), a new ISBN should be assigned. If the book cover is to be redesigned without changing the format and content of the original, it should keep the original ISBN. (See also "Reprints and Revisions.")

Note: It is redundant to say, as is commonly done, "ISBN number," since the N in the abbreviation already stands for "number." Just saying "ISBN" suffices.

Internet-Related Words

See "Computer- and Internet-Related Words."

Internet Resources

The Internet offers previously unimaginable tools for writers, researchers, editors, and proofreaders. Caution is necessary, of course, because of the amount of misinformation disseminated freely on the Internet, but the following websites have proven to be authoritative for specific purposes.

Foreign Names. For the spelling of foreign names, the public databases of the Central Intelligence Agency is extremely useful:

www.odci.gov/cia/publications/factbook/index.html
www.odci.gov/cia/publications/chiefs/index.html

Trademarks. To ascertain the accurate ownership of trademarks, check the website of the International Trademark Association:

www.inta.org/tmcklst.htm

Or check the Federal Government's list at:

www.uspto.gov/

US Geography. For the accurate spelling of US geographic locations that can't be found in *Webster's*, check the Federal Government's database:

mapping.usgs.gov/www/gnis

World Geography. For the accurate spelling of geographic locations worldwide that can't be found in *Webster's,* check:

164.214.2.59/gns/html/index/html

InterVarsity

To avoid confusion, the publisher and the Christian organization that go by this name in the US have recently standardized the spelling. Thus: *InterVarsity Press* and *InterVarsity Christian Fellowship.*

The organization that goes by that name in the United Kingdom used to hyphenate it (*Inter-Varsity*), but they now go by another name altogether: *UCCF—the Universities and Colleges Christian Fellowship.*

Introduction

An *introduction* is the final portion of a book's front matter, containing material pertinent to the main content of the book itself. The introduction is usually written by the author but can, on occasion, be written by someone else. If a well-known person has written the introduction, it is best to place that writer's name at the beginning of the introduction, right after the title, where it will be noticed. Otherwise, the author's name and a dateline (if used) should come at the end of the piece. If the introduction is written by the book's author, no signature or dateline is needed unless the writer requests it.

What distinguishes an introduction from a foreword or a preface is the degree of relatedness to the text itself. An introduction has a closer thematic connection to the content of the book and is more essential to the understanding of the text than a foreword or a preface, both of which can usually be left unread without limiting the reader's appreciation of the book. Of course, determining the level of relatedness to the text can be a highly subjective matter, but this principle should help: high level of relation to the text = introduction; low level of relation to the text = foreword (written by someone other than the author) or preface (written by the author). (See also "Foreword and Preface.")

Islamic Religious Terminology

As one of the three great monotheistic faiths, all of which ultimately claim their authority from Abraham, Islam is rapidly becoming more familiar in the West. With more than 840 million Muslims worldwide, Christians and Jews alike owe it to themselves to know more of the religion's history, culture, and customs. The following list shows only a few of the more common Islamic religious terms, with recommended spelling, capitalization, and styling, as well as some rudimentary definitions. (Also see "Jewish Religious Terminology.")

AH—the abbreviation of *anno Hegirae* ("in the year of the Hegira"); the beginning of the Islamic calendar, which began on July 16, AD 622. Like AD and BC, it is usually set in full caps without periods. Islamic scholars often use the abbreviations BCE (before the common era) to specify dates before the birth of Christ and CE (common era) to specify dates between the birth of Christ and 622. See *Hegira*.

Allah—the Arabic word for God; always capped

ayatollah—among various Shiite teachers and interpreters of the law, an ayatollah is the most learned and respected; the term is capped as a title when it precedes a proper name

fakir—a Muslim religious mendicant or, by extension, a Muslim or Hindu holy man noted for asceticism

fatwa—an opinion rendered by a religious leader on a matter of interpretation of the law; it is a recommended opinion but not necessarily legally binding on believers; occasionally spelled *fatwah*

five pillars of Islam, the—(sometimes capped) the five essentials of the Muslim faith: (1) belief that "there is no god but God, and Muhammad is his prophet"; (2) praying five times a day, facing Mecca; (3) giving alms; (4) fasting during Ramadan, the ninth month of the Islamic year; and (5) making at least one pilgrimage, or *hajj*, to Mecca, if possible

hajj—most Muslims attempt to make at least one pilgrimage to Mecca in the course of a lifetime. This pilgrimage is called a *hajj*, while the pilgrim is called a *hajji*

Hegira—Arab word meaning "flight"; always capped when referring specifically to Muhammad's flight from Mecca to Medina, AD 622. The Muslim calendar begins with that event; hence, AH (*anno Hegirae*, "in the year of the Hegira") for dates. Sometimes spelled *Hejira*. When lowercased, it means any escape from a dangerous situation, somewhat similar in sense to the Hebrew word *exodus*

imam—the prayer leader in a mosque; can also mean one who claims descent from Muhammad and serves as a religious leader with responsibility over a given region

Injeel—(capped) the NT Gospels

Islam—the term itself means "submission to God"

Islamic calendar—a lunar calendar that retrogrades in thirty-year cycles and is reckoned in terms of years since the Hegira (AD 622, which is termed 1 AH by Muslims)

jihad—literally, "the struggle along the path toward God," often implying one's personal struggle in the faith, though it is sometimes interpreted to mean armed conflict or holy war against one's enemies

Koran—see *Qur'an*

Muhammad—(c. 570–632) the founder of Islam and the receiver of the faith's holy scriptures, the Qur'an, in about 610. He is considered by Muslims the final prophet in a line of prophets that stretches back to Abraham

mujahideen—one who carries out a jihad; a holy warrior; sometimes synonymous with guerrilla fighter mullah—an interpreter or teacher of Islamic law; the term is capped as a title before a proper name

Qur'an (Koran)—the holy book, written in Arabic, believed by Muslims to be Allah's direct revelation to Muhammad; the form *Qur'an* is replacing *Koran*. Either is acceptable, though *Qur'an* is to be preferred whenever possible since it is the form used by most Muslim writers writing in English

Ramadan—the ninth month of the Islamic calendar, during which the faithful are required to fast

Sharia—the literal meaning is "the path to the water hole"; the term refers to Islamic law as a whole

sharif—a person of influence or importance in Muslim countries; originally refers to any descendent of Muhammad through his daughter Fatima

sheikh—a learned Muslim leader or chief; sometimes spelled *sheik*; the term is capped as a title before proper names

Shia (n.), Shiite (n. and adj.)—the branch of Islam that believes Ali and the Imams were Muhammad's legitimate successors; see *Sunni*

Sunna—the customary practices of Islam based on the extra-Qur'anic teachings of Muhammad

Sunni—the branch of Islam that adheres to the orthodox traditions and believes that the first four caliphs after Muhammad were his legitimate successors; see *Shia*

talib—a student of Islamic law

ulema—a group of Muslim scholars

Zaboor—(capped) the Psalms of the OT

Italics

Italic type, the right-leaning letters that accompany most typefaces, were first devised by the Renaissance Venetian printer Aldus Manutius for his series of Roman classics. Said to be inspired by the elegant handwriting of the Italian poet Petrarch, the type took up less space than ordinary roman type and allowed Aldus to produce readable, compact editions at a reasonable price. That sort of publishing, in fact, helped fuel the Renaissance itself.

Although Aldus set entire books in italics, they should be used with discretion in our time. Extended passages of italic type are not only more difficult to read than the roman type, but tests have shown that they slow the reader down considerably, even causing distraction, fatigue, and at times confusion. Entire sentences or paragraphs should thus not ordinarily be set in italics.

Nor should a careful writer need to use italics frequently for emphasis, although a word or phrase may occasionally be italicized when a specific emphasis will not be clear to the reader any other way. A dependence on italics for emphasis is a sign of poor writing.

Italics are indispensable, however, in some fairly defined situations.

Foreign Words and Phrases. When the author expects certain foreign words or phrases to be unfamiliar to the reader, they should be set in italics. But foreign words and phrases that have become common in English should not be italicized. As a general rule, those foreign expressions that appear among the main entries of *Merriam-Webster's Collegiate Dictionary* do not require italics. Those not listed in the main entries of *Webster's* or in the "Foreign Words and Phrases" section at the back of that dictionary are, in most cases, unfamiliar enough to require italics.

If an unusual foreign word or phrase is introduced as a way of conveying a specialized or technical meaning, it should be italicized when first defined. Thereafter it may be set in regular type.

Latin Terms and Abbreviations. With the exception of *sic*, which is always italicized, scholarly Latin terms and abbreviations should be set in roman. Even words requiring italics when spelled out should be roman when abbreviated. Consult *Webster's* and *CMS.*

> ibid.
> et al.
> q.v.
> i.e. (*id est*)

Thoughts. We no longer recommend that a person's thoughts, imagined words, and unspoken prayers (called *unspoken discourse*), when expressed in the first person, always be set in italics. There are two reasons for this. First, long stretches of italics can be difficult to read, and, second, italics can be mistaken for emphasis. Italics may be used when such thoughts are infrequent or cannot be conveyed without italics. Otherwise, thoughts should be expressed in roman type, with or without quotation marks, according to the author's preference.

> *I will lay my weapons upon the altar of Christ,* thought Ignatius as he rode toward Montserrat. [italic style for occasional use]
> "Dear Father," prayed Augustine silently, "make me pure—but not quite yet!" [quotation style]
> Ananais looked at the blind man and thought, Surely I have not been called to heal him! [roman, without quotation marks]

Dream Sequences, Flashbacks, and Other Narrative Devices in Fiction. Sometimes in fiction italics may be used to distinguish typographically between the simple past tense, in which the story is being told, and such things as dream sequences, flashbacks, and other fictional devices. If such devices are frequent or highly extended, the editor and author may want to consult with the book's designer or compositor so that either an alternate typographic setting may be sought or a typeface with a highly readable italic face may be chosen.

Words as Words. A word referred to as a word should be set in italics. Its definition may be set in roman type within quotation marks if it is a formal definition. But when a word is quoted from a specific context, quotation marks, not italics, should be used.

> Early Methodist ministers used the word *liberty* to describe an openness to God's Spirit in their preaching.
>
> By *feretory,* hagiographers mean "a shrine in which a saint's bones are deposited and venerated." [formal definition]
>
> The word *world* has various meanings in Scripture; in John 3:16, for instance, the Evangelist writes "world" to denote the inhabitants of our planet, not the broader cosmos.

Specialized Vocabulary. Technical terms or special terminology of any kind, especially when accompanied by a definition, are usually set in italics in the first reference and in roman type thereafter.

> Medieval theories of *impanation* asserted that the elements of Communion could be both the real presence of Christ and bread and wine at the same time. Impanation was condemned as heretical and is no longer propounded.

Titles. Italics are used for titles of certain works and for some names. (Compare the following list with the one given in "Quotation Marks, *In Titles.*") Italicize the titles of:

> Audio recordings, record albums, audiocassettes, compact discs, SRCDs, DVDs, etc.
> *Hallelujah! The Very Best of the Brooklyn Tabernacle Choir; Spirit of the Century*
> Books
> *The Lion, the Witch and the Wardrobe; Paul: A Novel; Fresh Wind, Fresh Fire*
> CD-ROMs (software programs, however, are set cap-lowercase, roman, with no quotes)
> *Compton's Interactive Bible; Zondervan International Bible Deluxe*
> Curriculum materials (in book or multimedia forms)
> *Marketplace AD 29; What's So Amazing about Grace Groupware*
> Ebooks
> *The Dawn Mistaken for Dusk; Riding the Bullet*
> Films, feature-length
> *Chariots of Fire; Shadowlands; The Prince of Egypt; The Apostle; The Lord of the Rings: The Fellowship of the Rings*
> Legal cases
> *Roe v. Wade; Brown v. Board of Education*
> Long poems or collections of poems
> *Paradise Lost; Songs of Innocence and Experience; A Scripture of Leaves*

Musical compositions, collections of
> *Preludes and Fugues; Sports et Divertissements; The Bay Psalm Book*

Newspapers, magazines, and newsletters (except for the initial *the* in running text)
> the *Christian Science Monitor; Mars Hill Review;* the *Christian Century*

Operas, musicals, ballets, and other performance-length musical compositions
> *Amahl and the Night Visitors; Godspell; The Nutcracker; The Symphony of Sorrows*

Paintings, sculptures, and other works of art
> *Self-Portrait in a Convex Mirror; David; The Bayeaux Tapestry; The Gates of Hell*

Plays
> *The Cocktail Party; The Producers; Shadowlands*

Ships and aircraft (though the designations USS, SS, and HMS are not italicized)
> USS *Constitution;* the space shuttle *Challenger;* the *Spirit of St. Louis*

Television and radio series, shows, and programs (though the names of individual episodes should be in quotation marks)
> *Joan of Arcadia, Touched by an Angel; All Things Considered*

Videocassettes and DVDs
> *Larry Boy and the Fib from Outerspace; The Sound of Music*

Web addresses/URLs
> *christianitytoday.com/*

Web-based magazines, ezines, email newsletters
> *Gadfly Online;* the *Faith and Imagination Newsletter* (but Web-based companies should be set in roman type like any company: Amazon.com, eBay)

The word *magazine* is set lowercase and in roman type when it is not part of the official name of a publication: *TIME* magazine; *Eternity* magazine; but *Parents' Magazine.*

The initial article of a title may be dropped when syntax warrants it, such as following a possessive noun or pronoun. An initial article should also be omitted if another article or an adjective precedes it.

> They planned on reading Tolkien's *Lord of the Rings* aloud. [*The* omitted]
> The powerful *Jesus I Never Knew* by Philip Yancey . . . [*The* omitted]

Added in Quotations. When specific words within run-in or block quotations are italicized for emphasis, the reader should be notified. An ascription, such as *italics mine* or *emphasis added*, should be placed in parentheses immediately after the quotation.

> Note the contrast in David's parallelism: "When *we* were overwhelmed by sins, *you* forgave our transgressions" (Ps. 65:3, italics mine).

For Titles of Specific Modern Editions of the Bible. When the title of a specific modern edition of the Bible is referred to, it should be set in italics, unlike the names of general versions of the Bible, which are set in roman type, especially when they appear in many editions and formats.

Specific Editions:

Good News Bible: The Bible in Today's English Version
The King James 2000 Edition
The Message
The New Testament in Modern English (J. B. Phillips)
The NIV Study Bible
The Oxford Annotated Bible: Revised Standard Version
Scofield Reference Bible: King James Version
Young's Literal Translation of the Bible

General Versions:

Breeches Bible
Jerusalem Bible
King James Version
New International Version
J. B. Phillips' paraphrase of the New Testament
Revised Standard Version
Today's English Version
Vulgate

The King James Version and the New American Standard Bible. In most editions of the King James Version of the Bible, italics are used to indicate words for which there are no direct correspondents in the original texts. The translators often added words to make sense of certain elliptical passages or to fill in words that were only implied in the original. In almost no case should these italics be reproduced when printing quotations from the King James Version. (For a fuller discussion of this topic, see "Quotations from the Bible, *Italics in the King James Version*.")

The *New American Standard Bible* follows the King James style; in addition, it uses italics anytime the Old Testament is quoted in the New. Again, these italics should not be reproduced when quoting the NASB.

> "And Pharaoh said unto his servants, Can we find *such a one* as this *is*, a man in whom the Spirit of God *is*?" [Gen. 41:38, as it appears in the KJV.]

> "And Pharaoh said unto his servants, Can we find such a one as this is, a man in whom the Spirit of God is?" [The same passage as it would be quoted.]

Jargon, Religious

Every religion develops its own unique vocabulary. It helps the faithful communicate with each other but often leaves those outside feeling excluded. So-called evangelical Christians have developed a vocabulary that is often opaque to non-Christians as well as to Christians outside evangelical circles. While much of this vocabulary may be unavoidable when communicating to a narrowly defined market, writers should be especially wary of using such Christian jargon when writing for a larger audience.

Unconsciously, some writers allow the often-outdated rhetorical language of sermons, hymns, and devotional literature to shape their prose, resulting in indefiniteness, lack of originality, and, at worst, insincerity. Like clichés, anachronisms, and archaisms, jargon has a legitimate and valuable purpose in the hands of a careful writer, but it can be an obstacle to good communication. Religious writing can only be strengthened as writers learn to find fresh and contemporary ways of expressing their ideas. Here are a few classic bits of evangelical jargon and cliché that should be used with discretion, if at all.

abundant life	epitome of evil
after God's own heart	eternal refuge
alive to the Spirit	eternal resting place
believe on (the name of the Lord)	eternal reward
better part of valor [or wisdom or whatever]	fervent prayer
	fleshly desires
born again	forever and ever
brothers and sisters in the Lord	from on high
burden on my heart	get into the Word
carnal desires	giant of the faith
cast a vision	God-fearing man [or woman]
Christian walk	God made known to me
crossed over (to die)	God revealed to me
daily walk, one's	God-shaped vacuum
den of iniquity	good Christian
depths of depravity	groanings of the spirit
depths of despair	grounded in the faith
desires of the flesh	grounded in the Word
desires of your heart	heart of the gospel
devout Catholic	heathen, the

heavenly angels
heavenly anthems
hedge of protection
hellfire and damnation
highest heavens
hopeless sinner
inspired Word of God
just pray (just ask)
laid upon my heart
let go and let God
life abundant
life-changing experience
life everlasting
life of sin
lift [someone] up in prayer
lift up the Lord
lusts of the flesh
meet his [or her] Maker
moved by the Spirit
of old [as in "Abraham of old"]
passions of the flesh
pearly gates
poor sinner
prayer warrior
precious blood of Jesus
prepare our hearts
primrose path
prodigal ways
realms of glory
rooted in the faith
rooted in the Word
saving knowledge of Christ
seventh heaven
share a verse [of Scripture]
sins of the fathers

snares of the Devil
sorely tempted
soul of humility
soul-stirring message
spiritual high
spiritual state
spoke to my heart
stand before the judgment seat
stars in one's crown
storms [tempests] of life
straight and narrow
take captive every thought
take it to the Lord
throughout eternity
time immemorial
traveling mercies
trials and tribulations
trophies of grace
trust and obey
unrepentant sinner
unspoken needs
unto eternity
uphold in prayer
urgings of the Spirit
vale of tears
victorious living
walk by faith
walk in the Spirit
walk with God
watch and pray
weeping and moaning
wicked ways
wiles of the Devil
wondrous ways of God
word of prayer

Jesu

Jesu is a Latinized form of the name Jesus. In English it is occasionally found in liturgical and literary contexts, especially when they have an especially Latinate character. Otherwise, its use is considered obscure and slightly affected. The term should be retained, however, when it is part of a Latin or formal title, as in J. S. Bach's "Jesu, Joy of Man's Desiring," Gabriel Fauré's "Pie Jesu," or St. Bernard's "Jesu Dulcis Memoria."

Jewish Holidays and Feasts

Jewish holidays and feasts can be baffling to those not familiar with the customs. The following brief description of the seven major seasons and holidays of the Jewish calendar should offer some clarification.

Rosh Hashanah (Jewish New Year) falls on the first and second days of the Hebrew month Tishri (September–October). After ten days of penitence, Yom Kippur is observed. Together, Rosh Hashanah and Yom Kippur are termed the *High Holy Days.*

Yom Kippur (Day of Atonement) is a day of praying for forgiveness for the sins of the past year and for fasting, observed on the tenth day of Tishri.

Sukkoth (Feast of Tabernacles) is the annual harvest celebration. This eight-day festival begins on the fifteenth day of Tishri. The day after the end of Sukkoth is Simhath, which celebrates the completion of the annual reading of the Torah. Also spelled *Sukkot.*

Hanukkah (Feast of the Dedication) is an eight-day festival commemorating the victory of Judas Maccabeus and the rededication of the temple in Jerusalem. It starts on the twenty-fifth day of Kislev (December) and incorporates the Festival of Lights, in which the eight candles of the menorah are lit. Sometimes spelled *Chunahak* or *Hanukah.*

Purim (Feast of Esther, or Feast of Lots) is a joyous festival commemorating the deliverance of the Persian Jews from a massacre as recounted in the Book of Esther. It is celebrated on the fourteenth day of Adar (February–March).

Passover (Pesach) commemorates the exodus of the Jews from Egypt. It is celebrated from the fourteenth to the twenty-second days of Nisan (March–April).

Shabuoth (Pentecost, or Feast of Weeks) takes place on the sixth and seventh days of Sivan (May–June) around the world, though only on the sixth in Israel. It is an agricultural festival during which the story of the grain harvest in the Book of Ruth is recounted. Secondarily, the festival commemorates the receiving of the Ten Commandments.

Jewish Religious Terminology

Judaism, along with its later offshoots, Christianity and Islam, is one of the world's three great monotheistic faiths. It is particularly important for Christians to understand the Jewish roots of their own faith, and the following list of Jewish religious terms provides some basic information. Such a brief list is unavoidably superficial and incomplete, but it offers a few of the most common terms, along with their recommended spelling, capitalization, and definitions.

bar mitzvah—when a Jewish boy reaches age thirteen, he is considered to be a morally responsible adult; he is then called a *bar mitzvah* (Hebrew: "son of the law"), as is the initiation ceremony that takes place at that time

bas mitzvah—when a Jewish girl reaches age thirteen, she, like a *bar mitzvah* (see previous entry) is considered a morally responsible adult; she is called a *bas mitzvah* (Hebrew: "daughter of the law"), or sometimes a *bat mitzvah*, which is also the name of the initiation ceremony that takes place

B'nai B'rith—the largest international Jewish service organization, founded in 1843 by Henry Jones, committed to training, charity, and education

Hasidism—a Jewish religious movement founded in about 1750, tending toward mysticism and stressing personal devotion over scholarly interpretation of the Scriptures

Kabbalah—a mystical method of interpreting the Hebrew Scriptures originating in the eleventh century and referring to the body of written literature that has grown up around it. Usually capped; also sometimes spelled *Cabala, Cabbala, Cabballah,* and *Kabalah.* In precise writing, usually used without an article

kipa—(also spelled *kippah*), a yarmulke, or skullcap

kittel—a white ceremonial robe in which the dead are wrapped; sometimes worn by worshipers during Yom Kippur; pronounced so that it rhymes with *little*

menorah—a ceremonial candelabra used in Jewish worship, accommodating seven or nine candles

mezuzah—a small scroll on which is written the texts of Deuteronomy 6:4–9 (beginning "Hear, O Israel: The LORD our God, the LORD is one"); 11:13–21 (beginning "So if you faithfully obey the commands . . ."); and the name *Shaddai.* In Jewish custom, this scroll is attached to the doorframe of a house as a reminder of one's faith. The word *mezuzah* literally means "doorpost"

midrash—stories told, sometimes with elaborations, from the Hebrew Bible; to teach a lesson in the Law or a moral principle

mitzvah—a commandment in Jewish law; the plural is *mitzvoth*, though *mitzvahs* is also common

Orthodox—refers to *Orthodox Judaism*; one of the principle movements within Judaism, teaching that the Law is divinely given and therefore immutable and without exception

patriarchs—Abraham, Isaac, Jacob; the founders and forefathers of the Jewish faith

phylactery—one of two small, leather, square boxes that contain passages from Scripture and are worn by Jewish men on the head and forearm during certain prayers

seder—a Jewish ceremonial meal served at the beginning of Passover as a commemoration of the exodus from Egypt

shofar—the ram's horn trumpet used on Jewish holidays; the plural of *shofar*, by the way, is *shofroth*

tetragrammaton—the four letters of the Hebrew alphabet that stand for God's personal name: YHWH, or JHVH

Yahweh—the name by which God is known (Ex. 3:14); used in place of his proper name, which is unknowable

yarmulke—(pronounced YAH-muh-kuh) Yiddish term for the skullcap. In the US the Hebrew term *kipa* is more often used. To avoid confusion, the English *skullcap* is the most convenient fallback

King James Version, Use of Italics in the

See "Quotations from the Bible: *Italics in the King James Version.*"

King James Version's Contributions to English

The King James Bible has been more influential than even the works of Shakespeare in shaping the way English speakers write and speak. Many common idioms come directly from the pens of the King James translators (and their heavy borrowings from the Wycliffe and Tyndale Bible translators before them), but it is surprising how often we forget their source, let alone remember the specific verse they are from. Here is a short reference guide for a few of the King James Version's most common idiomatic contributions to the English language, though note that the phrases below are the forms the words have taken in popular usage, not the exact phrasing in the Bible—for instance, we tend to say, "There's nothing new under the sun," while the KJV states, "There is no new thing under the sun."

Common Phrases from the King James Version

Phrase	Source
angels unawares, to entertain	Heb. 13:2
ask and you shall receive	Matt. 7:7
blind leading the blind, the	Matt. 15:14
bread on the waters, to cast	Eccl. 11:1
coals of fire upon someone's head, to heap	Prov. 25:21–22
cup runneth over, my	Ps. 23:5
dead bury the dead, let the	Matt. 8:21–22
drop in the bucket, a	Isa. 40:15
eye for an eye, an	Matt. 5:38 (Ex. 21:24)
eye to eye, to see	Isa. 52:8
fall from grace	Gal. 5:4
fat of the land, the	Gen. 45:18
filthy lucre	1 Tim. 3:8
fleshpots [of Egypt]	Ex. 16:3
fly in the ointment, a	Eccl. 10:1

Phrase	Source
glass darkly, through a	1 Cor. 13:12
green pastures	Ps. 23:2
hide one's light under a bushel, to	Matt. 5:15
house divided, a	Matt. 12:25
inner man, the	Eph. 3:16
iron sharpening iron	Prov. 27:17
kill the fatted calf, to	Luke 15:30
labor of love	1 Thess. 1:3
lamb among wolves, like a	Luke 10:3
land of milk and honey, a	Ex. 3:8
law unto oneself, a	Rom. 2:14
let my people go	Ex. 5:1
mighty are fallen, how the	2 Sam. 1:25
money is the root of all evil, love of	1 Tim. 6:10
mouths of babes, out of the	Ps. 8:2
multitude of sins	1 Peter 4:8
nothing new under the sun	Eccl. 1:9
pearls before swine, to cast	Matt. 7:6
powers that be, the	Rom. 13:1
respecter of persons, no	Acts 10:34
right mind, in one's	Mark 5:15
riotous living	Luke 15:13
root of the matter, the	Job 19:28
salt of the earth, the	Matt. 5:13
scales fall from one's eyes, to have the	Acts 9:18
shibboleth	Judg. 12:6
skin of one's teeth, by the	Job 19:20
stars in their courses, the	Judg. 15:20
suffer fools gladly, to	2 Cor. 11:19
sun go down on your wrath, don't let the	Eph. 4:26
thorn in the flesh, a	2 Cor. 12:7
threescore and ten (years)	Ps. 90:10
time for every purpose under heaven, a	Eccl. 3:1
tooth for a tooth, a	Matt. 5:38 (Ex. 21:24)
turn the other cheek, to	Matt. 5:39
valley of the shadow of death, the	Ps. 23:4
wages of sin is death	Rom. 6:23
wolf in sheep's clothing, a	Matt. 7:15
worthy of one's hire, to be	Luke 10:7

The influence of the King James Version is so pervasive that some phrases in English are commonly mistaken as coming from that Bible. Here are a few examples:

Phrases Sometimes Mistakenly Thought to Be Biblical

Phrase	Source
all that glitters is not gold	Chaucer (quoting a proverb)
amazing grace	hymn by John Newton
cleanliness is next to godliness	John Wesley (quoting a proverb)
dark night of the soul	book by St. John of the Cross
death's door, at	Book of Common Prayer
God helps those who help themselves	Benjamin Franklin, *Poor Richard's Almanac*
God's in his heaven (all's right with the world)	Robert Browning, "Pippa Passes"
God tempers the wind to the shorn lamb	Laurence Sterne, *Sentimental Journey*
have and to hold, to	Book of Common Prayer
in God we trust	on US coinage since 1865, but inspired by "Star-Spangled Banner"
instrument of thy peace, make me an	a prayer of St. Francis
land of the living, in the	Book of Common Prayer
little lamb, who made thee?	William Blake poem
milk of human kindness, the	Shakespeare, *Macbeth*
more things are wrought by prayer than this world dreams of	Tennyson, "Morte d'Arthur"
quality of mercy (is not strained), the	Shakespeare, *Merchant of Venice*
sickness and in health, in	Book of Common Prayer
snake in the grass, a	proverb
tender mercy	Book of Common Prayer
worldly goods, all one's	Book of Common Prayer

King James Version Versus *Authorized Version*

In the United States, the term *King James Version* (KJV) is more readily understood than the term *Authorized Version* (AV) as the name of the 1611 edition of the Holy Bible commissioned by King James I of England. *Authorized Version* is used primarily in the United Kingdom and its Commonwealth.

Large Print Books

The average adult reader with no visual impairment, or the reader with adequate vision correction, is capable of comfortably reading 9-point type with 2 points of leading, provided that the line lengths are not too long and the typeface is a standard text face. But nearly every reader will suffer some level of visual impairment as he or she ages. According to the National Association for Visually Handicapped (NAVH), more than 26 million Americans qualify as visually impaired; and as the baby boomers grow older, that number will increase.

Whether book and software publishers are up to the challenge posed by aging readers remains a question, though with the advent of book-on-demand printing and customized, downloadable texts, the technologies for producing large-print editions, sometimes euphemistically called *comfort editions*, are becoming less expensive.

Standards. Both the NAVH and the American Printing House for the Blind have established rigorous standards for the large-print book. Sadly, either because publishers are often ignorant of these standards or because they simply do not find them economically viable, many so-called large-print books do not meet these standards.

Often publishers photographically enlarge the pages of a book and deem it "large print" in a process called "shooting it up," even though that enlargement may not bring the type up to the large-print standard. Furthermore, many publishers do not print their own large-print editions but license them to specialty printers, some of which "shoot up" inexpensive editions that are not adequate in size or leading.

Most of the guidelines established by advocates for the visually impaired insist on 16- or 18-point type as the minimum. There is a preference for sans-serif types, which tend to blur less when read, although some scientific studies show that the difference between serif and sans serif is minimal. (Some studies marginally endorse serif typefaces as the more readable for average readers.)

(Times New Roman)
This is an example of a 16-point serif type

This is an example of an 18-point serif type

(Arial)
This is an example of a 16-point sans-serif type

This is an example of an 18-point sans-serif type

While the US Government Printing Office and the Library of Congress have yet to establish a standard for what constitutes a "large-print book," the following guidelines, provided by the NAVH, are useful. While not all of these standards are feasible for every book, they offer a target to shoot for and a helpful yardstick by which all so-called large-print books can be measured.

NAVH Standards and Criteria for Large Print Publications

1. No edition may exceed an overall size of 8-3/4" x 11-1/4", with a maximum sheet size of 8-1/2" x 11".
2. The finished book shall not exceed 1-1/4" in thickness, with a maximum weight of three pounds. (This does not apply to technical or reference books—that is, a dictionary, atlas, etc.)
3. An off-white or natural vellum or matte offset stock must be used to prevent glare.
4. Gutter margins should not be less than 7/8", with the outside margin smaller, but not less than 1/2".
5. Type size should not be smaller than 16 point—preferably an 18-point type should be maintained.
6. When resetting, it is recommended that a sans serif or modified serif be used. Helvetica, Century, or Garamond are examples of particularly good typefaces. It is recommended that medium type style be used with bold for titles, captions, etc. (See #11 for further information.)
7. Letter spacing, word spacing, and leading must be adequate in order to avoid crowded copy, as white space is of utmost importance to many of the visually impaired.
8. Density is extremely important, and copy that appears gray will not be acceptable.
9. The binding shall allow for as much flexibility as possible, with the hope that a loose spine will be employed in order to allow the book to lie as flat as possible. It is recommended that all books be side sewn for durability.
10. A vertical line must be used to separate columns.

11. If photographically enlarged from the original edition, broken letters must be avoided. Careful scrutiny of selections should be made either by the editorial department of the respective publisher, or NAVH will offer this service if small print editions are sent to us prior to the enlarging process. With easy accessibility of computer type, excellent large print can be prepared. It is recommended that, for most typefaces, a medium font be used with a laser printout of at least 400 DPI.

12. Signatures or tear sheets of all books that are to carry the *NAVH Seal of Approval* must be sent to NAVH prior to final printing for examination. (NAVH, 3201 Balboa Street, San Francisco, CA 94121; or NAVH, 22 West 21st Street, New York, NY 10010)

13. The NAVH seal shall appear on jackets (when used), as well as on either the front cover or on the copyright or credit page of each book. At least four copies of each completed book shall be given to NAVH.

Additional Standards. In addition to these standards, the following suggestions ought to be given serious consideration:

1. If a book is re-typeset or conceived of as a large-print book to begin with, it should be set ragged right to avoid as many words broken over lines as possible.

2. Ideally, the average line of type should contain no more than twelve to fourteen words. This helps the eye to "track back" to the next line most easily.

3. Numerals should be used for all numbers over ten. Research has shown that numerals are more easily read and understood than numbers that are spelled out.

4. Leading (space between lines) is as important as the typeface itself in readability. Most standards recommend leading at least one and a quarter to one and a half times the measurement of the type itself. That is, a 15- to 18-point leading for a 12-point type.

Large-Print Bibles. Because of the difficulty in producing truly large-print editions of the Bible, many publishers do not acknowledge the actual type size of the text in their promotional material, fearing, perhaps, that 10- or 11-point type will not sound like "large print" to those with visual impairments. In any case, the following list is made up largely of those Bibles for which the publishers do acknowledge the type size.

Holy Bible New Living Translation (2000, Tyndale, 12-point type)

Holy Bible: New Revised Standard Version Anglicized Edition, Containing the Old and New Testaments with the Apocryphal/Deuterocanonical Books (2000, Oxford, 12-point type)

KJV Holy Bible, Giant Print Reference Edition (2000, Zondervan, 14-point type)

KJV Giant Print Bible (1991, Nelson, 24-point type)

Life Application Study Bible: New Living Translation (2000, Tyndale, 12-point type)

Nelson Classic Giant Print Center-Column Reference Bible: KJV (1994, Nelson, 13-1/2–point type)

New American Standard Giant Print Bible (1998, Foundation Publications, 14-point type)

NIV Holy Bible Giant Print Reference Edition (1990, Zondervan, 14-point type)

NIV Large Print Reference Bible (1986, Zondervan, 12-point type)

NIV Thinline Bible, Large Print (1996, Zondervan, 10-point type)

Layperson

The terms *layperson* and *laypeople* have generally replaced the older terms *layman* and *laymen* as non-gender-specific terms. This manual recommends using the more traditional term *laity* whenever appropriate, since it refers to both men and women. *Laymen* and *laywomen* are best reserved for those instances when it is important to specify that a group of laypeople consists entirely of members of one sex or the other, as in *the leadership conference was attended by two hundred laywomen.*

Legal Deposit

The term *legal deposit* refers to the legally mandated provision of copies of published books and other material to a national library, such as the Library of Congress. In the United States every publisher is required, as a condition of copyright protection, to provide two copies of every copyrightable work to the Copyright Office of the Library of Congress within three months of publication. This also applies to foreign works that are published in the US by means of either distribution of imported copies or a new edition printed in the US.

For more details, contact the Copyright Office, Library of Congress, 101 Independence Avenue SE, Washington, DC 20559-6000; *www.copyright.gov* (this website also provides a means of searching copyright registrations from 1978 to the present). Phone: Public Information Office (202) 707-3000; Forms and Publications Hotline (202) 707-9100.

Legends, Periods with

See "Period, *With Captions and Legends.*"

Letters of the Alphabet as Words

See "Alphabet: Letters as Words."

Limited Edition, Certificate of

The *certificate of limited edition*, which is also called a *limit notice*, sometimes appears on the copyright page of gift books, deluxe editions, and other finely printed books to indicate that the print run of the edition is limited to a specific number of copies. This can often increase the collector value of such books. It is usually only done for first printings of the first edition, and only when the print run is relatively small (less than 1,000). It has been done for larger print runs, but the labor involved can be prohibitive. The notice often appears on its own page in the front matter, in which case it is called a *limit page*; or the information is included in the colophon at the back of the book.

The phrasing of the limit notice is not standardized but may take either of two general forms. First, the notice may specify how many copies were printed and provide a space or rule for an individual copy number to be written in. It is customary to write the copy number in pencil.

> This edition was printed in a limited edition of [NUMBER OF COPIES IN THE FIRST PRINTING], of which this copy is number [NUMBER OF INDIVIDUAL COPY].

Second, a limit notice may simply specify how many copies of the book were printed. This is more cost-efficient because it saves hours of tedious hand numbering.

> This volume is one of a limited edition of [NUMBER OF COPIES IN THE FIRST PRINTING] copies.

Extra copies of such editions that do not bear a limited edition number are referred to as "out of series."

Lists

See "Outlines and Lists."

LORD and *GOD* (Small-Cap Forms)

Many English versions of the Bible (KJV, RSV, NIV, and TNIV among them) use the cap-and-small-cap forms LORD and GOD to translate the Hebrew *Yahweh* (*YHWH* or *Jehovah*) and the regular lowercase form *Lord* and *God* to translate *Adonai* and other words denoting the deity. This is a useful distinction for Bible readers insofar as *Yahweh* tends to indicate greater personal intimacy on the part of the speaker than *Adonai*, which is a more formal mode of address. The question becomes how strictly to adhere to this distinction when quoting short passages from one of these versions. The following general guidelines should be adapted to the sensibilities and tastes of each publishing house:

In academic materials, Bible studies, works of theology, books of sermons, formal Bible exposition, and any writing that focuses on aspects of the Bible itself, the small-cap LORD and GOD style should be strictly maintained when quoting from a Bible version that uses that style.

In works of a highly popular or informal nature, such as devotionals, popular theology, fiction, biographies, and autobiographies, the small-cap style may be used at the joint discretion of the author and the editor. It does not, however, need to be maintained if there seems to be no compelling reason to adhere to it, since the distinction between LORD and *Lord* is lost on most readers and can even lead to confusion. For instance, many people think that the GOD form is simply used to give the word special emphasis, just as italics or capital letters might do. In such popular works, its presence can be superfluous. Furthermore, many readers mistakenly feel that the small-cap form lends the words more, rather than less, formality.

> When Genesis 2:15 says, "The LORD God took the man and put him in the Garden of Eden," the Hebrew word for "man," *adam*, may in fact be a pun on *adamah*, which means "ground." [academic usage]
>
> As an inveterate gardener, he adopted Genesis 2:15 as his favorite Bible verse: "The Lord God took the man and put him in the Garden of Eden to work it and take care of it." [informal, or popular usage]

If the cap-and-small-cap style is used in a work for a popular audience, a note of explanation should be given on the copyright page:

> In the following pages, the forms LORD and GOD, in quotations from the Bible, represent the Hebrew *Yahweh*, while *Lord* and *God* represent *Adonai*, in accordance with the Bible version used.

Such a notice is not needed in academic works for which the readership is more likely to be familiar with this typographic custom.

Magi

While the Gospels nowhere specify how many magi, who were probably astrologers, came to visit the infant Jesus, three different gifts are mentioned: gold, incense, and myrrh (Matt. 2:11). Out of that fact has grown the unreliable tradition that the magi themselves were three in number, referred to as *the three wise men* or *the three kings*. The term *magi* is the plural of the Latin *magus*, meaning "magician," or "sorcerer."

This manual recommends lowercasing the terms *magi, the three wise men*, and *the three kings* in most references, although they may be capitalized, as appropriate, in the traditional manner in such seasonal literary works as pageants, poetry, sermons, and Christmas stories.

During the Middle Ages, legends grew around these figures, and they even acquired names: (1) Melchior, king of Arabia, who brought gold; (2) Caspar, king of Tarsus, who brought frankincense; and (3) Balthazar, king of Ethiopia (depicted as having dark skin), brought myrrh.

Manuscript Preparation: Author Guidelines

Preparing the Manuscript. A book manuscript prepared for a publisher should be printed on one side only of standard 8-1/2-by-11-inch white paper, double-spaced, with approximately one-inch margins on all sides. Zondervan editors recommend, when possible, that authors use Times New Roman type in a font size of 12 points (what was called "pica" back in the days of the typewriter), a standard that results in approximately 350 words per page and facilitates the estimation of the total pages of the finished book. Colored printer papers, thin papers (such as onion skin), and erasable-bond papers are unacceptable. No staples, binders, or paper clips should be attached to any portion of the manuscript.

The page layout of the electronic version of a manuscript should conform to the same general standards as the paper version outlined in the previous paragraph. Many publishers prefer to receive the author's manuscripts in an electronic form (submitted on a disk or sent online) with or without an accompanying printout. If the contract does not specify a preferred form or format, a call to the editor is in order.

Electronic-only submissions are becoming more common, but formatting inconsistencies can be a problem. In the electronic version, the data should be as free of formatting as possible to allow the publisher to convert the data most easily. Authors should resist the temptation to design and format the manuscript to appear like a printed book. The plainer the better. For details, see *Formatting Conventions* below.

Many publishers require that both a paper copy ("hard copy") and an electronic copy be submitted. This is done for several reasons. While the electronic version is used for producing the book itself (by "capturing the keystrokes," as compositors say), the paper copy is used to make sure that no data has been corrupted or lost in the conversion of data from the author's computer to the publisher's. Sometimes, paragraph breaks, subhead levels, indents, nonroman characters, accents and diacritical marks, italics and other font changes, extracts, footnotes, and other formatting can be lost in the conversion process.

Authors sometimes wonder why the publisher can't simply print out their own paper copy from the submitted disk. The reason is that such a copy would only reproduce any mistakes that might have slipped into the publisher's possibly corrupted version. Clearly, in the not-too-distant future, technology will obviate the need for a hard-copy printout, but at this time they are still a valuable reference.

File System. For ease of conversion, the author's electronic manuscript should be prepared on a file system compatible, if possible, with the publisher's. Compatibility will vary from publisher to publisher, so the author should request an individual publisher's guidelines. Zondervan recommends Macintosh, DOS, or Windows-compatible systems. Saving files in a Rich Text format is required because other formats, such as Text (.txt) or ASCII, eliminate italic and bold characters as well as some formatting when converted to other systems.

One of the most efficient ways for an author to check the compatibility of the publisher's computer system is by using a sample disk. This disk should include at least one text file that contains all the book's elements (title page, part title page, chapter opening page, typical text page, subheads, etc.). This sample should be accompanied by a paper printout so that the compositor or editor can check to make sure that all the elements converted correctly.

Backup disks. The author should keep backup copies of any files sent to a publisher. Ideally, a copy should be kept on the author's computer hard drive as well as on a removable medium, CDR-W or other storage disk, such as a Zip disk.

Single or Multiple Files. Most books can be efficiently converted and edited when included in a single file. If the author's computer does not have the memory to conveniently allow an entire book to be placed on a single file, then the individual chapters of the book, or the other subdivisions, may be relegated to their own files. If the book is split into multiple files, however, a clear file-labeling system should be established. For convenience, a file-labeling convention should identify: (1) the abbreviated title, (2) the correct order of the files, and (3) the chapter or part of the book included in that file. We recommend the following labeling convention: TI00fm (in which TI = title; 00 = file number 00; fm = front matter). Although most systems now accept file names of more than eight characters, this labeling convention is still used as a way of standardizing file names and to encourage both brevity and clarity. Thus, a complete book might look like this:

TI00fm	(title/file number 00/front matter)
TI01ch01	(title/file number 01/chapter one)
TI02ch02	(title/file number 02/chapter two)
TI03ch03	(title/file number 03/chapter three)
TI04ch04	(title/file number 04/chapter four)
TI05ch05	(title/file number 05/chapter five)
TI06ch06	(title/file number 06/chapter six)
TI07ch07	(title/file number 07/chapter seven)
TI08epi	(title/file number 08/epilogue)
TI09rm	(title/file number 09/rear matter, such as an afterword or endnotes)
TI10in	(title/file number 10/index)

Formatting Conventions. As stated before, less formatting is better. The following tips should help:

1. Use the computer's basic word-processing software rather than any desktop-publishing software that might be available. The desktop formatting will only have to be stripped out later by the publisher and could contribute to errors when being converted between systems.
2. If possible, use 12-point Times New Roman as the default typeface.
3. Double space everything—all text, notes, bibliographies, captions, etc.
4. Paginate the manuscript consecutively from beginning to end, which for multiple files may require manually setting a new page number at the beginning of each file.
5. Use the word-wrap feature on the computer; that is, only place a return at the end of a paragraph and after a title or heading.
6. Use the computer's automatic indent function ("indent first line of paragraph" feature), if available, rather than inserting a tab or multiple spaces at the beginning of each paragraph.

7. Do not hyphenate words at the end of a line. Use hyphens only for compound words.

8. Use only one space between sentences or after a colon—not two.

9. Use three pound signs (# # #) to indicate any needed line or section breaks in the text. Though that symbol is likely to change in typesetting, it is the conventional symbol for text breaks in manuscripts.

10. Although other formatting is discouraged, it is best to use the computer's built-in functions for indicating underlined, italicized, and boldfaced text as well as superscripts and subscripts. Assuming that the files are saved in Rich Text format, these elements will not be lost.

11. Type all heads in cap-lowercase. Do not use all caps or boldface type for headings. To differentiate between various levels of headings within the text, either center the A-heads and flush-left the B-heads, or, if there are more than two levels of headings, use braces or parentheses to indicate the level before the heading: {A}, {B}, {C}, etc. If there is more complexity to the hierarchy of subheads than that, it may be best to indicate the levels on a paper printout of the manuscript, using the letters *A*, *B*, *C*, and so on. In any case, a consistent method of distinguishing various levels of subheadings should be used. Since the goal is to make the levels of subheads clear during the conversion of manuscripts from the author's to the publisher's software, it is preferred that the author not use pre-programmed formatting styles, since these can be lost in the conversion process.

12. Footnotes and endnotes should be marked by consecutive reference numbers in the text. Start over again with 1 at the beginning of each chapter if your software allows that. The text of endnotes (notes that appear at the end of the chapters or end of the book) should appear together in an attached notes file linked to the text document. Consult your editor if you are unsure about using footnotes versus endnotes.

13. Put complex tables, charts, and graphs in a separate file, especially if they require any formatting other than standard text. Indicate where each table goes within the text by a consecutive reference such as "TAB2 HERE."

14. Use the tab key rather than the spacebar to align tabular material.

15. If your book has artwork, indicate its placement in the text with a consecutive reference such as "FIG1 HERE." If artwork is stored on a disk, clearly label the disk with the software and hardware used to create the artwork. *Important*: Do not embed artwork into word-processing files. Put all captions in a separate file and number them so that they can easily be paired with the artwork with which they belong. Zondervan prefers Adobe Illustrator, EPS, or TIFF files.

16. Never type an l (el) when a 1 (one) is intended, or vice versa. By the same token, do not interchange 0 (zero) and O (oh).

Preparing Artwork. When the book includes artwork (or any graphic matter reproduced from another source), a clean photocopy of the original should accompany the paper manuscript, and its correct location should be noted in the pages. The author should keep the original on hand until such time as the publisher needs it for scanning (creating a digital file of the image), usually when the first set of proofs are run. In the electronic version of the manuscript, the artwork, if it is already digitized, should be segregated in a separate graphics file and not embedded in the word-processing document along with the written text. Inclusion of graphics files in a word-processing document will increase the likelihood of an inaccurate conversion of the data.

Preparing Tables and Charts. Simple tabular material such as charts and graphs may be inserted directly into the text, whether in the paper or electronic version. If the material is complex or involves nontype elements (such as line art, curved figures, or three-dimensional graph formatting), then it should be placed in a separate file to be inserted later (see previous paragraph on "Preparing Artwork"). If you can easily type the table, graph, or chart using the basic keys on the keyboard (letters, numbers, tabs, symbols), they should be included in the text. Anything more complex than that should be considered art and will need to be freshly created by the compositor, digitally scanned, or submitted in a separate graphics file.

Making Copies. Some publishers, Zondervan among them, require the author to provide two hard (paper) copies of the manuscript, one for editing and the other for review, cost estimate, and design. Other publishers request only one copy clean enough for photocopying; that is, it should be in dark type, with no cut-and-pasted material that might jam a copy machine and with all handwritten additions in black ink (not in pencil or blue ink). In all cases, the author should retain additional copies of both the printout and the electronic file.

Numbering Pages. Pages in both electronic and paper copies should be numbered consecutively throughout the book rather than beginning each chapter with page 1. Numbering may begin with either the body of the book or the front matter. If an author's computer does not allow for the consecutive numbering of all the pages throughout an entire manuscript, the pages should be numbered by hand in the upper right-hand corners of the hard copy. Such page numbers are conventionally circled to distinguish them from other numbers that might appear on the page.

Handling Notes. All notes, whether intended as footnotes, chapter endnotes, or book endnotes, should be grouped together in a separate section, preferably at the end of the manuscript. In most cases, the annotation feature of the major word-processing systems can easily be converted between the author and publisher.

General Matters of Style. The author is responsible for providing a clear and readable manuscript, communicating to the editor all matters of preference (especially when they conflict with the publisher's style) and distinctive features that may require the editor's special attention. General responsibilities for obtaining permission to quote from published sources, the accuracy of quoted material, complete and detailed references, and other such matters are delineated in this manual (see "Bible Permissions, Guidlines for Obtaining"). Before submitting a manuscript, however, the author should be familiar with any additional requirements specified by the publisher.

Quoting from the Bible. The author is responsible for checking the accuracy of all Bible references and the wording of quotations from the Bible before submitting the manuscript to the publisher. The author should also state the predominant Bible version used and indicate in the manuscript whenever a deviation occurs. When no translation is preferred, this manual recommends the *New International Version* as an accurate and accessible modern translation.

Quoting from Other Sources. The author is responsible for checking the accuracy of all quotations taken from other sources. The quotations should be reproduced exactly as they appear in the original source, with no style changes to make it conform with either the author's or the publisher's style. The primary exception to this rule is when antiquated spellings might confuse the reader. In those cases, the modern spelling may be substituted.

In the course of writing and researching, authors should be careful to note the sources for the borrowed material to save having to retrace their steps later. This is especially important if the quote will require a written permission (see "Permissions, Obtaining: Author Guidelines").

Using Greek and Hebrew. Since religious books often contain words and quotations from Greek and Hebrew, whose characters are not found on all word processors, the author is responsible for clearly hand-rendering such characters and any accompanying diacritical marks in their correct positions. Furthermore, since some photocopy machines may blur small handwritten characters, the author should send the hand-rendered original to the publisher and keep the copy. In many cases, transliteration may be preferable. For a list, see "Greek and Hebrew Transliterations."

Avoiding Gender Bias. Authors should strive to eliminate gender bias in their language. Such bias is often unintentional, and much of it rests on the use of anachronistic forms, obsolete terms, stereotyped gender assumptions, and unnecessary labeling. For guidelines and examples, see "Gender-Accurate Language."

Mass (Roman Catholic)

Mass is the liturgical ceremony in the Roman Catholic Church during which the Eucharist is celebrated. There are some fine points to the usage of the word that should be observed. *High Mass* contains singing and is, therefore, referred to as being *sung* not *said*. By contrast, *Low Mass*, which contains no singing, is *said* not *sung*. Both can be referred to as being *celebrated* or *offered*, but it is considered substandard to say that any Mass "took place" or "was held."

The terms *Mass*, *High Mass*, and *Low Mass* are usually capitalized, but they may be lowercased if the context warrants it.

Megachurch

Though often spelled with a hyphen, *megachurch* is most commonly spelled as one word, closed. This neologism can be defined as a large, rapidly growing fellowship of Christian believers, though in some contexts it has pejorative overtones.

Mid-Atlantic Style

Imposing an international standard of English for both the United States and the United Kingdom is idealistic in the extreme. But there are times when it is simply more economical to produce a single version of a book instead of two. The editors of *The Christian Writer's Manual of Style* suggest the following guidelines for what we somewhat jocularly call a *mid-Atlantic style*, which blends aspects of British and American style, if not seamlessly, at least coherently, to achieve a look that will minimize discomfort for readers of both nationalities and for other English-speaking readers around the world.

Mid-Atlantic style, which is also referred to as "world English style," should not be confused with "International English," which is a somewhat stripped down form of basic English, intended for foreign speakers who wish to be as widely understood in all parts of the English-speaking world as possible. International English teaches a broadly understood, basic vocabulary and allows for little regionalism or stylistic flair in either speaking or writing.

It Begins with the Author. By nature, writers universalize their experiences, and the best writers do so across cultures, even when translated into another language. In some cases, more regionally focused authors actually have better luck being understood in foreign translation than in another English-speaking country because a good translator works hard to find dynamic equivalents for all words and phrases that are unfamiliar to the foreign culture, whereas the same word or phrase can mean different things in various English-speaking countries.

When a book is likely to be sold in more than one English-speaking country, an author should be aware of the extent to which his or her own vocabulary, regional dialect, local references, and topical allusions might not be understood. Of course, this also applies to translations into other languages. The more a book is expected to be read abroad, the more the author needs to write for an international readership.

Allusions to television shows, for instance, should either be avoided or carefully explained since such shows differ from country to country and are often short-lived. Often celebrities, companies and corporations, stores, restaurants, and magazines in one country are unknown in another; and some anecdotes and written illustrations can be limited by their geography. For instance, while most Americans would recognize *Stonehenge* and *Westminster Abbey*, most of them would not understand the associations a British reader would have for *Iona* or *Blackpool*. By the same token, British readers who would readily understand references to the *Grand Canyon* and the *White House* might not be familiar with the *Twin Cities* or the *Bible Belt*.

Writers of nonfiction may well find a mid-Atlantic style more congenial than would novelists or poets, who often draw on dialect and regional vocabularies to give their writing color. Understandably, not all writers wish to have mid-Atlantic style thrust upon them. Fortunately for novelists and poets, most readers who pick up a novel or book of poems expect to be transported to another place in their imaginations and adapt easily to regional specificity. So in a sense they may actually be best left in the style of the country in which their book was written and published.

Asking any writer to be sensitive to international issues, however, is really no more burdensome than asking him or her to be sensitive to gender, ethnic, and racial issues in their writing. The obvious disadvantages of writing for a broader English market are usually outweighed by the increased potential for international sales.

It should be the publisher's responsibility to inform an author whenever a book is likely to be distributed in more than one English-speaking country or translated into another language. The following guidelines for a mid-Atlantic style may help.

Vocabulary. Even assuming an author writes for an international readership, specific vocabulary will still pose problems. Many common objects have different names in the British Isles and the United States, and many individual words have different meanings in those countries. Aside from making an effort to avoid the more obscure terms whenever possible, these differences should not be avoided altogether because they give the writing spontaneity and flair.

Therefore, this manual recommends that a book printed in mid-Atlantic English should adhere to the author's own vocabulary wherever possible. Often, more damage is done to the sense of a passage by trying to rewrite around a difficult word than by simply leaving it as it is. In rare cases, a particularly arcane word may be queried by the editor, but by and large, the author's word choice should be honored. While some readers stumble on an odd word or two, most readers quickly learn to interpret the meanings of unfamiliar words in their contexts.

In using this style, editors, copy editors, and proofreaders should not yield to the temptation to supply dynamic equivalents (*elevator* for *lift*, or *diaper* for *nappy*). They should respect the intelligence of readers who, in most cases, will understand a passage in spite of an unfamiliar word or two.

Phrasing, Syntax, Cadence, and Voice. Editors and proofreaders need to be sensitive not only to the author's word choice but to his or her national and personal style as well. Too often editors have an "ideal standard" of English style in their heads, whether British or American, and editing becomes a matter of conforming writers to that style. This is misguided and results in bland writing. Ultimately, if such editors were given enough leeway, their authors' voices would be indistinguishable from each other.

Good editing should allow authors to sound more like themselves—that is, different than anyone else. This allows writers freedom in the way they phrase sentences, order their words, establish a rhythm to their speech, and choose words. Unless an editor is certain that a specific usage is simply wrong in both British and American style and that both kinds of readers are likely to be confused, then that editor should not make the change. This is a good principle for all editing, not just for mid-Atlantic English.

Spelling. Like vocabulary and phrasing, an author's national spelling should be retained. Very few spelling differences between British and American cause problems for readers of mid-Atlantic English; the British *centre* is clearly understood to be *center* by Americans, just as the American *inflection* is understood to be *inflexion* by readers in the UK. Most readers quickly learn to "read over" such alternate spellings without much distraction.

Quotation Marks. The British generally use single quotation marks where Americans use double quotation marks, although some British publishers are now adopting the double quotation mark as their standard. Ultimately, English readers worldwide have no difficulty reading either system, and both are workable.

While the American style actually takes up slightly more space than the British style, this manual recommends US double quotation-mark style as more useful for a mid-Atlantic style, for the following reasons:

First, worldwide, more books are actually published in double-quotation style than in the single. Second, double quotation marks in some form or other are the norm for most other European nations as well as for countries around the world that have adopted those European languages. The French, Italians, and Spanish use the *guillemets*, which look like double angled quotation marks (« »). The Germans use double quotation marks (which curve the opposite direction than American marks), and the open quotation mark is set on the baseline („ “). While these systems are somewhat different than the American style, they are still closer to the American system than the single-quotation style. Finally, Scandinavians use a double-quotation system much like the American system. Most English readers in non-English-speaking countries find the American system closer to their own.

Punctuation with Quotation Marks. The use of punctuation with quotation marks differs in the US and the UK. This manual recommends that the British style of punctuation be used, especially when the readership is likely to be predominantly or at least half British. The British style has a certain inherent logic that makes it effective and easy to remember. If the readership is certainly going to be predominantly American, then the American style could be used. Ultimately, the two systems only differ in a couple instances, so this should not be a major change. See "British Style."

Dashes. We recommend using the British spaced en dash instead of the long em dash. This is less obtrusive, breaks more easily over lines, and is more pleasing to the eye (in our opinion). Many typographers have argued that the em dash draws too much attention to itself and creates a spotting effect on the page. So use the en dash with a word space on either side of it.

Numbering. Because of the enormous difference in vocabulary between British English and American English when it comes to large numbers, we recommend using numerals for *all* numbers above one hundred, including large round numbers. That means, for instance, saying *3,000,000* rather than *3 million*, since the latter term actually means quite a different number in the UK. If the numbers are simply too large to reproduce in all numerals, then a general note that clearly states which style is being used should be provided.

Dates. For books styled in mid-Atlantic English, this manual recommends the British style of spelling out dates (day/month/year, without commas) as the most universally understood worldwide: 28 August 2003.

Abbreviations. Mid-Atlantic style should use the British system of abbreviation, that is, avoiding periods wherever possible, especially when the missing letters are from the interior of a word and not the end (*Dr, Ltd, Mr, Mrs*, and so on).

Footnoting. Either the UK or the US style of footnoting can be employed; that is, beginning with 1 on every new page (UK) or beginning with 1 only at the beginning of every new chapter (US). Neither is more accessible to most readers than the other, so the style of origin should be retained. Using the author's style will also minimize for editors the busywork of converting styles.

Summary. Despite the long explanation above, mid-Atlantic style is basically simple for authors, editors, and proofreaders to grasp, especially those familiar with the main features of both British and American styles. In short, after asking the author to write or revise with an international English readership in mind, the publisher should:

1. Use the author's own style in matters of vocabulary, spelling, phrasing, syntax, footnoting, etc.; query the author when important references seem wholly opaque.
2. Use American style quotation marks.
3. Use British style in matters of dashes (spaced en dashes), punctuation, dates, and abbreviations.
4. Use numerals for all numbers over 100, even large rounded ones.

Misspelled Personal Names, Commonly

Some personal names, many of them common to religious books, especially those that use accents, can cause problems. Note the spellings, alphabetical order, accents, and particles of the following:

Ælfric—note the cap ligature (ash); *Aelfric* also acceptable
Andersen, Arthur—accounting firm; note *-en*
Andersen, Hans Christian—note *-en*
Andrewes, Lancelot—note *-es*
Bartók, Béla—note accents
Bashō, Matsuo—note accent; if accent not available, set simply o
Becket, Thomas à—note grave accent; alphabetized under "Becket" (unlike Thomas à Kempis, who is alphabetized under "Thomas"; see below)
Beckett, Samuel—note *tt*
Berkouwer, Gerrit
Bonhoeffer, Dietrich
Brontë, Charlotte and Emily—note umlaut
Buechner, Frederick
Bustanoby, André—note acute accent
Chardin, Pierre Teilhard de—alphabetized under "Chardin"
Crouch, Andraé—note acute accent
Cummings, E. E.—caps; the poet himself signed it that way, and the E. E. Cummings Society recommends adhering to that usage
de Gasztold, Carmen Bernos—alphabetize under "de Gasztold"
de Gaulle, Charles—alphabetize under "de Gaulle"
de Hueck, Catherine—alphabetize under "de Hueck"

Dostoyevsky, Fyodor—among the variant spellings, this one is preferred by *Webster's Eleventh* and *Webster's Biographical*

Eliot, John—Bible translator; note *l* and *t*

Eliot, T. S.—poet; note *l* and *t*

Elliot, Elisabeth—Christian author; note *ll* and *t*

Elliott, Ramblin' Jack—folksinger; note *ll* and *tt*

Fénelon, François—note acute accent and cedilla

FitzGerald, Edward—English poet (*Rubaiyat of Omar Khayyam*); note cap *G*

Foxe, John—martyrologist; note *-e*, though some old editions spell it *Fox*

Gilliland, Glaphré—note acute accent

Gogh, Vincent van—note lowercase *v*; alphabetized under "Gogh"

Guyon, Madame (Mme.)

Hammarskjöld, Dag—note umlaut

Héloïse—(of Abelard and Héloïse) note acute accent and umlauted *ï*; the *H*, by the way, is silent when pronounced

Jabba the Hutt—of *Stars Wars'* fame; note *tt*

Kierkegaard, Søren—note Danish *ø*

Küng, Hans—note umlaut

LaHaye, Tim and Beverly—note internal cap *H*

Li'l Abner—cartoon character; note position of apostrophe

MacDonald, George—Scottish writer; curiously, *Webster's Eleventh* and *Webster's Biographical* insist on lowercase *d*, but the author himself signed his name with a cap *D* (per Wade Center, Wheaton College, Wheaton, Illinois)

March, Fredric—no final *k*

Milosz, Czeslaw—pronounced *MEE-wosh, CHESS-lauv*

M'Intyre, David M.—*M'* is a contraction of *Mac*. In England the form used to be rendered with an apostrophe (*M'*) but no longer. This Christian writer's name is traditionally given in the contracted form.

Mother Teresa—not *Mother Theresa*

Müller, George—note umlaut; the spelling *Mueller* is also common and acceptable

Niebuhr, Reinhold

Schaeffer, Francis

Selassie, Haile

Ten Boom—with first name, "ten" is lowercased (Corrie ten Boom). As a family name it is capped (the Ten Boom family)

Teresa of Ávila—note acute accent over the capital

Thomas à Kempis—note grave accent; alphabetize under "Thomas" (unlike Thomas à Becket, who is alphabetized under "Becket"; see above)

Tolkien, J. R. R.—this is often mistakenly rendered *Tolkein*; and note space between initials

Truman, Harry S.—US president; although *S* was his full middle name, not an abbreviation, Truman himself put a period after it

Vergil—Roman poet; preferred to *Virgil*

Wesley, Susannah—note spelling of first name

Wycliffe, John—several spellings are common; this is preferred

Misspelled Words, A List of Commonly

In the following list, an asterisk (*) indicates those words that are common in religious works. The underscores show the common problem spots; that is, those letters that are often mistakenly dropped or replaced with other letters.

abscess
accidentally
accommodate
achieve
acknowledgment
algae
allotted
all right
analogous
annihilate
anoint*
archaeology
argument
banister
barbiturate
battalion
beggar
belligerent
bizarre
bouillon
broccoli
burglar
Cadillac
caffeine
calendar
camaraderie
canister
caress
Caribbean
catalyst
cemetery
chauffeur
colonnade
Colosseum, but coliseum (l.c.)
commitment
computer

confetti
connoisseur
consensus
coolly
crystal
deductible
defendant
demagogue
dependent
despicable
diarrhea
dilettante
discipline
dissect
drunkenness
ecstasy
embarrass
entrepreneur
entrust
erratic
eunuch
exalt (lift up)
exhilarate
existence
extension
exult (rejoice)
fluorescent
foreign
foresee
fulfill
fuselage
genealogy
government
grammar
guerrilla
guttural
gynecologist

gypsy
hangar (for airplanes)
harass
hemorrhage
holistic
inadvertent
indispensable
innate
innocuous
inoculate
iridescent
irrelevant
irresistible
judgment (no e)*
liaison
license
lightning
limousine
liquefy
machete
maintenance
manageable
maneuver
mannequin
margarine
marshal
mercenary
millennium*
minuscule
miscellaneous
misspell
mustache
necessary
newsstand
nickel
niece
Noxzema (skin cream)

occasion	principally	sheriff
occurrence	privilege	siege
pallid	proceed	sieve
parallel	prophecy (n.)*	skillful
paraphernalia	prophesy (v.)*	spigot
parishioners*	publicly (*not* -ally)	subpoena
pastime	questionnaire	supersede
perseverance	rarefied	temperamental
pharaoh*	raspberry	timbrel
Philippians*	recommendation	tonsillitis
Philippines	repentance	totally
phlegm	repetition	toxin
picnicking	resistance	tranquillity
pistachio	restaurateur (*no* n)	tyranny
pneumonia	rhythm	vacuum
Portuguese	ridiculous	vengeance
prairie	sacrilegious*	vilify
precede	scurrilous	weird
preferring	seize	wholly
prerogative	separate	yield
presumptuous	sergeant	zephyr

Mount Zion

See *Zion*.

Muhammad

The preferred form of the name of the founder of Islam is *Muhammad*, not *Mohammed* or *Mahomet*. See "Islamic Religious Terminology."

Muslim

The term *Muslim*, which is preferred to the outdated *Moslem* and the even more outdated *Mohammedan* and *Mussulman*, is both a noun, when referring to an individual adherent to the faith, and an adjective. When referring to the religion as a whole, use the noun and adjective forms *Islam* and *Islamic*. See "Islamic Religious Terminology."

New International Version: Bible Style

See "Bible Style: The New International."

Notes

Types of Notes. Textual annotations are of two general types: narrative notes and source notes.

Narrative notes, sometimes called *substantive notes*, are used for any comments that could not be appropriately incorporated into the text itself. They can define words or points, comment or expand on the text, provide explanations, refer the reader to other parts of the text, or provide information peripheral to the text.

> 1. Such was Jeremy Taylor's reputation that he was later referred to as the "Shakespeare of divines."
> 2. *Euphuistic* is used here to refer specifically to the ornate style of Elizabethan prose.

Source notes, also called *bibliographic notes*, inform the reader of the sources of quotations and other borrowed information; they can also refer the reader to works that might be of related interest. The term *source note* is now preferred to *bibliographic note* since sources can be of many types other than books.

> [3]A. C. Cawley, ed., *Everyman and Medieval Miracle Plays* (New York: Dutton, 1959), 79–108.
> [4]See also Leland Ryken, *Triumphs of the Imagination* (Downers Grove, Ill.: InterVarsity Press, 1979), and Walter Kaufmann, ed., *Religion from Tolstoy to Camus* (New York: Harper & Row, 1961).

Of course, narrative notes and source notes, it should be noted, are not mutually exclusive, for a single note can serve both purposes.

> [5]In many of his books Martin E. Marty attempts to get an overview of these tensions in the modern church. Perhaps the most representative of his works to date is Martin E. Marty, *Modern American Religion* (Chicago: Univ. of Chicago Press, 1986).

In Popular and Academic Books. Authors of popular books are encouraged to keep the number of narrative notes to a minimum, since annotations intrude upon the reader's attention and detract from its popular tone. In scholarly works narrative notes are often essential to clarify important and complex information, although when possible, the author should still try to keep the number of notes to a minimum. Source notes, of course, are commonly used in both kinds of books whenever quotations or other information has been borrowed from another source, although the presentation of such notes can differ greatly in each kind of book.

Citing in Text. A note is usually cited by a superscript number in the text next to the sentence or word to which the note refers. Where possible, the superscript number should be placed at the end of a sentence so as not to disrupt the reader's attention. While reference numbers in the text are always set in superscript numerals, the corresponding numerals attached to the note may be set in either superscript with no period or in regular type followed by a period. (Examples of both kinds are found in this section.) Symbol reference marks may be preferred to numerals in some cases (see *Symbol Reference Marks* below).

Footnotes, Chapter Endnotes, and Book Endnotes. Notes commonly appear in one of three places:

1. as footnotes at the bottom of the text pages
2. listed as chapter endnotes at the back of each chapter
3. as book endnotes at the back of the book

The Superscript Number. Whether the notes appear as footnotes, chapter endnotes, or book endnotes, superscript citations in the text should begin over again at 1 in every new chapter (or every page in British style). Superscript numbers should follow all punctuation marks except a dash and should be placed at the end of a sentence or a clause whenever possible. They should be placed at the end of a block quotation, not with the statement that introduces the block quotation. They should never be italicized. The use of symbols instead of numerals should be reserved for bottom-of-text-page footnoting only.

Superscript citation numerals should not be used in a line of display type or after a subheading. If a note applies to an entire chapter, it should be unnumbered and appear on the first page of the chapter as a footnote, whether or not the rest of the book is annotated in a footnote style.

Headings for Book Endnotes. In the endnotes section in the back matter of a book, the number and title of each chapter should appear as a heading for notes from that chapter so that those notes will be easier to locate.

The Hidden Endnote Style for Nonacademic Books. A relatively recent form of endnote, used almost exclusively for source notes, has become popular in the past decade. It is commonly referred to as the *hidden endnote* style and is used particularly in those books in which it is desirable to avoid the academic look of superscript footnote callouts. Hidden endnotes are arranged at the back of the book like ordinary endnotes, but instead of being referenced to superscript numbers in the text, the note itself is headed by the page number and the first word or words of the sentence or phrase to which it refers. Thus, no superscript numbers are given in the text at all. Like an index entry, the hidden endnote makes its own reference by using the page number and an associated word or words. Also like an index, this style of endnoting has to be done at the end of the production process when the pages have all been correctly set and flowed. Any change in pagination, obviously, would cause the page references of the hidden endnotes to shift.

Here are some examples of hidden endnote style:

[page] 33. *"This child is destined . . ."* Luke 2:34.

37. *"O here and now"*: W. H. Auden, *The Collected Poetry*. New York: Penguin Books, 1971, 443–44.

136n. *Muggeridge*. Malcolm Muggeridge, "Books," in *Esquire* (April 1972), 39. [The *n* indicates that the name is referenced in a footnote on that page.]

Footnoting Often Discouraged. Although some academic writers view footnotes as more scholarly than endnotes, many publishers are now discouraging the use of footnotes altogether for two reasons: (1) footnotes often unnecessarily distract the reader from the main argument of the book, and (2) the small type and narrow leading are often unattractive. Endnotes, it may be argued, are more of a distraction in that they force the reader to turn to the back of the book each time a superscript citation appears. But ideally, endnotes should be less distracting, for the reader can simply look up those notes that are of special interest.

Footnotes and Endnotes Together. In some cases, footnotes and endnotes might both be used in the same book. If the narrative notes are so closely related to the text that it is not appropriate to set them as endnotes, they should be set as footnotes. In such cases, the footnotes should be cited in the text by symbol reference marks (*, †, ‡, and so on). The endnotes are cited by superscript citation numbers. In books with few narrative footnotes, symbol reference marks should be used instead of superscript numbers.

Symbol Reference Marks. Symbol reference marks are used in the following sequence only if more than one note appears on a particular page. Otherwise the sequence begins with the asterisk on each new page.

* asterisk or star	§ section mark
† dagger	¶ paragraph mark
‡ double dagger	then the same marks doubled: **, ††, ‡‡, §§, ¶¶

Titles and Degrees of Authors. Titles and degrees are usually not given with author's names in source notes and should be included in narrative notes only if that information is pertinent.

Referencing Books. The following information should normally be included, as appropriate, in a source note that cites a book as the source:

Full name of author(s) or editor(s)
Title and subtitle of book
Full name of editor(s) or translator(s), if any
Name of series, and volume and number in the series
Edition, if other than the first
Number of volumes
Facts of publication: city (and state if city is not well known), publisher, and year of publication (all in parentheses)
Volume number
Page number(s) of the citation

6. Winthrop S. Hudson, *Religion in America,* 2d ed. (New York: Charles Scribner's Sons, 1973), 154.
7. John Calvin, *Institutes of the Christian Religion,* ed. John T. McNeill, 2 vols. (Philadelphia: Westminster, 1960), 2:1016.
8. Ruth A. Tucker and Walter Liefeld, *Daughters of the Church* (Grand Rapids, Mich.: Zondervan, 1987), 100–102.

Including State Names in Sources. For well-known cities, state names need not be used in notes or bibliographies. When in doubt, use the state name with cities.

Using the Shortened Form of the Publisher's Name. Delete such words as *Publisher, Inc., Co., Press,* and *Books.* The words *Press* and *Books* should be retained, however, when a publisher's name might be confused with its parent organization or another institution; for instance, the university presses or such publishers as Moody Press or InterVarsity Press. Also, it is best to use the longer form for university presses, although the article *the* should be dropped and the word *University* may be shortened to *Univ.* Thus, *the University of Chicago Press* could be rendered *Univ. of Chicago Press.*

References to Classical and Scholarly Works. References to classical and some scholarly works appearing in many editions may be designated by division numbers rather than page numbers. This enables citations to be located regardless of the particular edition an author uses. Different levels of division (such as book, section, paragraph, line) are indicated by numerals separated by periods. Commas, en dashes, and semicolons are used for multiple references just as they are in citing page numbers. The numerals are usually arabic. Using division numbers eliminates the need for volume and page numbers, but notes may contain both forms of notation if desired.

9Saint Augustine, *Confessions* 9.23–31. [book 9, sections 23 through 31]

10Eusebius, *The History of the Church* 1.2.15, 18. [book 1, section 2, paragraphs 15 and 18]

11William Langland, *Piers Plowman* 5.136–89; 15.1–49. [canto 5, lines 136 through 189; and canto 15, lines 1 through 49]

12John Calvin, *Institutes of the Christian Religion*, ed. John T. McNeill, 2.1.5. [book 2, chapter 1, paragraph 5]

13*The Didache*, 2.9.1 [part 2, section 9, line 1]

Referencing Periodicals. The following information should normally be included in giving an article from a periodical as the source:

Full name of author(s)
Title
Name of periodical
Volume and issue numbers
Date (in parentheses)
Page number(s)

Note that not all this information is available for every periodical. Popular newspapers and magazines often do not carry volume and issue numbers, and many articles do not carry a by-line. In such cases, as much of the above information as possible should be provided. Some manuals, like *The Chicago Manual of Style*, recommend that the date information of popular magazines be separated with commas rather than parentheses. That style is perfectly acceptable as long as it is consistently applied throughout a work. But since the line between scholarly journals and popular ones is sometimes thin, and since many works contain a mix of both kinds of references, we recommend staying with parentheses in all cases. Note also that a colon precedes page number(s) if volume and/or issue numbers are given; otherwise a comma is used.

14. James Johnson, "Charles G. Finney and a Theology of Revivalism," *Church History* 38 (September 1969): 357.

15. John H. Timmerman, "The Ugly in Art," *Christian Scholar's Review* 7, no. 2–3 (1977): 139.

16. Tom Carson, "Baring the Celtic Soul of U2," *Los Angeles Times Book Review* (March 27, 1988), 15.

17. "Bruce Cockburn: Singer in a Dangerous Time," *Sojourners* 17, no. 1 (January 1988): 28–35.

Referencing Websites. Many different styles of referencing websites have been offered by various organizations and style manuals. This manual recommends a style modified from that proposed by the Modern Language Association, which is also compatible with the general principles laid out in *The Chicago Manual of Style.* We recommend the style outlined below for a number of reasons, not the least of which is that the format generally resembles that already used for books and periodicals. Another reason is that it recommends providing an "access date," that is, the date on which the website itself was referenced. For most websites, the turnover rate for information and content is high, to say nothing of websites that are constantly disappearing while others are being created. Until authors grow more accustomed to referencing sources from the World Wide Web, however, this manual does not recommend an absolute insistence on providing access dates.

The following elements should be included where available or applicable.

Full name of author(s), first name, then last name
Title of page, entry, or article
Title of the larger work of which the entry or article may be a part (in italics)
Version or file number
Publication, posting, or last-revision date
The website's name (in italics)
The website's URL (in italics)
Access date (in parentheses)

18. Cal Thomas, "Have We Settled for Caesar?" *Is the Religious Right Finished? Christianity Online*: *www.christianity.net/ct/current/* (September 21, 1999).
19. John Bunyan, "The Author's Apology for His Book," *The Pilgrim's Progress.* Last updated May 27, 1999. *Christian Classics Ethereal Library*: *ccel.wheaton.edu* (August 4, 1999).

Referencing Software. Annotating works that are included on such software sources as CD-ROMs, floppy disks, and DVDs should generally be handled like ordinary book and periodical references. This is sometimes complicated because such materials often contain the equivalent of many different books. This situation also occurs in the print world and should be handled the same way, that is, by first referencing the work-within-the-larger-work and then referencing the larger work itself. See example, note 20, below.

Also, due to a lack of formatting standards, works included on many software sources, such as floppy disks, CD-ROMs, and DVDs, do not include page numbers. There have been calls in the academic community to impose standards so that all software includes page numbers. This urge, however, seems to be imposing the book paradigm on newer media, and it ignores the fact that most software compensates for its lack of page numbers by having some sort of search function so that individual words and phrases can be easily found. Even lacking this, most computers on which such software is viewed have their own search functions.

Ultimately, referencing software is not all that much different than referencing books or periodicals and need not be complicated. Simply include the following elements as appropriate.

Full name of author(s) or editor(s) (if known)
Title and subtitle of software package
Full name of editor(s) or translator(s)
Name of the software series, and volume and number in the series
Edition, if other than the first
Number of volumes
Facts of publication: city (and state if city is not well known), publisher, and
    year of publication (all in parentheses)
Volume number
Page number(s) of the citation (if known)

20. Matthew Henry, *Matthew Henry's Commentary on the Whole Bible* (1706–21), in *The Zondervan Bible Study Library: Scholar's Edition* CD-ROM, version 5.01.0025 (Grand Rapids, Mich.: Zondervan, 2002).
21. *Artsource 3.0: CD-ROM Clip Art Library* (Grand Rapids, Mich.: Zondervan, 2002).

The Use of Ibid." For both book and periodical references, *Ibid.* takes the place of the author's name, the title, and page number when all of that information is identical to the information in the immediately preceding note. If the author and title are the same but the page reference has changed, "Ibid." may be used with the new page reference. For books intended for a general or popular readership, authors are encouraged to use repeated short-form references instead of "Ibid." (See next paragraph for the proper elements of a short-form reference.) "Ibid." is most appropriately used in academic and scholarly books that contain a large number of citations.

[22] Nicholas Wolterstorff, *Art in Action* (Grand Rapids, Mich.: Eerdmans, 1980), 45.
[23] Ibid., 47.
[24] Ibid.

Note that "Ibid." is not italicized in notes.

Using Short-Form References. When a second reference occurs later than immediately following the first reference (in which case "Ibid." would not apply), a short-form reference should be used in both scholarly and popular works. This is preferred over the older system of using "op. cit." or "loc. cit." A short-form reference should include the author's last name, a shortened form of the title (if it is more than five words) that is sufficient to identify the book cited previously in a full note, and a page reference.

25. James Samuel Preus, *From Shadow to Promise: Old Testament Interpretation from Augustine to Young Luther* (Cambridge, Mass.: Belknap, 1969), 50.
26. Wolterstorff, *Art in Action*, 97.
27. Preus, *From Shadow to Promise*, 58.

Using Page Citations for Books and Periodicals. Whenever possible, exact page references should be given in lieu of using a single page number followed by *ff*. Such abbreviations as *vol.* and *p.* or *pp.* are unnecessary unless their omission will result in ambiguity.

State Abbreviations in Source Notes. Abbreviations of states in notes or bibliographies should be given in conventional form with a period. Two-letter postal forms should be reserved for actual mailing addresses. (See "Abbreviations; *States, Territories, Provinces, and Countries.*")

Numbers, Inclusive (Elision)

To indicate that an entire range of numbers is being referred to, an unspaced en dash is used between the numbers. These are called *inclusive numbers*. The second number may be elided (shortened) in many combinations, especially in year numerals and page references. Since the rules of elision are difficult to describe, the following examples should make them easier to grasp.

For date references:
2000–2004 [do not elide when first number ends in 00]
2000–2011 [do not elide when first number ends in 00]
1904–8
1905–13
1910–14
1914–18
1897–1901 [do not elide when century changes]
AD 374–79
379–374 BC [do not elide when used with BC]

For page numbers and bibliographic references:
2–3
22–23 [not 22–3]
100–107 [do not elide when first number ends in 00]
100–119 [do not elide when first number ends in 00]
101–5
110–25
151–58
1,081–87
12,483–515

Note, however, that numbers given in book titles should generally not be ellided. For instance: *The Collected Poems of T. S. Eliot, 1909–1962.*

Numbers: Spelling Out Versus Using Numerals

General Rule. Spell out numbers under one hundred and round numbers in hundreds, thousands, millions, billions, etc. Extremely large round numbers may be expressed in figures and units of millions or billions. Numerals should be used for all other numbers.

thirty-four	two million	2.4 billion	thirty-two thousand
fifteen hundred	1,876	195	385,000

Ordinal Numbers. The general rules for spelling out numbers versus using numerals also applies to ordinal numbers. In notes, tabular matter, and a few traditional expressions, a combination of numeral and suffix is used, without periods. There are a few situations in which numerals have become customary for ordinal numbers, for instance, in degrees or latitude. The correct numerical forms of the ordinal numbers are: 1st, 2nd, 3rd, 4th, 5th, 6th, 7th, 8th, 9th, 10th, and so on.

tenth grade 38th parallel
twenty-first century   *Words into Type*, third edition

He was the fifteenth person to receive the award.
He was the 115th person to receive the award.

Percentages. Numerals should be used with percentages regardless of the context. For most purposes, the word *percent* should be used with the numeral rather than the percent symbol (%), but in technical, statistical, or frequent usage, the % symbol should be used. Note that when the symbol is used, a word space should not be placed between the numeral and the symbol.

He graduated in the top 10 percent of his class. [common use]
Recent polls show that only 10% of the people polled favor the new policy. [technical, statistical, or frequent use]

Idioms and Common Expressions with Numbers. A handful of idiomatic expressions using numbers have gained currency. It is not always possible to formulate rules for such expressions, but the following list offers a few of the most common.

Fourth of July holiday, the Fourth
hundred-and-fifty percent, to give a (to work exceptionally hard; spell it out)
million, to look like a
9/11 attacks (spoken as "nine-eleven"), *or* the events of September 11

nine-to-five job, to work nine-to-five
twenty-four/seven (meaning night and day, seven days a week; also *24/7* in
informal contexts)

Measurements. To indicate dimensions, numbers are spelled out or set as numerals according to the context. The symbol × or the letter *x* may replace the word "by" in technical works but is discouraged in nontechnical writing.

three-by-five card *or* 3 x 5 card
8-¹/₂-by-11-inch paper

Parts of a Book. Use numerals for numbers referring to parts of a book. This is one of the more common exceptions to the rule that recommends spelling out words under one hundred.

The author makes three points in chapter 6, as indicated in table 3 on page 97.

The Beginning of a Sentence. A number should be spelled out at the beginning of a sentence. If this is cumbersome, rewrite the sentence so that it does not begin with the number.

Nineteen seventy-eight marked the five-hundredth anniversary of the birth of
Sir Thomas More.
The five-hundredth anniversary of the birth of Sir Thomas More was observed
in 1978.

Dialogue. Except for year dates, most numbers should be spelled out in dialogue. Numerals may also be used in specific cases in which numbers are so large that it would be impractical to spell them out.

"On October thirty-first, 1517," said the tour guide, "more than four hundred
and fifty years ago, Luther affixed his Ninety-five Theses to this very door."

Money. Monetary references should be spelled out or set in numerals according to the general rules for numbers given above. If many dollar amounts are given in close context, they should be set as numerals. When fractional and whole dollar amounts appear in close proximity to each other, zeroes should be placed after the decimals in the whole dollar amounts for consistency.

Hundreds paid twenty dollars each to hear Steven Curtis Chapman in person.
The deacons collected a total of $413.
The agent received $9.50, $22.00, and $28.00 for the three sales.

Age. Numbers indicating ages of persons should always be spelled out. Also note the correct hyphenation of the following forms.

the five-year-olds
a twenty-five-year-old woman
he was sixty years old
she lived to be one hundred and eleven

Groups of Numbers. If several numbers are given for several items in one general group, all the numbers should be handled in the same way. If the largest contains three or more digits, use figures for all.

With a choir of fifty people and a worship committee of more than thirty, why can we get only two people to take care of infants on Sunday?

There are 14 graduate students in the religion department, 61 in the classics department, and 93 in the romance languages, making a total of 168 in the three departments.

Street Addresses. In formal writing, streets that bear a number as the name should be spelled out. But house numbers or other numbers used in street addresses should always be given in figures.

Fifth Avenue   21 Forty-second Street
Fifty-second Street   221b Baker Street

Route Numbers. In both formal and informal writing, road and highway route numbers should always be shown in numerals.

Highway 61   M-21
Interstate 75, *or* I-75   Route 66

Numerals, Commas with

Always use the comma in numbers of four or more digits.

31,928   1,000   9,500
1,476   9,000   5,000,000

O and *Oh*

Most editors and writers know the difference between what's called "the vocative O" and the exclamation "oh." O, we are told, should be used when addressing people or invoking a deity (*O citizens of Rome, O Lord*) and *oh* reserved for expressions of surprise or sudden emotion (*Oh! you startled me!*). Caution should be used, however, because the vocative O, which suggests oratory, is rapidly disappearing. First, it has acquired something of a melodramatic and antiquated feeling in modern writing and is therefore largely used for humor or satire. Second, and perhaps more tellingly, it is used so little that many writers and readers simply mistake it for *oh*, that is, as an expression of heightened emotion, so that its vocative sense is lost. Some Bible translations, such as the TNIV, have altogether eliminated the use of the vocative O for these reasons.

Use *O*, of course, in any direct quotation, but otherwise use it cautiously. Stick with *oh*, which still communicates its intended meaning unambiguously.

Okay Versus *OK*

An arcane controversy that has generated furious debate among editors and grammarians is the question of which is correct: *OK, O.K.,* or *okay?*

As a general rule, this manual advises writers to use *okay* in text and dialogue. This stems largely from the fact that the so-called inflected forms of the spelled-out style are generally more accessible and less of an eyesore to most readers: *okayed, okaying, okays*. Few readers like the looks of *OKed, OKing,* or *OKs*. If the abbreviation is used, however, do not use periods.

The inimitable H. L. Mencken once referred to *okay* as "the most successful of all Americanisms."

Old Style and New Style Systems of Dating

See "Time and Dates, *Old Style and New Style.*"

-Ology

The suffix -ology, of course, means the "study of." The following list shows some of the common "-ologies" in the field of religion.

angelology—the study of angels and their theological implications

Christology—the study of the person and work of Christ

demonology—the study of demons and evil spirits

ecclesiology—the study of church architecture and ornament; also the study of church history

eschatology—the study of theories of how the world will end, the end times

hagiology—the study of saints' lives

hamartiology—the study of doctrines regarding sin

heortology—the study of the history and significance of holidays, festivals, and seasons of the church calendar

hymnology—the study of church hymns

martyrology—the study of martyrs and their sufferings

numerology—the study of numbers; often applied to the study of numbers in the Bible

pneumatology—the study of the doctrines regarding the person and work of the Holy Spirit

soteriology—the study of the doctrines of salvation, especially in regards to Christ's role in salvation

teleology—the study of first causes, especially arguments for the existence of God based on scientific observation

theology—the study of God and God's interactions with humans

typology—the study of types and symbols, especially as they relate to the Bible.

Orphans

See "Widows and Orphans."

Orthodox Versus Eastern Orthodox

See "Eastern Orthodox Versus Orthodox."

Outlines and Lists

An outline can help explain and organize information systematically and hierarchically so that it is most clearly understood by the reader. A list is nothing more than a simple, one-level outline.

Two major systems of multilevel outlining are recommended: the *traditional system* and the *decimal system*.

The Traditional System. This system is appropriate for short, informal outlines that might appear in popular or trade books. It is the one most readers are familiar with since primary-school days. Such outlines should follow this format:

I. C. S. Lewis [capital roman numeral with period]
    A. Writings [capital letter with period]
        1. Fiction [arabic numeral with period]
            a. The *Narnia* books [lowercase letter with period]
                (1) *The Lion, the Witch and the Wardrobe* [arabic numeral in parentheses]
                    (*a*) Characters [lowercase italic letter in parentheses]
                    (i) Aslan [lowercase roman numeral in parentheses]

The Decimal System. The decimal system is so-called because it uses a period between numbers, although the periods don't really function as true decimal points. They merely separate the levels of information. Decimal style is best used in formal presentations in which a very strict hierarchy needs to be understood, for instance, in scholarly, reference, and textbook settings. That said, the decimal system is most accessible when it does not go beyond two or three levels, since the multiplication of levels can be quite confusing (of course, the traditional system can be confusing as well). A decimal outline should follow this pattern:

1. C. S. Lewis
    1.1 Writings
        1.1.1. Fiction
            1.1.1.1. The *Narnia* books
                1.1.1.1.1. *The Lion, the Witch and the Wardrobe*
                    1.1.1.1.1.1. Characters
                        1.1.1.1.1.1.1. Aslan

Runover Lines. Runover lines in both numerical lists and outlines should begin under the first letter of the first word in the previous line.

1. Gregory contributes his support and energies to the formation of the papal states.
2. Gregory becomes a leading advocate of the missionary work in England.
3. Taken as a whole, Gregory's writings earn him the status of "Doctor of the Church."
    a. *The Book of Morals* is his most extensive commentary.
    b. To this day, his *Dialogues* continues to be considered his most influential work.

At Least Two Points. Each level of an outline must have at least two points.

Informal Outlines. In popular books where outlining is minimal, less formal, or not carried beyond the third level, it is acceptable to begin the outline with A. or 1., rather than the roman numeral. Of course, in single-level lists, only the arabic numbers (*1, 2, 3,* etc.) should be used.

Unnumbered Lists. Authors and editors sometimes feel that numbering the items in a list gives them legitimacy, but usually typographic bullets (•) or other graphic symbols can be used just as effectively to separate the items. Use numbers only when there is a specific reason to do so. (See also "Parentheses, *Numbered Lists.*")

Papers for Printing

Common Types. Several different kinds of paper are commonly used for printing:

Antique—A kind of rough-textured book paper that is usually used in high-quality letterpress printing. *Eggshell* is a smooth variety, and *vellum* is smoother. If the paper is *laid,* it was made on a fine wire screen, which left almost imperceptible lines on the paper. Otherwise, it is referred to as *wove.*

Bond—The paper most often used for stationery. It absorbs ink well because it is usually made with a high percentage of cotton-rag fibers, usually 25 to 50 percent.

Book paper—Standard book paper comes in many weights and in either smooth or antique (rough) finishes. It is the paper predominately used for the pages of books. It is made to rigid specifications so that thickness (pages per inch) can be accurately measured.

Coated paper—Often used in high-quality printing (aside from books), it is coated with chemical or clay surfactants so that the paper is more opaque and brighter. It may be gloss coated, dull coated, or machine finished (very smooth). Because the ink does not absorb, it is ideal for high-quality color printing.

Cover—Any of a variety of stiff, durable papers, either coated or uncoated, which are used for book covers.

Index paper—Index paper, which comes in either vellum or smooth finish, is less expensive than cover stock and is used for cards and inserts.

Newsprint—Used largely for newspapers. Made from ground wood pulp, it is sometimes called *groundwood paper.* Its advantage is its low cost, which is counterbalanced by its specked, off-white color, high absorbency, and impermanence.

Offset paper—This printing paper is specially "sized" (coated) to resist the tackiness of inks and the moisture involved in the offset printing process.

Uncoated—Uncoated paper is commonly used in printing. Whether sized or unsized, it is very smooth and can be made in a wide variety of textures and colors.

Untrimmed Fore Edge. Sometimes the outside edge of a book, called the *fore edge,* is left untrimmed, especially for some gift books and even, occasionally, for large books of high literary or academic pretension. This is intended to give the book an elegant, handmade feel, although it occasionally happens that some readers believe such rough edges are an error in the manufacturing process. If an untrimmed-edge effect is desired, check with the printer to see if they can achieve an irregular trim, avoiding the same pattern of peaks and valleys in the edges of the paper.

Deckle. A *deckled edge* is the feathery edge of a piece of handmade paper. A deckled edge is sometimes included when the fore edge is left untrimmed. This gives the book an even more handmade feel. Since most papers are machine made and therefore do not have a true deckled edge, printers sometimes simulate the deckle by folding and tearing the paper, giving a similar feathery edge to the page.

Parachurch

While the word *parachurch*, which should be lowercased, has yet to appear in most of the major dictionaries, it is in common use among church-going people in the United States and England. Most commonly the word is used as an adjective, as in *a parachurch organization*, but it is also used as a noun, as in *the ministries of the nation's parachurches.*

A parachurch is a religious-based organization, usually independent of traditional denominations, that was created to involve Christians in ministry, often a ministry that is beyond the scope of individual churches and denominations. Usually, parachurches are founded to achieve a very specific goal, such as providing wheelchairs to Third World countries or funding local food programs.

They have their roots in the early nineteenth century when groups of Christians would band together interdenomenationally for a specific purpose, such as to promote moral reform (as in the various abolition and temperance leagues), to print tracts, or to fund missionary endeavors.

Paragraphing Dialogue

When writing dialogue in both fiction and nonfiction, it is customary to set each speaker's words as a new indented paragraph. A possibly apocryphal story says that this custom was devised by the French novelist Balzac. Before his time, apparently, dialogue was commonly run into a single paragraph according to general subject and theme like any other paragraph. But Balzac, who wrote serialized novels for periodicals and was paid by the line, realized he could make more money by beginning a new paragraph each time the speaker changed.

Although it may violate our sense of editorial propriety, there are occasionally good reasons to run dialogue into a single paragraph. In some cases, it may be unavoidable because of the structure of the sentence. There is no reason, for instance, why a writer should not be able to write something like this:

> When Polyphemus asked, "Who are you?" Odysseus replied, "Nobody," and when the other cyclopes later asked Polyphemus, "Who was it who blinded you?" Polyphemus replied, "Nobody."

A writer may also run dialogue into a single paragraph to communicate a sense of hurry, humor, or repetition.

"Are you sure?" "Yes." "Absolutely?" "Yes." "Beyond a doubt?" "Yes." "Yes?" "Yes!"

Finally, it is common in children's picture books and books for beginning readers to make no distinction between paragraphs at all, so that all dialogue is run together. By and large, children's writers and editors feel that paragraphing, as a typographic device, is lost on young readers. To avoid confusion, the *said references* in such books need to be carefully managed to make clear who is speaking.

The disadvantage of running dialogue together is that it may confuse readers accustomed to the traditional method. But if it can be done to effect with no loss of clarity, then it is a legitimate, and often necessary, device. The paragraphing of dialogue is no different than any other rule of grammar and style: if there's a good reason to break it, do so. "Really?" "Yes!" (See also "Said References.")

Parentheses

Parenthetical Thought. Parentheses may be used to expand, comment on, explain, or define a point, or may be used to make an aside, whether or not it is closely related to the first part of the sentence. While commas and dashes can also be used to set apart parenthetical statements, commas are best used when an extremely close affinity exists between the inserted element and the rest of the sentence. Dashes that enclose a parenthetical idea, on the other hand, convey a heightened sense of energy, urgency, interruption, or immediacy.

> William of Ockham (remembered in the principle of "Ockham's Razor") left Avignon in 1328.
>
> Lancelot Andrewes, who was said to have kept Christmas all the year, was noted for his hospitality.
>
> For only love—which means humility—can cast out the fear which is the root of all war.—Thomas Merton

Numbered Lists. When lists are run into the text, parentheses are used around the numbers or letters. Do not use just one: 1), 2), 3), etc.

> Historians are usually careful to distinguish between (1) Macarius Magnes, (2) Macarius of Alexandria, and (3) Macarius of Egypt.

With Other Punctuation. Periods, question marks, and exclamation points should be placed outside a closing parenthesis when the parenthetical statement is inserted into a larger sentence, although a question mark or exclamation point should be placed inside the closing parenthesis when it is part of the parenthetical statement itself.

Periods, question marks, and exclamation points should be placed inside the closing parenthesis when the entire sentence is enclosed in parentheses.

> Elizabeth Fry's activities reflected the many social concerns of her time (such as slavery, missions among the Indians, and the poor).
>
> Dorothy Sayers published her first detective novel (could she have guessed how popular they would become?) just after establishing her teaching career.
>
> The Ephesus that Paul knew was the major trade center in the Roman province of Asia. (By AD 950 it had become a ghost town.)

With Font Changes. Parentheses should be set in the same font as the main text and not necessarily in the font of the material contained within the parentheses. Ordinarily this means that parentheses should be set in roman type unless they are used in an italicized title, heading, or display line or in a text sentence that is entirely italicized.

> Her memoir (*The Sculptor's Daughter*) recounts her life as the daughter of two artistically gifted parents. [parentheses in roman]
>
> The Latin form (*sacire*) ultimately comes from a Hittite word, meaning "to make sacred." [parentheses in roman]
>
> The title of the book was *How to Make (and Lose) a Million.* [Parentheses in italics as part of title]
>
> *Once again (for the twenty-fifth time!) the Curse of the Bambino had worked its ill luck this season.* [parentheses in italics as part of italicized sentence]

With Bible References. When a parenthetical Scripture reference immediately follows a Scripture quotation, place any needed punctuation after the parenthetical reference. If the quotation itself requires a question mark or exclamation point, it should be placed with the text regardless of what punctuation follows the parenthesis.

> "Jesus wept" (John 11:35), the shortest verse in Scripture, is often quoted out of context.
>
> "In the beginning God created the heavens and the earth. Now the earth was formless and empty" (Gen. 1:1–2).
>
> "Lord, are you going to wash my feet?" (John 13:6).

Particles with Proper Names

See "Capitalization, *Particles with Proper Names.*"

Performance Symbol

The *performance symbol* ℗ is sometimes called the "p-in-the-circle" symbol. This symbol is used to copyright sound recordings—mostly audio recordings, in the case of books.

The performance symbol does not serve as a copyright notice for any of the printed matter that accompanies the recording. A copyright symbol with a complete copyright notice should be provided to protect any printed matter that accompanies a sound recording, though, conversely, it should be understood that the © symbol does not protect the recording itself. For a more complete discussion of how the performance symbol is used, see William S. Strong's *The Copyright Book* (Cambridge, Mass.: MIT Press, 5th edition, 1999).

Period

As an End Stop. The period most commonly indicates the end of a declarative or imperative sentence.

With Initials and Abbreviations. The period is often used for initials and abbreviations, although some abbreviations do not use periods. (See "Abbreviations.")

J. I. Packer	BCP	OT
M.Div.	1 Thess.	FDR

With Numbers in Vertical Lists. When items are listed vertically, a period should follow the numbers or letters.

1. Susannah Wesley
2. Hannah More
3. Phoebe Palmer

With Vertical Lists of Sentences. In a vertical list, a period is used after each item only if at least one of the items is a complete sentence.

Among Whitefield's favorite themes were the following:
1. The boundlessness of God's love.
2. Man's misery without God.
3. Repentance is necessary for salvation.

With Captions and Legends. With photo captions and other descriptive copy attached to charts or graphic illustrations, a period is used only when such copy forms a complete sentence.

Illustration: Thomas Cromwell
Table 1: This chart traces the evolution of the reprints of the King James Version.

When Not to Use a Period. No period should follow titles, running heads, display type, bylines, chapter heads, or subheads that are set off from the text. When a sublevel head is run into the text, however, it should be followed by a period.

Permissions, Author Guidelines for Obtaining

General Procedures for Obtaining Permissions.* Under most contracts, it is the author's responsibility to obtain all permissions to reprint materials taken from other sources. (For Zondervan authors, this includes material taken from books published by Zondervan and its parent company, HarperCollins). The author should write for such permissions as soon as he or she decides to use any copyrighted material in the book. If the author waits too long and permissions are denied, the author may have to scramble at the last minute to find suitable substitutes, or the book's release date may have to be delayed until the permissions are granted. Also, if the permission fee required by the copyright owner is too high, the author may wish to delete or substitute other material. The author is also responsible for including full credit information in the manuscript whenever credit is required as a condition of the permission license.

A request for permission is not a commitment to use or pay for the material. If, after permission has been granted, the author decides not to use a given passage, it is a simple matter to inform the copyright holder, as a courtesy, that the material will not be used. The author need not pay for the permission until it is certain that the quote will actually be contained in the book, that is, after the editing stage.

If, as occasionally happens, the publisher's address is not given in the book from which the author is quoting, such references as *The Writer's Market* and *The Literary Market Place*, available at most libraries, are excellent resources for finding publishers' addresses for permission purposes. In some cases, the Internet may be a valuable tool in tracking down a specific publisher's address.

* The guidelines given in this section on "Obtaining Permissions" outline the internal editorial policies of Zondervan and are solely for the information of authors under contract with Zondervan. This information does not purport to give definitive legal advice and should not be relied upon by authors for that purpose. Zondervan's right in its sole discretion to decide which materials require permission in a given case is in no way limited by this "Obtaining Permissions" outline. Other publishers may have different guidelines, and the information given in this manual should not be referred to in connection with any book that a Zondervan author may be writing for another publisher. Zondervan's authors make certain representations and warranties regarding the content of their books and agree to indemnify Zondervan against certain claims relating to such content. Nothing in this section is intended to modify those obligations of the author or to reduce or restrict the rights and remedies available to Zondervan under its publishing agreements with authors.

Writers should be aware that the same need to obtain permissions also applies to information quoted or copied from an Internet source. The fact that a quotation has appeared on the Internet does not imply that it is in the public domain and can be quoted without obtaining a permission or paying a fee. Also note that frequent or extended use of passages from modern Bible versions or translations generally requires permission.

When writing for permission to quote from a printed source, the author should provide the publisher of the quoted material the following information:

1. The title and author(s) of the work from which the quote will be taken
2. A description or copy of the material to be quoted, along with an explanation of how the quotation will be used (a copy of the relevant page might be included)
3. An approximate total of the number of words to be quoted
4. The title and author(s) of the work in which the quote will be used
5. The projected publication date
6. The projected number of copies in the first print run
7. The projected retail price
8. A one-sentence synopsis of the work's subject

If the author has any difficulty finding any of the above information, the book's editor can usually help.

The author is responsible for rendering the borrowed material exactly as it appeared in the original, with no reworking of the spelling, punctuation, grammar, or general style. Occasionally, in works from the public domain, antiquated spelling, syntax, grammar, and punctuation may be modernized, although a declaration of such modernization, either as a footnote or as a general note on the copyright page, should be provided as a courtesy to the reader.

Public Domain. In 1976 Congress passed a new Copyright Act, which took effect on January 1, 1978. The new law recognized two different methods of measuring the duration of a copyright, depending on when the work was first published. In general, works first published in or before 1922 are now in the public domain, and no permission is required to reproduce them in the United States. Works first published in or after 1923 are protected for ninety-five years from the date of their initial publication. Works created and published after January 1, 1978, are copyrighted for the life of the author plus seventy years.

In addition, scientific and historical facts, general ideas and concepts, titles, names, short phrases and slogans, and most US government publications are also considered to be in the public domain. Written permission must be obtained to copy or closely paraphrase all copyrighted material unless the privilege of "fair use" can be invoked (see below).

Ownership of Copyrighted Material. Bear in mind that for a permission to be valid, it must be granted by the copyright owner, who controls the rights to the use the author wishes to make of the material. As a general rule, the author or original creator of the material is considered the copyright owner and usually holds the permission rights unless those rights have been assigned to another individual or entity (usually the publisher). The addressee of a letter or the owner of a photo negative or print does not necessarily control the copyright, even though he or she may possess the only available copy of that work. Authors should be sure to secure permission from the proper party.

Fair Use. In certain circumstances, the copyright law permits authors to use small amounts of copyrighted material without permission from the copyright owner. The fair use privilege is intended primarily for purposes of criticism, comment, news reporting, teaching, scholarship, and research.

There are no hard-and-fast rules that govern the application of fair use, since each instance has its own peculiar set of facts that must all be weighed in determining whether a use is a "fair use." Such a determination is made by taking into account the following factors:

1. The length of the quoted passage in relation to the length of the copyrighted work from which it is taken (not in relation to the work in which it is used by the borrowing author).
2. The qualitative significance of the passage in relation to the copyrighted work as a whole; that is, is the passage the "heart" of the copyrighted work or merely an incidental or minor segment?
3. The manner in which the borrowed passage is used: Is the passage used in an illustrative, critical, or instructive context? Or is the passage used merely in a gratuitous manner to spare the author the burden of creating his or her own original expression for the thought and ideas conveyed by the borrowed passage? Is the passage quoted within the text of the book for purposes of comment or criticism, or is it used as a window dressing, primarily to enliven the new piece of writing?
4. The nature of the copyrighted work from which the passage is taken: Is it a published or unpublished source? (The scope of the fair-use privilege is significantly reduced for unpublished works.) Is the passage factual and mostly informative in content, or is it more expressive and fanciful, more "literary"?
5. The effect of the use of the material on the potential market for the copyrighted work, including the market for granting rights and permissions to use the copyrighted work.

Although there are no easy formulas for analyzing the above factors and applying them to a given set of facts, in general, an author will usually have to obtain permission for the following uses of copyrighted material:

1. Prose quotations or the close paraphrasing of 300 words or more from any full-length book (either a single citation or the total of several shorter quotations from a single work);
2. Prose quotations or the close paraphrasing of 100 words or more from a short article or periodical piece;
3. More than 300 words from a full-length play or 100 words from a one-act play;
4. One or more lines of a poem, unless it is of epic proportion, in which case more lines may be used depending on their qualitative and quantitative relationship to the entire copyrighted work;
5. One or more lines from a song;
6. All photographs and illustrations (including cartoons);
7. Any table, diagram, or map that is copied or closely adapted;
8. More than a single line or two from any unpublished letter, memo, diary, manuscript, or other personal document. (Always bear in mind that the guidelines for unpublished material are much more restrictive than that for published material.)

If the author has any doubts about whether material used in a manuscript is properly considered fair use, he or she should be sure to advise the project's editor so the publisher's legal counsel can be consulted.

Finally, it is important to remember that although one need not obtain permission for fair-use material, credit should be attributed to the source of any quoted or closely paraphrased passage.

Quotations within Cited Material. In reprinting articles or long portions of a book (such as material in an anthology or a compilation), it is easy to overlook internal quotations from other sources. If reprinted material has been taken from another original source and it requires permission according to guidelines outlined here, the compiler or author must obtain separate permission for that material. This rule applies even to public domain material that contains copyrighted material within it. Thus, an author may need several permissions to reprint one passage or article.

Territories. Whenever the publishing house that plans to publish the author's book controls world rights to the book and plans to exploit any rights outside of the United States and Canada, permissions should be cleared for use throughout the world. If the author's publisher will not be exploiting the work beyond North America, permissions may be cleared for the United States and Canada only.

No Reply. If the author receives no reply within a reasonable period of time (usually about three weeks) from the publisher from whom he or she is seeking permission, a second request should be sent by registered mail, return receipt requested. If after several weeks the request is still outstanding, the author should try to call the publisher by phone. In some cases, the publisher will give a verbal permission over the phone and will tell the author the proper credit line to use. This may be acceptable, provided the author provides his or her publisher written confirmation of the permission granted within a short period of time after the phone call. If, despite the author's best efforts, permission still is not granted, the material should not be used without further advice from the legal department of the company publishing the author's book. In summary, "no reply" does not translate into a grant of permission.

Credit Lines and Source Notes. In the manuscript, the author must use the precise wording for the credit line as provided by the copyright holder as part of the grant of permission. If no wording is specified, include in a source note or on a permissions page the following information: author, book or article title, publisher or publication source, a copyright notice for the publication, and the notation "Reprinted by permission." The author should remember that he or she may also need to provide a proper source note for material that constitutes fair use even though permission did not need to be obtained.

Keeping Permissions Records. When permissions are complete, the author should send either copies or original records and correspondence to the editor with the final manuscript. The author should always keep a copy of the complete file for his or her own records.

The Publisher. The publisher is responsible for applying and securing proper copyright for new publications, and the publisher usually also retains the privilege of granting permission for the reprinting of excerpts as requested for use in other publications.

Permissions Notice

Any credit lines for permissions granted for materials quoted or used in the book should appear on the copyright page. If such permission notices are numerous or long, then they may be listed on a separate acknowledgments page either in the front or at the back of the book.

Permission-to-Copy Notice

Some books might benefit from allowing the reader, without special written permission from the publisher, to photocopy pages for personal use or, in educational situations, allowing teachers or group leaders to make copies for students or transparencies for use on an overhead projector. Books of copyright-free images, which contain material to be used in other publications, also fall into this category. Such books should provide a *permission-to-copy notice* on the copyright page, often in conjunction with the warning notice. (See "Warning Notice.") This might be beneficial in such books as:

workbooks intended for study groups
books of charts or tables that might be useful in educational situations
certain Bibles or Bible studies
books with content already in the public domain
reference books containing material expected to be copied by students
fill-in-the-blank books, so that the reader doesn't need to mark the book itself
books of copyright-free images, quotations, templates, or forms
books containing financial worksheets

The permission-to-copy notice is the publisher's way of informing the reader that such copying is allowed as well as defining any needed restrictions that apply. Such restrictions might include:

the number of copies the publisher will allow to be made of any given page
the maximum number of pages that can be copied from a single work
whether a credit line should be included on the copied text pages
how many graphic images may be used and how the credit line should read

A permission-to-copy notice, when given in conjunction with a warning notice, might read as follows:

No part of this publication may be reproduced, stored in a retrieval system, or transmitted in any form or by any means—electronic, mechanical, photocopy, recording, or any other—without the prior permission of the publisher, except as follows: individuals may make a single copy of a page (or a single transparency of a page) from this book for purposes of private study, scholarship, research, or classroom use only. Teachers may make multiple copies of a page from this book for classroom use only, not to exceed one copy per student in the class. Copies made for classroom use should provide the title of the book, the author's name, and the publisher's name on each copy.

Personal Names, Adjectives Derived from

Adjectives can be formed from any personal name. The most common method is to add an *-ian* to names ending in consonants (*Lewisian*—C. S. Lewis; *Barthian*—Karl Barth) and an *-an* to most names ending in vowels

(*Blakean*—William Blake; *Joycean*—James Joyce; *Tolstoyan*—Leo Tolstoy). With ancient Greek and Roman names, the suffix is often added to a root form of the name (*Aeschylean*—Aeschylus; *Lucretian*—Lucretius).

Some names are made into adjectives by adding an *-esque* ending (*Lincolnesque*—Abraham Lincoln; *Kafkaesque*—Franz Kafka), though there is no rule that spells out when this should be done. The *-esque* ending is especially common with artists' names (*Cézannesque*—Paul Cézanne; *Leonardesque*—Leonardo da Vinci), but there are many artists whose names take the traditional form (*Duchampian*—Marcel Duchamp; *Warholian*— Andy Warhol). When in doubt, check *Webster's*. If no reference to a proper form can be found, an author or editor should formulate his or her own according to the rules stated above.

Word List. There are numerous exceptions to these forms, however, and the following list shows some of the most common ones—as well as a few others in which something unusual needs to be noted.

Aaronic—Aaron (descended from Aaron)
Abrahamic—Abraham (in Genesis; descended from Abraham)
Adamic, or Adamical—Adam (in Genesis)
Bernardine—Bernard of Clairvaux
Byronic—Lord Byron
Calvinist, or Calvinistic—John Calvin
Ciceronian—Cicero
Daliesque—Salvador Dalí (note: no acute accent in the adj. form)
Dantesque—Dante Alighieri
Demosthenic—Demosthenes
Eliotian, or Eliotic—T. S. Eliot
Goyaesque, or Goyesque—Francisco de Goya
Homeric—Homer
Huxleian, or Huxleyan—Aldous Huxley
Johannine—John (the apostle)
Lucan—Luke (the gospel writer)
Markan, or Marcan—Mark (the gospel writer)
Marlovian—Christopher Marlowe
Matthean, or Matthaean—Matthew (the gospel writer)
Miltonic, or Miltonian—John Milton
Mosaic—Moses
Napoleonic—Napoleon Bonaparte
Neronic—Nero
Ockhamistic, Occamistic—William of Ockham, or Occam
Pauline—Paul (the apostle)
Petrine—Peter (the apostle)
Quixotic, or quixotic—Don Quixote
Rimbaldian—Rimbaud
Shavian—George Bernard Shaw (humorously contrived by the author himself)
Socratic—Socrates
Thoreauvian—Henry David Thoreau

Personal Names, Commonly Misspelled

See "Misspelled Personal Names, Commonly."

Piety, Pious, and Piousness

Some insist that *piousness* is a back formation of the word *pious* and should therefore not be used, the noun form properly being *piety*. This insistence is niggling, for most dictionaries list *piousness* as a legitimate word. Furthermore, *piousness* and *piety* can have slightly different shades of meaning.

What the dictionaries sometimes miss is that all three words, which used to suggest sincere devotion and assiduous faith, are now often used pejoratively. They hint at insincerity and self-conscious display in matters of faith. If anything, *piousness*, arguably, has a slightly more pejorative tone than *piety* in common usage.

Although these terms are not exclusively negative in contemporary usage, the careful writer must be aware that those words could be misunderstood by the reader to have a double sense, for instance, when referring to the "piety" of a some well-known person. A religious audience may understand something different by these words than a nonreligious audience might.

Pilgrims and Pilgrim Fathers

When capitalized, the word *Pilgrims* refers specifically to those who founded and lived in the Plymouth colony in Massachusetts. The term *Pilgrim Fathers* (capped), however, refers exclusively to those men who actually made the voyage from England aboard the *Mayflower*, and it implies the first generation of Pilgrim leaders in the colony.

Plagiarism

We used to think of the plagiarist as someone who knowingly steals another's writing and publishes it as his or her own original work. It was, and continues to be, an ethical taboo akin to stealing and lying. So why would a manual of style that calls itself "Christian" even need to exhort writers against this particular fault? The answer is this: in the age of the Internet, much, if not most, plagiarism is unconscious and can afflict the morally scrupulous every bit as much as the unscrupulous. How can plagiarism be unconscious?

Plagiarism in Research. Many writers do research on the World Wide Web, where everything from simple statistics to entire books can be downloaded at the push of a few keys. Often, at a project's research stage, a writer highlights a relevant bit of information, perhaps an entire article, from a website and copies it into a document on his or her own hard drive. Later, at the project's writing stage, the author opens the document and, if the extract has not been carefully annotated with an author and source, the writer can too easily assume it to be his or her own original writing. One can imagine the writer saying, "I had no idea I was so articulate!" Before you know it, the extracted passage has been cut-and-pasted into the final draft of the manuscript as the writer's own—unconsciously plagiarizing. It happens time and again, as many recent plagiarism cases can testify. Such inadvertent plagiarism has ruined careers.

Guidelines. Ignorance, though understandable, is nevertheless inexcusable. It is now more important than ever to keep accurate references for all material used in the research and writing of a book, whether from print or online sources. These guidelines should help:

1. *Annotate.* When gathering notes, information, and extracts for a writing project, keep detailed annotations as to author and source. Note the publication's title, date, publisher, and page number for all print sources and, additionally, the website address and date accessed for all online sources. Keep the annotations with the extracted material, not on a separate note card or computer file.

2. *Keep a Separate Research File.* Keep all downloaded or digitized research and quotations in documents reserved exclusively for those materials and completely separate them from any documents used for original writing.

3. *Put It in Quotes.* When a page is photocopied from a book, one can easily identify that material's source; such pages commonly have running heads or other identifying marks. But this is not true of material downloaded from the Internet. Therefore, make it a habit to put all downloaded material in quotation marks as soon as it is inserted into a research document. Remember to put an open quotation mark at the beginning of each new paragraph just as you would in a printed quotation. Coupled with careful author-date-publisher annotations, this should help the writer avoid thinking the extract is his or her own writing. Let the quotation mark be a visual signal that the material is from another source.

4. *Transfer with Care.* When digitally transferring a relevant quote or other passage to the body of the book, make sure that the quotation marks and annotations are always attached to it. Writers who carefully annotate their sources sometimes forget to transfer the annotations to the book file itself, after which they assume the writing is their own.

How Much Is Too Much? When it comes to conscious plagiarism, some writers wonder how many words constitute plagiarism, as though it were a matter of a simple word count. Is it plagiarism to steal a sentence, a phrase, two or three words? The answer is simple: if it is enough to cause the writer to ask the question in the first place, then it is probably too much. Taking as little as a unique two-word coinage from another author and crediting it as one's own can constitute, ethically and legally, plagiarism. The author's conscience should be the yardstick, and erring on the side of caution is advised.

Common Knowledge. While not crediting even a short phrase from another author may be considered plagiarism, using facts or ideas that are "common knowledge" is not. In your research, for instance, you might have found the exact diameter of the earth or a list of Shakespeare's plays. In those cases, the information is considered common knowledge, and you need not credit your source. To determine what is common knowledge, academic writers often use the "Rule of Five": if you can find five independent sources for the information you wish to use, then it is most likely common knowledge and defensible in a court of law as such.

Paraphrasing. Some writers think that paraphrasing is a surefire way of avoiding plagiarism. Sometimes this is the case, sometimes it is not, depending on the content and context of the original. For instance, if you paraphrase the Greek myth of Perseus as found in Graves' *Greek and Roman Myths*, then your own paraphrase is an original retelling of a traditional myth that is considered common knowledge. But if you paraphrase another author's retelling of that myth in which that author transforms the characters into farm animals, then your paraphrased version is a plagiarism since the uniqueness of the barnyard telling belongs to that original author. In such a case, credit should be given to the original author, and if the telling does not fall under the fair use guidelines (see "Permissions, Obtaining: Author Guidelines, *Fair Use*"), then permission should be obtained as well. Take another example: you write a detailed, five-page paraphrase of the plot of a particular episode of a television comedy. Even though this is your paraphrase, permission should be obtained and proper credit given to the original author.

Conclusion. Writers need to be especially careful when handling the intellectual property of others. Conscious or unconscious, plagiarism is a serious problem. Whoever said, "Stealing from one author is called 'plagiarism'; stealing from many authors is called 'research,'" certainly did not live in the computer age—a time in which "stealing from many authors is called 'the Internet.'"

(See also "Quotations," "Quoting from the Internet," and "Permissions, Obtaining: Author Guidelines.")

Plurals

English, as a conglomeration of languages, has developed a variety of ways of expressing plurals, which can be maddening for people trying to learn the language.

Regular Plurals with S. The most common method of forming the plural is by adding an *s* to the noun, such as *cats, trucks, seas,* or an *es* to the noun if it ends in with a sibilant *s, z, ch,* or *sh* sound, such as *tresses, buzzes, churches,* and *bushes.* These are called *regular plurals.*

Other Regular Plurals. While still ending in *s*, certain nouns require more modification in forming the plural, as seen in the following list:

words ending in *-y,* preceded by a consonant	change *y* to *ie,* and add *s*: *candies, countries, mercies*
words ending in *-uy*	replace *y* with *ie* and add *s*: *colloquies, obliquies*
some words ending in *-f* or *-fe*	replace with *-ves*: *elves, lives*
some words ending in *-o*	add *-es* to certain words ending in *-o*: *echoes, heroes, potatoes, tomatoes, zeroes*

Irregular Plurals. Irregular plurals follow no rules. Some of the most common, the majority of which have roots in Old English, are:

singular	plural
child	children
foot	feet
goose	geese
man	men
mouse	mice
ox	oxen
woman	women

Plural Form Same as the Singular. For some words, the plural form is the same as the singular. These are referred to as *zero plurals.* For example: *bison, cattle, deer, elk, fish, grouse, moose, salmon, sheep, shrimp, swine, tuna.* The word *fish,* by the way, uses *fishes* as a plural only when different kinds of fish are being referred to. Often nationalities take the zero plural as well: *Chinese, Japanese, Norse, Taiwanese, Sioux.*

Plurals Commonly Construed as Singular. In actual usage, both written and spoken, certain plural forms have come to be constructed as singulars. This is especially common with Latin plurals that have drifted into English, such as *data, agenda,* and *criteria.* For example, *the data is ready for review, the agenda is enclosed,* and *the criteria is simple* are acceptable in informal writing. Sometimes, using the correct Latin singular forms or using a plural noun can often sound stilted or pedantic: *the agendum is enclosed* or *the agenda are enclosed.* Stick with the colloquial, common forms. Still, in books of a high literary or academic standard, the precise formal forms may be used: *The data in the study are of three types . . .*

Of Single Letters. The plural forms of lowercase letters should end in *'s*: as in to *watch one's p's and q's.* The plurals of capital letters should end only in *s* unless that would lead to misreading: *Ps and Qs,* but *A's, U's.* In most ordinary text, the *'s* or *s* should be set in roman, even when the single letter is set in italic.

Poetry

Titles. The titles of most poems are set in roman and in quotation marks, although book-length poems should be italicized and not set in quotations. Most poem titles are capped according to the general rules for titles, but when a poem does not have a formal title and is identified by its first line, then the title is set sentence style.

> "Epistle to Be Left in the Earth"—Archibald MacLeish [ordinary poem]
> *Paradise Lost*—John Milton [book-length poem]
> "Because I could not stop for death"—Emily Dickinson [first line as title]

Quoted in Text. When poetry is quoted and set as an extract (block quotation) within a prose text, it should be set in the same typeface as the text, either the same size, or, more customarily, one or two points smaller in size. The smaller size is recommended to minimize the number of long lines that might need to be broken if the full text size were used.

Traditionally, and unless the designer has a different intention, the longest line of the poem is centered on the page and the rest of the poem is allowed to align accordingly. If a lot of poetry is quoted, however, or when more than one poem appears on a single page, the verses can all be aligned on a pre-established indent (usually one or two picas) to avoid the appearance of a ragged left margin. If the lines are especially long (as with Whitman's verse), the poetry can even begin at the left margin and runover lines set at a pre-established indent, although in such cases the poetry should be set in a different font or type size to distinguish it from the prose. Secondary leading before and after the extract are also recommended.

In books meant to project a high literary value, extracted poetry can be set in italics—another technique for squeezing long lines onto the page, since italics are more condensed than roman in most typefaces. Since italic fonts generally slow the reader down, some designers like to set poetry in italics, feeling that poetry should be read more slowly than prose. Other designers either avoid italic setting of poetry altogether or limit its use to those instances when poetry is quoted only sparingly.

As appropriate, two lines of quoted poetry may either be set as a block quotation or run into the text, using a spaced slash (/) to indicate the line breaks. Three or more lines of quoted poetry may also be run into the text with spaced slashes whenever the context calls for it.

Pontiff

The word *pontiff*, which is nearly always lowercased, refers exclusively to the pope of the Roman Catholic Church. It is from the Latin *pontifex maximus* ("supreme pontiff," with the Latin *pontifex* implying "bridge maker"). There have been other popes throughout history, in the Eastern church, for instance, but they are not referred to as *pontiffs*.

Possessives

Forming Common Possessives. Most proper names and common singular nouns form the possessive by adding *'s*. Exceptions are made for a few common phrases that, perhaps for the sake of euphony, have come to require an apostrophe only. Plural possessives are formed by adding an apostrophe only, except for words whose plurals do not end in *s*. In those cases, the plural possessive is formed by adding *'s* to the word.

> Remember Henry Ward Beecher's remark: All words are pegs to hang ideas on.
> For conscience' sake, Baxter allied himself with the Nonconformists.
> Parishioners' complaints did not hinder Susannah Wesley's evangelism.
> At first the disciples did not believe the women's story.

When the Word Ends in S. When proper names and singular nouns end in *s*, they still form their possessive in the same way as words that don't end in *s*. When in doubt, euphony and common pronunciation should be your guides. For instance, when you would not ordinarily pronounce an extra possessive *s*, only an apostrophe should be added in the written form.

Bliss's hymns	the Lewises' letters
the bus's exit	John Rogers' Bible
Dickens' *Life of Our Lord*	the truss's strength

Classical and Biblical Names. Determining the possessive forms for classical and biblical names ending in *s* is often a problem. No system is perfect, but euphony and common pronunciation should be adhered to. When the possessive *s* is ordinarily pronounced, add *'s*; if it is awkward to pronounce the possessive *s*, add an apostrophe only. The following rules should help. When the *s* represents the sound *z* at the end of the word (as in *Socrates* or *Thales*) or when the final *s* is immediately preceded by another *s* or *z* sound (as in *Augustus*, *Xerxes*, *Moses*, or *Jesus*), only an apostrophe should be added. When the *s* represents an *s* sound and is not immediately preceded by another *s* or *z* sound (as in *Cyrus*), *'s* should be added to form the possessive. Also, any classical or biblical name that is also a common modern name (like *James*), whether it ends in an *s* or a *z* sound, should form its possessive by adding *'s*.

Achilles' heel	Thales' philosophy
Ananias's house	Thomas's doubt
Jesus' disciples	Zacchaeus's tree
Ramses' dynasty	

For Feast Days. The names for feast days of saints are formed with the possessive.

All Saints' Day	Saint Patrick's Day
Saint Michael's Eve	Saint Valentine's Day

With Italicized Words. A possessive ending to an italicized noun should be set in roman.

John Timmer explains how the riches of the kingdom can be found in the *anawim*'s very poverty.
Sandy joined the *Banner*'s staff in 1980.

To Show Joint Possession. When a possessive needs to be formed for two or more persons in the same context, the following rules apply: (1) If one object is possessed mutually by all the people listed, only the final name needs to be in a possessive form; (2) if separate objects are possessed, each name should be in the possessive form. In some cases, rewriting may be called for if the distinctions are not otherwise clear.

Keil and Delitzsch's study [the book they wrote together]
Vaughan's and Herbert's poetry [their separate poetry]
my aunt's and uncle's books [their separate books]
my aunt's books and my uncle's books [rewritten]

With Phrases. Phrases or epithets of two or more words form possessives as long as they are not more than three or four words in length and no ambiguity results. Otherwise the sentence should be rewritten.

> the Evil One's devices
> the Good Shepherd's promises
> the Apostle to the Gentile's writings [ambiguous]
> the writings of the Apostle to the Gentiles [rewritten]

Collective Possessives. The plural possessive form is used when an object is described by the group of people that commonly control, own, or possess it. When the group commonly uses an object but no strict possession is implied, then it becomes an attributive form, and the possessive apostrophe is not used. A strict distinction cannot always be made between possessive and attributive forms, so each case should be decided using common sense and common usage as guides. Note first that the plural possessive is being used less often today altogether, and also that it is common for many groups and organizations to drop the possessive form in their official names or functions; in these cases, adhere to the group's preference.

> bishops' letter   writers guidelines
> realtors' association   Michigan Teachers Association
> nurses' station   Christian Booksellers Convention

Use of the Gerund. The possessive form is commonly used with gerunds.

> Peter's confessing that Jesus is the Christ . . .
> God's having gathered his people to himself . . .

Preface

See "Foreword and Preface."

Prefixes

Most prefixes are set closed, that is, without space or hyphen, when forming compound words. Exceptions are made when the prefix (1) precedes a numeral, (2) precedes a capital letter, (3) precedes an already compounded term, or (4) either duplicates letters that might cause misreading or forms a new word that might cause misreading. In those cases, a hyphen is usually placed between the prefix and the word, though an en-dash is generally inserted when a prefix defines an entire unhyphenated compound term rather than just the first word in that term.

Since many exceptions exist to both the exceptions and the general rule, it is always best to check *Webster's* when in doubt. If the word does not appear there, then the above rules should apply. The following examples should help make them clear. (See also "Hyphenation, *Prefixes and Suffixes.*")

counterculture, counterespionage, counterintuitive
   but Counter-Reformation [precedes a capital letter],
   counter-counterintelligence [to avoid *countercounter-*]
codirector, coworker [though *CMS* prefers *co-worker*], cowriter
   but co-colonize, co-edition, *and* co-op [all to avoid misreading]
midday, midcareer change, midlife, midterm election, midwinter
   but mid-1900s [precedes a numeral], mid-nineteenth century [precedes a
   compound term]
multifaceted, multitalented, multivolume set
   but multi-international *and* multi-instrumentalist [to avoid duplicated vowel]
postdated, postelection polls, postmodern
   but post-9/11 [precedes numeral], post-Christian society [precedes a
   capital letter], post-traumatic stress disorder [precedes compound term],
   post–Desert Storm [precedes compound term, note en-dash]
predate, predestination, preschool
   but pre-presentation ceremonies [to avoid *prepre-*], pre-engineered [to avoid
   duplicated vowel], pre-Socratic [precedes a capital letter], pre–World War II
   [precedes compound term, note en-dash]

Preparing Electronic Manuscripts

See "Manuscript Preparation: Author Guidelines, *Formatting Conventions.*"

Prepositions in Titles

Lowercase a preposition of any length in a title or subtitle unless the preposition is used adverbially or otherwise emphasized: *The Crusades through Arab Eyes*, and "Roaming through the Gloaming," but *The Prayer of Jabez: Breaking Through to the Blessed Life* and "All Through the Night." See also "Capitalization, *Titles.*"

Presentation Page

A *presentation page* is a separate page included at the beginning of some gift books and Bibles on which are provided blank lines to indicate who is giving the book to whom. A presentation page can be as simple as the words *To* and *From* followed by blank rule lines to be filled in or as complex as elaborately decorated pages, printed on elegant paper, and tipped in at the beginning of the book. In some cases, the flyleaf can be specially printed as a presentation page. Occasionally, the presentation page can take the place of the half title page.

Presentation pages can be prepared for special occasions, such as graduations, weddings, and baptisms, the text of which can include blank lines on which can be written such things as the date, location, witnesses, and other pertinent information. A wedding Bible or a graduation gift book should almost certainly include a presentation page.

Print-on-Demand

Print-on-demand (POD) refers to a method of book production that combines online downloadability with the aesthetic appeal of actual books. In the world of print-on-demand, the publisher does not need to store large print-runs in warehouses nor does the bookstore have to stock books on the shelves; rather, the publisher stores the text on a downloadable computer file, which can then be printed and bound on a special printing-and-binding device at a bookstore, a POD packager, or other central location.

At the time of this writing, print-on-demand technology is capable of producing relatively inexpensive paperback books, though they are still slightly more expensive than their traditional-print counterparts and trim sizes are generally limited to the standard trade-paper formats. Cheaper books in a larger variety of formats could well be possible in the near future. So far, print-on-demand has not threatened to replace traditional publishing, but it has become a serious alternative for many companies who wish to print but not to pay the high costs of inventory.

Author Aspects. Print-on-demand technology has received mixed reviews from authors. On one hand, it can prolong a book's availability, allowing readers to order copies long after the traditional print copies of the book have gone out of print. On the other hand, this prolonged availability can at times prevent authors from getting their rights back from the publishers so they can resell the book elsewhere. The book remains in a kind of "in-print limbo" in which only the potential of the printed book exists, not actual copies.

In the long run, as print-on-demand becomes more efficient, it should lower the cost of producing books and give the reader a greater variety from which to choose. It is especially valuable for small presses and niche publishers, who can avoid the high costs of warehousing large print runs.

Problem Words, A List of Common

The following is a list of recommended styles for words that are for one reason or another often problematic for writers, proofreaders, and editors. Also see "Brand Names," "Computer- and Internet-Related Words," "Gender-Accurate Language," "Hyphenation," "Misspelled Personal Names, Commonly," and "Misspelled Words, A List of Commonly."

Adrenalin—pharmaceutical trade name
adrenaline—body chemical
adviser—not *advisor*
A-frame (house)
air force, the
Air Force, US
anticommunist (n. and adj.)
anti-Zionist
appendixes—not *appendices*
arabic numeral
army, the
Army, US
Asian—not *Oriental* in referring to people
audiotape

babysit, babysitter (no hyphen)
backward
benefited
bestseller, bestselling (n. and adj.)—this is contrary to *Webster's*, which lists *best seller* and *best-selling*
Bible study (n. and adj., no hyphen)
black (racial designation, lowercase in most contexts)
born-again (adj.)
boyfriend
businesspeople
businessperson
businesswoman

café—note acute accent
canceled
catalog
cell phone (two words, short for *cellular telephone*)
Communism
communist (adj.)
Communist (n.)

communistic
Congo (not *the* Congo)
conservatism—lc
conservative—lc
copyedit (v.), copyediting
copyeditor
counseled—one *l*
counseling—one *l*
C-section—but note: *cesarean section*

Daddy, Dad—direct address
daddy, dad—indirect reference
Dark Ages, the
Depression, the—but *a depression*
diagramed—one *m*; but *diagrammable*
disc (compact disc, DVD, SACD, or phonograph record)
disk (computer hard drive or floppy disk)
DJ—capped with no periods; or spell out *dee-jay*
Down syndrome—rather than the former usage, *Down's syndrome*
Dr Pepper—soft drink; no period after *Dr*

Earth Mother
East Coast
e-church
email
Encyclopaedia Britannica—note the older *ae* form (but not ligature *æ*)
entrée
Episcopal—adj.
Episcopalian—n.
ezine

facade—the cedilla on the *c* is now commonly dropped
far-out (adj.)

fiancé (m.)
fiancée (f.)
flannelgraph—one word
footwashing
free world—lc
fulfillment
fullness
full-time (adj. and adv.), otherwise, *full time*

girlfriend
glamour
good-bye—though *goodbye* is becoming
  more common and acceptable
Gothic (style of art or type)
gothic novel
gray
Greater Chicago
grown-up (n. and adj.)

hangout (n.)
hang-up (n.)
Harper & Row—publisher preferred
  ampersand; now called HarperCollins
  (with no space)
Harper's—magazine; note possessive
health care (two words as both n. and adj.)
Hispanic (preferred to *Latin American*)
Holocaust—capped when it refers to Nazi
  murder of Jews
homeland
hometown

indexes (*not* indices)
InterVarsity Christian Fellowship—name of
  campus organization
InterVarsity Press—American publisher
Iron Curtain
italic type

Keystone Cops (capped)
kidnapped, kidnapper, kidnapping
kindergarten
kindergartner

labeled
latchkey child
Latin American (see *Hispanic*)
layman, laymen
layperson, laypeople
laywoman, laywomen
liberal—lc
liberalism—lc
lifestyle
life's work
Lloyds—banker; no apostrophe
Lloyd's of London—insurer; note
  apostrophe
loanword

mah-jongg—Chinese tile game; note
  hyphen and *gg*
maître d', short for *maître d'hôtel*
marines
Marines, US
matins (US)
mattins (UK)
medieval
megachurch
mid—set closed, as in *midcentury* or
  midterm, unless followed by numeral or
  compound, as in *mid-1800s* or *mid-
  nineteenth century* (see "Prefixes" for
  more details)
middle age
middle-aged (adj.)
Middle Ages, the
Midwest, midwestern
mind-set
M & M—candy brand name, note
  ampersand, spaces, and no periods
Mother, Mommy, Mom (direct address)
mother, mommy, mom (indirect reference)
Muhammad
Muslim

naive, or naïve—the umlaut is now
  commonly dropped
Native American (American Indian)

native American (person born in America)

navy

Navy, US

never-never land—imaginary place, from
Peter Pan; note lowercase

New World

New Year's Day

9/11 attacks (or *September 11 attacks*, but
not *nine-eleven* or *nine-one-one*)

Novocain—trade name for anesthetic

novocaine—generic chemical name for
anesthetic

Old World

Oriental (see *Asian*)

part-time (n., adj., and adv.)

peacemaking

percent

Ping-Pong—trademark; capped and
hyphenated as both adj. and n.

proofreader

proof text

renaissance, a

Renaissance, the

restroom

résumé, or resumé—note acute accents

Rolls-Royce—trade name; note hyphen.

roman numeral

roman type

roommate

shofar—Hebrew ram's horn; note: the plural
is "shofroth"

skeptic

South (Civil War)

Southwest

storytelling

Stryker frame—special bed for spinal-injured
patients; note cap *S*

Sunday school (n. and adj.)

teenage, teenager

Third World

timeline

totaled

toward (usually no final *s* in US style)

traveling, traveled

T-shirt—*T* is capped

T square—note no hyphen

twentieth century (n.), but twentieth-
century (adj.)

Ukraine (not *the* Ukraine)

un-Christian

uptight

videotape

V-8—brand name of vegetable juice

V-eight—eight-cylinder engine; *V* is capped;
eight spelled out

Vietnam, Vietnamese

V-neck—*V* is capped

Volkswagen—note *-en*

V-six—*V* is capped

Warner Bros.—second word is always
abbreviated

way-out (adj.)

Webster's—italic with apostrophe when
referring to *Merriam-Webster's Collegiate
Dictionary, Eleventh Edition*

West Coast

whiskey

white (racial designation, lowercased in
most contexts)

woolly

wordplay

word processor

world's fair—note possessive

worldview

World War I, World War II (not *World War
One* and *World War Two*)

worshiped, worshiper, worshiping

X-ray—verb (sometimes lowercased) and
noun; note hyphen

Prodigal

Because of its long association with the parable of the prodigal son, the word *prodigal* is mistakenly thought to mean "wandering," "straying," or "disobedient." The word in fact means "wasteful," "excessive," and "lavish," and it is not necessarily a term of condemnation. It can suggest "bounteousness," as in its close cognate, *prodigality*. For example, Nature's riches at harvest time can be described as *prodigal*, though *prodigious* (which suggests not quite as much excessiveness) would be the more conventional word.

A careful writer, therefore, should pay attention to the shades of meaning of these words. To refer to a runaway child as *a prodigal* is only true if that child has spent lavishly or wastefully.

Profanity

Does an author commit a sin when her fictional character uses vulgarity? Does an editor commit a sin by allowing an author to use a four-letter word in a book?

Christians must take seriously the biblical admonitions against coarse joking (Eph. 5:4), filthy language (Col. 3:8), and the misuse of God's name (Deut. 5:11), but when it comes to their use in writing, especially when those very words are needed to convey character or authentic setting in fiction, for instance, the issues are not entirely clear. Should offensive language of any kind be universally forbidden in Christian writing? Should honest portrayals of sin be avoided in books?

No human language is devoid of fringe speech, that is, words used largely to express extremes of pain, surprise, anger, and other emotions; create coarsely humorous or grotesque effects; or shock the listener or reader. Authors and editors alike should recognize not only the existence of "taboo words and phrases" but also their occasional necessity in effective communication. As many have noted, the writers of the Bible themselves freely used taboo language to make their points.

While such language offends some readers, individual words are, from a linguistic standpoint, simply objective signifiers and therefore morally neutral. Thomas Aquinas said that objects (and one imagines he would have included words) are neither good nor evil in themselves—only in the uses to which they are put by fallen humans.

Preferring not to alienate prospective buyers, many religious publishers request their authors to avoid all forms of taboo speech. When authors use such expressions, editors routinely eliminate such language at the editorial stage. This is wise if there is a likelihood of a deeply negative reaction among the book's ultimate audience. It is certainly counterproductive for any author to alienate readers. If a moral consideration is at issue, it is usually not so much in the words themselves as in the desire to avoid offending those who have paid money for the book.

This tacit censorship runs up against the author's First Amendment right to free speech, although, in a larger sense, editors at all publishing houses, secular and religious alike, make many decisions that are tantamount to censorship in an effort to accomplish the publisher's goal of communicating effectively to a given market. Ironically, many secular publishers censor an author's religious opinions (though they may euphemistically call it "toning down") if they are apt to offend a more general, nonsectarian readership. The very nature of publishing is imbued with implicit censorship, beginning with the fact that some manuscripts are accepted for publication and others are not. Still these conflicting rights of authors and publishers are serious matters, and it is best for the publisher and author to discuss them ahead of time.

For practical purposes, taboo and fringe speech can be roughly divided into six categories:

1. *Profanity*: using the names of persons of the Trinity in inappropriate ways, commonly called "cursing" or "taking God's name in vain."
2. *Scatology*: narrowly defined as insensitive or coarse, slang terms for bodily functions and waste products.
3. *Venery*: obscene words and expressions explicitly describing reproductive organs, body parts, or sexual acts.
4. *Vulgar Interjections*: taboo words used as expressions of sudden emotion. These are sometimes forms of profanity, scatology, or venery.
5. *Vulgar Epithets*: often colorful but socially unacceptable terms used pejoratively to describe individual people.
6. *Social Insensitivity*: words and expressions that inherently communicate a derogatory attitude toward people because of their race, gender, ethnic background, physical or mental challenge, or sexual orientation. This is elsewhere called "politically incorrect language" or "hate speech." (See "Ethnic and Racial Designations" and "Disability Designations.")

The issues are complex. Authors and publishers must decide for themselves how restrictive or how liberal they wish to be on these issues, and publishers should state their policy and expectations clearly in their contracts so that authors won't be blindsided later.

The following guidelines outline a middle path, adopted by Zondervan, which may be helpful to other producers of religious materials:

Zondervan does not allow its authors to use the most offensive examples from any of those six categories listed above—that is, those words and phrases recognized as strictly taboo by the largest proportion of Christian readers. The word *largest* should be emphasized here, because there exists a sizable "second tier" of language—sometimes referred to as *euphemisms* or *minced oaths*—that might offend some readers but not others. In such cases, our editors employ the criteria of *appropriateness*, of which there are two aspects.

First, is the language appropriate to the work itself? Is the taboo word necessary to convey a mood or an idea that cannot be conveyed otherwise? In fiction, particularly, strong language can be essential in characterizing people, providing a sense of realism, and describing the true nature of sin and evil.

Second, is the language appropriate to the primary intended readership? Not all books are for all readers. So we ask: Will the language be acceptable in its context by the largest number of readers for whom this book is intended? Obviously, judgment needs to be exercised, realizing, of course, that it may be impossible—to say nothing of useless—to produce a book that is wholly inoffensive to every possible reader. Often an overdelicate social propriety, not biblical mandate, is at stake.

Beyond specific words and phrases, some readers are offended by mature situations and discussions of sensitive topics. Issues of immorality and sin are central themes in many Christian books, especially fiction, and cannot be addressed effectively without allowing for realistic portrayal. Again, the criteria of appropriateness to the work and to the intended audience are applied, and judgment is used.

Ideally, such decisions cannot be made unilaterally by the editor or author alone. They are best discussed with the publisher's marketing experts and salespeople, who have a professional investment in seeing that work succeeds in reaching its audience. Such decisions might also be discussed with readers themselves, by way of focus groups or marketing surveys.

No book can please every reader. Nor should an author or publisher's goal be to produce a perfectly inoffensive book. Since definitive guidelines for the use of profanity, vulgar speech, and frank portrayals of evil are difficult to formulate, the best procedure is for the author and publisher to confer about the issues: Who will read the book? What are the costs of using offensive language in terms of reader trust and sales? Can effective alternatives be found for the offensive language?

These are difficult issues, but they must be confronted for the sake of the health of religious communication.

Prologue

Despite its name, a book's *prologue* is not part of the front matter but is actually the first element of the body matter. It is a separate section, usually falling immediately before the first chapter, in which the narrative background of the story is filled in. It is usually reserved for books of literary quality, such as fiction, drama, biography, history, and other nonfiction narratives. Its purpose is to show "what went before" the main action of the book, just as the epilogue informs the reader of what happened after the main action of the book.

The prologue should not be about the book itself but should function as a sort of pre–first chapter, filling in elements of the narrative before the story proper begins. Otherwise, if written by the author, it should properly be called a *preface*. A prologue is often written in the same voice as the rest of the book, that is, in the narrator's voice rather than the author's, when those voices are distinct. (See also "Foreword and Preface" and "Introduction.")

Pronunciation Guide

Although this manual can't hope to provide pronunciation helps for all the possible difficulties, the following list gives a few of the more common problem words found in Christian life and worship. They are a mix of proper names and biblical, historical, and contemporary words.

accidie—AHK-suh-dee
Baal—BAY-ul (pref.); or BAH-ahl
Babel—BAY-bul (pref.); or, pronounced as *babble*
Barth (Karl)—BART
Bede (the Venerable)—BEED
Boethius—bo-EE-thee-us
Böhme, Jacob—BURM, YAH-cub
Bonhoeffer, Dietrich—bon-HAWF-er, DEE-trick
Brueghel—BREW-gul (sometimes spelled *Breughel*)
Buber (Martin)—BOO-ber (not BYOO-ber)
Buechner (Frederick)—BEEK-ner
Caedmon—CADD-mun (not CAYD-mun)
Celtic (church)—KEL-tik (not SELL-tick)
Chardin, Teilhard de—char-DA(N), tay-YAR duh
Chrysostom—KRIS-us-tum (accent on first syllable)
Columba (Saint)—kuh-LUM-buh (accent on second syllable)
Comenius (John Amos)—koh-MEEN-ee-us (accent on second syllable)
Cynewulf—KIN-uh-wolf
de Gasztold, Carmen Bernos—de GAHZ-toe, CAR-men BARE-no
Hammarskjöld, Dag—HAHM-ur-shuld, DAHG
Héloïse—AY-lu-weez (the *H* is silent)

Kempe (Margery)—KEMP (one syllable)
Kuyper, Abraham—KY-per, AHB-ruh-hahm
Lucado (Max)—lu-KAY-do
Salome—suh-LOH-mee (pref.); or SAL-oh-may
slough—SLUE (rhymes with *clue*, in the US); SLAOU (rhymes with *cow*, in the UK)—as in Bunyan's "Slough of Despond" in *The Pilgrim's Progress*, and meaning a swamp or bog. The pronunciation SLUFF is a different word altogether, meaning "to shed."
Vondel, Joost van den—FOHN-dul, Yoost vahn den
Wangerin (Walter)—WAHNG-rin
Weil, Simone—VEY, see-MOAN
Wycliffe (John)—WICK-liff (not WHY-cliff)

Proofreading

The average 200-page book contains about 500,000 characters, that is, a half-million letters, spaces, and punctuation marks. Each one must be in exactly the right place if the book is to be error-free. A book that is 99 percent accurate will still contain five thousand typographical errors—about twenty-five errors per page. A book that is 99.9 percent accurate will still contain five hundred errors, or about two-and-a-half per page.

Because many casual readers spot a typo from time to time, they often feel that they would make excellent proofreaders—not realizing, of course, that proofreading is far more than just catching typos. Professional proofreaders can tell you in detail exactly how demanding and frustrating proofreading can be.

Even though proofreading is one of the most important jobs in publishing, proofreaders tend to get more recognition for their lapses than for their successes, and even though perfection is the standard, even experienced professionals can be expected to miss about one error every fifty pages.

Computers and Proofreading. Not long ago proofreaders feared their jobs were destined for extinction. Spell-checking software, they were told, would soon do to them what PCs had done to the typewriter. With the flush of confidence that accompanied the explosion of desk-top publishing systems, many techno-pundits predicted the demise of proofreading as a profession.

Now, more than twenty-five years into the computer-publishing revolution, proofreaders remain as invaluable as ever, though their function has changed in some interesting and unexpected ways. Computers catch the obvious typos and some grammar errors, but they have serious limitations. Imagine that a 200-page book has a thousand errors in a manuscript—about five per page. Even the best spell-checkers and grammar programs will only catch a certain percentage of those. Let's say that the spell-checker can identify 99 percent of them. In a 200-page book that means that there will still be one error every twenty pages that the human proofreader is expected to catch. It takes a proofreader as much time to find an error every twenty pages as it does to find five errors per page. The proofreader can't "ease up" simply because he or she knows there will be fewer errors in the book. Their tendency, in fact, will be to read even more closely and take more time because the errors, in a sense, will be harder to find.

But that just takes spelling errors into consideration. Computers can't find many contextual errors (singulars and plurals, for instance), mixed homonyms, format problems, and problems of word division.

Few companies now employ in-house proofreading staff. At the beginning of computerization, many publishers optimistically hired on-screen proofreaders, only to find, for whatever reasons, that such proofreading tended to be less accurate than its paper counterpart. Not only can some format problems be best identified on hard copy, but the simple word-for-word reading seems more accurate.

Like so many other jobs, proofreading has become largely an outsourced occupation. Most proofreaders are self-employed, and they combine such traditional functions as checking for correct spelling and punctuation with newer computerized functions, such as checking typesetting codes and managing spell-checking software.

Single-Copy Proofreading. Although paper continues to be the most common medium for proofreading, many changes have taken place due to computerization. The most noticeable has been the shift from double- to single-copy proofreading. Traditionally, a proofreader compared the newly typeset galleys (*live copy*) against an edited manuscript (*dead copy*). Now that editors and copy editors routinely perform their functions on the computer, often with no revision tracking, an authoritative paper copy showing the changes that have been made may not even exist. Computerization has rung the death knell of dead copy.

The proofreader, therefore, must become proficient at *single-copy proofreading* (also called *dry proofreading, straight proofreading,* or *railroading*), which is reading galley proofs with no manuscript against which to check. Single-copy reading can actually be more accurate because it allows the proofreader's eyes to focus solely on the live copy and eliminates the fatigue of constantly shifting the eyes between two copies. Still, many proofreaders tend to speed up when reading a single copy, a tendency that can result in greater inaccuracy. In any case, this new way of proofreading has made new demands on the proofreader.

Traditional proofreaders, when asked to read single copy, are often frustrated by not having a manuscript against which to check. They are now required to know more; they need to think more like editors by understanding just what an author intends to say, but they must also maintain their obsession with detail. The guides available to them to answer their questions are the following:

1. *Dictionary.* Most proofreaders who read single copy find they use the dictionary far more than when reading against dead copy. Proofreaders should get into the habit of looking up every word, even the most common, the spellings of which they are not completely certain. The proofreader should obtain a copy of the publisher's preferred dictionary and use it often.

   Proofreaders should also be aware that the computerized spell-checkers used by some publishers are often programmed to reference a dictionary other than the one the publisher purports to use for its house style. The differences—in such things as word breaks, first usage, alternate spellings, and hyphenation—can be significant. Proofreaders should always verify that they are, in fact, using the publisher's preferred dictionary, regardless of whether the publisher's spell-checker is being used.

2. *Style Manual.* Most publishers conform to one of the popular manuals of style, such as *The Chicago Manual of Style.* They will also commonly provide proofreaders with their own in-house style guides that summarize major rules and indicate variations from their chosen manual of style. The proofreader must be certain to have access to, and be thoroughly familiar with, these references.

3. *The Style Sheet.* Since editors often do not have a paper manuscript on which to indicate style decisions (for instance, whether to capitalize the deity pronoun or to use the serial comma), a style sheet should be used to inform a proofreader of these decisions, especially when they depart from the publisher's accepted dictionary or manual of style. Style sheets have always been an important strategy for communicating style decisions to everyone involved in a manuscript's development; style sheets are even more important for the proofreader of straight copy.

   If the proofreader has not been provided with an existing style sheet for the project, he or she should compile one and pass it along to the editor when the proofing is completed. That way, the proofreader can annotate all questions of fact, style, spelling, and grammar that might recur. When a style sheet is provided, the proofreader should feel free to add to it, so that the style sheet is a fluid document, charting the stylistic oddities of a book.

4. *Common Sense.* Proofreaders proficient at single-copy reading will tell you that they have had to develop a certain caginess. They learn to "read with the flow" of the manuscript. Even when no style sheet is provided, they can still figure out where variations from accepted style

were deliberately made. In a sense, they learn to second-guess both the author and the editor, though this, in turn, can lead to the added problem of incorrect second-guesses. The single-copy reader must learn when to query. With no authoritative manuscript, the potential exists for proofreaders to query too often, when in fact they might be able to answer their own questions by reading further in the manuscript.

Compensating for Spell-Checkers. The best proofreaders have learned to complement the computer rather than confront it; that is, they learn to specialize in what computer spell-checkers don't do well. For instance, since spell-checkers consistently catch the classic spelling bugbears (*anoint* rather than *annoint*, and *millennium* rather than *millenium*), proofreaders have learned to watch for errors that computerized spell-checkers are generally blind to:

1. *Homonyms.* So far, spell-checkers can't read contexts particularly well, though they have been getting more sophisticated in recent years. Homonyms used in the wrong place, such as *too*, *to*, and *two*, are usually invisible to the spell-checker, and because English has an extraordinarily high number of such words, the proofreader needs to be especially careful in making sure the correct option is used.
2. *Right Words in Wrong Contexts.* Spell-checkers know when a word is spelled wrong, but by and large they can't identify correctly spelled words used in the wrong place. For instance: *Wee fold thee truths too bee self-evident . . .*
3. *Transpositions.* Similar to right words in wrong contexts is the very common problem of transposition—adjacent words, the order of which has been reversed. Transpositions can be particularly hard to find because the mind tends to make sense of them unconsciously. For instance: *I wish I had than more one life to give for my country.*
4. *Font Changes.* Spell-checkers just don't care. Italic, bold, and roman are all the same to them (as it should be—who would want the spell-checker to flag you every time the font changed?). Proofreaders need to read especially carefully when the font changes—or when it should change but hasn't.
5. *Word Division.* This is a particularly troublesome problem because spell-checkers often *are* programmed to check for word division, but the computer's style is often at odds with the publisher's. Many spell-checkers accept two-letter breaks (*tru-ly*), while most publishers do not. By the same token, spell-checkers may be programmed according to the word-division style of one dictionary while the publisher may not accept that style.

6. *Formats.* Most book readers don't realize that checking page format is one of the proofreaders most time-consuming tasks—one that spell-checkers don't even pretend to check. Here is a short list: wrong folios, wrong or misplaced running heads or footers; wrong fonts; wrong hierarchy of headings and subheads; consistency of placement for all the elements; inconsistent leading between elements of type.

Proofreading Tips. Here are a few tips for the proofreader in this age of single-copy proofreading:

1. *Avoid speeding up when reading a single copy.* Some proofreaders even read aloud to keep from going too fast. Read word-for-word, or even syllable-for-syllable, look up all unfamiliar words, and check them letter-for-letter.
2. *Avoid getting caught up in the story.* Not only do dry proofreaders tend to speed up, but because they are focusing more closely on a single copy, a kind of hypnosis can occur. Proofreaders can easily become so absorbed in a narrative that they will wake up four pages later to realize that they haven't been looking for errors. If you find yourself enjoying the book, it may be a signal to reread.
3. *Back up every time an error is found.* Research shows that most errors that proofreaders miss are in close proximity to other errors that the proofreader caught. Every time an error is found, make it a habit to back up one or two lines before continuing the reading.
4. *Take a five-minute break every hour.*
5. *Keep a style sheet whenever the editor has not already provided you with one.* Or if the editor has given you a style sheet, feel free to add more items to it. Note all unusual words and names and any special grammar, punctuation, abbreviation, or symbol considerations. Also keep track of fonts, leadings, and specification changes for different elements of the book.
6. *Be particularly careful about font changes.* When italic material is called for, use common sense to ascertain where the italics are to end. Sometimes they will erroneously extend into copy that should be roman.
7. *Double-check all folios and running heads* to make sure they are all in the same font and consistent throughout the project.
8. *Watch for flags.* Flags are an editor's, author's, or compositor's annotations not intended to be part of the final book. Often a proofreader will assume that these obvious flags will be searched and caught by the editor or typesetter when, in fact, these flags were already missed.

The proofreader should mark anything, no matter how obvious, that is not intended to appear in print.

9. *Read syllable for syllable.* Many people claim that letter-for-letter proofreading (that is, letting the eye rest momentarily on each letter) is the only accurate method. This is customary for the reading of small amounts of copy, such as covers and flap copy, but it is too time-consuming for text. Other people use a word-for-word approach (letting the eye rest momentarily on each word), but this is usually not accurate enough. For general text proofreading, a syllable-for-syllable style that allows the eye to rest on each syllabic element of a word is encouraged.

10. *Vocalization.* Many proofreaders either say the words aloud as they visually check them or, more often, "pronounce" them mentally. This technique is called vocalization. The pronunciation, however, is not standard; it should vocalize every letter of the word, including silent letters. For instance, *knight* is vocalized "kuh-NIKT," pronouncing the silent *k* as well as the silent *gh*. This is done to verify that all silent letters, or otherwise tricky elements, are present.

Miscellaneous. Certain typefaces have idiosyncrasies which the proofreader and editor should be aware of. For instance, some Souvenir types, especially if slightly kerned, run *r* and *n* so closely together they may appear as an *m*. Baskerville and Bembo types usually seem smaller when compared with other faces in the same point size. Some faces have ligatures that don't quite run together. In many typefaces an *f* followed by a quotation mark, question mark, or close parenthesis will require a hair space (hr#) inserted between them, as will some opening parentheses followed by a capital *J*.

Tools of the Trade. Finally, beyond a pencil, the proofreader needs a number of other tools, most of which are the proofreader's responsibility if he or she is a professional freelancer. Below is a list of some essential tools and some optional ones.

Essential Tools

The publisher's preferred dictionary (Zondervan recommends *Merriam-Webster's Collegiate Dictionary, Eleventh Edition*)

The publisher's preferred style manual (Zondervan recommends both *The Chicago Manual of Style, Fifteenth Edition* and *The Christian Writer's Manual of Style*)

The publisher's preferred Bible version (a freelancer's library should contain, at least, the King James Version, the NIV, and the NRSV)

Optional Tools (handy but not essential)

a perpetual calendar (for checking dates and days of the week, past and future; these circular calendars can be found in science stores, in some Asian gift shops, and online)

ruled cards (these can be made from a piece of clear, thick plastic, along the top of which a strip of black tape has been placed, about a quarter inch wide; this allows the reader to isolate the current line but also to view the lines that follow)

ruler

calculator, to do the math

an analytical concordance (to check spellings in Bible references)

Merriam-Webster's Biographical Dictionary (a pocket edition is available; in this and the following three items, Merriam-Webster publications are recommended because they are generally compatible in spelling and style with their *Collegiate Dictionary*)

Merriam-Webster's Geographical Dictionary (a pocket edition is available)

Merriam-Webster's Medical Dictionary (a pocket edition is available)

Merriam-Webster's Dictionary of the Law

one-volume desk encyclopedia

dictionary of quotations

thesaurus

Proof Stages.

Since the advent of word processing, there can be as many as six proofreading stages in book production: printout, first proofs, second proofs or repros, page corrections, printer-ready disc (or camera copy), and silverprints (also called blues). These steps will vary from publisher to publisher. For those publishers who do follow these six stages, the printout stage is often skipped. When a printout is done, it is usually checked by the author. First proofs are assigned to a proofreader and are often checked simultaneously by the author. Second proofs are also assigned to a proofreader. The last three stages are usually checked by the editor in charge of the project.

1. *Printouts.* In computerized editing, printouts are sent to the author at the editor's discretion. This is usually done before first proofs have been run, and this step allows an author a chance to review the book for changes before seeing it in proofs. Printouts are especially helpful when heavy editing has been done or when many revisions are expected. Often scheduling does not allow time for a printout stage, in which case the author will be sent a copy of the first proofs on which to check for errors.

2. *First Proofs.* Ideally all mistakes should be discovered and corrected by the end of the first-proof stage, if not in the preceding printout stage.

In traditional proofreading, the proofreader checks the proofs (*live copy*) against the manuscript (*dead copy*) to ensure that proof copy corresponds word for word with the edited manuscript. With the advent of computer typesetting, however, it is not always possible to provide the proofreader with an accurate manuscript against which to check the typeset copy. In this case the proofreader must read the proofs without reference to an authoritative manuscript. This entails checking the accuracy of spelling against the dictionary, and checking for correct style against the publisher's accepted manual of style and any other references provided by the publisher. The proofreader is responsible to see that all typographical specifications (*specs*) called for by the editor are carried out correctly.

Correcting typographical errors is an important part of a proofreader's objective but by no means the only one. Just as important are errors in formatting. These kinds of errors should be marked in first proofs:

Poor spacing (between letters, words, illustrations, lines, and headings)
Wrong alignment or indentations
Incorrect placement, size, or typeface of headings
Wrong typeface or size of text area
Misspellings (refer to *Webster's Eleventh*)
Footnotes out of order
Incorrect reduction of footnotes or extracts
Poor word divisions
Makeup problems, that is, less than a full line on the first line of text, fewer than two lines below a heading at the bottom of a page, or fewer than four lines on a page ending a chapter

Every correction on a proof requires two marks; one in the text and one in the margin. A caret or slash is usually used to locate the error in the text; the appropriate proofreader's mark is then made in the margin. For standard symbols, see "Proofreading Symbols, Standard." Proofreaders should flag in the margin any cross-references within the book so that they can be filled in on final pages. They should also flag places where artwork (illustrations, charts, figures, and so on) will be needed.

The proofreader should use a red or blue pen (not black) and initial each proof page. This will certify that the proofreading is complete.

Ascertaining the style of each project and being consistent within that style are important parts of the proofreader's job because not all projects will conform to the most recognized or standard usage.

Proofreaders are limited in their right to make editorial changes but are encouraged to query the editor if a passage seems unclear in content or grammatical form or if factual information seems false. Proofreaders query the editor by placing a question mark to the far right of the margin, concisely noting the problem or suggested correction. Queries should be circled, and the page on which they occur should be marked with a paper clip or a sticky note. When the proofreader has a query, he or she should call the editor's attention to it by writing on the page in a different color ink. Marking queries on the pages themselves in a different color ink is preferable to affixing Post-It notes with queries written on them, since such tags can easily become separated from the pages. One approach might be to write the query in the margin in a different color ink and then attach a blank tag to the page to help the editor or compositor find it. In any case, avoid writing a query on an adhesive tag that could possibly fall off the page. If a query involves more than this type of short note, to avoid cluttering the proofs proofreaders can prepare a query sheet indicating the page and line on which their question occurs.

3. *Second Proofs.* At the second-proof stage the proofreader sees that each correction called for on first proofs has been made properly; if it has, it should be checked off. Usually the proofreader will be provided with both the first proofs and the author's corrections.

After checking that all corrections have been made, the proofreader reads through the entire project, marking any errors overlooked on first proofs and checking for sense, proper arrangement of material, and incorrect hyphenations that may have resulted from the previous corrections. The proofreader does not read line for line against the first proofs or the author's copy but may refer to either. Any inserted material that has not been proofread before this point should be carefully scrutinized.

Second proofs normally consist of completed pages with folios and running heads; these are checked for proper sequence, position, and typeface. The order and numbering of footnotes, both in the text and in the list of notes, is double-checked at this stage. The proofreader also makes sure all chapter titles and running heads are consistent with the titles given in the table of contents and inserts correct page numbers into the table of contents. Cross-references in the text are also filled in by locating the page reference in the manuscript and noting the material referred to and then finding this material and its final page number in the second proofs. The proofreader spot-checks page lengths and scrutinizes overall appearance, especially noting consistency in spacing. Queries should be few at this stage.

4. *Page Corrections.* Often when a correction is called for on second proofs, only the affected pages are reset and proofread. These corrected pages are usually proofread by the editor, who verifies that the corrections have been properly made. This involves looking up the page in the second proofs on which each correction is called for and scanning the material around the cor-

rection to ensure that no additional errors have been introduced. These corrected pages are then inserted into the final proofs by the typesetter.

5. *Format Check.* Once all the corrected pages have been assembled, the copy is checked one last time for accuracy. The overall page appearance is the main concern at this stage. The editor checks that all page corrections have been accurately made. The running heads and folios are examined for order and placement and are compared with the table of contents for consistency. Copyright information is double-checked. Chapter titles and artwork that have been pasted in are checked for proper placement and general appearance. The length of facing pages is closely examined. Many times the editor reads the bottom line of a page and the top line of the following page to ensure correct order of copy. This is the best opportunity to look at the big picture: Is the title correct on the title page? Is the author's name spelled correctly? Do the page numbers given on the table of contents really correspond to the actual chapters?

Once everything is deemed accurate and complete, the data is saved to a printer-ready disk and sent to the printer, or, in the case of noncomputerized printing, the camera copy is sent to the printer.

6. *Silverprints.* Also called blueprints or "blues," silverprints are contact prints made from negatives by the printer. These prints are checked by the editor for general appearance. After the editor makes sure that everything is in order and that all corrections have been made, the book is ready for the press. No changes can be made after the editor has approved silverprints because the next step is platemaking for the printing press.

Black spots and spots in letters caused by faulty negatives are circled for removal. Signature marks, located on the spine of each signature and used for collating the book, are checked for proper placement. Also, the pages should be checked at this stage to make sure that they are in the correct numerical sequence.

Problems that may not show clearly on camera-ready copy are often easily spotted in silverprints. For instance, inconsistency in space between a pasted-up line and adjacent lines, space between a running head and text, or straightness of pasted-in material are problems often not found until the silverprint stage. But changes on silverprints are costly and involve shooting new negatives. In fact, corrections become more troublesome and expensive to make with each successive stage of production, so it is important to examine proofs and materials carefully each time a project comes into the hands of an editor or proofreader. When corrections do need to be made on silverprints, the editor should mark the problem clearly and attach a paperclip to the page so that the long side of the paperclip extends onto the page of the correction.

Proofreading Abbreviations and Terms

Authors are sometimes mystified by the arcane terminology that proofreaders and editors have developed over the centuries. Here are a few of the most common, along with their meanings.

aa—author's alteration; any change made by the author after the type has been set

ad—advertisement

agate—a type size of about 5-$^1/_2$ points; once used in newspaper classified ads to save space

agate line—a vertical measurement of space in newspaper and advertising layout. Fourteen agate lines equals one vertical inch of space.

all caps—all capital letters

alley—the vertical white space between two columns of type

alphabet length—the length of a typeface's alphabet, usually in 6 point. Alphabet lengths of different faces can then be compared for copy-fit purposes.

alternate characters—alternatives for certain characters in some fonts. Alternate characters include swash characters, ligatures, kerned characters, and letters with longer or shorter ascenders and/or descenders.

antiqua—the German term for roman type

ascender—the stroke that ascends higher than the letter's x-height. Capital letters are considered ascenders as are the following lowercase letters: b, d, f, h, k, l, t.

author's proof—copy sent to the author for correction, often after all typographic errors have been corrected

back matter—same as rear matter; the portion of the book after the main text

bad break—a word that is incorrectly broken over a line; abbreviated *bb*

baseline—the imaginary line on which a line of type sits

b/b, or b to b—baseline to baseline (in measuring leading)

bf—boldface

black letter—a now little-used style of type; also called *Old English*, *gothic*, or *German* type

bleed—a graphic device in which an image or type is allowed to run off the edge of the printed page

blurb—promotional copy endorsing the book, used on the cover or in a catalog

body matter—the main text of the book, excluding the front and back matter

body type—type used for continuous reading, also called *text type*

border—any rule or decorative frame placed around the text on the page

box—a rule line placed around type or around an image

box head—a heading set within rules

break out—a quotation, sometimes extracted from the text itself, that is printed in display size for emphasis; sometimes boxed or placed between rules; also called a *drop quote* or *pull quote*

bullet—a typographic dot used to highlight elements in a list or to separate items on a line b&w—black and white

callout—the symbol or superior number inserted in a text to mark a foot- or endnote reference; also, a mark that a proofreader places in the margin as a reminder to check something (such as a footnote reference) later

cap—capital

caret—the proofreading symbol that means "insert"; looks like an inverted v

cast off (noun)—a sample of either the book's design or the rough calculation of the number of pages in the final book

cast off (verb)—to estimate the number of pages in the final printed book

c/lc—capital and lowercase

comp—comprehensive layout

c.q.—a marginal indication to the typesetter that a seemingly misspelled or odd word is actually correct; originally a Morse code abbreviation for *call to quarters*; in text, *sic* is used in the same way

c/sc—capitals and small capitals

cx, cxs—correction, corrections

dead copy, *also called* foul proof—old copies of the manuscript that have been superceded by newer, corrected copies, called *live copy*

descender—the stroke that descends below the baseline of a letter. The following letters are the descenders: g, j, p, q, y.

ea—editor's alteration; any change made by the editor after the type has been set

endpaper—the piece of paper glued to the inside of a book's cover

extract—a quotation set apart from the main text, usually in a smaller type size and with a narrower measure

fl l—flush left

fl r—flush right

flush—not indented

front matter—the portion of the book before the main text

H&J—hyphenation and justification

galley—any copy of the manuscript, usually before it has been flowed into typeset pages

gutter—the white space that runs along the interior of the book's spine between the text printed on the facing pages; the fold in a newspaper

hanging head—a running head that is set closer to the outer edge of the page than the text itself

hanging indentation—when the first line of a paragraph is set left and the remaining lines are indented.

head, heading—a line of type that stands as a title or description of a portion of the book

ital—italic type; the kind of type that slants to the right

jacket—dust jacket; the paper cover of a hardcover book

justify—to align type vertically on both the left and right margins

kill—to delete, either from a copy or from a digital archive

lc—lowercase; small (non-capital) letters

leaders—a horizontal series of dots intended to lead the eye from one element to another leading—the horizontal space between lines of type

legend—caption

letterpress—type of printing in which inked metal type prints directly on the paper

linecut—a black-and-white line illustration

makeup—the correct positioning of the elements on a page (a process now computerized)

margins—the blank areas that frame the text

masthead—a printed list of a periodical's editors and production personnel, along with other essential publication information

measure—the width of a single column of text

mechanicals—the final pasted up pages ready for printing (a process now wholly computerized)

negs—negatives

nut—an en space (term now antiquated)

OCR—optical character recognition

OE—Old English (black letter) type

OF—Old Face type

offset—a printing method in which a rubber blanket transfers an inked image to the paper

orphan—a broken word of four or fewer characters on a line by itself

OS—old style type

parens—parentheses

pe—printer's error

perfect binding—a binding process in which the folds are trimmed off the signatures and the loose pages are held together with glue

pi, px—pica, picas; a unit of printer's measurement. A pica is 12 points, and 6 picas is just a hair short of one inch.

point—1/12 of a pica, and about 1/72 of an inch

proof—a rough copy, often in low resolution, of printed material used to check for errors

pt, pts—point, points

QWERTY—standard keyboard layout

rear matter—the portion of the book after the main text

recto—right-hand page, with an odd number

repro—reproduction copy

rg rt, ragged right—type copy not aligned on the right margin

roman type—type that stands straight up

rule, rule line—a printed line

running head, running footer—a line at the top or bottom of a page bearing the book title, chapter title, author name, or folio

sig, or signature—a large printed sheet that, when folded, makes up several book pages (usually in multiples of 16 or 32 pages)

sink, or sinkage—dropping the text area lower on the page

slug—line spacing (term is now antiquated)

spec—specification

spread—two facing pages

ss, or s/s—same size

stet—Latin for "let it stand"

stripping—putting together the film to make book pages (now largely computerized)

subhead—the heading subordinate to a larger heading

subscript—letters or number that are set lower than the baseline of type

superscript—letters or numbers that are set higher than the baseline of type

text type—the typeface used for the text of a book

type page—the text and graphic area of the page, excluding the margins

typo—typographical error

uc—uppercase; capital letters

u/lc, or u&lc—upper- and lowercase

verso—left-hand page, with an even number

wf—wrong font

widow—four or fewer lines of type on a page at the end of a chapter

x-height—the height of the letter *x* in any given font. The following letters are all the x-height letters in the alphabet: a, c, e, i, m, n, o, r, s, u, v, w, x, z.

Proofreading Symbols, Standard

Insert Copy

e	Insert letter.
word	Insert a.
(See p.x)	Insert new copy.
ʒ	Insert ending letter.
b	Insert beginning letter.
#	Insert space.
⊙	Insert period.
↑	Insert comma.
;/	Insert semicolon;/
⊙	Insert colon:
=/	Insert hyphen. [born again]
em	Insert em dash, or long dash.
en	Insert en dash. [1898, 1963]
(/)	(Insert parentheses.)

[/]	[Insert brackets.]
•••	Insert ellipsis.
✓/ ✓ ✓	Insert quotation marks.
(slash)	Insert solidus, slash.
✓	Insert apostrophe [Buechners]
(accent) ✓	Insert accent. [cliché]
(set) ?	Insert question mark
(set) !	Insert exclamation point
✓	Insert superior number.

Delete Copy

✓	Delete character.
✓	Delete and close up.
✓	Delete word word.
✓	Delete line.

Replace Copy

e   Replace l/tter.

word   Replace term.

(cap)   capitalize letter or word.

(lc)   Lowercase letter or Word

(c/lc)   SET IN CAPS AND LOWERCASE.

(ital)   Set in italics.

(bf)   Set in boldface.

(rom)   Set in roman.

(sc)   Set in small caps.

(c/sc)   Set in caps and small caps.

(sp)   Spell out abbrev. number, or symbol.

Move Copy

(tr)   Transpose characters.

(tr)   words Transpose.

□   □Indent one em space.

⊏   ⊏ Move left.

⊐   Move right.

⊐⊏   Center.   ⊏

(align)   ‖ Align copy.

⌒   Close sp⌒ace.

(less #)   Less ∧ space.

¶   ¶ Start new paragraph.

(run-in)   Run lines together.

(break)   Break. Start on new line.

Other Symbols

(stet)   Let it stand as set.

(?)   Author or editor query.

(divi·sion)   Indicate correct word div- ìsion.

(Note)   Circle notations not meant to be set.

Fix Copy

(X)   Fix defective character.

(wf)   Correct wrong font.

(eq #)   Equalize ∧uneven ∧spacing.

/   **Slashes are used to:**

r/(lc)/⁄   Separate corections /in ar/ single line.

e ‖‖   Rpeat sam∧ corrction in a single ∧line.

Proofs: Author's Responsibilities

Most publishers provide an author with *proofs* at one or more stages of the manuscript's development. This section deals with the author's responsibility in regard to proofreading and checking that all corrections have been made and that the editorial changes are acceptable. For a more detailed description of proof-handling procedures and the responsibilities of the proofreader, see "Proofreading."

Production Stages. Although every publisher adheres to a slightly different routine, an edited manuscript generally passes through the following stages in the production process: pre-typeset galleys (sometimes called *printouts*), design and sample pages, composition, first proofs (also called first typeset galleys), second proofs (also called second typeset galleys or final proofs), printer's disk or camera copy, platemaking, press, silverprints, and binding.

Some publishers provide authors with galleys from one or more of the various proof stages. In these cases, it is still important that the author make major changes in the earlier, preferably pre-typeset, stages rather than in the later stages.

1. Pre-typeset Galleys. An editor may supply the author with a set of pre-typeset galleys, which are usually nothing more than a hard-copy printout of the editor's revised version of the manuscript, and indicate a date by which the author's revisions to those galleys should be returned. This is the computer-age equivalent of providing the author with a hand-marked-up copy of the edited manuscript for response and correction.

Computerized pre-typeset galleys may include "revision tracking," that is, the editor's annotations of all the changes that were made, but this is not always done since revision tracking can actually be an obstacle to checking the accuracy of copy.

The use of these pre-typeset galleys is an effective way to control costs as an author and editor polish a manuscript, especially when the author's or editor's revisions are expected to be extensive. In a sense, the author and editor are working to make the manuscript "letter perfect" before flowing the text into the designed and typeset format.

2. First Proofs. Often the editor will furnish the author with a set of first proofs (the first set of typeset pages) and indicate a deadline for returning them. Extensive or frequent revisions at this stage tend to be more costly, and as stipulated in the author's contract, these costs may be charged to the author if they exceed stated limits.

3. Final Proofs. An author will usually receive second or final proofs *only* if the book calls for an index. In this case, the author will be given a deadline by which to complete the compilation of the index. Manuscript revisions (other than the correction of typographical errors) are usually not permitted at this stage.

Prophecy and Prophesy

Be careful to distinguish between *prophecy* (a noun) and *prophesy* (a verb).

A false prophet may prophesy, but will his prophecy come to pass?

Protestant

The term is capped when referring to one of the denominations established during the Reformation to oppose the primacy of the pope or when referring to any other later, non-Catholic denomination that believes in justification by faith, the priesthood of all believers, and the Bible as the primary source of revelation. *Protestant* also refers to a member of such a denomination. The term *Protestantism* refers to that form of belief as a whole.

The term *Protestant* should not be used simply to mean non-Catholic, since that ignores the fact that Eastern Orthodoxy is both a non-Catholic and non-Protestant form of Christian belief. (See also *"Eastern Orthodox* Versus *Orthodox"* and *"Catholic."*) A Protestant, in other words, is a Christian believer who is neither Catholic nor Orthodox.

Psalms, Alternate Numbering of the

Writers, readers, proofreaders, and editors are often surprised to stumble upon the fact that there are two numbering schemes for some of the Psalms, one based on the Hebrew Bible and the other on the Septuagint. Care must be taken when quoting some Jewish and classic Christian authors' opinions about certain psalms because they may actually be referring to a different psalm altogether.

Some Roman Catholic Bibles formerly took their cue from the Vulgate, which followed the Septuagint numbering, in which all but twelve of the psalms are assigned a number one less than the number assigned to those psalms in most Protestant Bibles, such as the KJV and NIV. Many contemporary Roman Catholic Bibles, such as the JB, list both numbers: the Hebrew number first, followed by the Vulgate's number in parentheses.

Psalms 10 through 147. The psalms in question are Psalms 10 through 147. Psalms 9 and 10 in the Hebrew Bible (from which most Protestant Bibles take their numbering) are regarded as a single psalm, which is number 9 in the Septuagint and Vulgate. The scholarly arguments in favor of the Septuagint in this case are strong. Psalm 10 is the sole psalm among the first thirty-two that does not bear its own heading, suggesting it was meant to be part of the preceding psalm. Also, Psalm 9 begins an acrostic pattern that is continued in Psalm 10, as well as possessing a continuous theme and tone. Psalm 9 was probably split in the Hebrew Bible to facilitate its use in liturgical settings.

When Psalms 9 and 10 are considered a single unit, the psalms that follow it bear a different number, which is one less, according to Septuagint and Vulgate numbering. The famous Psalm 23, for instance, is actually Psalm 22 in the Septuagint and the Vulgate and in many Bibles based on them.

Psalms 114 through 116. Another difference occurs in Psalms 114–16. The Hebrew Bible considers Psalms 114 and 115 as two separate psalms, while the Septuagint folds them into a single psalm, which is numbered 113. Conversely, the next psalm, 116 in the Hebrew Bible, is separated into two in the Septuagint, where they are numbered 114 and 115. After those three psalms, the alternate numbering system continues until Psalm 147, which the Septuagint again divides into two, thereby reverting to the numbering system most familiar to Protestant readers for Psalms 148–50.

Other Differences. The Septuagint also adds the apocryphal Psalm 151, which does not appear at all in the Protestant Bible or the Vulgate but does appear in some Eastern Orthodox Bibles. Also the Septuagint has different verse numberings in many cases because it numbers the titles and headings that precede some of the psalms as verse 1, which none of the later Bibles, not even the Vulgate, do. So in many cases, the Septuagint Psalms have one more verse than later versions of the Bible.

What is true of most quotations from the Bible is especially true of Psalms: take no quotation for granted. Careful writers check their sources. The following chart should help.

Hebrew Bible (& Protestant Bibles)		Septuagint (& Vulgate & Some Roman Catholic Bibles)
1–8	=	1–8
9	=	9a
10	=	9b
11–113	=	10–112
114	=	113a
115	=	113b
116a	=	114
116b	=	115
117–146	=	116–145
147a	=	146
147b	=	147
148–150	=	148–150
(omitted)	=	151 (omitted in Vulgate)

Psalms, Traditional Groupings of

Certain groupings of OT Psalms have become so familiar as to have acquired names. Here are a few of the major groupings and the specific psalms that are included. Note that many of the groupings overlap.

The Alphabetic Psalms—Psalms 9, 10, 25, 34, 37, 111–112, 119, and 145. So called because they use an alphabetic device in their poetic structure.

The Asaphite Psalms—Psalm 73–83. Also called the *Psalms*, or *Songs, of Asaph*, so called because Asaph and possibly his descendents are attributed as the author(s). Psalm 50 may also have been included in this group.

The Great Hallel—in Jewish tradition, Psalm 136.

The Hallel—Psalms 113–118, which are customarily chanted at such Jewish festivals as Passover; also called the *Egyptian Hallel*. Sometimes Jewish tradition also refers to the *Songs of Ascents*, 120–134, as the *Hallel*.

The Hallelujah Psalms—Psalms 146–150. The last five psalms, all of which begin with "Praise the Lord."

The Penitential Psalms—Psalms 6, 32, 38, 51, 102, 130, 143. These are all psalms expressive of contrition, often spoken in times of illness and suffering. They are commonly used as texts for Ash Wednesday services. Unlike the other groupings, this set of psalms was created for Christian liturgical use and is not a grouping found in the Septuagint.

The Prayer of Moses—Psalm 90. This title does not mean that the patriarch Moses wrote the psalm but that it is imitative of his style.

The Psalm of Ethan—Psalm 89.

The Psalms of David—Psalms 3–9, 11–32, 34–41, 51–65, 68–70, 86, 103, 108–110, 122, 124, 131, 133, 135–145. These psalms are ascribed to David.

The Psalms of Solomon—Psalms 72 and 127. Like the Psalm of Moses, this ascription most likely means that these psalms imitate Solomon's style rather than asserting his direct authorship.

The Psalms of the Sons of Korah—Psalms 42–49, 84–85, 87–88.

The Songs of Ascents—Psalms 120–134. Also called the *Gradual Psalms* or the *Songs of Degrees* (KJV). They are probably so called because they were sung by Jewish pilgrims on their way to Jerusalem as they ascended Mount Zion.

Publishers' Names in Short Form, Religious

The following list is provided as a quick reference for the correct spelling and shortened form of some well-known religious publishers. Note that some cities are well-known enough to warrant the omission of state names.

Publisher Name	Location	Short Form
Abbey Press	St. Meinrad, Ind.	Abbey
Abingdon Press	Nashville	Abingdon
ACTA Publications	Chicago	ACTA
Accent Books	Colorado Springs	Accent
Alba House	Staten Island	Alba House

Albury Publishing	Tulsa	Albury
American Bible Society	New York	ABS
AMG Publishers	Chattanooga	AMG
Antioch Publishing Co.	Yellow Springs, Ohio	Antioch
Ascension Press	West Chester, Pa.	Ascension
Augsburg Fortress, Publishers	Minneapolis	Augsburg Fortress
Augustinian Press	Villanova, Pa.	Augustinian
Ave Maria Press	Notre Dame, Ind.	Ave Maria
Back to the Bible	Lincoln, Neb.	Back to the Bible
Baker Book House	Grand Rapids, Mich.	Baker
Ballantine/Wellspring	New York	Ballantine/Wellspring
Banner of Truth	Carlisle, Pa.	Banner of Truth
Baptist Publishing House	Texarkana, Tex.	Baptist
Barbour Publishing, Inc.	Uhrichsville, Ohio	Barbour
Bethany House Publishers	Bloomington, Minn.	Bethany House
Bob Jones University Press	Greenville, S.C.	Bob Jones
Broadman & Holman Publishers	Nashville	Broadman
Charisma House	Lake Mary, Fla.	Charisma House
Christianity Today International	Carol Stream, Ill.	Christianity Today
Christian Publications	Camp Hill, Pa.	Christian
Cistercian Publications	Kalamazoo, Mich.	Cistercian
College Press Publishing Co.	Joplin, Mo.	College Press
Concordia Publishing House	St. Louis	Concordia
Cook Communications Ministries	Colorado Springs	Cook
Cowley Publications	Cambridge, Mass.	Cowley
Crossroad Publishing Company, The	New York	Crossroad
Dake Publishing	Lawrenceville, Ga.	Dake
Destiny Image Publishers	Shippensburg, Pa.	Destiny Image
Discipleship Publications International	Billerica, Mass.	Discipleship
Discovery House Publishers	Grand Rapids, Mich.	Discovery House
Doubleday/Galilee	New York	Doubleday/Galilee
Eerdmans Publishing Co., Wm. B.	Grand Rapids, Mich.	Eerdmans
Evangel Press	Nappanee, Ind.	Evangel
Faith Library Publications	Tulsa	Faith Library
Focus on the Family Publishing	Colorado Springs	Focus on the Family
Fordham University Press	Bronx	Fordham
Foundation Publications	La Habra, Calif.	Foundation
Friends of Israel, the	Bellmawr, N.J.	Friends of Israel
Good News Publishers/ Crossway Books	Wheaton, Ill.	Good News/Crossway
Gospel Advocate Company	Nashville	Gospel Advocate
Gospel Light/ Regal & Renew Books	Ventura, Ca.	Gospel Light/ Regal & Renew
Group Publishing, Inc.	Loveland, Colo.	Group

Publisher Name	Location	Short Form
Guideposts	Carmel, N.Y.	Guideposts
HarperSanFrancisco	San Francisco	HarperSanFrancisco
Harrison House Publishers	Tulsa	Harrison House
Harvest House Publishers	Eugene, Ore.	Harvest House
Hendrickson Publishers, Inc.	Peabody, Mass.	Hendrickson
Herald Press	Scottdale, Pa.	Herald
Honor Books	Tulsa	Honor
Howard Publishing	West Monroe, La.	Howard
iExalt Inc.	Austin	iExalt
Ignatius Press	San Francisco	Ignatius
Inspirational Press	New York	Inspirational
InterVarsity Press	Westmont, Ill.	InterVarsity
Jewish Lights Publishing	Woodstock, Vt.	Jewish Lights
Kregel Publications	Grand Rapids, Mich.	Kregel
Liguori Publications	Liguori, Mo.	Liguori
Liturgical Press, The	Collegeville, Minn.	Liturgical
Loyola Press	Chicago	Loyola
Macmillan Co., The	New York	Macmillan
Mennonite Publishing House	Scottdale, Pa.	Mennonite
Moody Press	Chicago	Moody Press
Multnomah Publishers, Inc.	Sisters, Ore.	Multnomah
NavPress	Colorado Springs	NavPress
Nazarene Publishing House	Kansas City, Mo.	Nazarene
Nelson Publishers, Thomas	Nashville	Nelson
New City Press	Hyde Park, N.Y.	New City
New Hope Publishers	Birmingham	New Hope
New Life Publications	Orlando	New Life
Orbis Books	Maryknoll, N.Y.	Orbis
Our Sunday Visitor	Huntington, Ind.	Our Sunday Visitor
Oxford University Press	New York	Oxford
P&R Publishing Company	Phillipsburg, N.J.	P&R
Paraclete Press	Orleans, Mass.	Paraclete
Paternoster Publishing USA	Waynesboro, Ga.	Paternoster
Paulist Press	Mahwah, N.J.	Paulist
Penguin Putnam, Inc.	New York	Penguin Putnam
Plough Publishing House	Farmington, Pa.	Plough
Regina Press	Melville, N.Y.	Regina
Servant Publications	Ann Arbor, Mich.	Servant
Shaw Books	Colorado Springs	Shaw
Sheed & Ward Book Publishing	Franklin, Wis.	Sheed & Ward

Standard Publishing	Cincinnati	Standard
Sweet Publishing	Fort Worth	Sweet
Tyndale House Publishers, Inc.	Wheaton, Ill.	Tyndale House
Upper Room, The	Nashville	Upper Room
Victor Books	Colorado Springs	Victor
Walk Thru the Bible Ministries	Atlanta, Ga.	Walk Thru the Bible
Waterbrook Press	Colorado Springs	Waterbrook
Westminster John Knox Press	Louisville	Westminster
World Bible Publishers, Inc.	Iowa Falls	World
W Publishing Group	Nashville	W
YWAM Publishing	Seattle, Wash.	YWAM
Zondervan	Grand Rapids, Mich.	Zondervan

Punctuation

Punctuation with Font Changes. When more than one font is used in a sentence, all periods, commas, colons, and semicolons should be set in the predominant font of that sentence, not necessarily the font of the word adjacent to the punctuation mark. In most ordinary text settings, this means that periods, commas, colons, and semicolons will be set roman even when they immediately follow an italicized word. The rationale is that those particular punctuation marks are always signposts within the sentence and belong to the entire context not just a particular word.

Question marks and exclamation points, by contrast, can belong either to an entire sentence or to an individual word. Accordingly, question marks and exclamation points should be set in the same font as the element to which they belong. For instance, when the entire sentence is a question, the question mark should be in the same font as the sentence, even if it follows a word in another font.

Of course, all punctuation marks should be set in italics when they are part of an italicized title.

With paired punctuation marks, such as parentheses, brackets, and quotation marks, set the opening and closing marks in the same font as the predominant font of the context. If an italic quotation is on a line by itself, then the quotation marks should be set in italic. An exception should be made whenever a letter in the italicized word oversets (touches) the punctuation mark. In that case, either set the punctuation mark in italic or add a thin space to resolve the oversetting.

Newman followed the *Apologia*, written in 1864, with *Grammar of Assent*. [Both comma and period are in roman type.]

Newman's masterpiece (*Apologia pro vita sua*) was written in 1864. [Both the opening and closing parentheses are in roman type.]

Has he seen *The Greatest Story Ever Told*? [The question mark is in roman.]

Have you read *Where Is God When It Hurts?* [The question mark is in italic as part of the title.]

(see paragraph 6*a*) [The closing parenthesis is in roman type.]

"The prayer ended with a *Deo gratias*." [The period is in roman, and the closing quotation mark is in roman to match the opening mark.]

[*sic*]

An Alternate Method of Handling Punctuation with Font Changes. The rule outlined in the first paragraph of this section is a change from the former rule that recommended that periods, commas, colons, and semicolons be set in the same font as the word next to which they were set. This older rule is still perfectly valid and may be applied at the discretion of the author or editor. Consistent application of one rule or the other is the ideal, but the fact is that few, if any, readers can even distinguish between an italic comma and a roman one or understand the difference. This is to say that editors and proofreaders may have to live with a certain amount of inconsistency in this regard, especially in late proof stages, where correcting such minor errors that are unlikely to be noticed by readers would be both time-consuming and costly.

Abbreviations with Other Punctuation. When an abbreviation ends a sentence, the abbreviating period will also serve as the period to the sentence. All other punctuation, however, is used in combination with an abbreviating period.

The service began promptly at 11:00 a.m.

Is it true that the winner was R. J.?

Multiple Punctuation. When two different punctuation marks are needed in the same place in a sentence, only the more emphatic mark is used. In rare instances multiple punctuation may be advisable for clarity and expression.

In which poem does Hopkins write, "O world wide of its good!" [No final question mark is added.]

"What shall we do with Jesus?" Moody asked the congregation. [No comma is used after the question mark.]

The question Jesus asked Peter, Do you love me? was a reflection of the Great Commandment. [No comma is used after the question mark.]

Does he really believe you can serve both God and mammon! [No question mark is used, since the sentence is clearly interrogative.]

He really believes that?!

Multiple Punctuation with Titles. In references or in running text, when a title of a work ends in a question mark or an exclamation point, any period or comma that would ordinarily follow that title is dropped. Colons and semicolons, however, can be used after question marks or exclamation points in titles and should be retained.

> Morrison, Frank. *Who Moved the Stone?* London: Faber and Faber, 1930. [no period after the title]
>
> I spent the summer reading five of Philip Yancey's books: *Where Is God When It Hurts? The Jesus I Never Knew, What's So Amazing about Grace? The Bible Jesus Read,* and *Reaching for the Invisible God.* [no commas after titles with question marks; if there is concern that confusion will result, semicolons could be inserted to separate titles]
>
> He had read Francis Schaeffer's *How Then Shall We Live?*; it made a deep impression on him.

Open Versus Close Style. In general, this manual recommends an "open style" of punctuation (that is, minimizing punctuation as much as possible) in all books intended for a popular audience. This has been the trend in publishing for many years and is often characterized by the phrase "when in doubt, leave it out." Generally, a "close style" of punctuation should be reserved for books of a highly complex, polemical, or academic nature, such as textbooks, theological works, or reference works intended for scholars.

(See individual entries for each type of punctuation mark.)

Q

Question Mark

The question mark was developed by early printers from the first and last letters of the Latin word *questio*, which was originally rendered "₰" and later simplified to the form we know now.

In usage, a question mark always follows a direct question and, like the period and the exclamation point, is considered an *end stop*, that is, a punctuation mark primarily found at the end of a sentence, although there are exceptions.

When Used within a Sentence. Even though the question mark usually falls at the end of a sentence, sometimes it can be used within a sentence, for instance in fiction to show a character's thought-but-unspoken question or in quoted dialogue.

> *Why would she have said that?* he thought.
> "Why would she say that?" he said.

Sometimes a series of questions occurs within a sentence, and a question mark can appropriately be used with each.

> A good reporter asks who? what? where? when? and how?

Care must be taken in all these preceding cases because most autoformatting and grammar-checking computer programs, if activated, will automatically capitalize the first letter after all question marks.

Indirect Questions. No question mark should be used with indirect questions.

> The knights never asked the king why he wanted Thomas killed.
> All of us wondered who the new archbishop would be.

With Other Punctuation. A question mark is considered a "strong" punctuation mark and usually has precedence over any other mark of punctuation that might logically fall in the same place in the sentence. Only the exclamation mark is as strong, and to determine whether the question mark or exclamation mark takes precedence, the sense of the sentence should be considered. If the querying nature of the question is stronger than its surprise, or if the question is asked in anticipation of an answer, then the question mark should be used. If a strong declamatory question is meant to be largely rhetorical, then an exclamation point should be used.

In his terror, he yelled, "Who's there?" [an answer is expected]
With utter incomprehension, she shouted, "What do those people expect!" [declamatory and rhetorical]

In Titles. When a book title ends in a question mark, that question mark still takes precedence over any other punctuation, as in:

Philip Yancey's books include *Where Is God When It Hurts? The Jesus I Never Knew, What's So Amazing about Grace?* and *Reaching for the Invisible God.* [commas not used after question marks in the list]

Spanish Question Marks. In Spanish-language publishing worldwide, an inverted question mark (¿) precedes a question, and a regular question mark (?) follows it. There is no need to reproduce this device when translating a Spanish quotation into English, but the device should be retained when a quotation is given in the original language.

Questions, Internal

An *internal question*, sometimes referred to as an *embedded question*, is any question that is placed within the context of a declarative sentence but is not set apart with quotation marks. Formerly, the first word of an internal question was generally capitalized, just as it would be were it a direct quotation, but it is now more common to lowercase the first word, especially when the question is short or consists of a single word. A comma should still precede the question. Longer or proverbial questions, or questions that have a formal tone or internal punctuation may still be capitalized as appropriate.

She wondered, why haven't they called yet?
They shivered to think, what would Mrs. Grundy say?
The committee wanted to know: What did the president know and when did he know it? [capitalized because the question is longer and has a more formal sense]

Quotation Marks

For Direct Discourse. Quotation marks are most commonly used to set off material quoted from another source or to indicate dialogue. These uses, called *direct discourse*, should be distinguished from *indirect discourse*, which should not be set off by quotation marks.

> "Few individuals have done as much as St. Francis to show Christians the way of peace," wrote Morton Kelsey. [written source]
>
> The pastor responded, "In witnessing, remember that we are only beggars advising other beggars where to find food." [dialogue]
>
> G. K. Chesterton once referred to coincidences as spiritual puns. [indirect discourse]

Quotes within Quotes. In American style, double quotation marks are used for most purposes (though see both "British Style" and "Mid-Atlantic Style"). Single quotation marks are used almost exclusively to indicate quotes within quotes. If a further level of interior quotation is needed, double quotation marks are reverted to. Although single quotation marks are then placed within those, if needed, and so on alternately, such multiple levels of quotes-within-quotes should be avoided for obvious reasons.

> "The angel said to them, 'Do not be afraid'" (Luke 2:10).
>
> John read Job 42:1–4 aloud, "Then Job replied to the LORD: 'I know that you can do all things; . . . You said, "Listen now, and I will speak"'" (Job 42:1–2, 4).

For Irony, Slang, and Emphasis. Quotation marks are occasionally used when a word or phrase is meant to be ironic. Since a reader can easily misunderstand the writer's intention, the careful writer should be able to convey irony without this device. Slang words and jargon should only be placed in quotation marks when the author is trying to convey that they are not part of his or her normal vocabulary. Quotation marks are best used with slang words or colloquial expressions when a strong emphasis is desired; even then they should be used with discernment.

> He resented the church's insistence on a "free-will" offering. [ironic]
>
> She could not be sure to what extent he had been "born again." [jargon]

With Other Punctuation. When other punctuation marks are used with quotation marks, correct placement depends on the context. In direct discourse, for instance, periods and commas usually go inside a closing quote mark; question marks and exclamation points usually go inside closing quotes, although they may go outside if the sentence structure calls for it. As a general rule, colons and semicolons are placed outside.

To summarize: single marks go inside, double marks go outside, except for exclamation points and question marks, which can vary according to the context.

> As he read the creed he hesitated before saying, ". . . the quick and the dead";
> a more modern translation would read, ". . . the living and the dead."
> "'Why were you searching for me?' he asked. 'Didn't you know I had to be in
> my Father's house?'" (Luke 2:49).
> Why was the 1560 Geneva Bible called the "Breeches Bible"?

Block Quotations. Block quotations do not normally begin or end with quotation marks. Note, however, that block quotations should retain any and all quotation marks that appear in the original. Also, epigraphs (whether on a separate page or at the beginning of a chapter) and other quotations used for display should not be enclosed in quotation marks. Only those quotation marks that appear in the original should be retained in epigraphs.

Block quotations, whether prose, poetry, or song, should be placed in quotation marks when they are part of dialogue. Note that if the block quotation is also preceded by a spoken lead-in phrase or other words spoken by the same speaker, the block quotation does begin with a new opening quotation mark, just as if it were a new paragraph.

Interior Quotations. In the case of run-in quotations, use single quotation marks for quotes within the quote. But when only the interior quotation is excerpted, the single quotation marks are dropped as long as the context is clear.

> Revelation 22:20 reads, "He who testifies to these things says, 'Yes, I am
> coming soon.'" [quote within the quote]
> Remember what the Spirit of Christ said to John in Revelation 22:20: "Yes, I am
> coming soon." [no single quotes used]

With Yes *and* No. Except in direct discourse, the words *yes* and *no* do not need to be enclosed in quotation marks.

> Although saying yes to Jesus doesn't solve all of life's problems, saying no can
> be a bigger problem in itself.

In Titles. Certain titles of short works and pieces of larger works are set in quotation marks. Be sure to contrast this list with that found in "Italics, *Titles.*"

articles in periodicals
chapters in books
essays
hymns
individual television and radio programs (series are set in italics)
short musical compositions
short poems (anything less than small book length)
short stories
songs

He referred to the "Speaking Out" column in last month's *Christianity Today.*
PBS broadcast Muggeridge's television show "God's Spies" from his series *The Third Testament.*

Nicknames. Nicknames of people require quotation marks when used with the full name, but the nicknames should not be in quotation marks if used alone or with the last name only.

Christopher "Kit" Smart *but* Kit Smart
G. A. Studdert "Woodbine Willie" Kennedy *but* Woodbine Willie
William Ashley "Billy" Sunday *but* Billy Sunday

With Display Caps. At the beginning of a chapter, an opening quotation mark should not be used before any initial display capital that is larger than text size, though the closing quotation mark should be retained. This is customary in British and American typesetting because oversized quotation marks look awkward.

Foreign Quotation Marks. European-style quotation marks are often seen on the Internet and, rarely, in English-language publishing. Although such a famed typographer as Jan Tschichold advocated the use of modified French guillemets in English publishing, his recommendation has been universally ignored. There is no reason to retain foreign-style quotation marks in English, even in direct quotation from the original languages. There are two major alternate systems, the French and German.

Character (open/close)	Name	Example or Explanation
« »	French quotes; guillemets	the open and close quotation marks as used in French, Italian, and Spanish
„ "	German quotes	the open and close quotation marks as used in German; note that they are the reverse of English quotes, and the open quote sits on the baseline

Even if quoting those original languages in an English language context, convert all quotation marks, internal and external, to the American style.

Quotations

To prove a point, support an opinion, muster an argument, reference an authority, inject humor, or gloss the content of a chapter or book with an appropriate thought—all these can be accomplished with an appropriate quotation. As the writer of Proverbs somewhat unappetizingly says, "A word aptly spoken is like apples of gold in settings of silver."

Accuracy. Authors are responsible for reproducing all quotations in wording, spelling, capitalization, and punctuation exactly as they appear in the original printed sources. As a general rule, the style of a quoted passage should not be made to conform to the style of the book in which it will be used. Idiosyncrasies of spelling and capitalization in older works should be preserved; the word *sic*, enclosed in brackets, may be used after an obvious misspelling but should be used sparingly. In the case of works in the public domain, spelling or punctuation may be modernized for the sake of clarity, although a general note should inform the reader that this has been done.

The Pitfalls. Care should be taken to avoid some of the common pitfalls of quoting from other sources. Most importantly, the author should not quote so much from any single source so as to infringe upon that work's legal copyright protection unless the author is prepared to write for permission and possibly pay a fee. (See "Permissions, Obtaining: Author Guidelines, *Fair Use.*") The fair use defense can only be invoked when the total number of words from all the quotations from a single source fall within the guidelines. For instance, if an author quotes a source ten times, the total number of words from those quotes may well exceed the commonly accepted limit even if no single quote exceeds it.

Secondly, some authors feel that they cannot express an opinion without offering supporting quotations from other sources. Using too many quotations can be a distraction, even an annoyance, to the reader. The author should have faith in his or her own ability to convince the reader without having to depend on the authority of others. Quoting, in other words, should be used selectively, not as a stylistic end in itself.

Finally, some authors use quotations as a means of avoiding having to put an idea into their own words. Even if the quotation is within the fair use guidelines, its use may be questionable if the author has simply lifted another author's wording to avoid expressing the idea in a fresh and original way. This last pitfall is more subtle. The author, however, should take heart in knowing that most readers are interested in the author's own words and opinions, not those of others.

Allowable Changes. An initial letter may be changed to a capital or a lower-case letter to conform to the quotation's context within the new work, and a final punctuation mark may be changed to suit the syntax of the larger context.

Run-in Versus Block Quotations. A short quotation may be run into the text (called a *run-in quotation*). A longer quotation is set off from the text (a *block quotation* or *extract*) and is usually set in smaller type (usually one point smaller than text type) and with a narrower width. Generally a prose quotation of more than eight typed lines (five or six typeset lines) or more than a hundred words should be set as a block quotation. Any quotation shorter than that should also be set in block style if it runs to two or more paragraphs. If a series of short quotations are separated by text, then those quotations may best be set off as individual extracts.

Block quotations of a single paragraph need not be indented, but additional paragraphs should be indented.

Three or more lines of poetry are usually set as a block quotation. Two lines of poetry may either be set as a block quotation or run into the text with a spaced slash (/) indicating the line breaks. More lines of poetry may be run-in with spaced slashes whenever an extract setting might look odd to the reader or cause distraction.

Introductory Phrases for Block Quotations. When a block quotation is introduced by a word or phrase like *thus* or *the following*, that word or phrase should be followed by a colon. When a verb-of-saying introduces the block quotation, a comma is used. If it is introduced by a complete statement, a period should be used. When the introductory phrase forms a grammatically complete unit with the block quotation that follows it, no punctuation should be used. Usually the syntax of the introductory phrase will suggest the correct punctuation.

> The role of the pastor has been described thus: . . . [uses a colon]
> In his letter to Queen Ethelberga, Pope Boniface said, . . . [uses a comma]

O'Connor tells the legend of Saint Francis and the wolf of Gubbio. . . . [uses a period]

William Jay said in his book on prayer that . . . [run in without punctuation]

Crediting Block Quotations. The source of a block quotation may be credited in a footnote, an endnote, or a parenthetical reference after the quotation. In some cases, as in epigraphs, a dash may be used to inform the reader of the source.

I went very unwillingly to a society in Aldersgate Street, where one was reading Luther's preface to the Epistle to the Romans. About a quarter before nine, while he was describing the change which God works in the heart through faith in Christ, I felt my heart strangely warmed.

—John Wesley, *Journals*

Accurate Indenting of Poetry. It is the author's responsibility to make sure that quoted poetry is indented line-for-line as in the original. Sometimes, when a manuscript's data is converted from one software to another, indents can be eliminated. It is especially important in these cases for the author to provide the publisher with a hard copy of the manuscript so that the indents may be double checked.

Accurate Indenting of Hymns and Songs. Like poetry, hymns and other songs should also be indented correctly. For the rule regarding the correct indentation of hymns, see "Hymn Meters."

Centering Poetry and Songs on the Page. When poetry, verse, or song lyrics are set as block quotations, they are traditionally centered on the page according to the width of the longest line. In some books, however, the book's designer may have reasons to vary the setting; for instance, if a lot of poetry is quoted amidst blocks of prose, the designer may opt to set all the poetry left to avoid a shifting appearance of the quoted material on the page.

All people that on earth do dwell,
   Sing to the Lord with cheerful voice;
Him serve with fear, His praise forth tell,
   Come ye before Him and rejoice.
—John Hopkins, "The Old Hundredth"

Tenses for Verbs of Saying. Sometimes the question of tense arises with verbs of saying used with quotations. In most cases, logic and the context will dictate the tense. When in doubt, the best rule is this: An author spoke or wrote the work in the past, but the work itself speaks to us in the present.

Solomon said, "Remember your creator in the days of your youth" (Eccl. 12:1).

As Ecclesiastes says, "Remember your Creator in the days of your youth" (12:1).

Quotations from the Bible

In addition to the rules given for general quotations (see "Quotations"), some special rules should be observed when quoting from the Bible.

Familiar Phrases. The tendency in past decades has been to over-reference quotations from the Bible, as though one needed the authority of a reference to verify its existence, but this tendency should be avoided where appropriate. Familiar phrases from the Bible, for instance, need not be set apart by quotation marks or referenced in every instance. In fiction and dialogue it is generally not necessary to annotate a Bible quotation with a parenthetical reference; this would be distracting and unnecessary.

> We too can share the shepherds' wonder at hearing the good tidings of great joy. [no quotation marks or reference needed]
> When the Bible says, "God so loved the world . . . ," it means *all* the world. [no reference needed]
> "Have you not heard that 'God is love'?" [no reference needed in dialogue]

Using Brackets. When quoting the Bible, if the author needs to change an occasional word for clarity's sake, brackets are used to indicate the change. Obviously, this should be done with fidelity to the original meaning of the quote.

> "We love because [God] first loved us" (1 John 4:19).

Noting Repeated Changes in Style. The author may wish to change a particular word or words of a given translation throughout an entire manuscript. This may be done without brackets as long as a general note informing the reader of this change is given in the front matter or on the copyright page. For instance, an author may want to replace the words *thee, thou, thy,* and *thine* of the King James Version with *you* and *your*. A note informing the reader of this change should be provided. Such a note is also useful when the author wishes to change the capitalization style of the deity pronouns in the predominant Bible version or translation used.

With Ellipses. In most cases, an ellipsis should not be placed before or after a Bible verse or a portion of a verse, though one should be used whenever an interior portion is not quoted. If the quoted portion is a sentence fragment, however, or might be confusing to the reader otherwise, an ellipsis should be used. Introductory words such as *And, Or, For, Therefore, But, Verily,* and so on may be omitted from a Bible verse without inserting an ellipsis. In a sense, the reader is probably already aware, without the aid of an ellipsis, that other words precede and follow any given quotation. (See also "Ellipsis.")

"The God of all comfort . . . comforts us in all our troubles, so that we can comfort those in any trouble" (2 Cor. 1:3–4). [ellipsis needed because interior words are dropped]
"He that is not against us is on our part" (Mark 9:40 KJV). [The original reads: "For he that is not against us is on our part."]

LORD *Versus* Lord *and* GOD *Versus* God. In some versions of the Bible, the words *Lord* and *God* appear in small caps, with an initial cap (LORD, GOD). In books written in a familiar or popular vein, this cap-and-small-cap style need not be followed. In scholarly works, however, quotations from Scripture should reflect the typographical rendering of the version cited. (For a thorough discussion of this issue, see "*LORD and GOD* [Small-Cap Forms].")

Italics in the King James Version. Words that are italicized in the King James Version (KJV, or AV) should not be italicized when quoted in popular writing. The translators of the KJV used italics to indicate supplied words that do not have exact parallels in the original Greek or Hebrew. These italicized words only confuse the modern reader who might mistake them for words intended to be emphasized.

Small Caps and Italics in the New American Standard Bible. When passages from the Old Testament are quoted in the New Testament of the New American Standard Bible, the quotation is set in caps-and-small-caps, and it also follows the KJV device of setting supplied words in italics. When quoting from the NASB, all cap-and-small-cap quotations and italicized words should be rendered in regular text type, since the reasons for those faces will be unclear to the reader and, again, may be mistaken for emphasis.

Retaining Italics for Supplied Words. The italics in the KJV and NASB and other versions that use that device should only be retained in instances when it is important for the reader to know which are the "supplied" words in the given translation, such as in an academic discussion of Bible translating or in a scholarly work on interpreting the passages in the original languages.

Pronunciation Marks in the King James Version. Some editions of the KJV and other versions provide pronunciation marks with proper names. These marks should not be reproduced when quoting from that version.

Correct Paragraphing. Some versions, most notably the KJV, set each numbered verse as though it were a separate paragraph. Since this is merely a typographic convention, these verses, when quoted, should not be set as separate paragraphs but run together. Actual paragraph breaks in the KJV are indicated by the paragraph symbol (¶).

Verse Numbers. In most context, verse numbers should not be included within the quotation from the Bible. The primary exception is Bible studies in which it is important to distiguish where each verse begins and ends.

Spelling of Proper Names. In a written text, biblical proper names should follow the spelling of the primary Bible version used. When no primary translation is used, this manual recommends that proper nouns should follow the style given in the New International Version and Today's New International Version.

Hezekiah [NIV]	Ezekias [KJV]
Jehoshaphat [NIV]	Josaphat [KJV]

Ligatures. Because of the limitations of many typesetting systems, ligatures (such as *æ*) should be set as separate letters (*ae*) when quoting from Bible versions that use such ligatures. Ligatures tend to look antiquated and may cause confusion.

Quoting from the Internet

Writers commonly quote poems, songs, bits of humor, chatroom vignettes, personal stories, anecdotes, articles, and other material from Internet sources as if there are no ethical strings attached. "After all," some writers argue, "a dozen sites on the Internet quote it without permission, why can't I?" But remember this rule: Treat Internet sources just as you would treat print sources when it comes to quotations. (See the details of fair use and permissions under the entry "Permissions, Author Guidelines for Obtaining.")

Just because a funny story appears countless times on the Internet without crediting a source does not mean it is in the public domain. Such oft-repeated and uncredited Internet writings have often been reproduced without their original authors' permission, and to repeat them once more is to compound the theft.

By and large, unless an Internet quotation clearly falls under the *fair use guidelines* (again, see "Permissions, Author Guidelines for Obtaining."), plan on tracking down the author and obtaining written permission to use the quote from the author's publisher or (if no other copyright owner is available) from the author himself or herself. Be even more reserved with private emails and comments from chatroom discussions. Treat them just as you would treat unpublished letters, which means, don't quote them unless you have written permission from the original author. Remember that fair use does not usually apply to unpublished correspondence.

It is painful for a writer to see his or her work exploited for another's financial profit. So keep the Golden Rule in mind: Get permission from others, just as you would expect them to get permission from you—whether it's online or in print. (Also see "Plagiarism.")

Racial Sensitivities in Language

See "Ethnic and Racial Designations."

Readability

Readability is different than legibility. Most books are legible, that is, the basic letter forms are clear and distinguishable, but not all are readable. Readability has more to do with the book's impression on the reader's eye, the extent to which a book can be easily and comfortably read for extended periods of time or for a particular purpose, and the extent to which the type and design prevent fatigue from setting in.

While some of the following information is summarized in "Typography, The Elements of Basic Book," that section is intended for compositors and designers. This section on readability is more for authors and editors who are working with a publisher to produce the best possible book.

The Three Cardinal Rules of Readability.

1. Most serif faces are inherently more readable than most sans-serif faces. The serifs, that is, the small strokes added to a letter, are not just ornamental; they serve a purpose. Since they are mostly horizontal strokes, the lateral emphasis increases reading efficiency. Sans-serif type, which eliminates this horizontal emphasis, can force the eye to read more slowly than is comfortable. Hence, sans-serif faces are popular for display purposes (noncontinuous reading). In text, however, sans-serif faces can be the typographic equivalent of someone speaking too slowly. Most of us, when forced to listen or read slowly, lose interest.

One study showed that the average reader can read serif type 7 to 10 words per minute faster than sans-serif. This may not seem like much, but over a two-hour reading session, that could amount to a short chapter. Coupled with the fact that research also found that serif faces are more aesthetically pleasing to most readers than sans-serif faces, this would indicate that traditional serif faces are a better choice for continuous text reading.

2. Roman type is intrinsically more readable than italic, bold, expanded, or condensed. By its design, regular roman type contributes to the lateral flow. Other fonts, such as italic and bold, are used intentionally for emphasis because they disrupt lateral flow, causing the reader to pause. This is why many designers prefer not to set large blocks of type in italic or bold. Though roman type is the norm, there has been a temptation among some designers to "copy-fit" text by electronically condensing the font. This practice is inadvisable for any but the most experienced typographer for the simple reason that types were designed with a certain visual proportion, and thus to alter them electronically is to change their intrinsic character.

3. *Tight-to-moderate word spacing is more readable than loose word spacing.* Although there are exceptions to this rule, lateral flow is again the ideal. Wide spacing causes the eye to stop and start—the visual equivalent of stuttering. Also, when word spacings are too large, the likelihood of "rivers" (blotches of white space spanning two or more lines) increases. Rivers add an unattractive vertical element and distract the reader from lateral eye movement. When there is a choice between setting a line too tight or too loose, it is usually preferable to set it too tight. There is often resistance among editors to allowing tight lines, but in continuous reading, a tightly spaced line is less likely than a loose line to cause problems for the reader.

Three Additional Factors

1. *Type Size.* Many people assume that type size is the single most important factor in readability, but it is not. Type size, while important, is not as significant in readability as typeface, font, spacing, and line length. The average reader with normal or corrected eyesight can comfortably read even 6-point type as long as the line widths are within the 10-to-12-words-per-line range (that is, about 60 to 72 characters per line, counting spaces) and the leading is sufficient to keep the text from looking splotchy. It is usually an overlong line length and a too-tight leading that causes problems.

For average trade books, body types in sizes of 9 to 11 points are almost universally used. Those are the sizes that generally fill the ideal 10-to-12-words-per-line average for the line widths. A few faces tend to be small on the body (like Bembo), in which case 9-point type may be too small and 10- to 12-point type preferred.

2. *Line Length.* For type sizes in the 9- to 12-point range, an average of 10 to 12 words per line is ideal (assuming the average word is 5 characters plus a word space), or an average of 60 to 72 characters per line (counting spaces). Studies have shown that 72 characters per line is the threshold beyond which the reader begins to have trouble finding the next line of text ("tracking back"). When line lengths must run longer than an average of 72 characters per line, then an extra point or two of leading should be added to all text lines to give the reader more space and a better chance to find successive lines. Every character beyond 72 characters per line significantly decreases the readability of a text.

Text that averages fewer than 7 words per line also poses problems. (1) If the copy is justified, there is more chance of frequent word division and wide word spacing, and (2) since the reader has to shift the eyes back to the beginnings of lines more often, fatigue can set in. Such narrow widths are more legible when set ragged right and with perhaps a little more than standard leading.

3. *Leading.* Visually, the average space between lines (leading) should always appear larger than the average word space. If the word spaces are larger than the leading, then "rivers" (jagged lines of white running down the page) are most likely to form, and reading will become more difficult.

Overly wide leading can be as much of an eyestrain as too little, although it is best to err on the side of slightly too much than too little. Reference works and other works intended for short piecemeal reading do not need this extra leading.

Reading-Level Calculation

A number of different formulas exist for determining the reading level (by grade or by age) of written texts. Among the most common are the Gunning "FOG" Readability Test and the Flesch-Kincaid Formula. Those two, and a third one, the Powers-Sumner-Kearl Formula, which is primarily used for primary-school-age readers, are outlined briefly here.

Keep in mind that these tests offer only general guidelines, and their results can vary, depending on the samples that are chosen to begin with. Still, they allow an editor or author to calculate whether a piece of writing might possibly be more complex than the intended readership can handle. In publishing, the conventional wisdom is that books written for the general reader should be aimed no higher than at an eighth-grade reading level. Academic books, of course, would be expected to rate much higher, since their specialized vocabularies should already be understood by the intended readership. But for trade books for the general reader, these tests may come in handy.

The Gunning "FOG" Readability Test. This test is most accurate when measuring older elementary- and secondary-school-age groups. To find the reading level:

1. Select three samples of 100 words each.
2. Determine the average length of each sentence (that is, the total number of words divided by the number of sentences).
3. Then, in each sample, count the number of words containing 3 or more syllables, and find the average over the three samples.
4. To calculate grade level, add the average sentence length to the average number of words of 3 or more syllables. Multiply that sum by 0.4.
5. To calculate reading age in years, add 5 to the total in step four.

The Flesch-Kincaid Formula. This formula was devised as a standard test for use by the US Department of Defense and is appropriate for secondary school and adult reading. To find the reading level:

1. Take a sample of text, anywhere from 100 to 300 words long.
2. Determine the average number of words per sentence (total number of words divided by the number of sentences).
3. Determine the average number of syllables (total number of syllables divided by the total number of words).
4. To calculate grade level, multiply the average number of words per sentence by 0.39, and then multiply the average number of syllables by 11.8. Add those two numbers together and subtract 15.59.
5. To calculate reading age, subtract 10.59 years, instead of subtracting 15.59 as in step four.

The Powers-Sumner-Kearl Formula. This formula is most accurate for primary-school-age students, up to about age ten. To find the reading level:

1. Select one or more samples of 100 words each.
2. Find the average number of words per sentence and divide that by the number of total sentences (rounding to the nearest tenth).
3. Count the number of syllables in each 100-word sample, and average them.
4. To calculate grade level, multiply the average number of words per sentence by 0.0778; then multiply the average number of syllables (per 100 word sample) by 0.0455. Add those two numbers together, then subtract 2.2029.
5. To calculate age level in years, add 2.7971 instead of subtracting the 2.2029, as in step four.

Recto Versus Random Setting of Pages

Recto (right-hand) pages have odd folio numbers and *verso* (left-hand) pages have even numbers. (The numbers as printed on a book's pages are called *folios*.) Recto pages are always considered the dominant page in any spread. Except in unusual designs, most elements of a book's front and back matter are set recto, except for the copyright page, which is intentionally set as the verso of the title page. When space is a consideration, most elements of a book may be set verso, although it can sometimes diminish the aesthetic appeal and even the accessibility of the book.

The first chapter of the book should begin on a recto page. Ideally, each subsequent chapter should begin on a recto page (called *recto setting*), but the design and available space may require that such chapters begin on the next available blank instead, whether a recto or verso (called *random setting*). Part title pages are invariably set recto.

By and large, there is no reason for a recto page ever to be blank in any book, except for the unused pages at the end. Readers expect major parts of any book to begin on the right-hand page.

Recycled-Paper Statement

For books printed on recycled paper, a notice should be given on the copyright page. Although it is by no means mandatory, the industry standard formula, preceded by the recycled symbol, is:

() Printed on recycled paper

Red-Letter Editions of the Bible

Well over half of all modern editions of the Bible are printed so that the words of Jesus appear in red type. These are called *red-letter editions*. The device was formerly called *rubrication* and was used in a variety of print situations. A few *red-letter* concordances of the Bible also exist as well as some rare editions in which all the words of God in the Old and New Testaments are printed in red. A few style issues regarding red-letter editions of the Bible should be noted.

Punctuation. In red-letter editions, not only the words of Jesus but all punctuation (including quotation marks) associated with them are printed in red.

Verse Numbers and Annotations. As with punctuation, all verse numbers and superscript numbers or letters used as callouts for footnotes or cross-references should be set in red when they are part of the red-letter text. Red-letter is used only in the text of the Bible itself and not when the words of Jesus are quoted in footnotes, introductions, or other peripheral matter.

Said References. Said references attached to the words of Jesus, such as *he answered* or *he said*, should not be set in red.

The Epistles and Revelation. In several instances in the Epistles and in Revelation, words of Jesus that do not appear in the four gospels are quoted. Those words too are set in red type.

Printing Registration. In some printing processes, different colors of ink have to be printed in different passes through the press, which can result in slight misalignments called *poor registration*. It is common, in fact, to see red-letter editions of the Bible in which the red words of Jesus seem to sit on a baseline fractionally higher or lower than the rest of the text. Any time a red-letter edition is printed, the publisher and printer should make spot checks to ensure that the registration is remaining accurate and consistent.

References, Bible

An author should inform readers of which Bible translation, version, or paraphrase is being used predominantly in the course of a work. This notice may be given in the introduction, the preface, or any other place where it is not likely to be overlooked. In many cases, since extensive use of modern translations requires a permission notice and credit line, the copyright page is the most convenient place for stating the Bible version. The following form is acceptable, although the granting copyright holder may prefer a different form, in which case that form should be strictly adhered to.

> Unless otherwise noted, all Scripture references in this book are taken from the [Version], copyright © [year and copyright holder]. Used by permission of [permission grantor].

When an Alternate Bible Version Is Used. When a general note regarding a predominant Bible version has been provided, the author should not indicate the version when references to that version are made in the text. The reader should only be informed with an in-text reference when an alternate version is used. This is done by placing the abbreviation of the alternate version next to the Bible reference. These abbreviations are usually set in full caps without periods. (See "Bible Versions and Translations.") When used in combination with the Bible reference itself, these abbreviations should not be preceded by a comma. Abbreviations of Bible versions may also be used in running text and notes.

> "Love is patient, love is kind. It does not envy" (1 Cor. 13:4). [No version is cited; the predominant version in this case is the NIV.]
> "Loue is pacient & curteous, loue envyeth not" (1 Cor. 13:4 Coverdale).
> "Charity suffereth long, and is kind; charity envieth not" (1 Cor. 13:4 KJV).
> The musical qualities of the NIV, Coverdale, and KJV differ significantly. [in Text]

Personal Translations or Paraphrases. When an author uses a personal translation or paraphrase, this should be indicated in a general note at the beginning of the book (if it is the predominant version) or in a note attached to each specific reference. In the latter case, the phrase *author's translation* or *author's paraphrase* should suffice. Such a phrase, however, is best preceded by a comma.

> "Love is content to wait and is considerate. It's not envious" (1 Cor. 13:4, author's paraphrase).

Arabic Numerals. Use arabic rather than roman numerals for books of the Bible. It is preferable to write out the number if it begins a sentence.

> 1 Corinthians, *not* I Corinthians
> First John 4:7 tells us . . .

Chapter Only. When an entire chapter is referred to, it may be spelled out, although a numeral may be used if no confusion will result.

In the first chapter of Genesis . . . *or* In Genesis 1 . . .

Dialogue. Numerals may be used for Bible references in dialogue, although frequently the syntax requires they be spelled out.

"I'm sure," said the minister, "everyone here could recite John 3:16 by heart."
"Amanda Smith overcame her fear by remembering the third chapter of Galatians and the twenty-eighth verse."

Spelling Out Versus Abbreviating. Names of the books of the Bible may be abbreviated when a reference is enclosed in parentheses, especially when such references are numerous. Otherwise they should be abbreviated in text only in scholarly or reference works. See "Abbreviations: Bible Books and Related Material" for a complete list of abbreviations of books of the Bible.

The Abbreviations V. and VV. The abbreviation for *verse* is *v.*, and for *verses*, *vv.* These abbreviations should be used in parenthetical references only or when repeating the entire reference would seem cumbersome.

Later in the eleventh chapter (v. 45) John wrote, "In that place many believed in Jesus."

Abbreviations for Portions of Verses. In some scholarly works, when the author wishes to indicate that only a portion of a Bible verse is being referenced, the abbreviations *a, b, c,* etc. may be added to the reference; for example: *"Praise him in his mighty heavens" (Ps. 150:1c),* indicating that only the third line of the verse is being quoted. This practice is largely limited to academic works in which precision is required and is generally not recommended for popular or trade books.

The Colon in Scripture References. A colon separates chapter from verse.

Mark 2:17   1 Peter 3:12

The Semicolon in Scripture References. A semicolon separates one chapter-and-verse reference from another. If the second chapter-and-verse reference applies to the same book of the Bible, the name of the book should not be repeated.

John 3:3; 10:10; Acts 16:31

When to Use Spaces. No space should precede or follow a colon in a Bible reference. There should be space following but not preceding a comma or a semicolon.

The En Dash in Bible References. An en dash is used between consecutive verse numbers. A comma separates nonconsecutive numbers of the same chapter.

John 3:1–6   John 3:15–16   Acts 1:1–8, 13, 16

An en dash is also used to indicate several chapters of a Bible book inclusively in a reference or to indicate that a citation begins in one chapter and ends in another.

Gen. 1–11   Gal. 5:26–6:5

Obadiah, Philemon, Jude, 2 John, 3 John. These little books of the Bible receive their own entry because each contains but a single chapter, which makes referencing specific verses tricky. Some writers, for instance, attempt to reference the first verse of Jude as *Jude 1:1*, which has the disadvantage of implying that there are other chapters, and in the Bible itself, no reader will be able to find the first chapter of Jude. Other writers opt for *Jude 1*, which ambiguously suggests either the first chapter of Jude or its first verse.

Fortunately for persnickety editors, these books are so short as to be seldom referenced. Still, the clearest way of referencing verses from them in text is either *the first verse of Jude* or *verse 1 of Jude*. If the reference is parenthetical after a quotation, then use this form: (*Jude v. 1*), even though the abbreviation *v.* may not appear elsewhere in the manuscript. If the reference falls in a Scripture index or in some other place where columnar appearance needs to be maintained, then it is all right to use the form *Jude 1:1*.

When to Spell Out and When to Abbreviate Books of the Bible. Books of the Bible should be spelled out, not abbreviated, when the reference appears in running text or when the book alone is referred to. An exception may be made in scholarly or reference works that contain so many references to books of the Bible that abbreviations are needed for the sake of brevity. Also, if many references appear in parentheses, it is acceptable to abbreviate books of the Bible. Two standard styles of abbreviating books of the Bible are commonly accepted: one for general books as well as some academic books and another for scholarly books alone. For a complete list, see "Abbreviations: Bible Books and Related Material."

In references following block quotations from the Bible, the names of Bible books may be spelled out or abbreviated at the author's or editor's discretion, but the same form should be used consistently throughout a manuscript. Either of the following forms may be used:

> No, in all these things we are more than conquerors through him who loved us. For I am convinced that neither death nor life, . . . nor anything else in all

creation, will be able to separate us from the love of God that is in Christ Jesus our Lord. (Romans 8:37–39 NIV)

[or] . . . will be able to separate us from the love of God that is in Christ Jesus our Lord.

—Romans 8:37–39 NIV

Punctuation with Run-in Quotations. For run-in quotations that also require a chapter-and-verse reference, place the period or other punctuation after the closing parenthesis containing the reference. If the quotation contains a question mark or exclamation point, place it with the text and place any other needed punctuation after the closing parenthesis.

"Here is your king" (John 19:14).
"Take him away! Take him away! Crucify him!" (John 19:15).

Religionist

While the word *religionist* is now fairly rare, it has a long history in English. It is sometimes used to refer to any kind of religious believer, but it actually has an overtone of zealotry to it. A *religionist* is anything but lukewarm about his or her faith.

Religiose

Although sometimes mistakenly used as a synonym for the adjective *religious*, the word *religiose* has a pejorative connotation. A *religiose* person would tend to be overly religious, self-consciously pious, or embarrassingly sentimental about his or her faith. It's a perfectly good word when used correctly.

Religious as a Noun

The word *religious*, which is both the singular and plural form, was formerly used as a noun, referring to a person in a monastic order: *The religious wore the white habit of her order.* That usage is now archaic and is rarely understood by readers, causing confusion or misreading. It is best to avoid it.

Reprints and Revisions

Reprint. A *reprint* is a new printing of an existing book in which no major or substantive changes have been made. Customarily, reprints may contain corrections of errors. New copyright dates are not needed in the copyright notice for reprints, even if the corrections are extensive. A reprint is sometimes called a *new impression* or a *new printing*.

For a reprint, if no bibliographic information (title, number of pages, author, publisher, ISBN, etc.) other than the year of publication has changed, then a new CIP need not be applied for. (See "Cataloging in Publication Data [CIP].")

Revision. A book is considered a *revision* any time major substantive corrections are made or when any new material has been added. Any time anything *new* has been added to the text that would need the protection of copyright, then a new date should be added to the copyright notice on the copyright page. A revision is sometimes called a *new edition.* A new CIP and ISBN are required for all publications that are considered revisions.

Resurrection, the

See "*Crucifixion, the* and *Resurrection, the.*"

Revelation

The final book of the New Testament is *Revelation,* or *The Book of Revelation,* not *Revelations,* or *The Book of Revelations.* Even the book's author refers to it in the first verse as a single, unified vision. Curiously, an Internet search of the plural shows that the vast majority of online writers who make that common mistake tend toward conspiracy theories, New Age practice, or religious separatism.

Reverend

The title *reverend* is often misused in writing and conversation. In formal writing, it is comparable to the title *honorable*; both words should be accompanied by the article *the,* and neither word should be used with a last name alone (for instance: *Graham,* rather than *Rev. Graham*). In informal contexts, the article may be dropped, although this is considered colloquial.

The use of the word *reverend* as a noun is also colloquial and should be avoided in formal writing, since the word is properly an adjective. These colloquial uses are best reserved for dialogue or humor or as spoken address in those denominations that use the word alone as part of their tradition.

> Many listeners have been touched by the Reverend Gary Davis's songs.
> He introduced Reverend Wilkins to us. [colloquial; not for formal writing]
> "We spoke to the reverend about our marriage plans." [dialogue, colloquial, custom]

As the editors of *Success with Words* quip, "If in doubt, consult your clergyman." For more details on the formal use of the word *Reverend* and its abbreviation *Rev.,* see "Forms of Address, Religious."

Rights

See "Subsidiary Rights."

Roman Numerals

Not having a clear concept of zero as a number, the ancient Romans devised a complex numbering system that has, surprisingly, survived into the modern world. One minor advantage is that it employs fewer symbols (only seven) than our familiar arabic system (sometimes referred to as the Hindu-Arabic system, since it actually seems to have originated in India), which uses ten. The Romans could render all the numbers between 1 and 100 with just five different symbols, whereas it takes all ten in the arabic system. The disadvantage of roman numerals, of course, is the long strings of characters that result, which are highly confusing to modern readers. The year *1999* is *MCMXCIX* in roman numerals, almost twice as long as the version in arabic numerals. By contrast, the year *2000* is a simple *MM*, half the length of the arabic!

The Characters. The basic characters of the Roman numbering system are:

I (or i) = 1
V (or v) = 5
X (or x) = 10
L (or l) = 50
C (or c) = 100
D (or d) = 500
M (or m) = 1,000
$\bar{V}$ (or $\bar{v}$) = 5,000
$\bar{X}$ (or $\bar{x}$) = 10,000
$\bar{C}$ (or $\bar{c}$) = 100,000
$\bar{M}$ (or $\bar{m}$) = 1,000,000

Note: In the Middle Ages, the character Z was added to represent 2,000

How to Form Roman Numerals. When a small number appears to the right of a larger one, the smaller number is added to the larger one. Thus, *VI* is 6 (a 5 plus a 1). When a smaller number appears to the left of a larger number, the smaller number is subtracted from the larger. Thus, *IV* is 4 (a 5 minus a 1). This method of subtraction-according-to-position is called the *subtrahend system* and was actually introduced during the Renaissance. The ancient Romans would have rendered the number *4* as *IIII*.

With those basic rules, all the numbers can be formed except, as stated before, 0. A line over the characters *V*, *X*, *C*, and *M* multiplies the value of that character by one thousand.

With Names. Roman numerals are commonly used in text in the names of numbered kings and other royalty as well as popes: for example, *Henry VIII, James I,* or *Pope John XXIII.* This practice is extended to common family names, usually the child of someone who is already designated a *Jr.* Thus, the son of John Doe Jr. is John Doe III, who plans to name his son John Doe IV. As with *Sr.* and *Jr.,* it is best not to allow the roman numeral to be separated from the name over a line break.

With World Wars. Perhaps the most common place to find roman numerals in ordinary text is in references to the two major wars of the twentieth century: *World War I* and *World War II.* By extension, futurists also refer to *World War III.*

In Book Front Matter. Another common place where one finds roman numerals in publications is in the front matter of some books, usually scholarly or other books that want to achieve an air of authority and high quality. In these books, the front matter is paginated in roman numerals, while the main text of the book is paginated with arabic numerals (starting with 1). See "Folios" for details. It should be noted that when front matter is paginated using roman numerals, lowercase letters (*i, ii, iii, iv, v,* . . . *x,* etc.) are used.

For Publication Dates. On rare occasions one still sees the year of a book's publication shown on the title page in roman numerals. In some older books, *D* (the roman numeral for 500) was actually rendered *IƆ* and *M* (1,000) was *CIƆ.* Those were printing conventions only, the sole function of which seems to have been the further confusion of those already confused by roman numerals.

Using roman numerals for publication dates is largely an affectation in the twenty-first century and is not advised. Still, it might be considered for a book to which the designers or editors wish to grant a special aura of authority or importance, such as a Bible or a historical or biblical novel.

The Roman Catholic imprimatur, often displayed across from the title page or on a book's copyright page, usually bears a date in Latin, including roman numerals. Official pronouncements, especially religious ones, sometimes bear roman numeral dates, and filmmakers, for some reason, seem to have made it a tradition to set the release dates of their films in roman numerals—causing viewers to squint and calculate frantically as the credits roll by—though this practice is waning.

For Numbering Chapters and Parts. The use of roman numerals for numbering chapters of a book is almost universally discouraged by contemporary designers unless a certain classical mood is required. Even in that case, they should only be used when the book contains fewer than ten chapters. A reader should not have to puzzle out the numerals beyond X (ten). Parts of a book are more commonly designated with roman numerals, although that practice too has declined in popularity. Again, roman numerals should not be used if there are more than ten parts.

For Act Numbers in Plays. One of the most common places where roman numerals are still occasionally used is in referencing the number of an act in a theater piece, although *The Chicago Manual of Style* recommends a newer style of using arabic numerals only. If the older style is used, in which acts are referenced with roman numerals, capitalize the word *Act* and set scene numbers in arabic numerals, with the word *scene* lowercased: *The wedding masque in Act IV, scene 1 of Shakespeare's* The Tempest *suggests the play was written for a royal wedding.* Either the old or new style may be used, as long as they are used consistently within a publication.

For Books of the Bible. Do not use roman numerals for referencing books of the Bible (such as *I Samuel* or *II Corinthians*), even when they are used in the predominant version of the Bible being quoted. While many older editions of the KJV, for instance, use roman numerals, most recent editions of the KJV have dropped that style altogether.

For Appendixes. Formerly, roman numerals were commonly used to number the appendixes. Though this use is still acceptable, it is much rarer now than it once was. We recommend avoiding it unless there is a specific reason for doing so. Again, roman numerals should not be used if more than the numbers one through ten are needed.

Outlining. Roman numerals are often used for the primary levels in an outline, although that traditional system has in many places been supplanted by the so-called decimal system (1, 1.1, 1.1.1, etc.). See "Outlines and Lists."

In Columns. If roman numerals are set in a vertical column, as in a chart or a table of contents, they should be aligned on the right.

Recommendation. Though an interesting part of book history, roman numerals should probably be relegated to the same dust heap as gothic type. Except for when not using them might cause more confusion than using them, as with the names of regents and popes, roman numerals are usually best rendered as arabic.

Rubrication

See "Red-Letter Editions of the Bible."

Running Heads and Feet

A *running head* is a line of type set at the top of a text page (though omitted on a chapter opening page) that includes such information as the book title, part title, chapter title, or section head, and sometimes the author's name. A *running foot* (or *running footer*) appears at the bottom of the page. In some designs, in textbooks, for instance, the running head may appear in the side margin and incorporate several lines of type as well as a folio.

Like folios, running heads and feet do not usually appear on pages without text type, that is, on title pages, copyright pages, tables of contents, dedication pages, and so on. Running heads and feet are often dropped altogether in popular fiction and mass-market books to conserve space and to contribute to the narrative flow. Folios may appear on the same line as the running heads or separately.

Formatting. Traditionally, running heads display the book title on the verso pages and the chapter title on the recto pages, though this format is less common than it once was. Any number of combinations of book title, chapter title, part title, section heads, author names (for compilations), series title, or other elements may be used in the running heads. Generally, the element with the greater weight or importance is placed on the left-hand (verso) running head, which is a departure from the general style of beginning major book elements on recto pages. Since different types of books have different needs, the formatting and positioning of the running heads is flexible and should be determined by the designer in consultation with the book's editor.

Running heads are usually not set flush left unless they are sufficiently leaded since they can easily be mistaken for the first line of type on the page.

With Fiction. Customarily, works of fiction should not have running heads along the top of the page unless there is a specific reason for doing so. Often, novels have only chapter numbers with no chapter titles, which would leave only the book title to be included in the running head. It is too repetitive to have the book's title appear twice on every spread, and most authors would be abashed to have their name included in every spread. Also, novels tend to run long and running heads eat up valuable space. Finally, running heads can prove a distraction to the experience of reading fiction, disrupting the flow of the narrative with uselessly repeated material.

Sacraments

As many as thirty different rites and rituals have been deemed *sacraments* in the course of Christian history. Only seven, however, are widely recognized, and they are traditionally listed in this order:

1. The sacrament of baptism, *or* baptism
2. The sacrament of confirmation, *or* confirmation, *or* christmation (Eastern Orthodox)
3. The sacrament of the Eucharist, *or* the Eucharist; *also called* Holy Communion, Communion, the Lord's Supper, the Lord's Table, Mass, *or* Blessed Sacrament, *though this last term can refer to the service or the elements themselves*
4. The sacrament of penance, *or* penance, *or* confession
5. The sacrament of extreme unction, *or* extreme unction; *also called* anointing of the sick, *or* unction of the sick; *the term* last rites *is the popular term for this sacrament, but it is not one used by the clergy or theologians. The term* unction *is also commonly used, but there are other nonsacramental rites involving anointing with oil to which that term also applies.*
6. The sacrament of orders, *or* orders, *or* ordination
7. The sacrament of matrimony, *or* matrimony; *also called* the sacrament of marriage, *or* marriage

Note that for the majority of Protestant publications, the names of the sacraments should be lowercased except for those associated with Communion, or the Lord's Supper. Keep in mind that most Protestant churches only recognize baptism and Communion as sacraments (and sometimes not even those). If a publication is targeted for a Roman Catholic, Church of England, or Eastern Orthodox audience, then these terms should be capitalized according to their customs. The Eastern Orthodox Church recognizes these seven in addition to others, all of which are termed *mysteries*.

Said References

A *said reference* is the verb used to connect the subject of a sentence and a direct quotation: *said, asked, answered, shouted,* and so on.

Overusing Said. Diversity is good, and in dialogue, the word *said* can become repetitive. However, some writers, in attempting to avoid the overuse of the plain *said*, devise a wide array of alternate words that can actually prove counterproductive. First, it can lead to a humorous redundancy, as in *"I beg you!" she pleaded* or *"Why?" they queried.* Second, it can lead to the use of words that seem so unusual that they actually distract from the quotation: *"Never!" he countermanded,* or *"I believe so," she cogitated aloud.* The goal, rather, should be to keep the said reference from becoming too noticeable. Ideally, the quotation itself should convey the mood and emotion of the words and should not have to depend on any attached verbs.

The solution to the overuse of *said* is simply to replace it only occasionally with common words that will serve the purpose and to remember that a said reference is not always needed in closely written dialogue: *"That's how it will be," he said. "Why?" "Because I said so!"* When the speaker is unambiguous, as in most two-person dialogues, no reference is needed at all.

Writer William Zinsser has said that *said* is so common as to be nearly invisible to most readers, and it takes an extraordinary number of them used in a small space to become distracting.

Questions. The question sometimes arises whether one can *say* a question, as in: *"Why?" she said.* Only the writer's judgment and ear can determine this, but grammatically, there is no reason why questions cannot be "said." *To say* simply means to speak, and questions are spoken as much as are statements. For variety, however, *ask,* or any other verb suggesting a question, can be used as long as it doesn't seem noticeable or redundant in context.

Saint

Most manuals recommend spelling out the word *Saint* in text when used in place names or before the names of Christian saints: *Saint Paul, Minnesota,* as well as *Saint Paul the apostle.* It may, however, be abbreviated (*St.,* singular, and *SS.,* plural) whenever custom recommends it (*St. Louis*), wherever a lack of space requires it, or when the terms are repeated so often as to be distracting. It is capitalized before names (*Saint John*) but lowercased in general usage (*the prayers of the saints*).

Mainstream Protestant tradition tends not to use *Saint* before the names of Bible figures and figures from church history, preferring *the apostle Paul,* for instance, to *Saint Paul.* This usage may have something to do with Protestantism's emphasis on the sainthood of all believers and not singling out certain ones for special status. Roman Catholic, Eastern Orthodox, and high-church Anglican traditions tend to use *Saint* more often to describe Bible figures, early church figures, and the saints from their traditions, and the word should be used appropriately when writing for those traditions.

The French feminine form of the abbreviation, *Ste.,* is generally not used in English before the names of female saints. The feminine form *Sainte,* however, is retained in personal names (*Charles-Augustin Sainte-Beuve*) and geographical references (*Sainte-Foy*).

When used as part of a personal name, *Saint* should be abbreviated or spelled out according to the person's own preference: *Oliver St. John Gogarty*, but *Antoine de Saint-Exupéry*.

Sanctimonious

The word *sanctimonious* formerly meant sincerely devout, but it has now come to mean hypocritically devout. It and the forms *sanctimony* and *sanctimoniousness* are generally pejorative.

Savior Versus Saviour

Taking their cue from the King James Version of the Bible, many American writers cling to the British spelling *Saviour* when referring to Christ. This seems an affectation, especially in publications that are not closely tied to the KJV. For US audiences, use *Savior*.

Scripture Indexes

See "Indexes, *Scripture Indexes.*"

Scripture Versus Bible

Though most Christians view them as synonymous, the terms *Scripture* and *Bible* have subtly different emphases. *Bible* is the more plain-spoken and commonly used word of the two, both inside and outside the Christian subculture. For many secular readers, *Scripture* has an overtone of religious cant.

Additionally, the word *scripture* can refer to the sacred writings of other religions (the Qur'an, for instance). Even within Christian circles, *Scripture* can have a slightly artificial ring, since it has long been associated with the language of Victorian devotional literature. Both words are perfectly acceptable in most contexts, but the careful writer should be aware of their different shades of tone and the audience to which they are addressed. In general, this manual has opted to use the word *Bible*.

Notice that when referring to the Bible, the terms *Scripture* and *the Scriptures* should be capitalized. When referring to the religious writings in general or holy texts of other religions, the term *scriptures* is usually lowercased.

Bible is always capped unless it is used metaphorically to refer to books of importance in other fields: as in, The Chicago Manual of Style *is the bible of American publishing.*

See also "*Holy Bible.*"

Second Half-Title Page

The second half-title page, also called the *inside half-title page*, is, in form, identical to the half-title that appears on page 1 of most books, but it is used immediately before the main content (body matter) of the book, separating it from any front matter. Though optional in most books, it can be especially useful in works of fiction when it seems appropriate to create a sort of psychological threshold for the reader, passing from the preliminary pages into the story itself. Second half-title pages are less common in other types of works but may be appropriate as content and space allow. They can add a note of elegance to works of scholarship and books of high artistic quality. Not all fiction benefits from a second half-title page, and such a page may certainly be dropped if space is a consideration or if the book is already divided into parts, in which case the first part-title page serves as a convenient divider between the front matter and the text.

Selah

Although the word *selah* is used in thirty-nine of the Psalms as well as three times in Habakkuk 3, its meaning is not entirely clear. It seems to have been some sort of liturgical direction, such as a shift in tune or tempo, or an indication of a poetic division, an inserted interlude, or perhaps a stanza break.

It is sometimes quoted as having the meaning "so be it," much like the word *amen*. The word *selah* does not have that meaning, however, and is probably not useful for any purpose other than its inscrutable function in Psalms. (There is a funny scene in the John Huston movie *The Man Who Would Be King*, in which the character Michael Dravot makes a kingly pronouncement and, as if to seal its inviolable authority, punctuates it with an emphatic "Selah!")

Semicolon

Despite the fact that no less a writer than William Zinsser advised against the use of the semicolon (;), which he felt had a certain "nineteenth-century mustiness" about it, the semicolon is still commonly used by most writers because it serves some specific functions that no other punctuation marks do.

With Compound Sentences. A semicolon is used in the place of a conjunction between two independent clauses of a compound sentence. Such words as *then, however, thus, hence, indeed, therefore, moreover, consequently,* and *also* are thought of as transitional adverbs, not conjunctions, when they are used between independent clauses; therefore, these words are customarily preceded by a semicolon. The words *yet* and *so*, although also considered to be transitional adverbs, are now commonly preceded by a comma when used between independent clauses.

Commas, rather than semicolons, are used in a series of short, closely related clauses with no conjunction. Also, short antithetical clauses are separated by a comma instead of a semicolon.

> Mary Slessor knew the hardships of the mission field; she would have been appalled by the romantic image that eventually surrounded her work.
>
> Wilberforce thought of himself as a Christian above all else; moreover, he saw his abolitionist views as an outgrowth of his faith.
>
> God warned Adam and Eve about the consequences of sin, yet they disobeyed him.
>
> He got up, he took his mat, he walked away.
>
> It wasn't in John's gospel, it was in Mark's.

In Lists of Bible References. In lists of Bible references, a semicolon should be placed between separate chapter references or chapter-and-verse references. Verse references within chapters should be separated by commas.

> He noted the following: Luke 1:46–55; 2:14; and Acts 1:7–8.
>
> The readings for the morning were John 1:1–13, 15, and 29–34.

If only chapter numbers are referred to, however, then commas may be used to separate the items in the list.

> The morning service included Psalms 19, 20, and 23.
>
> Healing miracles can be found in Matthew 8, 9, 12, 15, 17, and 20.

With Internal Punctuation. When items enumerated in running text are particularly long or contain internal punctuation, semicolons should be substituted for commas in those cases when commas alone would not clarify the relationship of one item to another.

> Hannah More knew many of the famous people of her day: Samuel Johnson; Horace Walpole; David Garrick, who produced her plays; William Wilberforce, the abolitionist politician; and John Newton, who eventually became a major influence in her life.

With Namely, That Is, *Etc.* Before such expressions as *that is, namely, i.e.,* and *e.g.,* a semicolon may be used, depending on the context and the degree to which the continuity of thought is interrupted. Note, however, that use of such scholarly abbreviations as *i.e.* (*id est,* Latin for "that is") and *e.g.* (*exempli gratia,* Latin for "for example") is discouraged in nonacademic writing.

> Lewis wrote Greeves that he had crossed a major threshold in his life; that is, he had passed from "believing in God to definitely believing in Christ."
>
> These shape-note hymnals, e.g., *The Sacred Harp, Southern Harmony,* and their imitators, flourished throughout the South. [semicolon not needed]

Serial Comma

See "Comma, *With a Series of Elements.*"

Seven Deadly Sins, The

Thomas Aquinas (c. 1224–74), in his *Summa Theologica*, identified *seven chief*, or *capital*, sins to which humans commonly fall prey. They have come to be known as *the seven deadly sins*. To resolve debates concerning which are the true "seven deadly" ones, and in which order they are ranked, the following list is provided. Note that the term *seven deadly sins* is generally lowercased, as are the particular terms below, unless they are personified or used in an allegorical sense, as they often are in medieval literature. (See also "*Four Cardinal Virtues, The.*")

1. pride
2. covetousness, or greed
3. lust
4. envy
5. gluttony
6. anger
7. sloth (also called *accidie*)

Seven Sacraments, The

See "*Sacraments.*"

Signature Breaks, A Chart of Printer's

Book pages are not printed separately but are bundled together on large sheets, then folded and trimmed into sections, called *signatures*. In former times, a single sheet folded once, so as to create a total of four pages, was called a *folio* (as in the First Folio of Shakespeare's plays). Nowadays, our large presses most commonly accommodate sheets of paper that can contain either sixteen or thirty-two pages, though some mass-market books are printed on signatures of sixty-four pages. As a result, the total number of pages in nearly every book that is printed will be a multiple of sixteen, thirty-two, or sixty-four. The science of arranging the pages on the large sheet so that they appear in the correct order when folded and gathered is called *imposition.*

In the world of ebooks, of course, terms such as *signature* and *imposition* are meaningless terms since ebooks can contain any number of pages without blanks left over at the end.

The following chart shows the common page-lengths for most printed books. Printers and publishers refer to these as the "signature breaks."

16	208	400	592	784	976	1168	1360
_32_	_224_	_416_	_608_	_800_	_992_	_1184_	_1376_
48	240	432	624	816	1008	1200	1392
_64_	_256_	_448_	_640_	_832_	_1024_	_1216_	_1408_
80	272	464	656	848	1040	1232	1424
_96_	_288_	_480_	_672_	_864_	_1056_	_1248_	_1440_
112	304	496	688	880	1072	1264	1456
_128_	_320_	_512_	_704_	_896_	_1088_	_1280_	_1472_
144	336	528	720	912	1104	1296	1488
_160_	_352_	_544_	_736_	_928_	_1120_	_1312_	_1504_
176	368	560	752	944	1136	1328	1520
_192_	_384_	_576_	_768_	_960_	_1152_	_1344_	_1536_

Legend:
Signatures = 16 pages
Add or subtract 8 for half-signatures
Underscores = 32-page signatures

Small Caps

Small caps are letters that have the form of the capital letters but are only as tall as the letter x (the x *height*) in that particular face (A, B, C, D . . .). They are common in display type of all kinds and have some specific uses in text type, although they are becoming much less common than they once were. They are no longer recommended for abbreviations of historical eras (use full cap *AD, BC, BCE* . . . instead) or time designations (use *a.m., p.m.*), though the small-cap abbreviation style may be appropriate in those instances when a book needs to convey a mood of high artistic or literary quality. A general small-cap abbreviation style is one of those handy tools that designers or editors have at their disposal, and it is perfectly allowable when called for, though it should be applied consistently within any given project.

For Display Purposes. Some book designs call for small caps to be used for the opening word (after an initial capital), phrase, or sentence at the beginning of a chapter. Unless otherwise noted by the designer, all punctuation marks and capital letters should remain in regular type.

PHILLIP BLISS'S HYMNS WERE POPULAR AT D. L. MOODY 'S CAMPAIGNS.

In Phonetic Spellings. Small caps may be used to indicate an accented syllable in informal renderings of phonetic pronunciation.

> Eusebius (pronounced you-SEE-bee-us) is considered the father of church history.

For Special Emphasis. Small caps are sometimes used to indicate special emphasis in running text, similar to the way italics are used, though perhaps a bit more emphatic. In most cases, italics are preferred. Fiction writers often use small caps in dialogue to indicate that a character is shouting. When a writer wishes to indicate that words on a sign or other display format are in capitals, small caps are often used, though full caps are now more common.

In traditional typography, all-cap words were seldom used in running text, and small caps were usually used in their place for aesthetic reasons. All caps tend to look overbold and too widely spaced when used together, drawing too much attention to themselves on the page. In contemporary usage, however, this manual recommends the continued use of small caps for occasional emphasis in works of an academic or artistic nature, or where accuracy or an unusually high-quality page appearance is desired. In works of a popular nature, especially books of humor or fiction, all caps may be used for emphasis instead.

> From the bell tower of the cathedral, Quasimodo shouted, "SANCTUARY! SANCTUARY!" [Cap-lowercase italics would probably be preferable here, although all caps are now commonly used as well.]
>
> In big, bold letters, the notice on the back gate of the Compassionate Heart Church read, "NO TRESPASSING." [Indicating capital letters on a sign.]

For LORD and GOD, see "LORD and GOD (Small-Cap Forms)."

Solidus (Forward Slash)

For Alternatives. An unspaced solidus, which is also called *slash*, *forward slash*, *diagonal*, or *virgule*, may be used to indicate a pair of alternative words. In the case of alternative prefixes, however, the first prefix is given a hyphen and set apart.

> and/or   if/when   over- or underexposed

In most formal writing the use of solidus combinations like *and/or* is discouraged. The solidus should be spaced, however, when one or both elements on either side is a compound: for instance, *a late Romantic / early Modernist debate.*

With Dates and Times. An unspaced solidus or an en dash may be used to indicate that a season or other period of time spans two consecutive years, although the en dash is preferred.

winter 1620/21   fiscal year 1987–88

In Poetry. If two or more lines of poetry are run into the text, a solidus (with a word space on both sides) is used to indicate line breaks. Such a solidus may fall either at the end or the beginning of a line of type that has been broken by the typesetter's justification. (See also "Poetry.")

Many people who quote, "God moves in a mysterious way, / His wonders to perform" (from the hymn by William Cowper), mistakenly believe they are quoting the Bible.

In Internet Addresses. An unspaced solidus is commonly used as part of URLs (uniform resource locators), commonly known as *Internet addresses* or *webpage addresses*, as in *www.zondervan.com/interactive*. In such cases, the slash, also called the forward slash, should be distinguished from the back slash (\ ), which is used in computer programming.

Song of Songs Versus *Canticles*
See "*Canticles.*"

Sources

Use of the Word Bibliography. Increasingly, the word *bibliography* is being replaced by the word *sources*. This is because some people feel that *bibliography*, which has its etymological roots in the Latin word for "book," is outdated in this era of digital references and websites. An insistence on using the word *sources*, however, seems uselessly purist—first, because language thrives by accommodating new ideas and concepts; and second, even the word *sources* finds its origin in an etymological root meaning a "spring" of water, which is no better as a metaphor for new media than "book."

We recommend, therefore, that the editor and author maintain the traditional distinction between a bibliography and a source list. That is, a bibliography should list the significant works related to the topic of the book, to points discussed in the book, or to works on related topics. Its purpose is to inform the reader of other works that might be of interest. A source list, by contrast, is more limited, listing all works actually referenced in the text, quoted, or otherwise important to the author's research.

Proper Names in Bibliographies. In a bibliography, authors, editors, translators, or compilers of works are listed last name first, and the list is compiled alphabetically. No titles or degrees are used with names. When two or more names are given for a single entry, the first is listed last name first, a comma follows that name, and the other names are then listed first name first. If the bibliography is broken down under subheads, each section is alphabetized separately.

Citing Books. The following information should normally be included, where appropriate, in a bibliographical entry for a book:

> Full name of author(s) or editor(s), last name first
> Complete title of book (and complete subtitle, if any)
> Full name of editor(s) or translator(s), if any
> Name of series, and volume and number in the series
> Edition, if other than the first
> Number of volumes
> City where book was published (and state if city is not well known)
> Name of publisher
> Year of publication

> De Gasztold, Carmen Bernos. *Prayers from the Ark.* Trans. by Rumer Godden. New York: Viking, 1947.
> Johnson, James Weldon. *God's Trombones.* New York: Viking, 1927.
> Tennyson, G. B., and Edward E. Ericson Jr., eds. *Religion and Modern Literature: Essays in Theory and Criticism.* Grand Rapids, Mich.: Eerdmans, 1975.

As with notes, a shortened form for listing the publisher's name should be used. See "Notes, *Using the Shortened Form of the Publisher's Name*" and "Publisher's Names in Short Form, Religious."

Citing Periodicals. The following information should normally be included in a bibliographical entry for an article from a periodical:

> Full name of author(s) or editor(s), last name first
> Complete title of article (and complete subtitle if any)
> Name of periodical
> Volume number (and issue number if any)
> Date (in parentheses)
> Page number(s) of article

As in citing books, not all this information is available for every periodical. In such cases, as much of the information as possible should be provided. Note also that a colon precedes page number(s) if volume and/or issue numbers are given; otherwise a comma is used. Also note that, as with source notes, this manual of style recommends using parentheses rather than commas to set off the dates of popular references, which differs from *CMS,* which recommends using parentheses for journals and commas for general magazines. The reason for using a single periodical reference style is that reference lists in religious and popular works often contain a mix of scholarly and popular periodicals and also because it is often hard to distinguish between the two.

> Aeschliman, M. D. "Flickering Candles in the Winds of Woe." *Books & Religion* 15, no. 6 (Winter 1988): 3, 29.
> "Fighting Isms and Schisms." *Christian History* 4, no. 3 (1987): 29.
> Ubell, Earl. "Surgeon General C. Everett Koop Has an Idea: A Battle Plan to Save Your Life." *Parade* (April 10, 1988), 16–17.

Citing Webpages. The following information should normally be included in a bibliographical entry for material from a webpage:

> Full name of author(s), last name first
> Title of page, entry, or article
> Title of the larger work of which the entry or article may be a part (if applicable)
> Version or file number (if available)
> Date of publication, posting, or last revision (if available)
> The website's name (set in italics)
> The website's URL (set in italics)
> Access date (in parentheses) (if known)

> Loconte, Joseph. "How to Really Keep the Commandments in Alabama—and Elsewhere." Posted September 3, 2003. *Christianity Today Online. www.christianitytoday.com.* Accessed September 30, 2003.
> "Autumn Leaves." Posted September 5, 2003. *Daily Guideposts. www.guideposts.org.* (Accessed September 5, 2003.)

Citing Software. The following information should normally be included in a bibliographical entry for material from a software package, such as a floppy disk, CD-ROM, or DVD.

> Full name of author(s), last name first (if known)
> Complete title of work, page, or article within the software package
> Title of the software package of which the entry or article may be a part (if applicable)
> Full name of editor(s) or translator(s), if any
> Name of series, and volume and number in the series
> Edition, if other than the first
> City where the software was published (and state if city is not well known)
> Name of publisher
> Year of publication

> Carson, D. A., Douglas J. Moo, and Leon Morris. *Introduction to the New Testament.* In *Zondervan Bible Study Library 5.0: Scholar's Edition* CD-ROM. Grand Rapids, Mich.: Zondervan, 2003.

"For Further Reading" Lists. A less formal type of bibliography—a "For Further Reading" list—may be more appropriate than a thorough bibliography in some books. Such lists should follow the format of the formal bibliography but could conceivably contain only author and title. Most any book in print can be located in a library collection, ordered from a bookstore, or referenced on the Internet with only an author name and title as references. Of course, more information would help the reader in a "For Further Reading" list, but it is not necessary if an author wishes to avoid an overly academic appearance.

> Boyer, Robert H., and Kenneth J. Zahorski. *Vision of Wonder: An Anthology of Christian Fantasy.*
> Chesterton, G. K. *The Man Who Was Thursday.*
> L'Engle, Madeleine. *A Wrinkle in Time.*
> MacDonald, George. *The Princess and the Goblin.*

Design. Bibliographies and source lists may be set in a type size one or two points smaller than text size, to conserve space, though if they are very short, they are best set in the same size as the text.

Spacing between Sentences

As far as putting two word spaces between sentences—*don't!* Inserting a double word space was a common practice in Victorian typesetting and later typewriting, and it is still sometimes taught as standard keyboard typing procedure. The extra space, however, has no place in printed material. A standard, single word space is sufficient.

Spelling Out Words in Text

Occasionally, a writer needs to indicate how a word, or words, should be spelled out. This happens most frequently in dialogue. The common practice is to use capital letters separated by hyphens, for instance: *"My name is Smyth, spelled S-M-Y-T-H, if you please!"*

State Resident Names

In writing and editing, the question of the correct label for persons from different geographic regions often arises. Entire dictionaries have been written to deal with that question on a global scale (see Paul Dickson's book *Labels for Locals: What to Call People from Abilene to Zimbabwe,* Merriam Webster, 1997). The following list will answer that question for the fifty US states. In some cases, especially when the states themselves have not designated an official name, the recommended name below is followed in parentheses by a commonly used alternative. When in doubt, use the first option.

State	Resident	State	Resident
Alabama	Alabamian (Alabaman)	Missouri	Missourian
Alaska	Alaskan	Montana	Montanan
Arizona	Arizonan (Arizonian)	Nebraska	Nebraskan
Arkansas	Arkansan (Arkansawyer)	Nevada	Nevadan
California	Californian	New Hampshire	New Hampshirite
Colorado	Coloradan (Coloradoan)	New Jersey	New Jerseyan
Connecticut	Connecticutter		(New Jerseyite)
Delaware	Delewarean (Delewarian)	New Mexico	New Mexican
Florida	Floridian (Floridan)	New York	New Yorker
Georgia	Georgian	North Carolina	North Carolinian
Hawaii	Hawaiian (Islander)		(Tar Heel)
Idaho	Idahoan	North Dakota	North Dakotan
Illinois	Illinoisan	Ohio	Ohioan
	(Illinoisian, Illini)	Oklahoma	Oklahoman
Indiana	Indianan (Hoosier,	Oregon	Oregonian
	Indianian)	Pennsylvania	Pennsylvanian
Iowa	Iowan	Rhode Island	Rhode Islander
Kansas	Kansan	South Carolina	South Carolinian
Kentucky	Kentuckyan	South Dakota	South Dakotan
Louisiana	Lousianian (Lousianan)	Tennessee	Tennessean
Maine	Mainer	Texas	Texan
Maryland	Marylander	Utah	Utahn
Massachusetts	Massachusettsan	Vermont	Vermonter
	(Bay Stater)	Virginia	Virginian
Michigan	Michiganian	Washington	Washingtonian
	(Michigander)	West Virginia	West Virginian
Minnesota	Minnesotan	Wisconsin	Wisconsonite
Mississippi	Mississippian	Wyoming	Wyomingite

Style Sheet

Perhaps the most effective way for a copyeditor to communicate the many style decisions that were made in a particular publication is in a *style sheet*. This is a simple one- or two-page chart, listing all the grammar, capitalization, punctuation, and word choices made by the editor, especially those that are exceptions to standard style or not covered in a manual such as this one. Also, all proper names should be listed with their correct spelling and capitalization so that the editor and proofreader can check for consistency throughout the publication. If many proper names are used, they are probably best listed separately on a second page.

The Basic Form. The following is a blank style sheet as it might be set up for a typical Zondervan book.

Style Sheet for [Author and Title] _____

Text Style: US _____ UK _____ Mid-Atlantic _____

Predominant Bible version: _____ **Other versions used** _____

Deity Pronoun: lc _____ cap _____ **Spell out nos. over:** 100 _____ 10 _____

Ellipsis Style: 3-dot (fiction) _____ 3–4-dot (others) _____ Rigorous _____

Special Style Notes: _____

_____

_____

Word List:

ABCD   MNOP

EFGH   QRST

IJKL   UVWXYZ

Subsidiary Rights

A publisher pays the author for the right to publish the first edition of the author's book, but a number of other rights are often included in an author-publisher contract. These are called *subsidiary rights* and usually include the following: audio edition rights (tape or CD), book-club rights, educational rights (curriculum use), electronic rights (ebook, software, and Internet), film rights, foreign publication rights, paperback edition rights, reprint rights, serial rights, theater rights, and translation rights. In most cases, the publisher is in the best position to exploit those rights in the author's best interest, but an author may wish to retain some of them when he or she has an existing or special contact who is more likely than the publisher to exploit those rights.

Symbols, Christian

Many symbols have important and unique significance to Christians, having become common in Christian art and literature over the centuries. Such symbols are common in churches and cathedrals alike, spanning denominations and cultures. The list below details some of those symbols and their meanings.

Symbol	Meaning
alpha and omega	eternity of Christ
altar	Communion
altar of burnt sacrifice	OT sacrifice
anchor	hope
angel (man with wings)	Matthew
apple	fall of man
Ark of Covenant	OT worship
ax, vertical	Matthew
balances, pair of	justice
banner	victory
Bible, placed over sword	Paul
birds	human souls
book, open	Bible
book, with ax	Matthew
book, with knife	Bartholomew
butterfly	resurrection
candle	Christ
censer	worship
chalice	Communion
cherubim	angelic host
chi rho (XP form)	Christ
chi rho on mountain	Sermon on the Mount
circle	eternity
circles, three interwoven	Trinity
coins	Christ's betrayal, Judas
cross, inverted	Peter
cross, with crown	death and heavenly reward
cross (X form)	Andrew
crown	Christ's kingship, believer's reward
crown of thorns	Christ's suffering
dove	Holy Spirit, peace
dove, descending	Jesus' baptism
doves, seven	Holy Spirit
eagle, winged	John
eye, all-seeing (in triangle)	God the Father
fire, seven-tongued	Holy Spirit
fire, tongues of	Holy Spirit, Pentecost
fish (ichthys)	Jonah, *also* Christ
fish, three	Trinity
fish, two crossed	Andrew
fleur-de-lis	Trinity

Symbol	Meaning
grapes	Communion
griffin	Christ's dual nature
halo	divinity
hand, blessing with halo	God the Father
hand, from cloud	God the Father
hands, clasped	marriage, friendship
handsaw	James the Less
harp	praise
heart	love and service
heart, pierced with sword	Mary
IHC or IHS	Jesus
keys	Peter
knives, three	Bartholomew
lamb	Christ
lamp	knowledge and learning
lamps, seven	Holy Spirit
lantern	Christ's betrayal
lion, winged	Mark
menorah	Jewish worship
moneybag, open	charity
moneybag, shut	Christ's betrayal, Judas
moneybags, three	Matthew
Noah's ark	salvation
olive branch	peace
ox, winged	Luke
palm branch	triumphal entry into Jerusalem
peacock	immortality and resurrection
pelican	Christ's atonement
phoenix	resurrection
pomegranate	resurrection
rainbow	God's covenant
rooster	Peter
scallop shell	pilgrimage
scallop shell, with water	Jesus' baptism
scallop shells, three	James the Greater
scroll	Bible
serpent, on cross or pole	crucifixion
shamrock	Trinity
shepherd	Christ
ship	the church, also Jude
snake	fall of man, sin, Satan
snake, in chalice	John
star, five-pointed	Jesus

Symbol	Meaning
star of David	David, Jesus
tau cross	Matthew, *also* St. Anthony
Tower of Babel	sin, human pride
triangle	Trinity
tunic, camel-hair	John the Baptist
wheat, with tares	parable of weeds
wheat sheaves	Communion
whips, *or* barbed scourge	Christ's suffering

Symbols, Circle

A variety of "small letters inside circles" are commonly used in publishing to denote various legalities and rights. The most common are these:

© = the copyright symbol
® = the registered trademark symbol
℗ = the performance symbol

Table of Contents

A table of contents, also called a *contents page*, not only helps the reader find specific parts of a book but can also provide a convenient outline of the book's content, a fact the author and editor should keep in mind when devising the titles for the chapters and parts of the book.

Placement. It is customarily placed on the next recto page after the title page (and across from the copyright page), although the positioning can be shifted to accommodate limitations or special designs. When a table of contents runs across two pages, they can be conveniently set as a spread, beginning on a verso and ending on the facing recto, which will keep the reader from having to turn a page to get an overview of the book.

Elements and Setting. It should contain all the major divisions of a book: usually parts and chapters, along with their numbers and titles. Any front or back matter text (such as forewords, prefaces, introductions, appendixes, and so on) should be listed on the contents page, though often they are shown in a contrasting font (italics when the chapters are set in roman type).

The word *chapter* should not appear before the chapter numbers on the contents page. They are superfluous in most cases, as well as repetitive. In the same way, the word *page* should not appear at the top of the column of page numbers.

Style Considerations. Usually, the table of contents is set in the same type style as the text of the book, and the word *Contents* at the top of the page should echo the treatment of the chapter openers.

Leader dots were once commonly used to connect chapter titles with their appropriate page numbers but are now almost universally rejected as eyesores.

Unnumbered Part- and Chapter-Title Pages. There is also this question to consider: Since part-title and full-page chapter-title pages do not bear folio numbers, how should you reference those pages in a table of contents? The table of contents should not list the actual page number of the part- or chapter-title page but the folio number on which the actual text of that part or chapter begins. That may seem odd, but experience has shown that readers become less confused when this is done. It is best not to tell a reader that Part One begins on page 15 when a 15 is actually not printed on any page in the book. It is best to say in the table of contents that Part One begins on page 17, even though the actual title page appears on 15.

Tanak

See "Acronyms and Initialisms, *Note.*"

Telephone Numbers

In general, the following format is used in setting telephone numbers in text: *(123) 456-7890*, that is, with parentheses around the area code and a hyphen used internally. If an extension is used, the number should be set: *(123) 456-7890, ext. 123.*

Advocates for the visually impaired argue that a parenthesis can be too easily mistaken for a numeral 1. If a book, such as a large print book, is being set specifically for readers with visual impairments, then the telephone number may be set: *123-456-7890.* Consistency should be maintained in any case.

In Fiction. Often in the course of a fictional narrative a telephone or cellular phone number must be given, for instance, when a character tells another character how to reach him or her. Of course, the odds are high that any given made-up number may be a real one, which could prove an inconvenience to the actual person whose phone has that number. There was a recent case in which a telephone number was given in a popular movie, which resulted in several people, in different area codes, feeling harassed by unwanted calls.

The safest way to give a phone number in a novel is to give it the three-digit exchange *555* followed by any other combination of numbers (except for *1212*). Any area code can safely be used, if needed. The exchange *555* is reserved exclusively for directory assistance in the US, followed by the number *1212*, which should be avoided. But all other four-number combinations should be safe, and if a reader does attempt to dial the number, he or she will receive an "I'm sorry, your call cannot be completed as dialed" message.

Ten Commandments

The term *Ten Commandments* and its synonymous terms, *Decalogue* and *Commandments*, are always capitalized, even when used metaphorically, as in *the Ten Commandments of confrontation management.* When one commandment is singled out, it should be lowercased, as in *the fourth commandment* or *the commandment regarding the keeping of the Sabbath.*

The Ten Commandments are listed twice in the Old Testament: Exodus 20:1–17 and Deuteronomy 5:6–21, with some slight differences in wording between them. For instance, in the Deuteronomic version of the Tenth Commandment against covetousness, the "neighbor's wife" is listed first and separately, whereas in the version in Exodus, she is listed among the neighbor's possessions.

Care should be taken in referring to a specific commandment because not all denominations and translations agree in wording, emphasis, or even order. Also, a careful writer should not assume that the reader will remember the Commandments by number alone. For instance, it is better to refer to *the commandment prohibiting murder* rather than *the sixth commandment*.

Text Breaks

Commonly a fiction author needs to indicate the passage of time, a scene change, an introduction of a new point-of-view, or other shift in the narrative. The most convenient way of achieving this is with a *text break*. The shift is usually not so strong or sudden that the author wishes to begin a new chapter but merely wants to signal a change in direction in the current chapter. Nonfiction writers also use text breaks between major unheaded sections.

In preparing a manuscript, the author should use three spaced asterisks (* * *), also called an *asterism*, on a line by themselves to indicate the text break. Another form of the *asterism* is three pound signs (# # #). The author should inform the editor of the method he or she used to indicate the breaks.

A double space, or two returns, should not be used. Using a double space runs the risk of having the text break becoming lost or discarded when the data is converted to another word-processing system since many common editing programs delete double spaces as redundancies.

That Versus *Which*

Many writers, editors, and proofreaders insist that in relative clauses the word *that* be used when the sense is restrictive and the word *which* be used when the sense is nonrestrictive. A clause beginning with a restrictive *that* is set without commas, while a clause beginning with a nonrestrictive *which* should be set off with commas. This workaday rule, which makes life easier for editors and proofreaders, is certainly worth observing.

But before insisting on adherence to the *that/which* rule, it should be remembered that no English writer before the twentieth century made such a distinction. In 1926 H. W. Fowler noted in his *Dictionary of Modern English Usage* that the history of those terms was "a jumble," so he proposed that they be distinguished according to restrictive and nonrestrictive senses. Since then, due to the influence of Fowler's seminal work, the rule has been adopted as one of the absolutes of English grammar, with perhaps even more rigidity than Fowler had intended. It should be remembered that few average readers are able to distinguish between the two uses, and few are likely to be confused by a misplaced *that* or *which*.

Certain exceptions to the *that/which* rule, therefore, should be taken into account. First, although Fowler was himself British, his rule has become gospel primarily among American teachers of English and editors rather than among the British, who commonly use *which* in a restrictive sense. This manual does not recommend forcing a British writer to conform to American style, especially when a work is intended for a UK or combined UK and US audience (as in the "Mid-Atlantic Style" outlined elsewhere in this book).

Second, the word *that* is one of the most frequently used words in English, which means an editor must be sensitive to how often the word is repeated in a passage before insisting on changing a *which* to a *that*. If many *that*s already exist in close proximity, it is perfectly acceptable to allow a restrictive *which* to stand.

Finally, an editor or proofreader should be sensitive to the kind of writing in which *that* and *which* are being used. In poetry, for instance, one should not presume to impose the strict *that/which* distinction on the poet. The same would hold true for highly literary fiction and essays, where the music and rhythm of the author's words are as important to the sense as the actual meanings. In those cases, query the author if the usage of *that* and *which* might possibly confuse the reader. Otherwise, leave them as they are.

Thou and *Thee*

It is surprising how often pseudo–King James English is used in public prayers when persons of the Trinity are addressed as *Thou* and *Thee*. Originally these forms, being the ones used with one's family and closest friends (equivalent to the French informal *tu* and *toi*), were used for their intimacy and informality. Most modern users of these pronouns intend them to sound more respectful and reverent, as though addressing royalty. Furthermore, many casual users of these terms use them incorrectly, sometimes indiscriminately interchanging "*thou*," which is a subject ("Thou preparest a table before me" [Ps. 23:5]), and "*thee*," which is an object ("Unto thee, O Lord, do I lift up my soul" [Ps. 25:1]). Even a well-known pop singer, in his rendition of "Be Thou My Vision," mixes up his pronouns when he sings, "Naught be all else to me save that Thy art." Needless to say, one should avoid these forms except in quotations or when the intent is clearly humorous.

Thou adds special inflections to its verbs, *-est*, *-st*, and *-t*, familiar to anyone who reads Shakespeare or the KJV ("Thou anointest my head with oil" [Ps. 23:5]). To most ears, *thou* sounds particularly stilted when used with modern verb forms: *Thou knows my inmost thoughts.* The possessive form is *thy* ("thy rod and thy staff" [Ps. 23:4]), though it takes the form *thine* when followed by a vowel or an unpronounced *h* ("Thine eyes did see my substance" [Ps. 139:16]).

These archaic terms were until recently used occasionally by some Friends (Quaker) denominations, though with the awareness of their quaint character. They are also used in such popular expressions as *holier than thou* and in some old hymns and songs, such as "Come, Thou Long Expected Jesus" and "My Country, 'Tis of Thee." Obviously, such uses should be retained as the familiar ones to most ears.

Many modern hymnals, however, have taken the fairly easy step of rewriting many of the old hymns by replacing *thee* and *thou* with *you*, and *thy* and *thine* with *your*. If the archaic forms are used to complete a rhyme, however, as in Frances R. Havergal's "Take my life, and let it be / Consecrated, Lord, to Thee," then such rewriting is not usually attempted.

Three-Em Dash

See "Dash."

Time and Dates

Spelling Out Versus Numerals. Times of day are usually spelled out unless an exact moment of time is emphasized, in which case numerals are used.

The evening service ended at about half past seven.
Sunday school begins at 9:30 sharp, and the worship service begins at 11:00.

A.M. and P.M. This manual recommends that the abbreviations *a.m.* and *p.m.* be set in lowercase letters with periods. Small-cap abbreviation style (with or without periods) is still acceptable, however, when a sense of high literary or artistic quality needs to be conveyed to the reader.

The abbreviations *a.m.* and *p.m.* should be used only with numerical time designations that use a colon, for instance, *11:00 p.m.* rather than *11 p.m.* Furthermore, the words *morning, afternoon, evening,* and *o'clock* should not be combined with the designations a.m. or p.m.

10:45 in the morning	4:00 p.m.
10:45 a.m.	four o'clock in the afternoon

Eras. References to millennia, centuries, and decades should be spelled out. If numerals are used for decades, add an *s* with no apostrophe. In informal contexts the full number of a specific year is sometimes abbreviated with an apostrophe, for instance, with year designations for automobiles and for graduating classes.

second millennium BC	the 1740s
sixteenth century	a '57 Chevy
the seventies and eighties	the class of '01

Months. Do not abbreviate the names of the months in text, although they may be abbreviated in references or charts as follows:

Jan.	Apr.	July	Oct.
Feb.	May	Aug.	Nov.
Mar.	June	Sept.	Dec.

Days of the Week. Do not abbreviate days of the week in text. If a special situation, such as a chart or list, calls for an abbreviation, use the following:

Sun.	Mon.	Tues.	Wed.	Thurs.	Fri.	Sat.

Seasons. The names for the seasons, solstices, and equinoxes are lowercased. Seasons are capped, however, when they appear in periodical references.

fall (or *autumn*)	summer
fall (or *autumn*) equinox	summer solstice
spring	winter
spring equinox	winter solstice

James Galvin, "River Edged with Ice," *Orion* 21, Winter 2002.

AD and BC. The abbreviations *AD* and *BC* should be set in capital letters with no periods (though the small-cap style may still be used when appropriate). Place *AD* before a specific year reference, although it should follow a reference to an entire century. The abbreviation *BC* always comes after a century or year reference. For more details, see "*AD*" and "*BC*."

BCE and CE. In recent years the abbreviations *BCE* ("before the Common Era") and *CE* ("Common Era") have gained currency as more secular alternatives to the traditional *AD* and *BC*, the specifically Christian emphasis of which some people find offensive. See "*CE and BCE*" for a more complete discussion.

AH. In Islamic scholarship, *AH* (*anno Hegirae,* "in the year of the Hegira") designates the era after Muhammed's flight from Mecca in AD 622. (Also see "Islamic Religious Terminology.")

Dates. This manual recommends the "month day, year" style of rendering dates (the month and day are separated from the year by a comma). Other styles are common, however. Style 2, shown below, is the "day month year." Common in many scholarly and reference works, it is also the preferred style in the UK. Note that no commas are used in Style 2. Do not use the ordinal abbreviations *st, nd, rd,* or *th* after numeral figures in dates.

When a month or season designation is immediately followed by a year, a comma should not be used.

> Style 1 (US Style): On May 30, 1934, the Barmen Declaration was signed.
> Style 2 (UK Style): Wesley's conversion took place on 24 May 1738.
> Style 3: On the first day of September 1670, William Penn's trial began.

> December 25, *not* December 25th, but "December twenty-fifth" (in dialogue)
> William Booth's tent ministry in the East End began in July 1865.
> It all goes back to fall 2000.

Old Style and New Style. Many historical references distinguish between dates from the Julian calendar (which was established in 46 BC) and those from the Gregorian calendar by using the abbreviations *OS* (Old Style) and *NS* (New Style) respectively. Unless otherwise specified, all modern references are in New Style. The new calendar was established in 1582, although many Western countries did not adopt it until many years later. The Eastern Orthodox Church still dates its holidays by the older Julian calendar.

Dates in and around the year in which a specific country adopted the Gregorian calendar should be checked carefully. For instance, when Great Britain and the American colonies adopted the New Style system in 1752, two important changes took place. First, eleven days were dropped from the calendar (the day after September 2, 1752, was considered September 14, 1752). Also, January 1 was officially made the first day of 1752, whereas before that time March 25 (the Annunciation) had traditionally been considered New Year's Day in England. This is further confused by the fact that many people already considered January 1 to be New Year's Day.

In referring to years before 1752 in English history, dates between January 1 and March 24 are sometimes listed with a double-year designation. A solidus is used between the elided year numerals. Again, if no such designation is given, it can usually be assumed that a New Style date is being referred to.

> The storm at sea that lead to John Newton's conversion took place on March
>   21, 1748 NS (March 10, OS).
> The service took place on Epiphany, January 6, 1720/21.

When Does the Day Actually Begin? Although most modern Western cultures consider midnight to be the start of the new day, both Jewish and Christian traditions have considered sunset to be the start of the new day, which is why the eve of feast days are celebrated—they are, in fact, the beginning of the feast day itself. Thus, Christmas Eve, Halloween (the eve of All Saints' Day), John Keats' famous "Eve of Saint Agnes," Twelfth Night (the eve of Epiphany), and other eves are singled out for special celebration because they mark the beginning of the holiday itself. Inherent in this Jewish and Christian tradition, perhaps, is the idea that God brings light out of darkness, so that daylight always follows nighttime, a symbol of hope and resurrection. Curiously, the ancient Babylonians, Syrians, and Persians began the day at sunrise, while the ancient Egyptians began the day at noon. (See also "Hours, Biblical" and "*Watches of the Night.*")

Quaker System of Dating. In the Quaker system of dating, days and months are usually spelled out and lowercased. This system is not used much today but is common in Quaker writings of the past. Also, note that before 1752 the Quakers considered March to be the first month of the year.

> January ninth, or the ninth day of the first month.
> Nineteen-year-old George Fox left home on the ninth day, the seventh month, 1643. [September 9, 1643]

Title Changes

If the title of a work changes in a subsequent reprint or edition of a book (whether or not the book was originally published by that publisher), it is recommended that a notice of the original title be provided on the copyright page. This is also true for books that were previously published in another language. A notice giving the original title in the original language should appear on the copyright page.

The phrasing of such formulae is variable, but usually something like the following is used:

> Originally published in [YEAR] under the title . . .
> Previously published as . . .
> Originally published in [COUNTRY] under the title . . .

Although some publishers opt not to put the original title on the copyright page, all publishers are required by the Federal Trade Commission (FTC) to give a notice of the original title on both the front cover (or jacket) and the title page of the book. It should be displayed in a relatively prominent manner so that it might readily come to the attention of the reader.

The FTC also mandates that such a notice in the change of a title be mentioned in promotional copy (meaning primarily catalog copy) for the book. Such change-of-title notice is not generally required in consumer or trade advertising, unless, of course, it would benefit the marketing of the book to mention the original title.

If a foreign work is appearing in English for the first time, the FTC regulations do not require that the original foreign-language title appear on the cover or title page, though, as stated before, it is usually a courtesy to the reader to mention the original title on the copyright page.

If the specific English translation of a foreign work has previously appeared under another title, then the earlier English title should be provided on the front cover and title page as well as the copyright page.

If it is an entirely new translation of a work that has appeared in other translations, then any previous English titles need not appear, though the foreign title should still appear on the copyright page as a courtesy to the reader.

Title Page

A book's *title page*, which is page 3 in most books but can vary widely according to the design, usually carries these elements:

1. the complete title and subtitle of the book
2. the name of the author(s), as well as name(s) of any series editors, translators, compilers, etc.
3. whether the book is an unnumbered revised edition or a newly numbered revised edition
4. whether the book was previously published with another title
5. the name of the publisher(s) and sometimes the publisher's city or full address
6. the publisher's logo

Sometimes other elements are present, such as an epigraph, especially if it is closely related to the title, or such short author information as "the author of the bestselling . . ." Not present on the title page are running heads or folios. Most often, designers strive for typographic simplicity, elegance, and cleanness on a title page. It is, in a sense, a formal invitation to the reader to read the book. Typographically, it should echo the design of either the cover or the chapter opening pages.

Titles, Capitalization of

See "Capitalization, *Titles.*"

Titles, Prepositions in

See "Prepositions in Titles."

Titles of Common Texts of the World's Religions

Like the Bible, the names of the most common sacred and venerated texts of the world's religions are generally set in roman type. As with the Bible, however, any specific edition of such a work should be italicized as an ordinary book title: for instance, *The Essential Chuang Tzu* or *The Tao Te Ching: An Illustrated Journey.*

Unless an author has an alternate preference, this manual recommends the unaccented and unhyphenated forms of such titles (*Tao Te Ching*, rather than *Tao Tê Ching* or *Tao-te-ching*, for instance) whenever there is an alternative. Although we recommend the pinyin system for most Chinese words, an exception is made for most Chinese authors and religious works whose names are already long-established in a romanized form. For instance, *Tao Te Ching* rather than *Daodejing* (pinyin) and its legendary author *Lao Tzu* rather than *Laozi* (pinyin). (See "Chinese Transliteration.")

Here is a list of the most common titles in their preferred forms in English. Alternate titles are also given where those are known.

Akaranga Sutra—Jain

Anelects, the—Confucian; also called the Lun Yü

Atharva-Veda, the—Hindu; part of the Samhita, or Vedas

Avesta, the—Zoroastrian (sometimes wrongly called *the Zend-Avesta*)

Bhagavad-Gita, the—Hindu; part of the Mahabharata

Blue Cliff Record, the—Zen Buddhist

Book of Changes, the—Confucian; also called the I Ching; one of the Five Classics

Book of Filial Piety, the—Confucian; also called the Hsiao Ching

Book of History, the—Confucian; also called the Shuh Ching; one of the Five Classics

Book of Mormon, the—Mormon; subtitled Another Testament of Jesus Christ

Book of Rites, the—Confucian; also called the Li Ki; one of the Five Classics

Book of Songs, the—Confucian; also called the Shih Ching; its two parts are two of the Five Classics

Book of the Dead, the—Buddhist (The Tibetan Book of the Dead)

Brahmanas, the—Hindu

Chuang Tzu—Taoist; the writings of Chuang Tzu

Dhammapada, the—Buddhist

Doctrine of the Mean, the—Confucian; also called the Chung Yung

Doctrines and Covenants, the—Mormon

Egyptian Book of the Dead, the—Egyptian; also known as the Papyrus of Ani

Five Classics, the—Confucian

Gemara, the—Jewish; part of the Talmud; a commentary on the Mishnah

Granth Sahib—Sikh (Shree Guru Granth Sahib)

Great Learning, the—Confucian; also called the Ta Hsueh

Hadith, the—Muslim; usually capped, even though it is an oral body of work rather than a written document

Haggadah, the—Jewish; also spelled Aggada; the legends and stories section of the Talmud

Halakah, the—Jewish; the legal section of the Talmud

I Ching, the—Confucian; also called the Book of Changes; one of the Five Classics

Inner Chapters, the—Taoist; the oldest section of the writings of Chuang Tzu

Kalpa Sutra—Jain

Kojiki, the—Shinto

Koran, the—Muslim; see *Qu'ran*

Lao Tzu—Taoist; the Tao Te Ching and other writings attributed to Lao Tzu

Lotus Sutra, the—Mahayana Buddhist

Mahabharata, the—Hindu

Mishnah, the—Jewish; part of the Talmud

Nihongi, the—Shinto

Papyrus of Ani, the—Egyptian; also known as the Egyptian Book of the Dead

Pearl of Great Price—Mormon

Pentateuch, the—Jewish

Qur'an, the—Muslim; also spelled *Koran* and *Quran,* though *Qur'an* is the preferred English form

Rig-Veda, the—Hindu; part of the Samhita, or Vedas

Sama-Veda, the—Hindu; part of the Samhita, or Vedas

Samhita, the—Hindu; the four Vedas together

Spring and Autumn Annals, the—Confucian; one of the Five Classics

Sunna, the—Muslim; usually capped, even though it is an oral body of work rather than a written document

Sun Tzu—Taoist; also called the Art of War

sutra—Buddhist; capped only if a specific one is named

Talmud, the—Jewish

Tanak, the—Jewish

Tao Te Ching, the—Taoist; attributed to Lao Tzu

Torah, the—Jewish

Tripitaka, the—Buddhist

Upanishads, the—Hindu; the final portion of the Vedas

Veda, or Vedas, the—Hindu

Vimalakirti Sutra, the—Mahayana Buddhist

Wen Tzu, the—Taoist; later writings attributed to Lao Tzu

Yajur-Veda, the—Hindu; part of the Samhita, or Vedas

Today's New International Version: Bible Style

See "Bible Style: The New International Version."

Trademarks and Trade Names

See "Brand Names."

Trim Sizes for Books, Common

Although books can be trimmed in almost any size, from the 1-$^3/_8$ x 2-$^5/_{16}$–inch *We the People: Two Hundred Years of the Constitution* by R. C. Bellas (Xavier Press, 1987) to the 10-$^3/_4$ x 14-$^1/_2$–inch *Leonardo Da Vinci* (Istituto Geografico da Agostino, 1956), the smallest and largest books, respectively, on my shelves, a few sizes have become standard throughout the book industry. These sizes tend to be the least expensive to produce since many printers have preset their presses and production equipment to conveniently handle them. These trim sizes generally apply as well to print-on-demand books, which have so far merely imitated the sizes and shapes of books already familiar to readers.

The following chart shows the common US book trim sizes and their common descriptions and purposes.

Common US Trim Sizes

Width x height in inches	Common description	Type of books sometimes associated with this size
4-$^3/_{16}$ x 6-$^3/_4$	"mass market" paperbacks	Traditional "pocketbook"; often printed on lower-grade paper; often has an ephemeral feel.
5-$^5/_{16}$ x 8	trade paper small hardcovers	Standard trade paper books; small hardcover and gift books; small novels
5-$^1/_2$ x 8-$^1/_2$	trade paper hardcovers	Many trade paper books and hardcovers; standard hardcover fiction size.
6 x 9	hardcovers some lengthy books	"Blockbuster" fiction and best-seller potential; important books that make a statement.
7-$^3/_8$ x 9-$^1/_8$	large size	Slightly larger than average book; workbooks, "lifestyle" books
8 x 9-$^1/_8$	large "square" format	"coffee table books"

Two-Em Dash

See "Dash."

Typographic Symbols, Common

The following typographic symbols are more or less common in contemporary publishing and printing, and although some seem a bit antiquated, their presence persists in most word-processing type fonts. The least used ones (like @, the "at symbol") have found a new life in the Internet age. An asterisk in the list below indicates that a more complete discussion can be found in this manual under a separate heading for that symbol. (Also see individual punctuation marks: "Period," "Comma," etc.)

Symbol	Name	Function
&	*ampersand	sign for "and"; a typographic form of the Latin *et* (also called the *tironian sign*)
§	section mark	shows the beginning of a section of writing; a stylized double *s*, for the Latin *signum sectionis* ("sign of a section")
☞	fist (or *index hand*)	printer's symbol, meaning "note this"
¶	paragraph symbol (or *blind p*)	indicates the beginning of a paragraph; common in the KJV
( )	*parentheses (or *round brackets*)	to indicate parenthetical thought or statement
[ ]	*brackets (or *square brackets*)	to show parenthetical statement within parentheses
{ }	*braces (or *curly brackets*)	used to group consecutive lines together
*	asterisk	for footnotes and itemizing elements in a list
* * * or * * * or # # #	asterism (or *triple asterisk*)	used to indicate minor breaks in text
†	dagger (or *obelisk*)	the first level of symbol footnoting
‡	double dagger	the second level of symbol footnoting
#	number sign (or *pound sign*)	still occasionally used for numbers, but now mostly used as a select key on telephone keypads
$	dollar sign	US currency
¥	yen sign	Japanese currency
€	euro sign	European currency
%	percent sign	used for percentages; abbreviation of the Latin *per centum* (per one hundred); used mostly in scientific or technical contexts

Symbol	Name	Function
/	*solidus	for uses, see "Solidus (Forward Slash)"
<	less-than sign	used in mathematical settings
=	equal sign	used in mathematical settings
>	greater-than sign	used in mathematical settings
@	at symbol	formerly little used as an abbreviation to mean *at* or *approximately*; now universally used to designate email addresses
\	back slash	used primarily in computer programming
™	trademark symbol	to show that the trademark is legally protected
©	copyright symbol	to show that the material is legally copyrighted
®	registered trademark symbol	to show that the trademark is legally registered

Typography, The Elements of Basic Book

A book's cover and its interior design serve two quite different purposes. The cover is essentially an advertisement, a billboard that quickly conveys in word, color, and image a sense of the book's content and the promise it holds for the reader. It should therefore draw attention to itself. It is the one place in book design, says biblio-scholar Douglas C. McMurtrie, in which "fancy can run riot."

The interior, or text, design of a book serves a different function. Ideally, it should be attractive but not distracting. In her book *The Crystal Goblet*, famed book designer Beatrice Ward compared interior typography to a wine glass. It should have sufficient beauty in itself, but not so much that it distracts from the color and taste of the wine. In a sense the reader looks through a book's type directly to the author's thoughts. To the extent that the design is noticed or is distracting, a portion of the author's content will be lost.

The design, interior and exterior alike, must also cohere as a whole, and there must be a reason for all design decisions. As designer Philip Brady says in his book *Using Type Right*, "Literally no element that goes into creating a visual message . . . is neutral. Each element is a signal acting as either a friend or a foe to getting the message across" (3).

Nor should the designer indulge in design for design's sake. Design can only be approached with the reader in mind. "In planning a book," wrote Eric Gill in his *Essay on Typography*, "the first questions are: who is going to read this, and under what circumstances?" (106).

Most of the elements of basic book typography given below are for the text of the book, not its cover, title pages, front or back matter, or chapter opening pages. General rules for display typography cannot be so easily summarized because, like advertising, book covers and even chapter openers are subject to rapidly changing trends, experimentation, and creativity on the part of the designer. Rules for text type are simpler. These principles have remained relatively unchanged over the centuries because they have proven to promote optimum reading speed with a minimum of fatigue, especially for long periods of sustained reading. Still, rules can be broken when there is a good reason to do so. Marshall Lee observed, in his *Bookmaking*, "There is only one rule in design: *If it works, it's good*" (90).

Type Size. The size of the text type for most books, whether for children who read at a fifth-grade reading level and above or for adults, is 9-, 10-, 11-, or 12-point type. For faces that have a small x-height, 11- and 12-point types predominate; while 9- and 10-point predominate for faces with a large x-height. Books that are termed "large-print" should have a type size of 16- or preferably 18-point or larger. Their relative sizes are shown here:

9-point Garamond:

As I walked through the wilderness of this world, I lighted on a certain place where was a Den, and I laid me down in that place to sleep: and, as I slept, I dreamed a dream. I dreamed, and behold, I saw a man clothed with rags, standing in a certain place, with his face from his own house, a book in his hand, and a great burden upon his back. I looked, and saw him open the book, and read therein; and as he read, he wept, and trembled; and, not being able longer to contain, he brake out with a lamentable cry, saying, *What shall I do?* (John Bunyan, the opening words of *The Pilgrim's Progress*, 1678)

10-point Garamond:

As I walked through the wilderness of this world, I lighted on a certain place where was a Den, and I laid me down in that place to sleep: and, as I slept, I dreamed a dream. I dreamed, and behold, I saw a man clothed with rags, standing in a certain place, with his face from his own house, a book in his hand, and a great burden upon his back. I looked, and saw him open the book, and read therein; and as he read, he wept, and trembled; and, not being able longer to contain, he brake out with a lamentable cry, saying, *What shall I do?* (John Bunyan, the opening words of *The Pilgrim's Progress*, 1678)

11-point Garamond:

As I walked through the wilderness of this world, I lighted on a certain place where was a Den, and I laid me down in that place to sleep: and, as I slept, I dreamed a dream. I dreamed, and behold, I saw a man clothed with rags, standing in a certain place, with his face from his own house, a book in his hand, and a great burden upon his back. I looked, and saw him open the book, and read therein; and as he read, he wept, and trembled; and, not being able longer to contain, he brake out with a lamentable cry, saying, *What shall I do?* (John Bunyan, the opening words of *The Pilgrim's Progress*, 1678)

12-point Garamond:

As I walked through the wilderness of this world, I lighted on a certain place where was a Den, and I laid me down in that place to sleep: and, as I slept, I dreamed a dream. I dreamed, and behold, I saw a man clothed with rags, standing in a certain place, with his face from his own house, a book in his hand, and a great burden upon his back. I looked, and saw him open the book, and read therein; and as he read, he wept, and trembled; and, not being able longer to contain, he brake out with a lamentable cry, saying, *What shall I do?* (John Bunyan, the opening words of *The Pilgrim's Progress*, 1678)

16-point Garamond:

As I walked through the wilderness of this world, I lighted on a certain place where was a Den, and I laid me down in that place to sleep: and, as I slept, I dreamed a dream. I dreamed, and behold, I saw a man clothed with rags, standing in a certain place, with his face from his own house, a book in his hand, and a great burden upon his back. I looked, and saw him open the book, and read therein; and as he read, he wept, and trembled; and, not being able longer to contain, he brake out with a lamentable cry, saying, *What shall I do?* (John Bunyan, the opening words of *The Pilgrim's Progress*, 1678)

Type Weight. A medium weight typeface, that is, with line strokes that are neither too light nor too heavy, is best for standard book setting. The most commonly used medium weight faces are Times New Roman, Bembo, and Garamond.

Boldface. Avoid boldface type in text whenever possible, except for headings, display type, and cross-referencing in reference works. (**These words are in boldface.**) Bold type in text tends to distract the reader from the content and make the page look splotchy, and large portions of boldface text can even cause the type to appear blurred. Use italic for emphasis instead.

Italic. While italic is commonly used for emphasis, its use should be kept to a minimum. (*These words are in italic.*) Large blocks of text in italics are difficult to read, and they decrease speed and comprehension levels.

Serif and Sans-serif Typefaces. Scientific research indicates that serif typefaces may be marginally more readable than sans-serif, although familiarity may be more of a factor than physiology. (This is a serif typeface, and this is a sans-serif typeface.) Anecdotal evidence from readers shows that serif faces are almost universally preferred for long periods of sustained reading. When in doubt, stick with the traditional serif fonts.

Lowercase and Uppercase Type. Standard cap-lowercase type should be used for text in books. (This line is set in cap-lowercase.) It is best to avoid even occasional use of all-cap type whenever possible because all-cap type decreases "word-shape recognition," slows the reading, and takes up thirty percent more space. It can also distract the reader and break the spell of the reading experience itself. In most cases when emphasis is required, italics can be used as effectively as all-caps. In those cases in which all-capital letters are needed, most traditional typographers recommend the use of small caps instead.

Calligraphy Fonts. These should be used only for display, never for continuous reading. Occasionally, when the author or editors wish to convey the general impression of handwritten text, a calligraphy font can be used in small doses. They are often quite beautiful but are unreadable for more than the occasional word or sentence.

This is a calligraphy font.

Type on the Spine of the Book. It is customary in the US to set spine type so that it reads from top to bottom, or, to put it another way, so that it reads from left to right when the book is laid flat with the front cover facing up.

Ligatures. Whenever ligatures are available for a font, they should be used, especially in display type, titles, and headlines. Most computer typesetters will automatically add the ligature characters in the typesetting process, although many recent fonts seemed to have been designed without them. Here are the most common ligatures in English: Æ, æ, Œ, œ, ff, ffi, ffl, fi, and fl.

Numbers and Numerals. Scientific research shows that arabic numerals are more readable than the same numbers spelled as words, even for numbers under one hundred. This manual recommends abiding by the customary rule of spelling out numbers of under one hundred, but it does make an exception for books intended for young adults, in which we recommend spelling out numbers under ten. Use numerals for all the rest.

Reverse Type. In striving for unique effects, some less-experienced designers will set light type or small fonts on dark backgrounds ("white on black"). This should be avoided. However, reverse-type technique can be quite effective when used with heavy type or display fonts.

Mixing Typefaces. Contrast and compatibility are the key words for mixing two or more different typefaces, and such a mix of fonts should usually be limited to front matter, chapter openers, running heads, back matter, and display type. For readability of text matter, however, a single face should be relied on.

Line Width and Average Word-Per-Line Counts. For maximum readability, the line width on the page of standard text type should be between 18 and 24 picas. Some designers use this rule: Maximum width should never be more than twice the font size. Thus, 24 picas would be the maximum width for a 12-point type.

Ideally, the average words-per-line count should be between 8 and 12, though readability begins to be sacrificed when the lines average much more than 13 or 14 words per line. This is not only because the typeface is smaller at that word count but also because the eye has a harder time "tracking back" to the next line of text while reading, which promotes fatigue. Lines that are too short (less than 8 words) can be just as fatiguing, however, because the eye is having to shift right-to-left much more often than in standard setting. To ascertain the average words-per-line, select ten full lines of text (exclude first and last lines of paragraphs), add up the total number of words, and divide by ten. The average word-per-line count of this paragraph you are now reading is 13.7.

Leading. The space between lines of standard serif text settings should be between one and four points, depending on the typeface used, its weight, x-height, and other factors. Dark types, boldface type, and most sans-serif types require more leading for maximum readability. Here is the same sample from Bunyan's *Pilgrim's Progress*, this time in 12-point type with four different leadings.

With 1 extra point of leading:

As I walked through the wilderness of this world, I lighted on a certain place where was a Den, and I laid me down in that place to sleep: and, as I slept, I dreamed a dream. I dreamed, and behold, I saw a man clothed with rags, standing in a certain place, with his face from his own house, a book in his hand, and a great burden upon his back. I looked, and saw him open the book, and read therein; and as he read, he wept, and trembled; and, not being able longer to contain, he brake out with a lamentable cry, saying, *What shall I do?* (John Bunyan, the opening words of *The Pilgrim's Progress*, 1678)

With 2 extra points of leading:

As I walked through the wilderness of this world, I lighted on a certain place where was a Den, and I laid me down in that place to sleep: and, as I slept, I dreamed a dream. I dreamed, and behold, I saw a man clothed with rags, standing in a certain place, with his face from his own house, a book in his hand, and a great burden upon his back. I looked, and saw him open the book, and read therein; and as he read, he wept, and trembled; and, not being able longer to contain, he brake out with a lamentable cry, saying, *What shall I do?* (John Bunyan, the opening words of *The Pilgrim's Progress*, 1678)

With 3 extra points of leading:

As I walked through the wilderness of this world, I lighted on a certain place where was a Den, and I laid me down in that place to sleep: and, as I slept, I dreamed a dream. I dreamed, and behold, I saw a man clothed with rags, standing in a certain place, with his face from his own house, a book in his hand, and a great burden upon his back. I looked, and saw him open the book, and read therein; and as he read, he wept, and trembled; and, not being able longer to contain, he brake out with a lamentable cry, saying, *What shall I do?* (John Bunyan, the opening words of *The Pilgrim's Progress*, 1678)

With 4 extra points of leading:

As I walked through the wilderness of this world, I lighted on a certain place where was a Den, and I laid me down in that place to sleep: and, as I slept, I dreamed a dream. I dreamed, and behold, I saw a man clothed with rags, standing in a certain place, with his face from his own house, a book in his hand, and a great burden upon his back. I looked, and saw him open the book, and read therein; and as he read, he wept, and trembled; and, not being able longer to contain, he brake out with a lamentable cry, saying, *What shall I do?* (John Bunyan, the opening words of *The Pilgrim's Progress*, 1678)

Justified and Unjustified Text Setting. For ease or speed of reading, little difference exists between justified (aligned on both margins) setting and unjustified (aligned on the left, ragged on the right). The issues are mostly aesthetic. Justified setting is the more common of the two, though unjustified setting is increasingly being used. This present paragraph was set in unjustified setting while the others on this page are justified.

One-Column and Two-Column Text. Where space is a problem, especially in reference works and textbooks, setting the type in a two-column rather than a one-column format can be not only more compact but also more readable. Obviously, many genres, such as fiction, do not lend themselves well to two-column setting, but even in those cases, creative designers have achieved attractive, readable design using two columns.

As I walked through the wilderness of this world, I lighted on a certain place where was a Den, and I laid me down in that place to sleep: and, as I slept, I dreamed a dream. I dreamed, and behold, I saw a man clothed with rags, standing in a certain place, with his face from his own house, a book in his hand, and a great burden upon his back. I looked, and saw him open the book, and read therein; and as he read, he wept, and trembled; and, not being able longer to contain, he brake out with a lamentable cry, saying, *What shall I do?* (John Bunyan, the opening words of *The Pilgrim's Progress*, 1678)

Indention. Commonly, the indention that comes at the beginning of every paragraph is about two to three ems. Sometimes, for gift books, experimental works, and very short works, an extra line of space can be inserted between paragraphs, although indentions are usually not used in combination with the extra line spaces between paragraphs.

Gutter. The margins that run along the center of the book when it is opened should be wide enough so that type does not curve when the book is opened. Curving type on too-wide line lengths decreases reading speed considerably. One test is this: Can you photocopy facing pages of the book without having to crack the spine to get a legible image of the words?

Outside Margins. Adequate margins should be maintained on the outside left and right margins of any book, even mass market editions. The simple reason is that they allow for the reader to hold the book open with the thumbs. Most of us have had the frustrating experience of having a book snap shut because we were holding the book delicately on the edges when the margins were of insufficient size.

U

Unspoken Discourse

A person's thoughts, imaginings, and unspoken prayers (called *unspoken discourse*), when expressed in the first person, are best set in roman type, either with or without quotation marks, according to the author's preference and the reader's perception. An internal capital letter may be used when the unspoken discourse begins in the middle of a sentence. This is a shift from the former style of expressing unspoken discourse in italics. Occasional unspoken discourse may still be set in italics, of course, especially when it is difficult to distinguish between the narrative matter and the unspoken thoughts. Still, a skillful writer will be able to communicate interior monologue without the use of italics.

> "Surely, this is the East Indies," thought Columbus as he gazed out at the tropical islands. [with quotation marks]
>
> Though hardly wealthy, the woman looked at her life and thought, What have I done to deserve such blessings? [without quotation marks, with a capital indicating the beginning of the thought]

URLs

See "Webpage Addresses (URLs)."

V

Vertical Lists, Numbering

See "Outlines and Lists" and "Period, *With Numbers in Vertical Lists*."

W

Warning Notice

A *warning notice* is a statement, usually included on a book's copyright page, that unequivocally notifies the reader that reproducing material from the book, no matter what the form of reproduction, is illegal. It is by no means mandatory for the publisher or author to provide a warning notice since the current copyright laws are sufficient to protect the book without it. Still, its use is recommended. (See "Copyright Page.")

The following formula is fairly standard throughout the publishing industry, though the phrasing may be made more or less threatening as appropriate:

All rights reserved. No part of this publication may be reproduced, stored in a retrieval system, or transmitted in any form or by any means—electronic, mechanical, photocopy, recording, or any other—except for brief quotations in printed reviews, without the prior permission of the publisher.

Note that the "all rights reserved" notice can be conveniently incorporated into the warning notice. (See "All Rights Reserved Notice.") When a warning notice is given, it is also important to give the publisher's address on the copyright page so that readers know where to write if they do wish to obtain the permission of the publisher to quote portions of the text.

If space is a problem, a shorter formula may be used:

All rights reserved. No part of this publication may be reproduced, stored in a retrieval system, or transmitted in any form or by any means except for brief quotations in printed reviews, without the prior permission of the publisher.

Or the even simpler:

All rights reserved. No part of this publication may be reproduced without the prior permission of the publisher.

In some cases, the publisher may want to qualify the warning notice so that copying of some pages is allowed in certain clearly defined situations. This is done by adding a *permission-to-copy notice* to the warning notice. (See "Permission-to-Copy Notice.")

Watches of the Night

In modern usage, the term *watches of the night* (or, less correctly, *watches in the night*) is archaic, though when it is used, it is often used incorrectly. In

Bible times, the night hours were divided into *watches*, though they take slightly different forms in the Old and New Testaments. *Watch* refers to the guards or soldiers whose duty was to keep watch during designated periods of the night. In the OT, the Israelites observed three watches of about four hours each (varying with the seasons), so that when Gideon blows his trumpet "at the beginning of the middle watch" (Judg. 7:19), it means about four hours after sunset. In the NT, the Romans observed four watches of about three hours each (varying with the seasons), so that when Jesus walks on the water "about the fourth watch of the night" (Mark 6:48), it means just before dawn.

Israelite Watch	Modern Equivalent (approximate)
first watch	6:00 p.m. to 10:00 p.m.
second watch	10:00 p.m. to 2:00 a.m.
third watch	2:00 a.m. to 6:00 a.m.

Roman Watch	Modern Equivalent (approximate)
first watch	6:00 p.m. to 9:00 p.m.
second watch	9:00 p.m. to 12:00 p.m.
third watch	12:00 p.m. to 3:00 a.m.
fourth watch	3:00 a.m. to 6:00 a.m.

Webpage Addresses (URLs)

The location of a specific website on the Internet can be found using its *webpage address*, or *web address*. The technical term for that address is the initialism *URL*, which stands for "uniform resource locator," though that full name should not be used because most people familiar with the abbreviation have no idea what it stands for. The terms *webpage address* and *web address* should be used in most ordinary communication rather than the more technical term *URL*. Note, however, that the abbreviation is pronounced as an initialism (*U-R-L*), not as a word (*"earl"*), and its plural is *URLs* (with a lowercase *s*).

Conventions for Setting in Text. It is common for authors to provide web addresses in text, whether referring to their own personal websites, the websites used in their research, or websites that might be of interest to their readers. Because of the unique construction of URLs and, often, their excessive length, problems in setting sometimes arise. The following guidelines should help.

1. Set web addresses, whether in lists or in text, in italics.

> *www.zondervanbibles.com/home.asp*
> *www.bookwire.com/bookwire/*

2. Do not use the prefix *http://* in the web address. It is the assumed prefix to all URLs and is not needed in references to a webpage. Say *www.zondervan.com/books/* rather than *http://www.zondervan.com/books/* in references to that page.

3. If a webpage address needs to be broken over a line of text, break it only at a convenient slash and do not add a hyphen.

> *www.zondervan.com/features/books/*
> *0310205719/default.htm*

If it is necessary to break an address at some place other than a slash, break it before any other punctuation. For instance, don't allow a dot to stand at the end of the first line, where it might appear to be a period, but place at the beginning of the second line.

> *www.zondervan.com/features/books/0310205719/default*
> *.htm*

4. Some people suggest that a webpage address not be allowed to fall at the end of a sentence or major clause because the sentence's own punctuation might be mistaken as part of the address itself. Most readers, however, will not have a problem distinguishing a "dot" from a period in context. It is okay to follow a webpage address with a period, comma, or question mark. If there is some reason to feel that placing a punctuation mark immediately after a webpage address will result in serious misreading or confusion, then a thin space between the address and the mark may be inserted.

> He finally found the book at *www.chapitre.com/accueil.htm* .
> Have you accessed *www.copyeditor.com/default.asp?id=3* ?

For more information on how to render web addresses as bibliographic references, see "Sources, *Citing Webpages.*"

Other Problems. One disadvantage of providing webpage addresses in printed material is that those addresses go out of date very quickly. It is frustrating to try to access a page on the Internet only to find that it no longer exists, and defunct address references can make a book seem prematurely outdated. There may be no solution to this other than referencing addresses selectively and carefully, using primarily those that are from larger, well-established organizations.

Website Names

In both references and text, the names of websites should be styled according to the same rules that apply to print sources. The title of an online periodical, for instance, should be italicized (for example, *Salon.com*), while the name of an online company should be set in roman (for example, Amazon.com). Though the distinction is sometimes hard to perceive, it is a distinction that must also be made in the non-Internet world (for example, *Time* magazine and Time Inc.).

Websites, Citing

See both "Sources, *Citing Webpages*" and "Webpage Addresses (URLs)."

Western Wall Versus Wailing Wall

Modern Israelis prefer the term *Western Wall* to the term *Wailing Wall* for that portion of the old temple in Jerusalem to which it refers (once believed to be part of Solomon's original temple but actually of a much later date), and there is no reason not to respect this preference. The change is meant to symbolize the Jews' new hope after emerging from the tragedies of history.

Widows and Orphans

The terms *widow* and *orphan* are often used interchangeably, but they describe distinct typographic situations. A typographic *widow* is defined as any last line of a paragraph that is allowed to stand apart from the rest of the paragraph, for instance, on the top of the following page or after an inserted graphic or sidebar. Most typesetting systems are programmed with preset "widow conditions" that calculate the lines-per-page so that, ideally, one line of a paragraph alone will never carry over to the next page.

The term *widow* also applies to the ends of chapters. In most circumstances, one- or two-line widows are never allowed to stand alone on an otherwise blank page. Three- to four-line widows should be strongly discouraged but may only be allowed if absolutely no other typographic option is available. Ideally, the last page of any chapter should have at least five lines of type on it.

A typographic *orphan* is a broken word or a short word of four or fewer characters that is allowed to stand alone on a line at the end of a paragraph. Usually there is a typographic solution to this situation, either by reducing the word space in the previous lines to bring the short word up or by expanding the word spaces to force more characters down to the last line. In most cases, reducing or expanding the letter space in the previous line or lines should not be done, since the resulting appearance usually draws more attention to itself than the original orphan. As a last resort, the editor has the option of editing out a word or rewriting a portion of the paragraph to eliminate the problem. Obviously, this should be done with caution and only when the orphan is likely to be a distraction to the reader.

Word Division

Word division is often a puzzle. The major dictionaries themselves occasionally differ on how properly to hyphenate words that are forced to break over lines of text. *Webster's Collegiate Dictionary*, for instance, breaks words according to pronunciation, whereas *The Random House College Dictionary* tends to divide them according to etymological derivation, or root word. Also, the standard style manuals do not accept all dictionary word divisions as legitimate for typesetting purposes—for instance, syllables of two letters are shown in all dictionaries, but they are seldom allowed to be used for line breaks in type. Add to these confusions the fact that computer typesetters generate their own word divisions in two ways: from the computer's own programmed dictionary and by a logic program, neither of which may correspond to the publisher's preferred style. To sort out this confusion, some guidelines might be helpful.

Use a Standard Reference and Stick with It. This manual recommends the rules for word division found in *The Chicago Manual of Style, Fifteenth Edition* (sections 7.33–7.45). These rules define which dictionary breaks are and are not legitimate for typesetting purposes. These include:

1. Do not allow two-letter breaks at the beginning of a line of type, though they are acceptable at the end of a line: for example, do not allow *enchant-er*, but *en-chanter* is acceptable.
2. Do not accept *-le* divisions (*liquid l*), as in *peo-ple*, *bot-tle*, *hum-ble*, *spar-kle*, *arti-cle*. (*CMS* now accepts these as legitimate breaks.)
3. Do not allow a word to break over two pages. Recto-to-verso breaks should never be allowed, though verso-to-recto breaks can occasionally be permitted when no other option works efficiently.
4. Do not allow a portion of a broken word to stand on a line by itself at the end of a paragraph. (Also see "Widows and Orphans.")
5. Do not break words of one syllable.
6. Words that already contain a hyphen should be broken only at the existing hyphen whenever possible: *twenty-three*, not *twen-ty-three*.
7. Words that begin with prefixes are best broken after that prefix whenever possible: *dis-equilibrium* rather than *disequi-librium*.
8. Compound words should be broken between the root elements whenever possible: *proof-reading* rather than *proofread-ing*.
9. Do not allow breaks that will cause misreading, as in *Anti-gone*, for example.

But Allow for Occasional Flexibility. You'll note that many of the rules in this section say "whenever possible." That should be taken to mean that an awkward break is preferable to a line of type that is either too loose or too tight. Common sense should be used, and the question should always be asked: What option will cause the least disruption for the reader?

As long as the conditions set out in *CMS* are met, some publishers even accept word divisions that conform to the style of any major dictionary. For instance, *righteous* may be broken either *righ-teous* (*Webster's* "pronunciation" style) or *right-eous* (*Random House College Dictionary's* "root word" style), and a publisher may accept both as legitimate. This liberality is often a compromise of style and quality, and should be avoided in high-quality editing. In many cases, however, such flexibility is necessary, since even a slight adjustment in line length at late proof stages can cause a paragraph, chapter, or even an entire book to rejustify. Little adjustments can snowball into expensive changes. Also, many computer spell-checkers and human proofreaders don't know the differences between the styles of various dictionaries. Most readers won't notice a slight and occasional inconsistency in word division.

Dividing Personal Names. Avoid dividing personal names whenever possible. If it is unavoidable, it is better to break a last name than a first name. Always try to keep a middle initial with the first name, and never separate the initials of the first and middle names; never allow *C. / S. Lewis*, for instance. By the same token, do not allow designations such as *Jr., Sr., II, III*, etc. to be separated from the name: do not allow *Henry / VIII*, for instance.

Numbers. Occasionally very large numbers set in numerals need to be broken over two lines of type. Break large numbers after a comma as long as that comma does not follow a single digit. Never break a numeral after a decimal point. Do not use a hyphen to indicate a numeral broken over a line. Simply drop the rest of the number to the next line.

Webpage Addresses. As described in the entry "Webpage Addresses (URLs)," webpage addresses should be broken after slashes whenever possible. Otherwise, break the address before any other internal punctuation marks, such as the "dot." As with numerals, no hyphen should be added to indicate the break since the hyphen could be mistaken as part of the address. The second element should simply be dropped down to the next line.

Keep Style Sheets. Freelance editors and proofreaders should be familiar with the publisher's preferred style of word division. Also, the proofreader, especially the one who reads the first set of typeset proofs, should keep a style sheet listing any problematic word divisions encountered.

World-English Style

See "Mid-Atlantic Style."

Xmas

The abbreviation *Xmas* (sometimes spelled *Exmas*) for Christmas should be avoided in formal writing. It is appropriate only for advertising copy and is usually considered substandard even there. Oddly enough, the abbreviation has a long and established history in English, dating back to its Old English form used in the *Anglo-Saxon Chronicle* of the twelfth century. The *X* is actually the Greek letter *chi* and has been used as a symbol for the name of Christ (*Christos*) since the first century.

Ye

The archaic *ye* was originally the second person plural pronoun, and *thou* was the second person singular pronoun. Both were used as subjects of sentences, while *you* and *thee* were the respective objective cases. In modern English, all these forms became simply *you*, which can be singular or plural, subject or object. While the KJV uses *ye* almost exclusively as a plural pronoun, as in "Blessed be ye poor" (Luke 6:20), the word eventually came to be used as a highly formal way of addressing one person, still occasionally seen in ecclesiastical and devotional writing, though considered excessively archaic. (See also "*Thou* and *Thee*.")

The word *ye* as it appears in some pseudo-antiquated names, such as Ye Olde Carde Shoppe, should not be confused with the *ye*, the outmoded second person plural. Early printers rendered the Middle English word *þe*, which means *the*, as *Ye* since the thorn character, *þ*, representing the *th* sound, was not available in their typecases. Any use of *ye* as an article is now considered almost wholly jocular.

Year of Publication

An accurate statement of the year of a book's first publication is needed at two points in the publishing process. First, it is needed in the copyright notice on the copyright page, where it is placed with the copyright symbol © (or word *copyright*) and the name of the copyright holder. Second, it is needed after the book is published and the book is officially registered with the Library of Congress and the US Copyright Office. (See "Copyright Holder and Copyright Owner"; "Copyright Notice"; and "Copyright Page.")

Ends of Years. In both cases, care should be taken, especially at the ends of years. For instance, a book may be in the publisher's warehouse in December but not actually in the stores until January. So which year is used for the publication date? The best rule is to go by the actual in-stock date, that is, the year the book actually arrived in the publisher's warehouse.

It generally causes no problem if the date is off by a year one way or the other in the copyright notice, although the US Copyright Office should be notified of the correct date when registering the copyright itself. If a wrong date was given to the Library of Congress when applying for CIP information (for instance, if the book is inadvertently delayed), they should be notified of the change as soon as possible.

Zealot

When lowercased, the term *zealot* means a fanatical believer in any cause (as in *a zealot for campaign-contribution reform*). When capitalized, it refers specifically to the religo-political Jewish sect of the first century that opposed Rome's military occupation of Palestine.

Zion

From the Hebrew word meaning "hill," *Zion* is a common biblical name for Jerusalem, named specifically for the hill on which the City of David was built. In the context of some Christian devotional literature, it has come to mean, metaphorically, the people of God themselves. John Bunyan, in his *Pilgrim's Progress*, uses *Mount Zion* as a synonym for heaven, or the celestial city. Since that time, *Zion*, or *Mount Zion*, has been popularly used in the language of hymns and sermons to mean heaven. A careful writer should clarify which context is intended: the earthly city of biblical times, the worldwide family of believers, or the heavenly abode of God and the saints.

Acknowledgments

First, I would like to thank my wife, writer and dancer Shelley Townsend-Hudson, who helped shape the previous edition of this book.

The original advisory board for this revision of *The Christian Writer's Manual of Style* was Stan Gundry, Mary McNeil, and Jim Ruark, to whom I am very grateful for all their help and guidance. I would also like to thank Gina Dorn, Angela Scheff, and Todd Sprague for their careful copyediting; Dawn Anderson, Becky Danley, Carol Ann Hiemstra and Elizabeth Yoder for their excellent proofreading. And extra big bows of gratitude go to Jim Ruark, who tirelessly edited version after version of this manuscript and serves as a mentor for all the editors at Zondervan; to Beth Shagene for her masterly interior design and composition; to Holli Leegwater for her elegant cover design; to Sue Brower and her marketing team for assuring that this book reaches its readers; and to Todd Sprague, Autumn Miller, Hannah Notess, and Carol Ganzevoort, who patiently reviewed the final galleys.

Special thanks are also due to Tim Beals for his profound scholarship into early English Bible translations; Jean Bloom, for checking the pages and keeping this and all Zondervan books on schedule; Amy Boucher-Pye, who not only assisted with delineating British style but also coined the handy term *mid-Atlantic style*; Jody DeNeef, who has labored to adapt this material for online use; Kristy Manion, for ably organizing the Bible permissions information; Bob Leeman for his knowledge of and advice on postal style; Brian Phipps for his expertise on Eastern Orthodoxy; Robin Schmitt, who organized the previous *CMS (14)* updates; Barbara Scott, who reviewed and edited the information about children's books; Shari Vanden Berg and Ben Irwin, who reviewed, corrected, and expanded the Bible-related material; and Verlyn Verbrugge, for his vast knowledge of Greek, Hebrew, and all matters biblical and academic.

This revision also springs from the collective wisdom of the following people: Karen Ball, Randy Bishop, Scott Bolinder, Jeff Bowden, Dirk Buursma, Greg Clouse, Lyn Cryderman, Britt Denison, Gwen Ellis, Paul Engle, Sara Fink, Heather Gemmen, Jane Haradine, Mark Hunt, Sue Johnson, Jack Kuhatschek, Cindy Hays Lambert, Dave Lambert, John Sloan, Lori VandenBosch, Sandy VanderZicht, Joe Vriend, and the many readers who wrote to us about their stylistic preferences.

Furthermore, this book was built on the foundation laid by numerous former Zondervan editors, designers, and freelancers who helped to compile the previous editions. We wish to preserve their memory here because they are this book's earliest caretakers: Joe Allison, Rachel Boers, Mary Bombara, Nelle Brinks, Al Bryant, Linda DeVries, Cheryl Forbes, Sue Hall, Paul Hillman, John Iwema, Tammy Johnson, Doug Johnston, Nia Jones, Julie Link, Martha Manikas-Foster, Judith Markham, Mary McCormick, Becky Omdahl, Jan Ortiz, Dallas Richards, Louise Rock, Judy Schafer, Michael Smith, Gerard Terpstra, Randy Tucker, Ed van der Maas, Ed Viening, and Bob Wood.

Bibliography

A. Standard References

The Chicago Manual of Style, Fifteenth Edition. Chicago: Univ. of Chicago Press, 2003.

Merriam-Webster's Collegiate Dictionary, Eleventh Edition. Springfield, Mass.: Merriam-Webster, 2003.

The NIV Study Bible. Grand Rapids: Zondervan, 1985.

The SBL Handbook of Style: For Ancient Near Eastern, Biblical, and Early Christian Studies. Peabody, Mass.: Hendrickson Publishers, 1999.

B. English Usage, Style, and Grammar

Bernstein, Theodore M. *Dos, Don'ts & Maybes of English Usage.* New York: Random House, 1999.

Follett, Wilson. *Modern American Usage: A Guide.* Revised by Erik Wensberg. New York: Hill & Wang, 1998.

Gordon, Karen Elizabeth. *The Deluxe Transitive Vampire: The Ultimate Handbook of Grammar for the Innocent, the Eager, and the Doomed.* New York: Pantheon, 1993.

————. *The New Well-Tempered Sentence: A Punctuation Handbook for the Innocent, the Eager, and the Doomed.* New Haven: Ticknor & Fields, 1993.

Paxson, William C. *The New American Guide to Punctuation.* New York: Signet, 1996.

Shaw, Harry. *Errors in English and Ways to Correct Them.* New York: Harper-Collins, 1993.

————. *Punctuate It Right!* New York: HarperCollins, 1994.

Shertzer, Margaret. *The Elements of Grammar.* New York: Macmillan, 1996.

Strunk, William, Jr., and E. B. White. *The Elements of Style.* 3d ed. New York: Macmillan, 1979.

C. Writing, Revising, and Editing

1. General

Appelbaum, Judith. *How to Get Happily Published: A Complete and Candid Guide.* 5th ed. New York: HarperCollins, 1998.

Atchity, Kenneth. *A Writer's Time: A Guide to the Creative Process, from Vision through Revision.* New York: W. W. Norton, 1995.

Barzun, Jacques. *On Writing, Editing and Publishing.* 2d ed. Chicago: Univ. of Chicago Press, 1986.

———. *Simple and Direct: A Rhetoric for Writers*. Rev. ed. Chicago: Univ. of Chicago, 1994.

Boswell, John. *The Awful Truth about Publishing: Why They Always Reject Your Manuscript . . . and What You Can Do about It*. New York: Mainstreet, 1997.

Cheney, Theodore A. Rees. *Getting the Words Right: How to Revise, Edit and Rewrite*. Cincinnati: Writer's Digest, 1990.

Flesch, Rudolf. *The Art of Readable Writing*. New York: Macmillan, 1977.

Plotnik, Arthur. *The Elements of Editing: A Modern Guide for Editors and Journalists*. New York: Macmillan, 1997.

Zinsser, William. *On Writing Well: The Classic Guide to Writing Nonfiction*. 6th rev. ed. New York: HarperCollins, 1998.

2. Religious

Aycock, Don M., and Leonard George Goss. *The Christian Writer's Book: A Practical Guide to Writing*. North Brunswick, N.J.: Bridge-Logos, 1996.

Gentz, William H. *The Religious Writer's Marketplace: The Definitive Sourcebook*. Rev. ed. Philadelphia: Running Press, 1985.

Stuart, Sally E. *Christian Writer's Market Guide 2003*. Wheaton, Ill.: Shaw, 2003. Updated annually.

D. Special Aspects of Writing and Editing

1. Copyediting

Butcher, Judith. *Copy-editing: The Cambridge Handbook for Editors, Authors and Publishers*. New York: Cambridge Univ. Press, 1992. (UK style)

Judd, Karen. *Copyediting: A Practical Guide*. 2d ed. Menlo Park, Calif.: Crisp Publications, 1992.

2. Proofreading

Anderson, Laura Killen. *Handbook for Proofreading*. Lincolnwood, Ill.: VGM Career Horizons, 1990.

Graham, Leland. *Building Proofreading Skills*. Nashville, Tenn.: Incentive, 1999.

Hall, Max. *An Embarrassment of Misprints: Comical and Disastrous Typos of the Centuries*. Golden, Colo.: Fulcrum, 1995.

May, Debra Hart. *Proofreading Plain and Simple*. Franklin Lakes, N.J.: Career Press, 1997.

Smith, Debra A., and Helen R Sutton. *Powerful Proofreading Skills: Tips, Techniques, and Tactics*. Menlo Park, Calif.: Crisp, 1994.

Smith, Peggy. *Letter Perfect: A Guide to Practical Proofreading*. Alexandria, Va.: Editorial Experts, 1995.

———. *Mark My Words: Instruction and Practice in Proofreading*. 3d ed. Alexandria, Va.: Editorial Experts, 1997.

Sullivan, K. D. *Go Ahead, Proof It!* Hauppauge, N.Y.: Barron's, 1996.

3. Indexing

Bonura, Larry S. *The Art of Indexing*. New York: John Wiley and Sons, 1994.

Mulvany, Nancy C. *Indexing Books*. Chicago: Univ. of Chicago Press, 1994.

Wellisch, Hans H. *Indexing from A to Z*. Bronx, N.Y.: H. W. Wilson, 1996.

4. Copyright

Fishman, Stephen. *Copyright Handbook: How to Protect and Use Written Work*. 4th ed. Berkeley: Nolo Press, 1997.

Wilson, Lee. *The Copyright Guide: A Friendly Handbook for Protecting and Profiting from Copyrights*. New York: Allworth Press, 1996.

5. British Style

Butcher, Judith. *Copy-Editing: The Cambridge Handbook for Editors, Authors and Publishers*. Cambridge: Cambridge University Press, 1992.

Ritter, R. M. *The Oxford Style Manual*. Oxford and New York: Oxford University Press, 2003.

Index